THE FOOTBALL FACT BOOK

JACK ROLLIN

GUINNESS PUBLISHING

About the author

Jack Rollin was born in London in 1932 and educated at King's, Harrow. There he played football, while later at Westcliff-on-Sea High School it was rugby. Within ten days of joining the Royal Air Force he was playing in a Welsh Cup tie for RAF Bridgnorth!

His playing career was ended in 1958 by an ankle injury but by then he had already covered the 1954 World Cup in Switzerland as a freelance journalist. For ten years he edited the football weekly magazine *Soccer Star* and its monthly companion *World Soccer*, before working for BBC Television's *Match of the Day*.

A member of the Association of Football Statisticians, he is currently the editor of *Rothmans Football Yearbook* and reports football regularly for the *Telegraph* newspapers.

His previous books include:
England's World Cup Triumph (1966)
A Source Book of Football (1971)
The History of Aldershot Football Club (1975)
The Guinness Book of Soccer Facts and Feats
  (1978, 1979, 1980, 1981, 1983)
World Cup Guide (1982)
Soccer Who's Who (1984, 1986, 1989, 1990)
Soccer at War 1939–45 (1985)
Soccer Records (1985, 1988)
Soccer Shorts (1988)
The World Cup 1930–1990 (1990)

The author is married to June and has a daughter Glenda. He would like to thank Mavis Suckling for her editorial assistance in compiling certain sections of this book.

Editor: Charles Richards
Design and Layout: Ken Vail Graphic Design
Cover design: David Roberts
Picture research: Julie O'Leary

Published in Great Britain by Guinness Publishing Ltd,
33 London Road, Enfield, Middlesex

Typeset in 9/11pt Helvetica
by Ace Filmsetting Ltd, Frome, Somerset
Printed and bound in Great Britain by The Bath Press, Bath

British Library Cataloguing in Publication Data
Rollin, Jack *1932–*
    The football fact book
    1. Great Britain. Association football, history
    I. Title
    796.334'0941

ISBN 0-85112-901-3

Contents

Introduction

This is the first edition of *The Football Fact Book*, the natural successor to the *Guinness Book of Soccer Facts and Feats* and *Soccer – The Records* series. It combines the best and most popular elements of both in a single volume, bringing all the records, facts and statistics right up to date.

At domestic level there are factual stories, chiefly of an unusual nature, covering all Football League and Scottish League clubs as well as a comprehensive directory of both competitions, showing a variety of information including honours and other achievements. The most recent figures concerning ground capacities are also included as the game moves towards an era of all-seated stadia.

Thirteen of the most popular local derby encounters are also detailed season by season and include the clashes on Merseyside between Liverpool and Everton, the North London rivalry of Arsenal and Tottenham Hotspur and the auld firm meetings involving Celtic and Rangers through the years.

Each FA Cup Final has a potted story-line revealing the outstanding feature of the game in question and for the Football League championship there is an analysis of each club's success with a summary of its playing record and other statistical points of interest.

At international level there is a full record of the respective national teams from the British Isles up to and including the 1990 World Cup, which along with the European Championship is featured strongly. Moreover, with English clubs being re-admitted to Europe following the ban imposed after the Heysel Stadium tragedy in 1985, it is of special interest that there is an up-to-date list of all matches played not only by English teams, but those from Scotland, Wales, Northern Ireland and the Republic in the three major European competitions. In addition the European Cup final details are also included along with those from the Cup-Winners' Cup and UEFA Cup.

Woven in with the facts are sections of stories concerning goalscoring feats and there are also fascinating snippets of information from countries around the world. However major records are not forgotten either and there is a section devoted to them.

BRITISH FOOTBALL   A–Z

In 1985–86 **Aberdeen** were unbeaten in all their cup-ties yet only won two of their three major knock-out competitions. They won the Skol Cup without conceding a goal in six games, completed a domestic cup double by winning the Scottish Cup from another six matches, one of which was drawn, and played six European Cup games. Although they were undefeated in Europe, they lost the quarter-final tie to IFK Gothenburg on the away goals rule. In addition, the Dons won the Tennent's Sixes competition and the BP Youth Cup.

In 1970 **Airdrieonians** became the first club in Scotland to have a match decided on penalty kicks, in a Texaco Cup tie against Nottingham Forest. It was the second leg of the first round on 28 September at Broomfield Park. The first leg had been drawn 2–2 and that was the score at the end of extra time in the return. Airdrie won 5–2 on penalties.

Albion Rovers had a wretched time in Division One during 1948–49. They lost their opening three games but on 28 August 1948 they beat Falkirk 2–0 at home, followed it by drawing 4–4 at Hibernian and then held Celtic 3–3 at home. But the draw at Hibs proved to be the only point they managed away from home all season. Their only other points came from two home wins, as they beat Morton 2–1 and Aberdeen by the same score. They were relegated with eight points. However they did manage to win a first round Scottish Cup tie, 2–1 at Hamilton Academical, and one Scottish League Cup match, 2–1 at home to Falkirk. In the League they scored 30 goals in 30 games but conceded 105.

Aldershot were unbeaten in all 23 Division Four matches and one League Cup tie at home in the 1977–78 season. They won 15 League games at the Recreation Ground and drew eight plus another draw in the League Cup. But they were let down by their away form which produced only four wins and eight draws. They missed promotion by one place and two points, finishing fifth.

Alloa were the last unbeaten team in the Scottish League in 1984–85 after 13 matches. Their first defeat in Division Two was sustained at Montrose on 10 November when they lost 2–1. A run of four defeats in March–April cost them the chance of the championship, but they did finish second behind Montrose.

Arbroath made an encouraging start to the 1960–61 season after promotion from Division Two. In the League Cup they finished top of their qualifying section, defeated Division One opponents Raith Rovers over two legs in the quarter-finals and then lost 3–0 to Third Lanark in the semi-final. But in the League they had a disastrous beginning, losing 11 of their first 13 games, and an even more calamitous ending during which they failed to win one of their last 14 fixtures. Away from home they took only two points from drawn games.

On 26 May 1989, **Arsenal** needed to beat Liverpool by a margin of at least two goals at Anfield to achieve their first championship success since 1971. Liverpool, the leaders, had not lost in 18 League games and Arsenal had seen their advantage slip after taking just one point from their last two home matches. A 2–0 win or a similar margin of victory would give Arsenal the title by virtue of having scored more goals than Liverpool, as both teams would have identical goal difference. It was the closest race for the championship since Arsenal had gone to Old Trafford in 1952 faced with the unlikely prospect of winning by seven goals to deprive Manchester United of the title. Then Arsenal had lost 6–1, but this time they went ahead after 52 minutes through Alan Smith and scored a dramatic second goal in the last minute with Michael Thomas obliging.

Michael Thomas (light shirt) scores Arsenal's dramatic last-minute second goal to clinch the 1988–89 championship at Anfield against Liverpool (Allsport)

Aston Villa had the unusual experience of achieving more points than they scored goals in 1968–69 in Division Two. In their 42 matches they hit only 37 goals but obtained 38 points. Only once did they manage to score as many as three in a game when they defeated Sheffield United 3–1 on 1 March. But they had four teams beneath them and they escaped relegation. However, it was a short-lived reprieve for in 1969–70 they finished second from bottom with 29 points, having scored only 36 goals.

Ayr United hold a record of six Division Two championships and three runners-up places before the reorganisation of the League into three divisions in 1975–76. In 1958–59 they acheived a club record 60 points from 36 games and finished top, 19 points ahead of second-placed Arbroath. They were the only Scottish League club that season to score over a century of goals. Of their 115 in Division Two, Peter Price scored 37 and four other players shared 61 between them. Ayr were beaten only once in their first 18 League games from which they took 32 points.

John Hughes helped to rescue Berwick Rangers from last position in the Scottish Division Two during 1988–89 with some consistent scoring feats (Tweeddale Press Group)

After losing 2–0 at Wrexham on 31 December 1933, **Barnsley** completed 21 Division Three (North) matches without defeat, taking 37 points and winning the championship. They scored 118 goals and all five regularly-used forwards reached double figures. Top scorer with 31 was Abe Blight, a 21-year-old signed from Blackhill in the North West Durham League, for whom he had scored 65 goals in the previous season. He was a miner at Annfield Plain. Dickie Spence and Tubby Ashton scored 19 goals each, Harold Andrews 18 and Jackie Smith 12.

Berwick Rangers won only one and drew another of their first 17 League matches in 1988–89 and were firmly fixed at the bottom of the Second Division. But they lost only one other match – the last of the season – and avoided finishing at the foot of the table.

Birmingham City also obtained more points than goals in Division Two during 1947–48, but won the championship. They scored 55 goals, which produced 59 points, and their defence conceded only 24 goals. Ten of their games ended in goalless draws. But they began the season by losing 3–2 at home to Barnsley. The following season they scored 36 goals and achieved 37 points, avoiding relegation by four points. In 1949–50 they finished bottom of Division One with 28 points after scoring 31 goals.

Simon Garner established a goalscoring record for **Blackburn Rovers** in the 1988–89 season. He took his aggregate total to 144 goals to overhaul the record set by Tommy Briggs of 140 League goals between 1952 and 1958. Garner finished the season with 20 goals, his second best total. He scored 22 in 1982–83 having made his debut in the 1978–79 season. In 1954–55 Briggs had scored 33 goals for Rovers.

Blackpool obtained exactly twice as many points away from home as at Bloomfield Road in Division One matches in 1966–67. They won only one and drew five on their own ground, but had five wins and four draws on their travels. They failed to score in ten home matches, scoring only 18 times in 21 attempts. They finished bottom with 21 points. Despite achieving 58 points the following season, a record total for a club not promoted from Division Two at the time, they missed out by 0.23 of goal average.

The 11 players who formed **Bolton Wanderers'** 1958 FA Cup wining team cost only signing-on fees. Five of them were England internationals: Eddie Hopkinson, Tommy Banks, Nat Lofthouse, Ray Parry and Doug Holden.

Simon Garner established a new scoring record for Blackburn Rovers in the 1988-89 season (Sporting Pictures)

Bournemouth achieved 97 points in 46 Division Three matches in 1986-87. They owed their total to a fine home record which saw them drop just six points. Only Gillingham won at Dean Court, beating Bournemouth 2-0 on 2 December. Brentford and Blackpool drew 1-1 there and Port Vale 0-0. Bournemouth remained unbeaten in their last 11 games. Three players reached double figures for the season; Carl Richards was leading marksman with 11, followed jointly by Trevor Aylott and David Puckett with ten each, in a total of 76 goals.

In 1948-49 **Bradford City** had to call upon the services of 40 different players in Division Three (North). They finished bottom and were forced to seek re-election. One of the few playing successes of the season was centre-forward Jimmy Brown, who arrived from Motherwell in November and proceeded to score 11 goals in 20 League games including a hat-trick against Hull City. But in August 1949 he was transferred to Queen of the South.

Brechin City suffered three 10-0 defeats in the 1937-38 season, all away from home; against Cowdenbeath on 20 November, Albion Rovers on 15 January and Airdrieonians on 12 February. They conceded 139 goals in their 34 Division Two games and finished bottom with 12 points.

In 1900-01 **Brentford** became champions of Division Two of the Southern League without losing a match and conceding only 11 goals. They had to apply for election to Division One but were refused and only subsequently gained admission when Gravesend dropped out.

Although **Brighton and Hove Albion** finished the 1950-51 season in a reasonable 13th place in Division Three (South) they had a season of ups and downs in the League. On 11 November they were beaten 7-0 at Reading and the following week lost 6-0 at home to Plymouth Argyle. But on 18 April they recorded a 9-1 win over Newport County, their highest score.

Bristol City met Aldershot in the FA Cup second round on 10 December 1988 at the Recreation Ground, Aldershot. Aldershot led 1-0 until Carl Shutt equalised in injury time. The replay at Ashton Gate three days later finished 0-0 after extra time. Then it was back to Aldershot on December 20. Aldershot again led 1-0 when Shutt again equalised in injury time to force extra time. The game finished 2-2 and two days later it was back to Ashton Gate for the thrid replay. A goal by Shutt after just ten minutes settled the tie which took 420 minutes to complete.

Bristol Rovers can claim to have had an exciting FA Cup run before they entered the Football League in 1920. In 1901-02 they figured in ten matches and knocked out several notable clubs including neighbours Bristol City, Swindon Town, Millwall and Middlesbrough before being beaten 1-0 at home by Stoke City, but only after a masterly display by Stoke's international goalkeeper Leigh Roose.

On 2 May 1960 **Burnley** defeated Manchester City 2-1 at Maine Road to go to the top of Division One for the first time in the season and became champions by a point from Wolverhampton Wanderers. They had lost 6-1 to Wolves on 30 March 1960. To achieve the title, Burnley had to take five points from their last three games and the final one was played when the other contenders had completed their programme. Only two members of the professional staff had cost transfer fees: Jimmy McIlroy and Alex Elder, both from Glentoran.

The most successful period in the history of **Bury** was around the turn of the century. Even before they were elected to the League in Division Two in 1894, they had already displayed their cup-fighting prowess, by winning the Lancashire Cup in 1892, on first entry. However, in the FA Cup they were twice successful, in 1900 and 1903; in the latter competition they were especially impressive, scoring 12 goals, including six in the final, and not conceding one themselves. During the same period the club had some respectable seasons in Division One. They were fifth in 1900–01, seventh in 1901–02 and eighth in 1902–03.

Cambridge United benefited from an eight-second own goal on 3 January 1977 at Torquay, conceded by Pat Kruse. It is a Football League record. They went 2–0 ahead before half-time, again from an own goal, but the Division Four game ended 2–2. Cambridge won the championship that season.

Cardiff City were twice deprived of championship successes in Divisions One and Two on goal average. In 1920–21, when they finished second to Birmingham their average was 1.843 compared with Birmingham's 2.078. In 1923–24 they lost the Division One title to Huddersfield Town whose 1.818 was marginally better than Cardiff's 1.794. Had goal difference been in operation at the time, Cardiff would not have won Division Two in 1920–21, but they would have overtaken Huddersfield Town in 1923–24. Although both teams had identical figures of +27, Cardiff would have won the title by scoring one more goal than their rivals.

However, Cardiff's subsequent experience was dramatic. In 1925 they were runners-up in the FA Cup before becoming the first and only club outside England to win the trophy in 1927. But in 1928–29 they were relegated to Division Two and two seasons later fell into Division Three (South). Worse followed, as in 1933–34 they finished bottom and had to apply for re-election. But they were unanimously voted back, along with Bournemouth, and the one non-league club applying, Folkestone, received no votes.

The turnover of players on either side of the Second World War was well illustrated by the example of **Carlisle United**. From the last full peace-time season in 1938–39 only Alec Taylor, a centre-half signed from Scottish junior circles, made appearances in 1946–47. He was also one of three Carlisle players to appear in the two abortive games of 1939–40, before the war intervened, and return to the team afterwards.

The other two were goalkeeper David Jones signed from Stoke City in 1939 and outside-right Ronnie Dellow, recruited from Tranmere Rovers the same year. Carlisle did complete the first regional wartime season of 1939–40 but did not return until 1945–46. All three made guest appearances for other clubs during the war period.

Celtic can claim to have won their first Scottish League game, defeating Hearts 5–0 at Tynecastle on 23 August 1890, but only after Renton's record was expunged from the competition, as the Celts had lost a home game 4–1 to Renton on 16 August. That eventful initial season also saw the club have four points deducted for fielding goalkeeper Bell without proper registration.

When Ralph Allen established a record for goalscoring at **Charlton Athletic** during the 1934–35 season, he achieved the total of 27 goals in only 18 games in Division Three (South). Transferred to Charlton from Brentford in October 1934 he scored both goals in a 2–1 win over Clapton Orient on 27 October and set up the new record against Queen's Park Rangers on 23 February. But he only added five more goals to his total before the end of the season. With Brentford he had scored 149 goals in three seasons for the reserves,

Chelsea achieved 99 points in 46 Division Two matches in 1988–89. They lost only five games and though they conceded 50 goals, exactly half at home and away, they scored 96 goals. They finished as champions, 17 points clear of the runners-up Manchester City. However, their achievement was all the more remarkable as they failed to win any of their first six games, from which they took just three points. From then on they lost only twice and between 29 October and 8 April they were unbeaten in 27 matches. Kerry Dixon was leading scorer with 25 goals, including four in a 5–3 win over Barnsley, but Gordon Durie hit five goals in a 7–0 win at Walsall and scored 17 altogether. Graham Roberts' total of 15 included 12 penalties and Kevin Wilson was the fourth player to reach double figures with 13 to his credit. Chelsea failed to score in only three games.

In June 1931 **Chester** applied for election to the Third Division (North) along with Nelson and Rochdale, the retiring clubs, plus another non-league representative Manchester Central. The opening voting produced the following result: Rochdale 47 votes, Nelson 27, Chester 27 and Manchester Central 4. A second ballot involving the tied clubs gave Chester 28 to Nelson's 20.

In 1904 **Chesterfield** added Town to their title and finished fifth in Division Two. The following season they were third from bottom, and again in 1906–07. In the next two seasons they were second from bottom and failed to gain re-election on the last occasion. They reverted to plain Chesterfield and eventually returned to the League in Division Three (North) in 1921.

In 1950–51 **Clyde** were relegated from Division One. They lost all of their opening four fixtures and scraped just four points from the first nine games. There was a partial recovery in December and January during which 13 points were gained, only to be followed by a run of six points from 11 matches. Yet a win in the last game against Celtic could have saved them.

Clydebank became the first club to reach the Scottish Premier Division from Division Two in successive seasons. In 1975–76 they finished top of Division Two on goal difference from Raith Rovers. The following season they were runners-up to St Mirren in Division One. Unfortunately their first season in the Premier Division resulted in relegation as the bottom club.

Vic Keeble was the first **Colchester United** player to score a hat-trick in the Football League, a feat he acheived in a spell of only 12 minutes. Signed from local sources in 1947 after an unsuccessful trial with Arsenal, he was later transferred to Newcastle United for £15,000 in February 1952 and moved to West Ham for £10,000 in October 1957.

Although **Coventry City** had to wait until 1986–87 before they won the FA Cup, their initial impact in the competition was made while they were still members of the Southern League, when in 1909–10 they reached the last eight. In the first round they won 2–1 away to Preston North End (Div. 1), had a 1–0 success at fellow Southern League side Portsmouth in the second round and beat Nottingham Forest (Div. 1) 3–1 at home in the third round. In the fourth round they lost 2–0 at home to Everton (Div. 1).

Because of severe weather conditions, **Cowdenbeath** were unable to play any home matches for 94 days in the 1985–86 season. The blank period lasted from 30 November to 5 March. Their last home game before the long lay-off was a 2–1 defeat against Stirling Albion and on their return to active duty at Central Park they were beaten again, this time 1–0 by Dunfermline Athletic.

Before being elected to Division Two of the Football League in 1892, **Crewe Alexandra** reached the semi-final of the FA Cup. In the 1887–88 season they had a 5–0 first round win over Druids, then won 1–0 at Northwich Victoria. They had a bye in the third round, then drew 2–2 with Swifts, who were subsequently disqualified! In the fifth round they defeated Derby County 1–0, then won 2–0 at Middlesbrough in the sixth. In the semi-final they were beaten 4–0 by Preston North End, who the following season completed the first League and Cup double.

The 1970–71 season was not a particularly memorable one for **Crystal Palace**. They finished 18th in Division One, but a fourth round League Cup replay against Arsenal at Highbury, after a 0–0 draw at Selhurst Park, was something special. A goal in each half from Gerry Queen and Bobby Tambling from the penalty spot gave Palace a 2–0 win. Arsenal went on to achieve a League championship and FA Cup double.

Derby County were unbeaten in the first 16 Division One matches of 1948–49. During this period they failed to score just once and in one spell conceded only one goal in seven games. The run came to an end at Newcastle on 13 November 1948 where they lost 3–0 to United. This was the start of a slump in which Derby lost 11 of 19 games. But a late improvement in which they dropped only one point from a possible 14 took them into third place.

David Jones scored a hat-trick on his debut for **Doncaster Rovers** against Rochdale in an away game in Division Four on 11 November 1989. Rovers won 3–1. Jones had previously had League

David Jones (extreme right) tries a shot in a crowded goalmouth in a match for Doncaster Rovers against Torquay United on 17 March 1990. He made a hat-trick scoring debut for Rovers earlier in the season (Doncaster Rovers FC)

experience with Burnley, Leyton Orient and Bury as well as being on Chelsea's books. But it was when he went to Ipswich Town on trial at the start of the 1989–90 season that he revealed his full name of David Jones-Quartery. However he has continued to play as 'the boy Jones'.

The Division One match between **Dumbarton** and Vale of Leven on 12 December 1891 was abandoned in the second half with Dumbarton leading 8–0. Several Vale players had already left the field exhausted by driving rain and a hailstorm. The result was allowed to stand.

Although **Dundee** achieved 32 points from 38 games in Division One in 1937–38, they were relegated. One more point and they would have finished 14th instead of 19th. There were six clubs on 33 points, only one of whom had a better goal average than Dundee. They also managed 32 points when relegated from the Premier Division in 1975–76 on inferior goal difference to two other clubs, one of which was Dundee United.

At the beginning of the 1989–90 season, Jim McLean of **Dundee United** was the longest serving one-club manager in British football, having been appointed in 1971. During this period the club achieved the following honours: Premier Division championship 1982–83; Scottish League Cup 1980, 1981; UEFA Cup runners-up 1987; European Cup semi-finalists 1984.

Dunfermline Athletic made their debut in the Scottish League Division Two in 1912–13 and immediately had a lengthy run in the Scottish Qualifying Cup. By the time the first round proper had been reached, Dunfermline had managed to play just four League fixtures compared with as many as 19 by their fellow members in Division Two. To their credit they struggled through the fixture list and at the end of the season finished just one place and a point behind the leaders Ayr.

East Fife are the only Division Two club to have won the Scottish Cup and the Scottish League Cup. In 1938 they won the Scottish Cup beating Kilmarnock 4–2 after a 1–1 draw and in 1948 they took the League Cup, also after a replay, defeating Falkirk 4–1 after a 1–1 draw.

East Stirling and Albion Rovers were fulfilling a Division Two fixture at Merchiston Park on 2 April 1904 when torrential rain rendered the pitch unplayable after ten minutes. After consultation with both captains, the referee agreed that a friendly

Jim McLean is the longest serving manager with Dundee United having taken up his position with the club in 1971 (Allsport)

could be played, but this was abandoned after an hour with Albion leading 4–2. The spectators were unaware of the non-competitive arrangement, but four weeks later East Stirling won the rearranged match 4–0.

Everton achieved 90 points in 42 Division One matches in 1984–85. They clinched the championship on 6 May by beating Queen's Park Rangers 2–0 at Goodison Park, with five games still to be played. Prior to that they had lost just five times, but then found themselves beaten on three more occasions before the end of the season. Everton had started badly, losing their opening two games, but enjoyed a run of 18 without defeat from 26 December to 8 May, during which only two points were dropped. Of Everton's 88 goals, 65 were shared by five players who reached double figures. Graeme Sharp scored 21, Trever Steven 12, Adrian Heath and Kevin Sheedy 11 each with defender Derek Mountfield contributing ten. Everton failed to score in just four games, two of these after they had won the title.

Spectators at St James's Park for the last Division Three (South) match of the season on 4 May 1935 watched a goalless first half between **Exeter City** and Aldershot. The final score was a win for Exeter, 8–1!

The youngest player to captain a Scottish League side is Gary Gillespie. He was 17 years 179 days old when he led **Falkirk** for the first time against Stenhousemuir in a Division Two match on 31 December 1977. He remained club captain until his transfer to Coventry City in March 1978.

Forfar Athletic won promotion for the first time in 1983–84. They made a highly satisfactory beginning to the campaign, remaining unbeaten in their first 14 fixtures. Having attained first place they were never headed and suffered just three isolated defeats, all away. Achieving 63 points, Forfar were 16 in front of the Division Two runners-up, East Fife.

On 18 May 1982 **Fulham** were at home to Lincoln City in the last Division Three fixture of the season, requiring one point to gain promotion, their opponents needing to win to overtake them. The match ended in a 1–1 draw. The following season on 14 May 1983 Fulham fulfilled their last Division Two game of the campaign away at Derby County. Fulham had to win to be promoted again, while County were striving to avoid relegation. With two minutes remaining, Derby were leading 1–0 when the crowd encroached onto the pitch thinking the referee had blown for full-time. The official had to take the teams off and when it proved impractical to restart the game, he abandoned it. Fulham appealed for a replay but to no avail.

While **Gillingham** were still known as New Brompton (they changed their name in 1913) they were involved in a marathon FA Cup tie with Woolwich Arsenal (who ironically shortened their name in 1913). It was a third qualifying round tie which began on 28 October 1899, at the Manor Ground, then Arsenal's home ground. The game ended in a 1–1 draw. They replay was also drawn 0–0 before the second replay took the teams to Millwall. Again the teams were level at 2–2 which sent them to Tottenham for the third replay. Once more there was a 1–1 draw until the tie moved nearer to Gillingham with the fourth replay staged at Gravesend. This time New Brompton won 1–0. At the time New Brompton were members of the Southern League, Woolwich Arsenal in Division Two of the Football League.

Fred Smith scored four goals in seven minutes for **Grimsby Town** in a Division Three (North) match against Hartlepools United on 15 November 1952. His goals came in the 14th, 17th, 19th and 21st minutes of a 7–0 win.

Although Albert Valentine set up the **Halifax Town** scoring record in 1934–35 with 34 goals in Division Three (North), his individual effort in the following season was more remarkable. He scored 29 goals, representing more than half of Halifax's total of 57. Valentine had been signed from Macclesfield after previous League service with Chester, Crewe Alexandra and Cardiff City.

Hamilton Academical were members of the Scottish Combination League when they gained admission to the Scottish League in October 1897, after Renton were forced to withdraw having completed only four fixtures in Division Two. Hamilton finished second from bottom.

On 10 February 1990 **Hartlepool United** beat Stockport County 5–0 in a Division Four game at the Victoria Ground, Hartlepool. On 15 September 1989, Stockport had beaten Hartlepool 6–0 at Edgeley Park. The previous occasion on which Hartlepool had scored five times in a League game had been on 3 April 1985, when they had beaten Stockport County 5–1.

Hearts highest scoring local derby with Hibernian was on 21 September 1935. They were four goals ahead by half-time and took a 5–0 lead shortly afterwards. From then the scoring went: 6–0, 6–1, 6–2, 6–3, 7–3 and finally 8–3.

Mel Pejic overhauled Chris Price's record of 330 League appearances for **Hereford United** during 1989–90. Price had achieved his total between 1976–86.

Goalscoring was not a problem for **Hibernian** in 1959–60. In Division One they were top scorers with 106 goals, of which Joe Baker scored 41. The reserves did even better with 129 League goals in their competition. But Hibs failed to obtain a point in the League Cup qualifying competition and made an indifferent start to the League programme. From the beginning of January until the end of the season they won just three games, conceding 85 goals overall, and were unable to finish higher than seventh.

Although the League aggregate goalscoring record for **Huddersfield Town** is equally shared by George Brown and Jimmy Glazzard with 142 goals, Glazzard would be well ahead if wartime regional matches were included. From 1943–44 to 1945–46 he scored 33 League and League War Cup goals in 98 matches. Brown's career at Huddersfield began in May 1921 when he was signed from Mickley, and ended in May 1929 when he was transferred to Aston

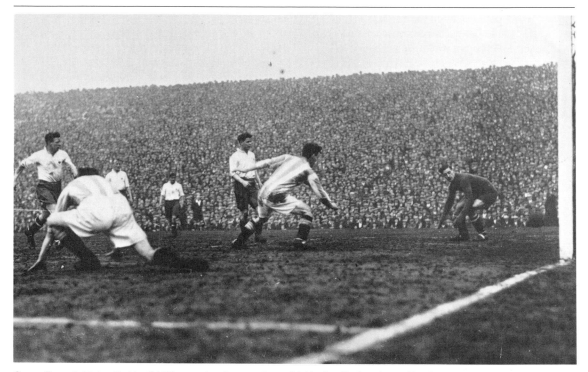

George Brown holds two Huddersfield Town goalscoring records on a joint basis with other players. Here (centre, striped shirt) he scores his fourth and his team's fifth goal in the 20th minute of their FA Cup sixth round tie with Tottenham Hotspur in March 1928. Huddersfield led 6–0 at half-time and won 6–1 (Ian M. C. Thomas)

Villa. During this period he scored 159 League and Cup goals in 229 games. Glazzard was signed in October 1943 from the Altofts club and his peace-time League and Cup tally was 154 in 321 outings. He equalled Brown's 142 total on 28 April 1956 at Leeds Road in a 3–1 win over Bolton Wanderers, which unfortunately did not save Huddersfield from relegation to Division One on goal average. Glazzard might well have added to his total but for playing many matches at inside-forward rather than centre-forward.

The nearest that **Hull City** came to achieving Division One status was in 1909–10. They finished third, one point behind the champions Manchester City and level on points with Oldham Athletic, who finished runners-up, and Derby County who were fourth. Hull's last game of the season was at Oldham where they needed just one point for promotion. Instead they lost 3–0. That season must have caused reporters some confusion as Hull had the brothers Browell, Andy and George, Davy and Dan Gordon, plus the unrelated Smiths, Jackie, Joe (known as Stanley to avoid confusion!) and Wally as well as Tim and Gordon Wright.

Ipswich Town made rapid progress towards Football League status in the 1930s. In 1934–35 they were still playing in the Southern Amateur League along with teams such as the Civil Service, Catford Wanderers and a variety of Banks: Barclays, Lloyds, Midland, Westminster and even the Bank of England. They were even managing to play in the AFA (Amateur) Cup and the FA Cup in the same season. After finishing fourth that season they switched to the Eastern Counties league in 1935–36, finishing sixth, and entered the Southern League in 1936–37 after turning professional. They won the championship at the first attempt and applied for election to the Third Division (South). The result of the poll was: Exeter City 40 votes, Aldershot 34, Ipswich Town 34. Exeter and Aldershot were re-elected. Although Ipswich only finished third in the Southern League in 1937–38, they finished with 36 votes at the AGM of the Football League compared with Walsall's 34 and Gillingham's 28 and were elected.

On 13 May 1989, the last day of the season, **Kilmarnock** beat already-relegated Queen of the South 6–0 on their opponents's ground at Palmerston Park, but still went down themselves on goal difference. Clyde survived at Killie's expense having beaten St Johnstone 2–0, by a goal difference of just one. In Kilmarmarnock's win, Willie Watters had scored five times.

As a new club, **Leeds United** had to enter the preliminary rounds of the FA Cup in 1920–21. On 11 September Leeds found themselves drawn at home to Boothtown in the extra-preliminary round of the competition on the same day as they were required to fulfill a Division Two fixture at Leicester City. The reserves played in the cup tie and won 5–2, while the first team won 3–1. Leeds were fined £50 by the Football Association for fielding a second team but were allowed to repeat the process in the next round when they were drawn away to Leeds Steelworks, who conceded home advantage and were beaten 7–0. At the same time the FA made it clear that in future rounds Leeds would be required to field a full-strength team. Leeds then withdrew from the competition, unbeaten.

Leicester City had a brief flirtation with European football in 1961–62. They began well enough in the Cup-Winners' Cup first round, winning 4–1 away to Glenavon and completing the tie with a 3–1 success at home. In the second round they managed a 1–1 draw with Atletico Madrid at Filbert Street, the Spaniards only equalising in the last minute. In Madrid they succumbed 2–0 after stubborn resistance, with goalkeeper Gordon Banks saving one of two Atletico penalties. The Spanish side went on to win the trophy.

Leyton Orient showed remarkable spirit in gaining promotion to Division One behind Liverpool in the 1961–62 season. Settling down in October they had a run of 16 games with only one defeat and from the end of November the O's remained in second place. Their home and away record was identical with 11 wins and five drawn games in each. On the last day of the season, 28 April, Orient were at Brisbane Road against Bury while Sunderland travelled to Swansea. Orient won 2–0 while Sunderland could only draw 1–1, giving the London club a point advantage.

On 16 September 1935 Alf Horne played a true captain's game for **Lincoln City** in their Division Three (North) fixture against Stockport County. He converted three penalties in a 3–0 win.

Liverpool achieved 90 points in 40 Division One matches in 1987–88. They lost just twice and remained unbeaten at home. In fact they did not lose until their 30th match when neighbours Everton beat them 1–0. The run equalled Leeds United's 29

undefeated games from the start of the 1973–74 season. Only six opposing teams scored at Anfield, Manchester United achieving the best result in a 3–3 draw, and just nine goals were conceded there. Liverpool went to the top of the table on 17 October and though they were headed briefly on 21 November, they regained the lead a week later and retained it. Of the 87 goals scored, John Aldridge hit 26 of them, including ten penalties. John Barnes and Peter Beardsley were joint second with 15 goals each. Liverpool failed to score in only four games.

On 6 February 1988, **Luton Town** beat Oxford United 7–4 at Kenilworth Road in a First Division match. It was the highest aggregate of goals scored in the division since Chelsea defeated Newcastle United 6–5 in September 1958.

When **Maidstone United** played at Gillingham on 26 December 1989 in the first Football League derby game in Kent, they were nearer to 'home' than in the reverse fixture. Maidstone's ground is situated at Dartford, 25 miles from Maidstone, while Gillingham is half the distance away. Maidstone won this historic Division Four game 2–1.

On 14 June 1947 **Manchester City** completed their final game of an extended season prolonged because of bad weather, against already-relegated Newport County. George Smith scored all five City goals in a 5–1 win to equal a club individual record. That season had seen 2.2 million spectators attend fixtures at Maine Road. The ground hosted both City and United home games, an FA Cup semi-final replay between Liverpool and Burnley plus the Rugby League Challenge Cup Final.

Manchester United had five seasons in the European Champions' Cup and never failed to reach at least the semi-final stage on each occasion. In 1967–68 they progressed to the final, beating Benfica 4–1 at Wembley. During this period they won 26 games, drew seven and lost eight. Their highest win was 10–1 against Anderlecht on 26 September 1956, their heaviest defeat 4–0 against AC Milan on 14 May 1958 in the second leg of their post-Munich semi-final.

In 1950–51 **Mansfield Town** finished runners-up in Division Three (North) and also reached the fifth round of the FA Cup. At home in the League they remained unbeaten and conceded only 19 goals. No team scored more than two goals at Field Mill where Mansfield dropped only six points. No other team in the entire League was unbeaten that season at home. Player-manager Freddie Steele was an inspirational leader and was one of four forwards to reach double figures. But for dropping 11 of the first 16 away points, they might well have done even better. That same season the ground record attendance was broken when 20 374 watched the FA Cup fourth round tie against Sheffield United.

Meadowbank Thistle were unlucky not to win promotion to the Premier Division in 1987–88. Although they finished the season four points behind Division One champions Hamilton Academical, they had the opportunity to finish top themselves near the end of the term. Unfortunately with only three points out of a possible ten, their chance was lost. Hamilton themselves managed only two points from their last four games. Normally, runners-up position would have guaranteed promotion, but with Premier Division reorganisation taking place, only one team went up to replace the three being relegated.

On 25 April 1953 **Middlesbrough** needed at least one point to be sure of avoiding relegation when they met Manchester United in a Division One match at Ayresome Park. They had not beaten United since the war, having lost 12 and drawn only one of their previous meetings. But two early goals from Wilf Mannion and an injury to United's Jack Rowley put Middlesbrough on the way to victory which was completed in the second half at 5–0 with Lindy Delapenha, Johnny Spuhler and Arthur Fitzsimons adding the other goals. Middlesbrough won their last game of the season 4–1 at Portsmouth to finish as high as 13th.

Millwall won the championship of Division Three (South) in 1937–38 despite an indifferent start to the season which saw them take just one point from their opening three games. They were not beaten again for ten matches but last all three games in December. However they lost just once in the last 16 outings, finishing with six successive victories.

In 1986–87 **Montrose** used five different goalkeepers in their last five games in Division One. Of these matches they won two, lost two and drew one. But they were still relegated at the end of the season.

In the 1987–88 season **Morton** won only three of their 44 Premier Division matches and drew another ten. Of the 27 goals they scored, all but nine of them came in the opening 12 games. In all they failed to score in 27 attempts. They finished bottom and were relegated.

Wilf Mannion of Middlesbrough and England was often referred to as the text-book inside-forward. His career was long and varied. After joining Middlesbrough in September 1936 from South Bank St Peters he spent 18 years at the club before retiring in June 1954. He returned to play for Hull City in December 1954 and subsequently for Poole Town, Cambridge United, Kings Lynn, Haverhill Rovers and after a spell working at Vauxhall Motors in Luton he became player-manager of Earlestown before finally hanging up his boots in 1962 (Evening Gazette, Middlesbrough)

Motherwell were leading Celtic 2–0 with eight minutes of the 1931 Scottish Cup final remaining. But Jimmy McGrory reduced the deficit for Celtic and in the last minute Motherwell centre-half Alan Craig headed a cross from Celtic winger Bertie Thompson into his own goal with no opponent near him. Celtic won the replay 4–2.

On 26 December 1933 **Newcastle United** scored four goals in five minutes at Everton in a Division One match which they won 7–3. After losing 2–0 at Portsmouth in their next game on 30 December they played at home to Liverpool on New Year's Day and hit seven goals in the last 30 minutes to win 9–2.

Sharing their County Ground with Northamptonshire Cricket Club has caused beginning and end-of-season problems for **Northampton Town**. In 1963, the year of the big freeze, the ground switched back to football twice after cricket had started. On 9 May, Northampton beat Carlisle United 2–0 to achieve the Third Division championship and on 24 May they defeated Hull City 3–0.

Norwich City achieved promotion for the first time in 1933–34 when they won the championship of Division Three (South). They scored 88 goals, 71 of which were contributed by five players: Jack Vinall (21), Billy Warnes (21), Ken Burditt (14), Thomas Scott (9) and Rod Williams (6), the latter making just eight appearances. After losing 3–2 at Clapton Orient on 30 December 1933, City remained unbeaten in their next 16 matches. They lost only one of their last 20. Goalkeeper Norman Wharton kept a clean sheet on 16 occasions and City's five away defeats were the fewest in the entire League.

Alex Higgins was the first **Nottingham Forest** player to score as many as five goals in a competitive match. He did so in an FA Cup tie against Clapton Orient in 1890–91. Forest won 14–0 away, a record for an away cup-tie. Higgins scored four goals on two occasions that season in the Football Alliance against Darwen and Crewe Alexandra, a hat-trick against Newton Heath in the same competition plus another in the FA Cup against Sunderland Albion. The following season Higgins hit four in the Alliance against Lincoln City and another League hit-trick against Grimsby Town. Between September 1890 and April 1894 he scored 89 in 107 matches for the club.

For many years **Notts County** was thought to be the oldest Football League club, having been formed in 1862, and indeed the club celebrated its centenary in 1962. However the researches of Keith Warsop have subsequently revealed that the club was on a haphazard basis, playing little more than practice matches. The meeting which put the club on a firm footing was held at the George IV Hotel in December 1864 when they became known as the Notts Football Club. But the club has played more Football League matches than any other, reaching 3656 at the end of the 1989–90 season. Moreover they remain the oldest.

In 1988–89 Roger Palmer set a goalscoring record for **Oldham Athletic** when he reached his 113th League goal for the club. The previous record had been established by Eric Gemmell with 110 goals between 1947 and 1954. Palmer was signed from Manchester City in the 1980–81 season.

Although **Oxford United** became the first club from Division Four to reach the sixth round of the FA Cup in 1963–64, they had actually played more games in 1953–54 when they managed to get to the fourth round while still outside the League. As members of the Southern League, they were required to enter the

Roger Palmer has scored more League goals than any other Oldham Athletic player in history (Sporting Pictures)

competition in the first qualifying round. They beat Aylesbury United 2–1, Maidenhead United 4–0, Chesham United 2–0, Wealdstone 3–0, Harwich & Parkeston 3–2, Millwall 1–0 after a 3–3 draw, and Stockport County 1–0 after a 0–0 draw. In the fourth round they were beaten 4–2 by Bolton Wanderers, then members of Division One. That season Oxford finished runners-up in the Southern League and won the Southern League Cup.

Inconsistency has been a continuing factor in the history of **Partick Thistle**. The 1950–51 season was no exception. They finished sixth in Division One and of the five clubs above them only Aberdeen took full points from them. In addition they twice beat Rangers, the runners-up, and held champions Hibernian in both meetings. But they lost to both relegated clubs Clyde and Falkirk.

While **Peterborough United** were still members of the Midland League and with only one defeat all season, they played an FA Cup first round match at home to Ipswich Town, then in Division Three (South). With ten players boasting League experience, Peterborough deservedly won 3–1. A ground record crowd of 20843 attended. In 1959–60 Ipswich had reached Division Two and found themselves drawn at home to Peterborough in the third round of the competition. United won again, this time 3–2. Peterborough were elected to the League the same year.

On Boxing Day 26 December 1930, **Plymouth Argyle** defeated Cardiff City 5–1 in a Division Two game at Home Park. The Argyle players then spent over ten hours in a train during an all-night journey to Liverpool for a match against Everton at Goodison Park. Everton were fresh, having not had a game the previous day. The visiting players arrived at 6 am, in torrential rain. Then the Argyle team had four hours sleep before arriving at Goodison to find half a gale blowing and the centre of the pitcy so wet that the toss-up had to be made on the touchline! Result: Everton 9 Plymouth Argyle 1.

Bill Thompson scored only two goals in his Football League career but they were of vital significance for Portsmouth. He is seen here taking a practice throw-in while with Bournemouth (Colorsport)

Portsmouth had to win the last match of the 1949–50 season to retain their Division One title. They were forced to use Bill Thompson at centre-forward as deputy for the injured Ike Clarke. It was his first match for the senior side as a forward, though he had played at wing-half and centre-half as well as full-back. Aston Villa were the opponents at Fratton Park, while Wolverhampton Wanderers were playing already-relegated Birmingham City hoping for

Pompey to drop at least a point in order to snatch the title for themselves. Thompson, who had not scored a goal before, scored in the first minute. But news that Wolves were also ahead was the prelude for a half-time score at Molyneux of 5–0. Portsmouth led 2–0 at the break and went on to win 5–1, Thompson scoring another goal, while Wolves were 6–1 winners. Both teams had 53 points but Portsmouth became the first team since Huddersfield Town in 1923–24 to win the championship on goal average and the first to succeed in consecutive years since Sheffield Wednesday twenty years earlier. Portsmouth's goal average was 1.947, while Wolves' was 1.551. The two goals by Thompson were the only ones he scored for the club.

Port Vale had a disturbed time in their early years of membership in Division Two. They lost their status in 1896 and spent two years in the Midland League. In 1897–98 they were drawn in the FA Cup against Sheffield United who had been runners-up in Division One during the previous season. After a 1–1 draw, Port Vale beat United 2–1 in extra time in the replay, their opponents going on to win the League championship.

Preston North End won their first League game 5–2 against Burnley on 8 September 1888 and remained unbeaten in any first-class game until 21 September 1889 when they were beaten 5–3 away to Aston Villa. They had achieved the League and Cup double during this sequence of one year and 13 days.

Queen of the South won only two First Division matches in 1988–89, both by 2–1; one at home to Forfar Athletic, the other at Meadowbank Thistle. They managed just 12 points but had two of these deducted for a breach of rules. They were relegated.

Queen's Park scored 13 goals against Queen of the South in the 1956–57 season and two of their players produced hat-tricks. At Hampden Park, Queen's Park won 7–0 with Hunter Devine scoring three, while at Palmerston Park in a 6–1 victory, it was Junior Omand who hit a trio of goals.

George Goddard's club record of 37 League goals in one season for **Queen's Park Rangers** has stood for 60 years. In Division Three (South) in 1929–30 he not only topped the club scoring list but was the leading marksman in the division. Born at Gomshall near Guildford, he had originally combined amateur football for Redhill with work in a local bus garage. He turned professional in 1926 for Rangers and was transferred to Wolverhampton Wanderers in December 1933, having taken his total of League goals to 172, another record intact at Loftus Road. He later played for Sunderland and Southend United where he combined playing with shopkeeping in London.

Raith Rovers won a five-goal Scottish Cup second round tie against Clyde on 11 February 1950 without one of their players scoring. Three Clyde players put through their own goal. Raith won 3–2.

On 23 November 1984 **Rangers** signed a 14-year-old Catholic schoolboy, John Spencer. Previously the only known Roman Catholic to have actually played for the club had been Laurie Blyth between 1951 and 1953. But in July 1989 Rangers paid £1.2 million to Nantes for the Catholic striker Mo Johnston, formerly with Celtic. On 4 November 1989 Johnston scored the only goal of the game against Celtic at Ibrox Park in the 88th minute, before a crowd of 41 598.

Steve Hetzke was not only the youngest player to make his debut for **Reading** at the age of 16 years 191 days in a Division Four game at Darlington on 18 December 1971, he also wore the following shirt numbers during his career at Elm Park until 1982: 2, 3, 4, 5, 6, 7, 9, 10, 11 and 12. He was also nominated emergency goalkeeper during 1974–75, though he was not called upon to appear in that position.

Rochdale enjoyed their longest FA Cup run in 1989–90. They reached the fifth round for the first time in their history and did not concede a goal before losing 1–0 to Crystal Palace at Selhurst Park. In the first round they won 1–0 away to Marine, in a game switched to Anfield. They then beat Lincoln City 3–0 at home, while in the third they had a 1–0 win over Whitley Bay, again at Spotland. Another home success 3–0 against Northampton Town, saw them through to the fifth round.

Rotherham United began their 1928–29 fixtures in Division Three (North) at Bradford City. They were beaten 11–1. But two days later they beat Lincoln City 3–2 in their first home game. Apart from losing 10–1 at Gateshead on 16 March, they did not concede more than four goals in any other game. They finished 16th.

At the end of the 1988–89 season, **St Johnstone** handed over Muirton Park – their ground since 1924 – to the Asda supermarket chain, in exchange for Asda building them a £4.4 million stadium on land owned and presented to the club by Bruce McDiarmid, a life-long supporter. The site was on the outskirts of Perth and is known as McDiarmid Park. It has a 10 000 all-seated capacity with an adjacent all-weather surface for club and community use.

St Johnstone became the latest club in Britain to move to a new ground when they opened the McDiarmid Park stadium at the beginning of the 1989–90 season (St Johnstone FC)

Ian Ferguson scored an extra-time winner for **St Mirren** in the 1987 Scottish Cup Final against Dundee United in the 110th minute. The club was in its 110th year.

On 4 October 1989 in the second leg of their Littlewoods Cup second round tie, **Scarborough** beat Chelsea 3–2, having drawn the first leg 1–1 at Stamford Bridge. Chelsea were then lying fourth in Division One. But in the third round Scarborough lost 7–0 away to Oldham Athletic of Division Two and proceeded to lose the next six Division Four matches.

In 1934–35 while still members of the Midland League, **Scunthorpe United** were drawn away to Coventry City of Division Three (South) in the first round of the FA Cup. Scunthorpe were outclassed and lost 7–0. It was not the end of a glimpse of the trophy itself that season though, nor was it the last Cup meeting with Coventry. Sheffield Wednesday won the FA Cup and in a Hospital Cup game against United at the end of the season, they paraded the trophy around the ground. In the first round of the competition in 1935–36 Scunthorpe were again paired with Coventry, who if anything, were in better form than the previous season. But

thanks to heroic goalkeeping by Gordon Young and an opportunist goal at the other end, Scunthorpe earned a replay at home following this 1–1 draw. A crowd of 7 084 turned up for the game but after 30 minutes Coventry were leading 2–0. Scunthorpe, though, scored three times before the interval and again ten minutes from the end to win 4–2. Coventry went on to win the Third Division (South) championship that season.

There have been six examples of two **Sheffield United** players scoring hat-tricks in the same match:
6 April 1896 – United 8 Bury 0 (Harry Harwood and Walter Egan)
1 January 1926 – United 11 Cardiff City 2 (David Mercer and Harry Johnsdon)
9 December 1939 – United 7 Notts County 1 (Jack Pickering and Collin Collindridge)
6 December 1941 – United 9 Lincoln City 0 (Charlie Thompson and Harold Barton)
27 January 1945 – United 10 Lincoln City 2 (Walter Rickett and Albert Nightingale)
17 September 1988 – United 6 Chester City 1 (Brian Deane and Tony Agana)

Sheffield Wednesday have four times regained First Division status the season after being relegated. They achieved this feat in 1899–1900, 1951–52,

Sheffield United's scoring duo of Tony Agana (left) and Brian Deane scored prolifically during the 1988–89 season (Sporting Pictures)

A stalwart for Sheffield Wednesday for two decades was Redfern Froggatt who achieved England international honours while serving the Owls (JR)

1955–56 and 1958–59. In each season they were champions of the Second Division. No other League club has had as many immediate returns to Division One. Redfern Froggatt, who had 20 years with the Owls, played in three of these successful seasons and also helped in a fourth. In 1958–59 he captained the team and produced his highest total of League goals, with 26 to his credit.

Shrewsbury Town had two eventful first seasons in the Football League. Elected in 1950–51 in the expansion programme for the Third Division, they played in the Northern section and finished 20th. Because they were required to play in the preliminary rounds of the FA Cup, they opted out of the competition. The following season they were transferred to the Southern section of Division Three and finished 20th again.

On 1 October 1951 **Southampton** staged what they claimed to be the first competitive football match under floodlights in Britain. It was a Football Combination fixture against Tottenham Hotspur and attracted a crowd of 13 654. Spurs won 1–0.

Southend United's best season in the Third Division (South) was in 1949–50. Apart from losing their opening game 2–0 at Notts County, they were top of the table on 3 September after beating Bristol Rovers 3–1 at Southend Stadium, on goal average from Northampton Town. It was the first time since the 1931–32 season that they had headed the division. That season they finished third. On 6 May 1950 Southend needed to win at Leyton Orient to secure the runners-up position behind Notts County. They drew 2–2 and were resigned to third place on goal average after achieving the same number of points as Northampton.

Stenhousemuir called upon the services of 45 different players in the 1986–87 season including seven goalkeepers. They finished third from bottom in Division Two but had the satisfaction of winning the Stirlingshire Cup for the first time in 12 years by beating Stirling Albion 1–0.

On 5 September 1987 the first competitive match in Scotland played on artificial turf was staged at Annfield Park; **Stirling Albion** drew 1–1 with Ayr United in the Second Division game.

Stockport County have four times provided the leading goalscorer in Division Three (North). Joe Smith (38 goals) in 1927–28, Frank Newton (36) in 1929–30, Alf Lythgoe (46) in 1933–34 and Jackie Connor (30) in 1954–55 all headed the division's scorers. Lythgoe's total is a club record. He was working on the railway at Crewe when he was told to choose between his job and football. He signed for Crewe Alexandra but was considered too small for a centre-forward and allowed to drift out of the League to Whitchurch, Sandbach, Congleton and Ashton National until Stockport recruited him in May 1931, at the age of 20. In October 1934 he was transferred to Huddersfield Town having continued his exceptional scoring form at the start of that season with 15 goals, in 11 outings, including five in one game. He then scored on his Huddersfield Town debut against Sheffield Wednesday, finishing the season on 21 goals. Returning to Stockport in March 1938 he was unable to save them from relegation to the Third Division (North), but was their leading scorer on 20 League goals in 1938–39. Off the field he was an accomplished jazz drummer.

It had been assumed that **Stoke City** derived their origin from as long ago as 1863. But recent research by Wade Martin, the club's historian, put the formation as 1868, when a couple of Old Carthusians apprenticed at the North Staffordshire Railway Company formed Stoke Ramblers with some of their workmates. Forty years later Stoke went bankrupt and a new club was formed.

Stranraer completed 28 Second Division matches between September and April in 1987–88 without a win. This dismal run included 15 successive defeats. They won only four League games, scored 34 goals in 39 matches and finished bottom with 16 points. They used 43 different players during the season.

Sunderland were the first to score a century of goals in the Football League. They achieved exactly 100 in 30 matches during their second Division One championship in 1892–93. Fifty-eight goals were scored at home. Their highest win was 8–1 against West Bromwich Albion and on four other occasions they scored six goals. John Campbell was top scorer with 28 goals, and three players with the forename James also reached double figures: Hannah, Gillespie and Millar with 18, 12 and 11 goals respectively. In the previous season, when they had achieved their first championship, they had become known as 'The Team of all the Talents', their usual line-up consisting almost entirely of Scottish players. The exception was Tom Porteous, signed from Kilmarnock but born in England.

In 1948–49 when **Swansea Town** (later Swansea City) won the championship of Division Three (South), the club established a number of records: 17 wins in succession at home; six wins in a row away; 27 wins during the season; the highest number of points (62) and the most successive games without conceding a goal (5). Top scorer was Stan Richards, newly signed from Cardiff City. He had a history of knee injuries and it was rumoured he could not train properly because of them. But he managed 26 goals in 32 appearances.

Swindon Town achieved 102 points in 46 Division Four matches in 1985–86, a Football League record. They owed their total to a fine home record which saw them drop only five points. Strangely enough their sole defeat at the County Ground arrived on the opening day of the season when Wrexham beat them 1–0. Only Port Vale in a 0–0 draw on 23 March and Scunthorpe United in a 1–1 draw on 12 April escaped defeat afterwards on Swindon's territory. They achieved promotion on 8 April by beating Chester City 4–2 at home with seven matches still to play. Of their 82 goals, Charlie Henry was leading scorer on 18, followed by Colin Gordon with 17, then Peter Coyne and Bryan Wade with ten each. Swindon's achievement was surprising in view of the fact that they lost five of their first eight games and were in 21st place on 28 September. But from 12 January until the end of the season they were unbeaten in a run of 21 games.

Torquay United failed to win promotion from Division Three (South) in 1956–57 on goal average. With three matches remaining Colchester United, Ipswich Town and Torquay were all in contention for the one promotion place. But in their last but one game, Colchester were beaten and Ipswich could only draw, leaving Torquay, who had won their match, one point above Ipswich and two ahead of Colchester. On the last day of the season, 1 May 1957, Ipswich travelled to Southampton and Torquay to Crystal Palace. The Ipswich match kicked-off 45 minutes earlier than the game at Palace. Ipswich won 2–0, but Torquay could only manage a 1–1 draw. Torquay's goal average was .48 inferior to Ipswich.

On 16 March 1912, **Tottenham Hotspur** beat Liverpool 2–1 at Anfield in a Division One match. They did not repeat their success until 16 March

A goal by Garth Crooks for Spurs in March 1985 ended a long sequence of disappointment for the club at Liverpool (Associated Sports Photography)

1985 when a second half goal from Garth Crooks gave Spurs a 1–0 victory.

Tranmere Rovers achieved promotion for the first time in the 1937–38 season. They finished top of the Third Division (North) two points ahead of Doncaster Rovers. The defence which conceded 41 goals in 42 games did not let in more than two goals in any one match, but the attack which scored 81 almost hit a rate of 2:1.

Justifiably considered as one of the most outstanding FA Cup 'giant-killing' performances of all time was the 2–0 win achieved by **Walsall** of Division Three (South) over Division One Arsenal on 14 January 1933 in a third round tie. Walsall repeated the feat in a Milk Cup fourth round tie at Highbury on 29 November 1983 when they beat Arsenal 2–1. But even before the turn of the century, Walsall had managed to record better results against Arsenal when both teams were in Division Two. The sides met 14 times between 1894–95 and 1900–01 and Walsall won six of their seven home games: 4–1, 5–3, 3–2, 4–1, 2–0 and 1–0. Overall Arsenal managed just five wins and three draws.

Watford scored only 27 League goals in 1987–88. Their leading marksman was Luther Blissett with four. Their highest win was 3–0 against Oxford United who finished one point below them in the First Division. Both teams were relegated. But in a Littlewoods Cup second round tie, the Hornets won 3–0 in the first leg at Darlington and 8–0 in the return at Vicarage Road. They reached the fourth round of the Littlewoods and the sixth round of the FA Cup.

West Bromwich Albion were the first British club to win a match in the Soviet Union. They played a three-match tour in June 1957, drawing 1–1 with Zenit Leningrad on 2 June, beating Dynamo Tbilisi 3–0 on 7 June and finishing with a 4–2 win over CSKA Moscow, the Central Army club, on 12 June. Derek Kevan scored five of Albion's goals. In May 1978 Albion became the first European professional team to visit the People's Republic of China, winning all five games with a goals tally of 16–1. Cyrille Regis was the top scorer with six goals.

West Ham United winger Ken Tucker earned the nickname of 'sprayer' after some supporters noticed that a report on one of the club's games had referred to him 'spraying passes to colleagues'. He scored a hat-trick on his debut in 1947–48 but did not score another senior goal until 1951–52. His 31 goals in 84 games were spread over ten seasons as follows: 3, 0, 0, 0, 5, 3, 0, 0, 14, 16.

Wolverhampton Wanderers became the first Football League club to have won the championship of all four divisions by taking the Third Division title in 1988–89. The previous season they had won the Fourth Division championship. In 1931–32 they were Second Division champions for the first time and achieved the first of their Division One honours in 1953–54. Wolves were League champions again in 1957–58 and 1958–59 and added another Second Division title in 1976–77.

Wigan Athletic were twice involved in close selection finishes at the AGM of the Football League before they gained admission. In 1950 Wigan and Workington each achieved the same number of votes on the first ballot, only for Scunthorpe United to overtake them both on the second vote. Wigan did manage to do better in 1978, but only after again tying on the first ballot with Southport, both clubs receiving 26 votes. In the re-run Wigan achieved 29 to Southport's 20.

Wimbledon won the FA Cup in 1988 in their 11th season as a member of the Football League and only their second in Division One. Their victims were: West Bromwich Albion (H) 4–1, Mansfield Town (A) 2–1, Watford (H) 2–1, Luton Town (at White Hart Lane) 2–1 and Liverpool (at Wembley) 1–0. Lawrie Sanchez scored the only goal in the final and goalkeeper Dave Beasant saved a John Aldridge penalty.

Wrexham have provided more international players for Wales than any other club in the British Isles has supplied for one of the four home international teams. At the beginning of the 1989–90 season there had been a total of 76 who had worn the colours of Wales while on the books of the oldest club in the Principality.

The oldest player to turn out in a League game for **York City** was Matt Middleton, who kept goal at the age of 42 years 6 months. In the 1949–50 season he missed only four matches in Division Three (North). But after a poor start, the team struggled and on the last day of the season travelled to New Brighton needing a win to avoid seeking re-election. But they were beaten 3–1 and were forced to apply after finishing bottom for the first time since they had entered the League in 1929. Middleton had previously played for Bradford City, Plymouth Argyle, Sunderland, Southport and Boldon Colliery Welfare. Born in Jarrow he was the brother of another goalkeeper, Ray Middleton.

Directory of Football League Clubs

Ground	Capacity[1] & record attendance	League career		Honours (domestic) League	Cup
ALDERSHOT (1926) Red, blue trim/blue					
Recreation Ground High Street Aldershot GU11 1TW 116×76 yd	12 000 19 138 v Carlisle FA Cup 4th Rd replay, 28 January 1970	1932–58 Div. 3(S) 1958–73 Div. 4 1973–76 Div. 3	1976–87 Div. 4 1987–89 Div. 3 1989– Div. 4	Highest placing 8th Div. 3 1974	FA Cup never past 5th Rd League Cup never past 3rd Rd
ARSENAL (1886) Red, white sleeves/white					
Arsenal Stadium Highbury London N5 1BU 110×71 yd	47 193 73 295 v Sunderland Div. 1 9 March 1935	1893–1904 Div. 2 1904–13 Div. 1	1913–15 Div. 2 1919– Div. 1	Div. 1 Champions 1931, 1933, 1934, 1935, 1938, 1948, 1953, 1971, 1989, Runners-up 1926, 1932, 1973, Div. 2 runners-up 1904	FA Cup winners 1930, 1936, 1950, 1971, 1979 Runners-up 1927, 1932, 1952, 1972, 1978, 1980 League Cup winners 1987 Runners-up 1968, 1969, 1988
ASTON VILLA (1874) Claret, light blue trim/white					
Villa Park Trinity Road Birmingham B6 6HE 115×75 yd	42 039 76 588 v Derby Co FA Cup 6th Rd 2 March 1946	1888 (founder member of League) 1936–38 Div. 2 1938–59 Div. 1 1959–60 Div. 2 1960–67 Div. 1	1967–70 Div. 2 1970–72 Div. 3 1972–75 Div. 2 1975–87 Div. 1 1987–88 Div. 2 1988– Div. 1	Div. 1 Champions 1894, 1896, 1897, 1899, 1900, 1910, 1981 Runners-up 1889, 1903, 1908, 1911, 1913, 1914, 1931, 1933, 1990. Div. 2 Champions 1938, 1960 Runners-up 1975, 1988 Div. 3 Champions 1972	FA Cup winners 1887, 1895, 1897, 1905, 1913, 1920 1957 (joint record) Runners-up 1892, 1924 League Cup winners 1961, 1975, 1977 Runners-up 1963, 1971
BARNSLEY (1887) Red/white					
Oakwell Ground Grove Street Barnsley S71 1ET 110×75 yd	30 099 40 255 v Stoke City FA Cup 5th Rd 15 February 1936	1898 elected to Div. 2 1932–34 Div. 3(N) 1934–38 Div. 2 1938–39 Div. 3(N) 1946–53 Div. 2 1953–55 Div. 3(N).	1955–59 Div. 2 1959–65 Div. 3 1965–68 Div. 4 1968–72 Div. 3 1972–79 Div. 4 1979–81 Div. 3 1981– Div. 2	Div. 3(N) Champions 1934, 1939, 1955 Runners-up 1954 Div. 3 runners-up 1981 Div. 4 runners-up 1968	FA Cup winners 1912 Runners-up 1910 League Cup never past 5th Rd

¹ Ground alterations and safety recommendations have meant capacities are in a constant state of change. Those listed here were in operation for the 1989–90 season, and follow the 15 per cent reduction in terrace capacity enforced after the Hillsborough tragedy.

² Three points for a win was introduced from the start of the 1981–82 season; club points records are given for both two and three points.

Most League points²	goals	Record win	Highest number of League goals for club in total	in a season	Most League appearances for club	Most capped player

ALDERSHOT

| 57, Div. 4 1978–79 75, Div. 4 1983–84 | 83, Div. 4 1963–64 | 8–1 Gateshead Div. 4 13 September 1958 | Jack Howarth 171, 1965–71 1972–77 | John Dungworth 26 Div. 4 1978–79 | Murray Brodie, 461, 1970–83 | Peter Scott 1, N. Ireland 1979 |

ARSENAL

| 66, Div. 1 1930–31 76, Div. 1 1988–89 | 127, Div. 1 1930–31 | 12–0 v Loughborough T. Div. 2 12 March 1900 | Cliff Bastin 150, 1930–47 | Ted Drake 42 Div. 1 1934–35 | David O'Leary 501, 1975–90 | Kenny Sansom 77, England 1980–88 |

ASTON VILLA

| 70, Div. 3 1971–72 78, Div. 2 1987–88 | 128, Div. 1 1930–31 | 13–0 v Wednesbury Old Athletic FA Cup 1st Rd 30 October 1886 | Harry Hampton 215, 1904–15 | Pongo Waring 49 Div. 1 1930–31 | Charlie Aitken 561, 1961–76 | Peter McParland 33, N. Ireland 1954–61 |

BARNSLEY

| 67, Div. 3 (N) 1938–39 74, Div. 2 1988–89 | 118, Div. 3 (N) 1933–34 | 9–0 v Loughborough T. Div. 2 28 January 1899 Accrington Stanley Div. 3(N) 3 February 1934 | Ernest Hine 123, 1921–26 1934–38 | Cecil McCormack 33 Div. 2 1950–51 | Barry Murphy 514, 1962–78 | Eddie McMorran 9, N. Ireland 1950–52 |

Ground	Capacity & record attendance	League career		Honours (domestic) League	Cup

BIRMINGHAM CITY (1875) Blue, white trim/white, blue trim

| St Andrews Birmingham B9 4NH 115×75 yd | 27 689 66 844 v Everton FA Cup 5th Rd 11 February 1939 | 1892–94 Div. 2 1894–96 Div. 1 1896–1901 Div. 2 1901–02 Div. 1 1902–03 Div. 2 1903–08 Div. 1 1908–21 Div. 2 1921–39 Div. 1 1946–48 Div. 2 1948–50 Div. 1 | 1950–55 Div. 2 1955–65 Div. 1 1965–72 Div. 2 1972–79 Div. 1 1979–80 Div. 2 1980–84 Div. 1 1984–85 Div. 2 1985–86 Div. 1 1986–89 Div. 2 1989– Div. 3 | Div. 2 Champions 1893, 1921, 1948, 1955 Runners-up 1894, 1901, 1903, 1972, 1985 | FA Cup runners-up 1931, 1956 League Cup winners 1963 |

BLACKBURN ROVERS (1875) Blue-white halves/white

| Ewood Park Blackburn BB2 4JF 116×72 yd | 17 819 61 783 v Bolton W FA Cup 6th Rd 2 March 1929 | 1888 (founder member of League) 1936–39 Div. 2 1946–47 Div. 1 1947–57 Div. 2 | 1957–66 Div. 1 1966–71 Div. 2 1971–75 Div. 3 1975–79 Div. 2 1979–80 Div. 3 1980– Div. 2 | Div. 1 Champions 1912, 1914 Div. 2 Champions 1939 Runners-up 1958 Div. 3 Champions 1975 Runners-up 1980 | FA Cup winners 1884, 1885, 1886 1890, 1891, 1928 Runners-up 1882, 1960 League Cup semi-finalists 1962 |

BLACKPOOL (1887) Tangerine, white trim/tangerine

| Bloomfield Road Blackpool FY1 6JJ 111×73 yd | 9 760 39 118 v Manchester U Div. 1 19 April 1952 | 1896 elected to Div. 2 1899 failed re-election 1900 re-elected 1900–30 Div. 2 1930–33 Div. 1 1933–37 Div. 2 | 1937–67 Div. 1 1967–70 Div. 2 1970–71 Div. 1 1971–78 Div. 2 1978–81 Div. 3 1981–85 Div. 4 1985–90 Div. 3 1990– Div. 4 | Div. 1 runners-up 1956 Div. 2 Champions 1930 Runners-up 1937, 1970 Div. 4 runners-up 1985 | FA Cup winners 1953 Runners-up 1948, 1951 League Cup semi-finalists 1962 |

BOLTON WANDERERS (1874) White/navy blue

| Burnden Park Bolton BL3 2QR 113×76 yd | 25 000 69 912 v Manchester C FA Cup 5th Rd 18 February 1933 | 1888 (founder member of League) 1899–1900 Div. 2 1900–03 Div. 1 1903–05 Div. 2 1905–08 Div. 1 1908–09 Div. 2 1909–10 Div. 1 1910–11 Div. 2 1911–33 Div. 1 | 1933–35 Div. 2 1935–64 Div. 1 1964–71 Div. 2 1971–73 Div. 3 1973–78 Div. 2 1978–80 Div. 1 1980–83 Div. 2 1983–87 Div. 3 1987–88 Div. 4 1988– Div. 3 | Div. 2 Champions 1909, 1978 Runners-up 1900, 1905, 1911, 1935 Div. 3 Champions 1973 | FA Cup winners 1923, 1926, 1929, 1958 Runners-up 1894, 1904, 1953 League Cup semi-finalists 1977 |

Most League points	goals	Record win	Highest number of League goals for club in total	in a season	Most League appearances for club	Most capped player
BIRMINGHAM CITY						
59, Div. 2 1947–48 82, Div. 2 1984–85	103, Div. 2 1893–94	12–0 v Walsall Town Swifts Div. 2 17 December 1892 Doncaster Rovers Div. 2 11 April 1903	Joe Bradford 249, 1920–35	Walter Abbott 34 Div. 2 1898–99	Frank Womack 491, 1908–28	Malcolm Page 28, Wales 1971–79
BLACKBURN ROVERS						
60, Div. 3 1974–75 77, Div. 2 1987–88, 1988–89	114, Div. 2 1954–55	11–0 v Rossendale United FA Cup 1st Rd 13 October 1884	Simon Garner 162, 1978–90	Ted Harper 43 Div. 1 1925–26	Derek Fazackerley 596, 1970–86	Bob Crompton 41, England 1902–14
BLACKPOOL						
58, Div. 2 1929–30, 1967–68 86, Div. 4 1984–85	98, Div. 2 1929–30	7–0 v Preston North End Div. 1 1 May 1948	Jimmy Hampson 247, 1927–38	Jimmy Hampson 45 Div. 2 1929–30	Jimmy Armfield 568, 1952–71	Jimmy Armfield 43, England 1959–66
BOLTON WANDERERS						
61, Div. 3 1972–73 78, Div. 4 1987–88	96, Div. 2 1934–35	13–0 v Sheffield United FA Cup 2nd Rd 1 February 1890	Nat Lofthouse 255, 1946–61	Joe Smith 38 Div. 1 1920–21	Eddie Hopkinson 519, 1956–70	Nat Lofthouse 33, England 1951–58

Ground	Capacity & record attendance	League career		Honours (domestic) League	Cup

AFC BOURNEMOUTH (1899) All red

Ground	Capacity & record attendance	League career		League	Cup
Dean Court Ground Bournemouth Dorset BH7 7AF 112×75 yd	11 375 28 799 v Manchester U FA Cup 6th Rd 2 March 1957	1923 elected to Div. 3(S) 1970–71 Div. 4 1971–75 Div. 3	1975–82 Div. 4 1982–87 Div. 3 1987–90 Div. 2 1990– Div. 3	Div. 3 Champions 1987 Div. 3(S) runners-up 1948 Div. 4 runners-up 1971	FA Cup never past 6th Rd League Cup never past 4th Rd

BRADFORD CITY (1903) Yellow with claret trim/claret

Ground	Capacity & record attendance	League career		League	Cup
Valley Parade Ground Bradford BD8 7DY 110×76 yd	14 814 39 146 v Burnley FA Cup 4th Rd 11 March 1911	1903 elected to Div. 2 1908–22 Div. 1 1922–27 Div. 2 1927–29 Div. 3(N) 1929–37 Div. 2 1937–61 Div. 3 1961–69 Div. 4	1969–72 Div. 3 1972–77 Div. 4 1977–78 Div. 3 1978–82 Div. 4 1982–85 Div. 3 1985–90 Div. 2 1990– Div. 3	Div. 2 Champions 1908 Div. 3 Champions 1985 Div. 3(N) Champions 1929 Div. 4 runners-up 1982	FA Cup winners 1911 League Cup never past 5th Rd

BRENTFORD (1889) Red-white stripes/black

Ground	Capacity & record attendance	League career		League	Cup
Griffin Park Braemar Road Brentford Middlesex TW8 0NT 111×74 yd	10 850 39 626 v Preston NE FA Cup 6th Rd 5 March 1938	1920 (founder member of Div. 3) 1921–33 Div. 3(S) 1933–35 Div. 2 1935–47 Div. 1 1947–54 Div. 2 1954–62 Div. 3(S)	1962–63 Div. 4 1963–66 Div. 3 1966–72 Div. 4 1972–73 Div. 3 1973–78 Div. 4 1978– Div. 3	Div. 2 Champions 1935 Div. 3(S) Champions 1933 Runners-up 1930, 1958 Div. 4 Champions 1963	FA Cup never past 6th Rd League Cup never past 4th Rd

BRIGHTON & HOVE ALBION (1900) Blue-white stripes/blue

Ground	Capacity & record attendance	League career		League	Cup
The Goldstone Ground Old Shoreham Road Hove, Sussex BN3 7DE 112×75 yd	18 493 36 747 v Fulham Div. 2 27 December 1958	1920 (founder member of Div. 3) 1921–58 Div. 3(S) 1958–62 Div. 2 1962–63 Div. 3 1963–65 Div. 4 1965–72 Div. 3	1972–73 Div. 2 1973–77 Div. 3 1977–79 Div. 2 1979–83 Div. 1 1983–87 Div. 2 1987–88 Div. 3 1988– Div. 2	Div. 2 Runners-up 1979 Div. 3(S) Champions 1958 Runners-up 1954, 1956 Div. 3 runners-up 1972, 1977, 1988 Div. 4 Champions 1965	FA Cup runners-up 1983 League Cup never past 5th Rd

BRISTOL CITY (1894) Red/white

Ground	Capacity & record attendance	League career		League	Cup
Ashton Gate Bristol BS3 2EJ 115×75 yd	25 271 43 335 v Preston NE FA Cup 5th Rd 16 February 1935	1901 elected to Div. 2 1906–11 Div. 1 1911–22 Div. 2 1922–23 Div. 3(S) 1923–24 Div. 2 1924–27 Div. 3(S) 1927–32 Div. 2 1932–55 Div. 3(S)	1955–60 Div. 2 1960–65 Div. 3 1965–76 Div. 2 1976–80 Div. 1 1980–81 Div. 2 1981–82 Div. 3 1982–84 Div. 4 1984–90 Div. 3 1990– Div. 2	Div. 1 runners-up 1907 Div. 2 champions 1906 Runners-up 1976 Div. 3(S) Champions 1923, 1927, 1955 Runners-up 1938 Div. 3 runners-up 1965, 1990	FA Cup runners-up 1909 League Cup semi-finalists 1971, 1989

Most League points	goals	Record win	Highest number of League goals for club in total	in a season	Most League appearances for club	Most capped player

AFC BOURNEMOUTH

Most League points	goals	Record win	Highest number of League goals for club in total	in a season	Most League appearances for club	Most capped player
62, Div. 3 1971–72 97, Div. 3 1986–87	88, Div. 3 (S) 1956–57	11–0 v Margate FA Cup 1st Rd 20 November 1971	Ron Eyre 202, 1924–33	Ted MacDougall 42 Div. 4 1970–71	Ray Bumstead 412, 1958–70	Colin Clarke 6, N. Ireland 1986

BRADFORD CITY

63, Div. 3 (N) 1928–29 94, Div. 3 1984–85	128, Div. 3 (N) 1928–29	11–1 v Rotherham United Div. 3(N) 25 August 1928	Bobby Campbell 121, 1981–84, 1984–86	David Layne 34 Div. 4 1961–62	Cec Podd 502, 1970–84	Harry Hampton 9, N. Ireland 1911–14

BRENTFORD

62, Div. 3(S) 1932–33 Div. 4 1962–63 68, Div. 3 1981–82, 1988–89	98, Div. 4 1962–63	9–0 v Wrexham Div. 3 15 October 1963	Jim Towers 153, 1954–61	Jack Holliday 38 Div. 3(S) 1932–33	Ken Coote 514, 1949–64	Dai Hopkins 12, Wales 1934–39

BRIGHTON & HOVE ALBION

65, Div. 3(S) 1955–56 Div. 3 1971–72 84, Div. 3 1987–88	112, Div. 3(S) 1955–56	10–1 v Wisbech FA Cup 1st Rd 13 November 1965	Tommy Cook 113, 1922–29	Peter Ward 32 Div. 3 1976–77	Tug Wilson 509, 1922–36	Steve Penney 17, N. Ireland 1984–89

BRISTOL CITY

70, Div. 3(S) 1954–55 91, Div. 3 1989–90	104, Div. 3(S) 1926–27	11–0 v Chichester FA Cup 1st Rd 5 November 1960	John Atyeo 314, 1951–66	Don Clark 36 Div. 3(S) 1946–47	John Atyeo 597, 1951–66	Billy Wedlock 26, England 1907–14

Ground	Capacity & record attendance	League career		Honours (domestic) League	Cup

BRISTOL ROVERS (1883) Blue-white quarters/white

| Twerton Park, Bath 112 × 75 yd | 9 813 38 472 v Preston NE FA Cup 4th Rd 30 January 1960 (at Eastville, Bristol) | 1920 (founder member of Div. 3) 1921–53 Div. 3(S) 1953–62 Div. 2 | 1962–74 Div. 3 1974–81 Div. 2 1981–90 Div. 3 1990– Div. 2 | Div. 3(S) Champions 1953 Div. 3 Champions 1990 Runners-up 1974 | FA Cup never past 6th Rd League Cup never past 5th Rd |

BURNLEY (1882) Claret-blue/white

| Turf Moor Burnley BB10 4BX 115 × 73 yd | 25 000 54 775 v Huddersfield T FA Cup 3rd Rd 23 February 1924 | 1888 (founder member of League) 1897–98 Div. 2 1898–1900 Div. 1 1900–13 Div. 2 1913–30 Div. 1 | 1930–47 Div. 2 1947–71 Div. 1 1971–73 Div. 2 1973–76 Div. 1 1976–80 Div. 2 1980–82 Div. 3 1982–83 Div. 2 1983–85 Div. 3 1985– Div. 4 | Div. 1 Champions 1921, 1960 Runners-up 1920, 1962 Div. 2 Champions 1898, 1973 Runners-up 1913, 1947 Div. 3 Champions 1982 | FA Cup winners 1914 Runners-up 1947, 1962 League Cup semi-finalists 1961, 1969, 1983 |

BURY (1885) White/navy blue

| Gigg Lane Bury BL9 9HR 112 × 72 yd | 8 500 35 000 v Bolton W FA Cup 3rd Rd 9 January 1960 | 1894 elected to Div. 2 1895–1912 Div. 1 1912–24 Div. 2 1924–29 Div. 1 1929–57 Div. 2 1957–61 Div. 3 | 1961–67 Div. 2 1967–68 Div. 3 1968–69 Div. 2 1969–71 Div. 3 1971–74 Div. 4 1974–80 Div. 3 1980–85 Div. 4 1985– Div. 3 | Div. 2 Champions 1895 Runners-up 1924 Div. 3 Champions 1961 Runners-up 1968 | FA Cup winners 1900, 1903 League Cup semi-finalists 1963 |

CAMBRIDGE UNITED (1919) Amber/black

| Abbey Stadium Newmarket Road Cambridge CB5 8LL 110 × 74 yd | 10 218 14 000 v Chelsea Friendly 1 May 1970 | 1970 elected to Div. 4 1973–74 Div. 3 1974–77 Div. 4 1977–78 Div. 3 | 1978–84 Div. 2 1984–85 Div. 3 1985–90 Div. 4 1990– Div. 3 | Div. 4 Champions 1977 Div. 3 runners-up 1978 | FA Cup never past 5th Rd League Cup never past 4th Rd |

CARDIFF CITY (1899) Blue/white

| Ninian Park Cardiff CF1 8SX 114 × 78 yd | 19 300 57 800 v Arsenal Div. 1 22 April 1953 | 1920 elected to Div. 2 1921–29 Div. 1 1929–31 Div. 2 1931–47 Div. 3(S) 1947–52 Div. 2 1952–57 Div. 1 1957–60 Div. 2 1960–62 Div. 1 | 1962–75 Div. 2 1975–76 Div. 3 1976–82 Div. 2 1982–83 Div. 3 1983–85 Div. 2 1985–86 Div. 3 1986–88 Div. 4 1988–90 Div. 3 1990– Div. 4 | Div. 1 runners-up 1924 Div. 2 runners-up 1921, 1952, 1960 Div. 3(S) Champions 1947 Div. 3 runners-up 1976, 1983 Div. 4 runners-up 1988 | FA Cup winners 1927 Runners-up 1925 League Cup semi-finalists 1966 |

Most League points	goals	Record win	Highest number of League goals for club in total	in a season	Most League appearances for club	Most capped player
BRISTOL ROVERS						
64, Div. 3(S) 1952–53 93, Div. 3 1989–90	92, Div. 3(S) 1952–53	7–0 v Swansea T Div. 2, 2 Oct 1954 Brighton & HA Div. 3(S) 29 Nov 1952 Shrewsbury T Div. 3, 21 Mar 1964	Geoff Bradford 245, 1949–64	Geoff Bradford 33 Div. 3(S) 1952–53	Stuart Taylor 545, 1966–79	Neil Slatter 10, Wales 1983–85
BURNLEY						
62, Div. 2 1972–73 80, Div. 3 1981–82	102, Div. 1 1960–61	9–0 v Darwen Div. 1 9 January 1892 Crystal Palace FA Cup 2nd Rd replay 27 January 1909 New Brighton FA Cup 4th Rd 26 January 1957 Penrith FA Cup 1st Rd 17 November 1984	George Beel 178, 1923–32	George Beel 35 Div. 1 1927–28	Jerry Dawson 530, 1906–29	Jimmy McIlroy 52, N. Ireland 1951–63
BURY						
68, Div. 3 1960–61 84, Div. 4 1984–85	108, Div. 3 1960–61	12–1 v Stockton FA Cup 1st Rd replay 2 February 1897	Craig Madden 129, 1978–86	Craig Madden 35 Div. 4 1981–82	Norman Bullock 506, 1920–35	Bill Gorman 11, Eire 1936–38
CAMBRIDGE UNITED						
65, Div. 4 1976–77 73, Div. 4 1989–90	87, Div. 4 1976–77	6–0 v Darlington Div. 4 18 September 1971 Hartlepool United Div. 4 11 February 1989	Alan Biley 74, 1975–80	David Crown 24 Div. 4, 1985–86	Steve Spriggs 416, 1975–87	Tom Finney 7, N. Ireland 1979–80
CARDIFF CITY						
66, Div. 3(S) 1946–47 86, Div. 3 1982–83	93, Div. 3(S) 1946–47	8–0 v Enfield FA Cup 1st Rd 28 November 1931	Len Davies 128, 1920–31	Stan Richards 30 Div. 3(S) 1946–47	Phil Dwyer 471, 1972–85	Alf Sherwood 39, Wales 1946–56

Ground	Capacity & record attendance	League career	Honours (domestic) League	Cup

CARLISLE UNITED (1903) Blue/white

Brunton Park	16 267	1928 elected	1974–75 Div. 1	Div. 3 Champions	FA Cup never
Carlisle	27 500 v	to Div. 3(N)	1975–77 Div. 2	1965	past 6th Rd
CA1 1LL	Birmingham C	1958–62 Div. 4	1977–82 Div. 3	Runners-up 1982	League Cup
117 × 78 yd	FA Cup 3rd Rd	1962–63 Div. 3	1982–86 Div. 2	Div. 4 runners-up	semi-finalists
	5 January 1957	1963–64 Div. 4	1986–87 Div. 3	1964	1970
	and Middlesbrough	1964–65 Div. 3	1987– Div. 4		
	FA Cup 5th Rd	1965–74 Div. 2			
	7 February 1970				

CHARLTON ATHLETIC (1905) Red/white

Selhurst Park	30 484	1921 elected	1972–75 Div. 3	Div. 1 runners-up	FA Cup winners
London SE25 6PH	75 031 v	to Div. 3(S)	1975–80 Div. 2	1937	1947
110 × 74 yd	Aston Villa	1929–33 Div. 2	1980–81 Div. 3	Div. 2 runners-up	Runners-up
	FA Cup 5th Rd	1933–35 Div. 3(S)	1981–86 Div. 2	1936, 1986	1946
	12 February 1938	1935–36 Div. 2	1986–90 Div. 1	Div. 3(S)	League Cup
	(at The Valley)	1936–57 Div. 1	1990– Div. 2	Champions 1929,	never past
		1957–72 Div. 2		1935	4th Rd

CHELSEA (1905) Royal blue/blue

Stamford Bridge	36 364	1905 elected	1963–75 Div. 1	Div. 1 Champions	FA Cup winners
London SW6 1HS	82 905 v	to Div. 2	1975–77 Div. 2	1955	1970
114 × 71 yd	Arsenal Div. 1	1907–10 Div. 1	1977–79 Div. 1	Div. 2 Champions	Runners-up
	12 October 1935	1910–12 Div. 2	1979–84 Div. 2	1984, 1989	1915, 1967
		1912–24 Div. 1	1984–88 Div. 1	Runners-up	League Cup
		1924–30 Div. 2	1988–89 Div. 2	1907, 1912, 1930,	winners 1965
		1930–62 Div. 1	1989– Div. 1	1963, 1977	Runners-up
		1962–63 Div. 2			1972

CHESTER CITY (1884) Royal blue/white

Moss Rose Ground	10 000	1931 elected	1975–82 Div. 3	Div. 3(N)	FA Cup never
London Road	20 500 v	to Div. 3(N)	1982–86 Div. 4	Runners-up 1936	past 5th Rd
Macclesfield	Chelsea	1958–75 Div. 4	1986– Div. 3	Div. 4	League Cup
Cheshire SK11 7SP	FA Cup 3rd Rd			Runners-up 1986	semi-finalists
	replay				1975
	16 January 1952				

CHESTERFIELD (1866) Blue/white

Recreation Ground	11 638	1899 elected	1936–51 Div. 2	Div. 3(N)	FA Cup never
Chesterfield	30 968 v	to Div. 2	1951–58 Div. 3(N)	Champions	past 5th Rd
S40 4SX	Newcastle U	1909 failed	1958–61 Div. 3	1931, 1936	League Cup
112 × 72 yd	Div. 2	re-election	1961–70 Div. 4	Runners-up 1934	never past
	7 April 1939	1921 elected to	1970–83 Div. 3	Div. 4 Champions	4th Rd
		Div. 3(N)	1983–85 Div. 4	1970, 1985	
		1931–33 Div. 2	1985–89 Div. 3		
		1933–36 Div. 3(N)	1989– Div. 4		

Most League points	goals	Record win	Highest number of League goals for club in total	in a season	Most League appearances for club	Most capped player
			CARLISLE UNITED			
62, Div. 3(N) 1950–51 80, Div. 3 1981–82	113, Div. 4 1963–64	8–0 v Hartlepool United Div. 3(N) 1 September 1928 Scunthorpe United Div. 3(N) 25 December 1952	Jimmy McConnell 126, 1928–32	Jimmy McConnell 42 Div. 3(N) 1928–29	Alan Ross 466, 1963–79	Eric Welsh 4, N. Ireland 1966–67
			CHARLTON ATHLETIC			
61, Div. 3(S) 1934–35 77, Div. 2 1985–86	107, Div. 2 1957–58	8–1 Middlesbrough Div. 1 12 September 1953	Stuart Leary 153, 1953–62	Ralph Allen 32 Div. 3(S) 1934–35	Sam Bartram 583, 1934–56	John Hewie 19, Scotland 1956–60
			CHELSEA			
57, Div. 2 1906–07 99, Div. 2 1988–89	98, Div. 1 1960–61	13–0 v Jeunesse Hautcharage Cup-Winners' Cup 1st Rd 29 September 1971	Bobby Tambling 164, 1958–70	Jimmy Greaves 41 Div. 1 1960–61	Ron Harris 655, 1962–80	Ray Wilkins 24, England 1976–79
			CHESTER CITY			
56, Div. 3(N) 1946–47 Div. 4 1964–65 84, Div. 4 1985–86	119, Div. 4 1964–65	12–0 v York City Div. 3(N) 1 February 1936	Gary Talbot 83, 1963–67 1968–70	Dick Yates 36 Div. 3(N) 1946–47	Ray Gill 408, 1951–62	Bill Lewis 7, Wales 1894–98
			CHESTERFIELD			
64, Div. 4 1969–70 91, Div. 4 1984–85	102, Div. 3(N) 1930–31	10–0 v Glossop North End Div. 2 17 January 1903	Ernie Moss 161, 1969–76, 1979–81, 1984–86	Jimmy Cookson 44 Div. 3(N) 1925–26	Dave Blakey 613, 1948–67	Walter McMillen 4, N. Ireland 1937–38

Ground	Capacity & record attendance	League career	Honours (domestic) League	Cup
COLCHESTER UNITED (1937) Blue/white				
Layer Road Ground Colchester CO2 7JJ 110 × 71 yd	6 480 19 072 v Reading FA Cup 1st Rd 27 November 1948	1950 elected to Div. 3(S) 1958–61 Div. 3 1961–62 Div. 4 1962–65 Div. 3 1965–66 Div. 4 1966–68 Div. 3	1968–74 Div. 4 1974–76 Div. 3 1976–77 Div. 4 1977–81 Div. 3 1981–90 Div. 4 1990– GMVC	Div. 4 runners-up 1962	FA Cup never past 6th Rd League Cup never past 5th Rd
COVENTRY CITY (1883) Sky blue and white/navy blue				
Highfield Road Coventry CV2 4GU 112 × 76 yd	26 218 51 457 v Wolverhampton W Div. 2 29 April 1967	1919 elected to Div. 2 1925–26 Div. 3(N) 1926–36 Div. 3(S) 1936–52 Div. 2	1952–58 Div. 3(S) 1958–59 Div. 4 1959–64 Div. 3 1964–67 Div. 2 1967– Div. 1	Div. 2 Champions 1967 Div. 3 Champions 1964 Div. 3 (S) Champions 1936 Runners-up 1934 Div. 4 runners-up 1959	FA Cup winners 1987 League Cup semi-finalists 1981, 1990
CREWE ALEXANDRA (1877) Red/white				
Football Ground Gresty Road Crewe CW2 6EB 112 × 74 yd	7 200 20 000 v Tottenham H FA Cup 4th Rd 30 January 1960	1892 (founder member of Div. 2) 1896 failed re-election 1921 re-elected to Div. 3(N)	1958–63 Div. 4 1963–64 Div. 3 1964–68 Div. 4 1968–69 Div. 3 1969–89 Div. 4 1989– Div. 3	Highest placing 10th Div. 2 1893	FA Cup semi-finalists 1888 League Cup never past 3rd Rd
CRYSTAL PALACE (1905) Red-blue/red				
Selhurst Park London SE25 6PU 110 × 74 yd	31 439 51 801 v Burnley Div. 2 11 May 1979	1920 (founder member of Div. 3) 1921–25 Div. 2 1925–58 Div. 3(S) 1958–61 Div. 4 1961–64 Div. 3 1964–69 Div. 2	1969–73 Div. 1 1973–74 Div. 2 1974–77 Div. 3 1977–79 Div. 2 1979–81 Div. 1 1981–89 Div. 2 1989– Div. 1	Div. 2 Champions 1979 Runners-up 1969 Div. 3 runners-up 1964 Div. 3(S) Champions 1921 Runners-up 1929, 1931, 1939 Div. 4 Runners-up 1961	FA Cup runners-up 1990 League Cup never past 5th Rd
DARLINGTON (1883) White/white				
Feethams Ground Darlington DL1 5JB 110 × 74 yd	10 932 21 023 Bolton W League Cup 3rd Rd 14 November 1960	1921 (founder member of Div. 3(N) 1925–27 Div. 2 1927–58 Div. 3(N) 1958–66 Div. 4	1966–67 Div. 3 1967–85 Div. 4 1985–87 Div. 3 1987–89 Div. 4 1989–90 GMVC 1990– Div. 4	Div. 3(N) Champions 1925 Runners-up 1922 Div. 4 runners-up 1966	FA Cup never past 5th Rd League Cup never past 5th Rd

Most League points	goals	Record win	Highest number of League goals for club in total	in a season	Most League appearances for club	Most capped player
COLCHESTER UNITED						
60, Div. 4 1973–74 81, Div. 4 1982–83	104, Div. 4 1961–62	9–1 v Bradford City Div. 4 30 December 1961	Martyn King 131, 1959–65	Bobby Hunt 37 Div. 4 1961–62	Micky Cook 613, 1969–84	None
COVENTRY CITY						
60, Div. 4 1958–59 Div. 3 1963–64 63, Div. 1 1986–87	108, Div. 3(S) 1931–32	9–0 v Bristol City Div. 3(S) 28 April 1934	Clarrie Bourton 171, 1931–37	Clarrie Bourton 49 Div. 3(S) 1931–32	George Curtis 486, 1956–70	Dave Clements 21, N. Ireland 1965–71
CREWE ALEXANDRA						
59, Div. 4 1962–63 78, Div. 4 1988–89	95, Div. 3(N) 1931–32	8–0 v Rotherham United Div. 3(N) 1 October 1932	Bert Swindells 126, 1928–37	Terry Harkin 34 Div. 4 1964–65	Tommy Lowry 436, 1966–78	Bill Lewis 12, Wales 1890–92
CRYSTAL PALACE						
64, Div. 4 1960–61 81, Div. 2 1988–89	110, Div. 4 1960–61	9–0 v Barrow Div. 4 10 October 1959	Peter Simpson 154, 1930–36	Peter Simpson 46 Div. 3(s) 1930–31	Jim Cannon 571, 1973–88	Paddy Mulligan 14, Eire 1972–75 Peter Nicholas 14, Wales 1979–81 Ian Walsh 14, Wales 1979–81
DARLINGTON						
59, Div. 4 1965–66 85, Div. 4 1984–85	108, Div. 3(N) 1929–30	9–2 v Lincoln City Div. 3(N) 7 January 1928	Alan Walsh 90, 1978–84	David Brown 39 Div. 3(N) 1924–25	Ron Greener 442, 1955–68	None

Ground	Capacity & record attendance	League career	Honours (domestic)	
			League	Cup

DERBY COUNTY (1884) White/black

| Baseball Ground Shaftesbury Crescent Derby DE3 8NB 110 × 75 yd | 24 000 41 826 v Tottenham H Div. 1 20 September 1969 | 1888 (founder member of League) 1907–12 Div. 2 1912–14 Div. 1 1914–15 Div. 2 1915–21 Div. 1 1921–26 Div. 2 1926–53 Div. 1 | 1953–55 Div. 2 1955–57 Div. 3(N) 1957–69 Div. 2 1969–80 Div. 1 1980–84 Div. 2 1984–86 Div. 3 1986–87 Div. 2 1987– Div. 1 | Div. 1 Champions 1972, 1975 Runners-up 1896, 1930, 1936 Div. 2 Champions 1912, 1915, 1969, 1987 Runners-up 1926 Div. 3(N) Champions 1957 Runners-up 1956 | FA Cup winners 1946 Runners-up 1898, 1899, 1903 League Cup semi-finalists 1968 |

DONCASTER ROVERS (1879) White with red trim/red

| Belle Vue Ground Doncaster DN4 5HT 111 × 76 yd | 7 759 37 149 v Hull City Div. 3(N) 2 October 1948 | 1901 elected to Div. 2 1903 failed re-election 1904 re-elected 1905 failed re-election 1923 re-elected to Div. 3(N) 1935–37 Div. 2 1937–47 Div. 3(N) 1947–48 Div. 2 | 1948–50 Div. 3(N) 1950–58 Div. 2 1958–59 Div. 3 1959–66 Div. 4 1966–67 Div. 3 1967–69 Div. 4 1969–71 Div. 3 1971–81 Div. 4 1981–83 Div. 3 1983–84 Div. 4 1984–88 Div. 3 1988– Div. 4 | Div. 3(N) Champions 1935, 1947, 1950 Runners-up 1938, 1939 Div. 4 Champions 1966, 1969 | FA Cup never past 5th Rd League Cup never past 5th Rd |

EVERTON (1878) Blue/white

| Goodison Park Liverpool L4 4EL 112 × 78 yd | 41 366 78 299 v Liverpool Div. 1 18 September 1948 | 1888 (founder member of League) 1930–31 Div. 2 | 1931–51 Div. 1 1951–54 Div. 2 1954– Div. 1 | Div. 1 Champions 1891, 1915, 1928, 1932, 1939, 1963, 1970, 1985, 1987 Runners-up 1890, 1895, 1902, 1905, 1909, 1912, 1986 Div. 2 Champions 1931 Runners-up 1954, 1989 | FA Cup winners 1906, 1933, 1966, 1984 Runners-up 1893, 1897, 1907, 1968, 1985, 1986, 1989 League Cup runners-up 1977, 1984 |

EXETER CITY (1904) Red-white stripes/black

| St James Park Exeter EX4 6PX 114 × 73 yd | 9 260 20 984 v Sunderland FA Cup 6th Rd replay 4 March 1931 | 1920 elected to Div. 3 1921–58 Div. 3(S) 1958–64 Div. 4 1964–66 Div. 3 | 1966–77 Div. 4 1977–84 Div. 3 1984–90 Div. 4 1990– Div. 3 | Div. 3(S) runners-up 1933 Div. 4 Champions 1990 Runners-up 1977 | FA Cup never past 6th Rd League Cup never past 4th Rd |

Most League points	goals	Record win	Highest number of League goals for club in total	in a season	Most League appearances for club	Most capped player

DERBY COUNTY

| 63, Div. 2 1968–69 Div. 3(N) 1955–56, 1956–57 84, Div. 3 1985–86 Div. 3 1986–87 | 111, Div. 3(N) 1956–57 | 12–0 v Finn Harps UEFA Cup 3rd Rd First leg 15 September 1976 | Steve Bloomer 292, 1892–1906 1910–14 | Jack Bowers 37 Div. 1 1930–31 Ray Straw 37 Div. 3(N) 1956–57 | Kevin Hector 486, 1966–78, 1980–82 | Peter Shilton 34, England 1987–90 |

DONCASTER ROVERS

| 72, Div. 3(N) 1946–47 85, Div. 4 1983–84 | 123, Div. 3(N) 1946–47 | 10–0 v Darlington Div. 4 25 January 1964 | Tom Keetley 180, 1923–29 | Clarrie Jordan 42 Div. 3(N) 1946–47 | Fred Emery 406, 1925–36 | Len Graham 14, N. Ireland 1951–58 |

EVERTON

| 66, Div. 1 1969–70 90, Div. 1 1984–85 | 121, Div. 2 1930–31 | 11–2 v Derby County FA Cup 1st Rd 18 January 1890 | Dixie Dean 349, 1925–37 | Dixie Dean 60 Div. 1 1927–28 | Ted Sagar 465, 1929–53 | Kevin Ratcliffe 48, Wales 1980– |

EXETER CITY

| 62, Div. 4 1976–77 89, Div. 4 1989–90 | 88, Div. 3(S) 1932–33 | 8–1 v Coventry City Div. 3(S) 4 December 1926 Aldershot Div. 3(S) 4 May 1935 | Tony Kellow 129, 1976–78, 1980–83, 1985–88 | Fred Whitlow 33 Div. 3(S) 1932–33 | Arnold Mitchell 495, 1952–66 | Dermot Curtis 1, Eire 1963 |

Ground	Capacity & record attendance	League career		Honours (domestic) League	Cup

FULHAM (1879) White/black

Craven Cottage	18 304	1907 elected	1968–69 Div. 2	Div. 2 Champions	FA Cup
Stevenage Road	49 335 v	to Div. 2	1969–71 Div. 3	1949	runners-up 1975
Fulham	Millwall Div. 2	1928–32 Div. 3(S)	1971–80 Div. 2	Runners-up 1959	League Cup
London SW6 6HH	8 October 1938	1932–49 Div. 2	1980–82 Div. 3	Div. 3(S)	never past
110 × 75 yd		1949–52 Div. 1	1982–86 Div. 2	Champions 1932	5th Rd
		1952–59 Div. 2	1986– Div. 3	Div. 3 runners-up	
		1959–68 Div. 1		1971	

GILLINGHAM (1893) Royal blue/white

Priestfield Stadium	19 581	1920 (founder	1958–64 Div. 4	Div. 4 Champions	FA Cup never
Gillingham	23 002 v	member of Div. 3)	1964–71 Div. 3	1964	past 5th Rd
114 × 75 yd	QPR	1921 Div. 3(S)	1971–74 Div. 4	Runners-up 1974	League Cup
	FA Cup 3rd Rd	1938 failed	1974–89 Div. 3		never past
	10 January 1948	re-election	1989– Div. 4		4th Rd
		1950 re-elected			
		to Div. 3(S)			

GRIMSBY TOWN (1878) Black-white stripes/black

Blundell Park	18 496	1892 (founder	1948–51 Div. 2	Div. 2 Champions	FA Cup
Cleethorpes	31 657 v	member of Div. 2)	1951–56 Div. 3(N)	1901, 1934	semi-finalists
South Humberside	Wolverhampton W	1901–03 Div. 1	1956–59 Div. 2	Runners-up 1929	1936, 1939
DN35 7PY	FA Cup 5th Rd	1903–10 Div. 2	1959–62 Div. 3	Div. 3(N)	League Cup
111 × 74 yd	20 February 1937	1910 failed	1962–64 Div. 2	Champions	never past
		re-election	1964–68 Div. 3	1926, 1956	5th Rd
		1911 re-elected	1968–72 Div. 4	Runners-up 1952	
		to Div. 2	1972–77 Div. 3	Div. 3 Champions	
		1920–21 Div. 3	1977–79 Div. 4	1980	
		1921–26 Div. 3(N)	1979–80 Div. 3	Div. 3 runners-up	
		1926–29 Div. 2	1980–87 Div. 2	1962	
		1929–32 Div. 1	1987–88 Div. 3	Div. 4 Champions	
		1932–34 Div. 2	1988–90 Div. 4	1972	
		1934–48 Div. 1	1990– Div. 3	Runners-up 1979	

HALIFAX TOWN (1911) Blue with white trim/blue

Shay Ground	5 656	1921 (founder	1969–76 Div. 3	Div. 3(N)	FA Cup never
Halifax	36 885 v	member of	1976– Div. 4	runners-up 1935	past 5th Rd
HX1 2YS	Tottenham H	Div. 3(N))		Div. 4 runners-up	League Cup
110 × 70 yd	FA Cup 5th Rd	1958–63 Div. 3		1969	never past
	14 February 1953	1963–69 Div. 4			4th Rd

HARTLEPOOL UNITED (1908) Blue/blue

The Victoria Ground	9 675	1921 (founder	1968–69 Div. 3	Div. 3(N)	FA Cup never
Hartlepool	17 426 v	member of	1969– Div. 4	runners-up 1957	past 4th Rd
110 × 75 yd	Manchester U	Div. 3(N))			League Cup
	FA Cup 3rd Rd	1958–68 Div. 4			never past
	5 January 1957				4th Rd

Most League points	goals	Record win	Highest number of League goals for club		Most League appearances for club	Most capped player
			in total	in a season		

FULHAM

Most League points	goals	Record win	in total	in a season	Most League appearances for club	Most capped player
60, Div. 2 1958-59 Div. 3 1970-71 78, Div. 3 1981-82	111, Div. 3(S) 1931-32	10-1 v Ipswich Town Div. 1 26 December 1963	Bedford Jezzard 154, 1948-56	Frank Newton 43 Div. 3(S) 1931-32	Johnny Haynes 594, 1952-70	Johnny Haynes 56, England 1954-62

GILLINGHAM

Most League points	goals	Record win	in total	in a season	Most League appearances for club	Most capped player
62, Div. 4 1973-74 83, Div. 3 1984-85	90, Div. 4 1973-74	10-0 v Chesterfield Div. 3 5 September 1987	Brian Yeo 135, 1963-75	Ernie Morgan 31 Div. 3(S) 1954-55 Brian Yeo 31 Div. 4 1973-74	John Simpson 571, 1957-72	Tony Cascarino 3, Eire 1985

GRIMSBY TOWN

Most League points	goals	Record win	in total	in a season	Most League appearances for club	Most capped player
68, Div. 3(N) 1955-56 79, Div. 4 1989-90	103, Div. 2 1933-34	8-0 v Darlington FA Cup 2nd Rd 21 November 1885	Pat Glover 182, 1930-39	Pat Glover 42 Div. 2 1933-34	Keith Jobling 448, 1953-69	Pat Glover 7, Wales 1931-39

HALIFAX TOWN

Most League points	goals	Record win	in total	in a season	Most League appearances for club	Most capped player
57, Div. 4 1968-69 60, Div. 4 1982-83	83, Div. 3(N) 1957-58	7-0 v Bishop Auckland FA Cup 2nd Rd replay 10 January 1967	Ernest Dixon 129, 1922-30	Albert Valentine 34 Div. 3(N) 1934-35	John Pickering 367, 1965-74	None

HARTLEPOOL UNITED

Most League points	goals	Record win	in total	in a season	Most League appearances for club	Most capped player
60, Div. 4 1967-68 70, Div. 4 1985-86	90, Div. 3(N) 1956-57	10-1 v Barrow Div. 4 4 April 1959	Ken Johnson 98, 1949-64	William Robinson 28 Div. 3(N) 1927-28	Wattie Moore 447, 1948-64	Ambrose Fogarty 1, Eire 1964

Ground	Capacity & record attendance	League career		Honours (domestic) League	Cup

HEREFORD UNITED (1924) White/black

| Edgar Street Hereford HR4 9JU 111×74 yd | 13777 18114 v Sheffield W FA Cup 3rd Rd 4 January 1958 | 1972 elected to Div. 4 1973–76 Div. 3 1976–77 Div. 2 | 1977–78 Div. 3 1978– Div. 4 | Div. 3 Champions 1976 Div. 4 runners-up 1973 | FA Cup never past 4th Rd League Cup never past 3rd Rd |

HUDDERSFIELD TOWN (1908) Blue-white stripes/white

| Leeds Road Huddersfield HD1 6PE 115×75 yd | 32000 67037 v Arsenal FA Cup 6th Rd 27 February 1932 | 1910 elected to Div. 2 1920–52 Div. 1 1952–53 Div. 2 1953–56 Div. 1 1956–70 Div. 2 1970–72 Div. 1 | 1972–73 Div. 2 1973–75 Div. 3 1975–80 Div. 4 1980–83 Div. 3 1983–88 Div. 2 1988– Div. 3 | Div. 1 Champions 1924, 1925, 1926 Runners-up 1927, 1928, 1934 Div. 2 Champions 1970 Runners-up 1920, 1953 Div. 4 Champions 1980 | FA Cup winners 1922 Runners-up 1920, 1928, 1930, 1938, League Cup semi-finalists 1968 |

HULL CITY (1904) Black and amber/black

| Boothferry Park Hull HU4 6EU 112×75 yd | 17932 55019 v Manchester U FA Cup 6th Rd 26 February 1949 | 1905 elected to Div. 2 1930–33 Div. 3(N) 1933–36 Div. 2 1936–49 Div. 3(N) 1949–56 Div. 2 1956–58 Div. 3(N) 1958–59 Div. 3 | 1959–60 Div. 2 1960–66 Div. 3 1966–78 Div. 2 1978–81 Div. 3 1981–83 Div. 4 1983–85 Div. 3 1985– Div. 2 | Div. 3(N) Champions 1933, 1949 Div. 3 Champions 1966 Runners-up 1959 Div. 4 runners-up 1983 | FA Cup semi-finalists 1930 League Cup never past 4th Rd |

IPSWICH TOWN (1878) Blue/white

| Portman Road Ipswich Suffolk IP1 2DA 112×70 yd | 31100 38010 v Leeds United FA Cup 6th Rd 8 March 1975 | 1938 elected to Div. 3(S) 1954–55 Div. 2 1955–57 Div. 3(S) 1957–61 Div. 2 | 1961–64 Div. 1 1964–68 Div. 2 1968–86 Div. 1 1986– Div. 2 | Div. 1 Champions 1962 Runners-up 1981, 1982 Div. 2 Champions 1961, 1968 Div. 3(S) Champions 1954, 1957 | FA Cup winners 1978 League Cup semi-finalists 1982, 1985 |

LEEDS UNITED (1919) White/white

| Elland Road Leeds LS11 0ES 117×76 yd | 33235 57892 v Sunderland FA Cup 5th Rd replay 15 March 1967 | 1920 elected to Div. 2 1924–27 Div. 1 1927–28 Div. 2 1928–31 Div. 1 1931–32 Div. 2 1932–47 Div. 1 | 1947–56 Div. 2 1956–60 Div. 1 1960–64 Div. 2 1964–82 Div. 1 1982–90 Div. 2 1990– Div. 1 | Div. 1 Champions 1969, 1974 Runners-up 1965, 1966, 1970, 1971, 1972 Div. 2 Champions 1924, 1964, 1990 Runners-up 1928, 1932, 1956 | FA Cup winners 1972 Runners-up 1965, 1970, 1973 League Cup winners 1968 |

Most League points	goals	Record win	Highest number of League goals for club in total	in a season	Most League appearances for club	Most capped player

HEREFORD UNITED

| 63, Div. 3 1975–76 77, Div. 4 1984–85 | 86, Div. 3 1975–76 | 6–0 v Burnley Div. 4 24 January 1987 | Dixie McNeil 88, 1974–77, 1982 | Dixie McNeil 35 Div. 3 1975–76 | Mel Pejic 351, 1980–90 | Brian Evans 1, Wales 1973 |

HUDDERSFIELD TOWN

| 66, Div. 4 1979–80 82, Div. 3 1982–83 | 101, Div. 4 1979–80 | 10–1 v Blackpool Div. 1 13 December 1930 | George Brown 142, 1921–29 Jimmy Glazzard 142, 1946–56 | Sam Taylor 35 Div. 2 1919–20 George Brown 35 Div. 1 1925–26 | Billy Smith 520, 1914–34 | Jimmy Nicholson 31, N. Ireland 1965–71 |

HULL CITY

| 69, Div. 3 1965–66 90, Div. 4 1982–83 | 109, Div. 3 1965–66 | 11–1 v Carlisle United Div. 3(N) 14 January 1939 | Chris Chilton 195, 1960–71 | Bill McNaughton 39 Div. 3(N) 1932–33 | Andy Davidson 520, 1952–67 | Terry Neill 15, N. Ireland 1970–73 |

IPSWICH TOWN

| 64, Div. 3(S) 1953–54 1955–56 83, Div. 1 1981–82 | 106, Div. 3(S) 1955–56 | 10–0 v Floriana (Malta) European Cup 1st Rd 25 September 1962 | Ray Crawford 203, 1958–63, 1966–69 | Ted Phillips 41 Div. 3(S) 1956–57 | Mick Mills 591, 1966–82 | Allan Hunter 47, N. Ireland 1972–80 |

LEEDS UNITED

| 67, Div. 1 1968–69 85, Div. 2 1989–90 | 98, Div. 2 1927–28 | 10–0 v Lyn Oslo (Norway) European Cup 1st Rd 17 September 1969 | Peter Lorimer 168, 1965–79, 1983–86 | John Charles 42 Div. 2 1953–54 | Jack Charlton 629, 1953–73 | Billy Bremner 54, Scotland 1965–75 |

Ground	Capacity & record attendance	League career		Honours (domestic) League	Cup

LEICESTER CITY (1884) Blue/white

| City Stadium
Filbert Street
Leicester LE2 7FL
112×75 yd | 26 770
47 298 v
Tottenham H
FA Cup 5th Rd
18 February 1928 | 1894 elected
to Div. 2
1908–09 Div. 1
1909–25 Div. 2
1925–35 Div. 1
1935–37 Div. 2
1937–39 Div. 1
1946–54 Div. 2
1954–55 Div. 1 | 1955–57 Div. 2
1957–69 Div. 1
1969–71 Div. 2
1971–78 Div. 1
1978–80 Div. 2
1980–81 Div. 1
1981–83 Div. 2
1983–87 Div. 1
1987– Div. 2 | Div. 1 runners-up
1929
Div. 2 Champions
1925, 1937, 1954,
1957, 1971, 1980
Runners-up 1908 | FA Cup
runners up 1949,
1961, 1963, 1969
League Cup
winners 1964
Runners-up 1965 |

LEYTON ORIENT (1881) All red

| Leyton Stadium
Brisbane Road
Leyton
London E10 5NE
110×80 yd | 18 869
34 345 v
West Ham U
FA Cup 4th Rd
25 January 1964 | 1905 elected
to Div 2
1929–56 Div. 3(S)
1956–62 Div. 2
1962–63 Div. 1
1963–66 Div. 2 | 1966–70 Div. 3
1970–82 Div. 2
1982–85 Div. 3
1985–89 Div. 4
1989– Div. 3 | Div. 2 runners-up
1962
Div. 3 Champions
1970
Div. 3(S)
Champions 1956
Runners-up 1955 | FA Cup
semi-finalists
1978
League Cup
never past
5th Rd |

LINCOLN CITY (1883) Red-white stripes/black

| Sincil Bank
Lincoln LN5 8LD
110×75 yd | 10 369
23 196 v
Derby Co
League Cup 4th Rd
15 November 1967 | 1892 (founder
member of Div. 2)
1908 failed
re-election
1909 re-elected
1911 failed
re-election
1912 re-elected
1920 failed
re-election
1921 re-elected
1921–32 Div. 3(N)
1932–34 Div. 2 | 1934–38 Div. 3(N)
1948–49 Div. 2
1949–52 Div. 3(N)
1952–61 Div. 2
1961–62 Div. 3
1962–76 Div. 4
1976–79 Div. 3
1979–81 Div. 4
1981–86 Div. 3
1986–87 Div. 4
1987–88 GMVC
1988– Div. 4 | Div. 3(N)
Champions
1932, 1948, 1952
Runners-up
1928, 1931, 1937
Div. 4 Champions
1976
Runners-up 1981 | FA Cup never
past 5th Rd
(equivalent)
League Cup
never past
4th Rd |

LIVERPOOL (1892) Red/red

| Anfield Road
Liverpool L4 0TH
110×75 yd | 39 772
61 905 v
Wolverhampton W
FA Cup 4th Rd
2 February 1952 | 1893 elected
to Div. 2
1894–95 Div. 1
1895–96 Div. 2
1896–1904 Div. 1 | 1904–05 Div. 2
1905–54 Div. 1
1954–62 Div. 2
1962– Div. 1 | Div. 1 Champions
1901, 1906, 1922,
1923, 1947, 1964,
1966, 1973, 1976,
1977, 1979, 1980,
1982, 1983, 1984,
1986, 1988, 1990
(record)
Runners-up
1899, 1910, 1969,
1974, 1975, 1978,
1985, 1987, 1989
Div. 2 Champions
1894, 1896, 1905,
1962 | FA Cup winners
1965, 1974, 1986,
1989
Runners-up
1914, 1950, 1971,
1977, 1988
League Cup
winners 1981,
1982, 1983, 1984
Runners-up
1978, 1987 |

Most League points	goals	Record win	Highest number of League goals for club		Most League appearances for club	Most capped player
			in total	in a season		
						LEICESTER CITY
61, Div. 2 1956–57 70, Div. 2 1982–83	109, Div. 2 1956–57	10–0 v Portsmouth Div. 1 20 October 1928	Arthur Chandler 259, 1923–25	Arthur Rowley 44 Div. 2 1956–57	Adam Black 528, 1920–35	Gordon Banks 37, England 1963–66
						LEYTON ORIENT
66, Div. 3(S) 1955–56 75, Div. 4 1988–89	106, Div. 3(S) 1955–56	8–0 v Crystal Palace Div. 3(S) 12 November 1955 Rochdale Div. 4 20 October 1987 Colchester United Div. 4 15 October 1988	Tom Johnston 121, 1956–58, 1959–61	Tom Johnston 35 Div. 2 1957–58	Peter Allen 432, 1965–78	John Chiedozie 8, Nigeria 1978–80
						LINCOLN CITY
74, Div. 4 1975–76 77, Div. 3 1981–82	121, Div. 3(N) 1951–52	11–1 v Crewe Alexandra Div. 3(N) 29 September 1951	Andy Graver 144, 1950–55, 1958–61	Allan Hall 42 Div. 3(N) 1931–32	Tony Emery 402, 1946–59	David Pugh 3, Wales 1900–01 George Moulson 3, Eire 1948
						LIVERPOOL
68, Div. 1 1978–79 90, Div. 1 1987–88	106, Div. 2 1895–96	11–0 v Stromsgodset (Norway) Cup Winners' Cup 17 September 1974	Roger Hunt 245, 1959–69	Roger Hunt 41 Div. 2 1961–62	Ian Callaghan 640, 1960–1978	Emlyn Hughes 59, England 1970–79

Ground	Capacity & record attendance	League career		Honours (domestic)	
				League	*Cup*

LUTON TOWN (1885) White/black

| 70-72 Kenilworth Road Luton LU1 1DH 110 × 72 yd | 13 023 30 069 v Blackpool FA Cup 6th Rd replay 4 March 1959 | 1897 elected to Div. 2 1900 failed re-election 1920 elected to Div. 3 1921-37 Div. 3(S) 1937-55 Div. 2 1955-60 Div. 1 | 1960-63 Div. 2 1963-65 Div. 3 1965-68 Div. 4 1968-70 Div. 3 1970-74 Div. 2 1974-75 Div. 1 1975-82 Div. 2 1982- Div. 1 | Div. 2 Champions 1982 Runners-up 1955, 1974 Div. 3 runners-up 1970 Div. 4 Champions 1968 Div. 3(S) Champions 1937 Runners-up 1936 | FA Cup runners-up 1959 League Cup winners 1988 Runners-up 1989 |

MAIDSTONE UNITED (1897) Amber/black

| Watling Street Dartford Kent DA2 6EN 110 × 75 yd | 5 250 5 006 v Carlisle United Div. 4, 5 May 1990 | 1989 elected to Div. 4 | | Highest placing 5th, Div. 4, 1990 | FA Cup never past 3rd Rd League Cup never past 1st Rd |

MANCHESTER CITY (1887) Sky blue/white

| Maine Road Moss Side Manchester M14 7WN 117 × 76 yd | 46 000 84 569 v Stoke City FA Cup 6th Rd 3 March 1934 | 1892 elected to Div. 2 as Ardwick FC 1894 elected to Div. 2 as Manchester C 1899-1902 Div. 1 1902-03 Div. 2 1903-09 Div. 1 1909-10 Div. 2 1910-26 Div. 1 1926-28 Div. 2 | 1928-38 Div. 1 1938-47 Div. 2 1947-50 Div. 1 1950-51 Div. 2 1951-63 Div. 1 1963-66 Div. 2 1966-83 Div. 1 1983-85 Div. 2 1985-87 Div. 1 1987-89 Div. 2 1989- Div. 1 | Div. 1 Champions 1937, 1968 Runners-up 1904, 1921, 1977 Div. 2 Champions 1899, 1903, 1910, 1928, 1947, 1966 Runners-up 1896, 1951 | FA Cup winners 1904, 1934, 1956, 1969 Runners-up 1926, 1933, 1955, 1981 League Cup winners 1970, 1976 Runners-up 1974 |

MANCHESTER UNITED (1878) Red/white

| Old Trafford Manchester M16 0RA 116 × 76 yd | 50 726 70 504 v Aston Villa Div. 1 27 December 1920 | 1892 elected to Div. 1 as Newton Heath. Changed name 1902 1894-1906 Div. 2 1906-22 Div. 1 1922-25 Div. 2 | 1925-31 Div. 1 1931-36 Div. 2 1936-37 Div. 1 1937-38 Div. 2 1938-74 Div. 1 1974-75 Div. 2 1975- Div. 1 | Div. 1 Champions 1908, 1911, 1952, 1956, 1957, 1965, 1967 Runners-up 1947, 1948, 1949, 1951, 1959, 1964, 1968, 1980, 1988 Div. 2 Champions 1936, 1975 Runners-up 1897, 1906, 1925, 1938 | FA Cup winners 1909, 1948, 1963, 1977, 1983, 1985, 1990 Runners-up 1957, 1958, 1976, 1979 League Cup runners-up 1983 |

Most League points[2]	goals	Record win	Highest number of League goals for club		Most League appearances for club	Most capped player
			in total	in a season		

LUTON TOWN

Most League points[2]	goals	Record win	Highest number of League goals for club (in total)	(in a season)	Most League appearances for club	Most capped player
66, Div. 4 1967–68 88, Div. 2 1981–82	103, Div. 3(S) 1936–37	12–0 v Bristol Rovers Div. 3(S) 13 April 1936	Gordon Turner 243, 1949–64	Joe Payne 55 Div. 3(S) 1936–37	Bob Morton 494, 1948–64	Mal Donaghy 58, N. Ireland 1980–89

MAIDSTONE UNITED

73, Div. 4 1989–90	77, Div. 4 1989–90	5–1 v Aldershot Div. 4 1 January 1990	Steve Butler 21, 1989–90	Steve Butler 21 1989–90	Mark Golley 45, 1989–90	None

MANCHESTER CITY

62, Div. 2 1946–47 82, Div. 2 1988–89	108, Div. 2 1926–27	10–1 v Huddersfield Town Div. 2 7 November 1987	Tommy Johnson 158, 1919–30	Tommy Johnson 38 Div. 1 1928–29	Alan Oakes 565, 1959–76	Colin Bell 48, England 1968–75

MANCHESTER UNITED

64, Div. 1 1956–57 81, Div. 1 1987–88	103, Div. 1 1956–57 1958–59	10–0 v Anderlecht (Belgium) European Cup Prelim Rd 26 September 1956	Bobby Charlton 199, 1956–73	Dennis Viollet 32 Div. 1 1959–60	Bobby Charlton 606, 1956–73	Bobby Charlton 106, England 1958–70

Ground	Capacity & record attendance	League career		Honours (domestic) League	Cup

MANSFIELD TOWN (1910) Amber/blue

| Field Mill Ground
Quarry Lane
Mansfield
Notts
115 × 72 yd | 10 468
24 467 v
Nottingham F
FA Cup 3rd Rd
10 January 1953 | 1931 elected
to Div. 3(S)
1932–37 Div. 3(N)
1937–47 Div. 3(S)
1947–58 Div. 3(N)
1958–60 Div. 3
1960–63 Div. 4 | 1963–72 Div. 3
1972–75 Div. 4
1975–77 Div. 3
1977–78 Div. 2
1978–80 Div. 3
1980–86 Div. 4
1986– Div. 3 | Div. 3 Champions
1977
Div. 4 Champions
1975
Div. 3(N)
Runners-up 1951 | FA Cup never
past 6th Rd
League Cup
never past
5th Rd |

MIDDLESBROUGH (1876) Red/white

| Ayresome Park
Middlesbrough
Teesside
115 × 75 yd | 25 000
53 596 v
Newcastle U
Div. 1
27 December 1949 | 1899 elected to
Div. 2
1902–24 Div. 1
1924–27 Div. 2
1927–28 Div. 1
1928–29 Div. 2
1929–54 Div. 1
1954–66 Div. 2 | 1966–67 Div. 3
1967–74 Div. 2
1974–82 Div. 1
1982–86 Div. 2
1986–87 Div. 3
1987–88 Div. 2
1988–89 Div. 1
1989– Div. 2 | Div. 2 Champions
1927, 1929, 1974
Runners-up 1902
Div. 3 runners-up
1967, 1987 | FA Cup never
past 6th Rd
League Cup
semi-finalists
1976 |

MILLWALL (1885) Blue/white

| The Den
Cold Blow Lane
London SE14 5RH
112 × 74 yd | 21 000
48 672 v
Derby Co
FA Cup 5th Rd
20 February 1937 | 1920 (founder
members of Div. 3)
1921 Div. 3(S)
1928–34 Div. 2
1934–38 Div. 3(S)
1938–48 Div. 2
1948–58 Div. 3(S)
1958–62 Div. 4
1962–64 Div. 3 | 1964–65 Div. 4
1965–66 Div. 3
1966–75 Div. 2
1975–76 Div. 3
1976–79 Div. 2
1979–85 Div. 3
1985–88 Div. 2
1988–90 Div. 1
1990– Div. 2 | Div. 2 Champions
1988
Div.3(S)
Champions
1928, 1938
Runners-up 1953
Div. 3 runners-up
1966, 1985
Div. 4 Champions
1962
Runners-up 1965 | FA Cup
semi-finalists
1900, 1903, 1937
League Cup
never past
5th Rd |

NEWCASTLE UNITED (1882) Black-white stripes/black

| St James' Park
Newcastle-upon-
Tyne
NE1 4ST
115 × 75 yd | 33 530
68 386 v
Chelsea Div. 1
3 September 1930 | 1893 elected
to Div. 2
1898–1934 Div. 1
1934–48 Div. 2
1948–61 Div. 1 | 1961–65 Div. 2
1965–78 Div. 1
1978–84 Div. 2
1984–89 Div. 1
1989– Div. 2 | Div. 1 Champions
1905, 1907, 1909,
1927
Div. 2 Champions
1965
Runners-up
1898, 1948 | FA Cup winners
1910, 1924, 1932,
1951, 1952, 1955
Runners-up
1905, 1906, 1908,
1911, 1974
League Cup
runners-up 1976 |

Most League points	goals	Record win	Highest number of League goals for club in total	in a season	Most League appearances for club	Most capped player
MANSFIELD TOWN						
68, Div. 4 1974–75 81, Div. 4 1985–86	108, Div. 4 1962–63	8–0 v Scarborough FA Cup 1st Rd 22 November 1952	Harry Johnson 104, 1931–36	Ted Harston 55 Div. 3(N) 1936–37	Rod Arnold 440, 1970–83	John McClelland 6, N. Ireland 1980–81
MIDDLESBROUGH						
65, Div. 2 1973–74 94, Div. 3 1986–87	122, Div. 2 1926–27	9–0 v Brighton & HA Div. 2 23 August 1958	George Camsell 326, 1925–39	George Camsell 59 Div. 2 1926–27	Tim Williamson 563, 1902–23	Wilf Mannion 26, England 1946–51
MILLWALL						
65, Div. 3(S) 1927–28 Div. 3 1965–66 90, Div. 3 1984–85	127, Div. 3(S) 1927–28	9–1 v Torquay United Div. 3(S) 29 August 1927 Coventry City Div. 3(S) 19 November 1927	Derek Possee 79, 1967–73	Richard Parker 37 Div. 3(S) 1926–27	Barry Kitchener 523, 1967–82	Eamonn Dunphy 22, Eire 1966–71
NEWCASTLE UNITED						
57, Div. 2 1964–65 80, Div. 2 1983–84, 1989–90	98, Div. 1 1951–52	13–0 v Newport County Div. 2 5 October 1946	Jackie Milburn 178, 1946–57	Hughie Gallacher 36 Div. 1 1926–27	Jim Lawrence 432, 1904–22	Alf McMichael 40, N. Ireland 1949–60

Ground	Capacity & record attendance	League career	Honours (domestic) League	Cup

NORTHAMPTON TOWN (1897) Claret with white trim/white

Ground	Capacity & record attendance	League career	Honours (domestic) League	Cup
County Ground Abington Avenue Northampton NN1 4PS 112 × 75 yd	11 907 24 523 v Fulham Div. 1 23 April 1966	1920 (founder member of Div. 3) 1921 Div. 3(S) 1958–61 Div. 4 1961–63 Div. 3 1963–65 Div. 2 1965–66 Div. 1	1966–67 Div. 2 1967–69 Div. 3 1969–76 Div. 4 1976–77 Div. 3 1977–87 Div. 4 1987–90 Div. 3 1990– Div. 4	Div. 2 runners-up 1965 Div. 3 Champions 1963 Div. 3(S) runners-up 1928, 1950 Div. 4 Champions 1987 Runners-up 1976	FA Cup never past 5th Rd League Cup never past 5th Rd

NORWICH CITY (1902) Yellow/green

Ground	Capacity & record attendance	League career	Honours (domestic) League	Cup
Carrow Road Norwich NR1 1JE 114 × 74 yd	24 284 43 984 v Leicester City FA Cup 6th Rd 30 March 1963	1920 (founder member of Div. 3) 1921 Div. 3(S) 1934–39 Div. 2 1946–58 Div. 3(S) 1958–60 Div. 3 1960–72 Div. 2	1972–74 Div. 1 1974–75 Div. 2 1975–81 Div. 1 1981–82 Div. 2 1982–85 Div. 1 1985–86 Div. 2 1986– Div. 1	Div. 2 Champions 1972, 1986 Div. 3(S) Champions 1934 Div. 3 runners-up 1960	FA Cup semi-finalists 1959, 1989 League Cup winners 1962, 1985 Runners-up 1973, 1975

NOTTINGHAM FOREST (1865) Red/white

Ground	Capacity & record attendance	League career	Honours (domestic) League	Cup
City Ground Nottingham NG2 5FJ 115 × 78 yd	31 920 49 945 v Manchester U Div. 1 28 October 1967	1892 elected to Div. 1 1906 Div. 2 1907 Div. 1 1911–22 Div. 2 1922–25 Div. 1	1925–49 Div. 2 1949–51 Div. 3(S) 1951–57 Div. 2 1957–72 Div. 1 1972–77 Div. 2 1977– Div. 1	Div. 1 Champions 1978 Runners-up 1967, 1979 Div. 2 Champions 1907, 1922 Runners-up 1957 Div. 3(S) Champions 1951	FA Cup winners 1898, 1959 League Cup winners 1978, 1979, 1989. 1990 Runners-up 1980

NOTTS COUNTY (1862*) Black-white stripes/black

Ground	Capacity & record attendance	League career	Honours (domestic) League	Cup
County Ground Meadow Lane Nottingham NG2 3HJ 114 × 74 yd	21 097 47 310 v York City FA Cup 6th Rd 12 March 1955	1888 (founder member of League) 1893–97 Div. 2 1897–1913 Div. 1 1913–14 Div. 2 1914–20 Div. 1 1920–23 Div. 2 1923–26 Div. 1 1926–30 Div. 2 1930–31 Div. 3(S) 1931–35 Div. 2	1935–50 Div. 3(S) 1950–58 Div. 2 1958–59 Div. 3 1959–60 Div. 4 1960–64 Div. 3 1964–71 Div. 4 1971–73 Div. 3 1973–81 Div. 2 1981–84 Div. 1 1984–85 Div. 2 1985–90 Div. 3 1990– Div. 2	Div. 2 Champions 1897, 1914, 1923 Runners-up 1895, 1981 Div. 3(S) Champions 1931, 1950 Runners-up 1937 Div. 3 runners-up 1973 Div. 4 Champions 1971 Runners-up 1960	FA Cup winners 1894 Runners-up 1891 League Cup never past 5th Rd

* firm basis from 1864

Most League points	goals	Record win	Highest number of League goals for club in total	in a season	Most League appearances for club	Most capped player
NORTHAMPTON TOWN						
68, Div. 4 1975–76 99, Div. 4 1986–87	109, Div. 3 1962–63 Div. 3(S) 1952–53	10–0 v Walsall Div. 3(S) 5 November 1927	Jack English 135, 1947–60	Cliff Holton 36 Div. 3 1961–62	Tommy Fowler 521, 1946–61	E Lloyd Davies 12, Wales 1908–14
NORWICH CITY						
64, Div. 3(S) 1950–51 84, Div. 2 1985–86	99, Div. 3(S) 1952–53	10–2 v Coventry City Div. 3(S) 15 March 1930	Johnny Gavin 122, 1945–54, 1955–58	Ralph Hunt 31 Div. 3(S) 1955–56	Ron Ashman 592, 1947–64	Martin O'Neill 18, N. Ireland 1981, 1982–83
NOTTINGHAM FOREST						
70, Div. 3(S) 1950–51 74, Div. 1 1983–84	110, Div. 3(S) 1950–51	14–0 v Clapton FA Cup 1st Rd 17 January 1891	Grenville Morris 199, 1898–1913	Wally Ardron 36 Div. 3(S) 1950–51	Bob McKinlay 614, 1951–70	Martin O'Neill 36, N. Ireland 1972–80
NOTTS COUNTY						
69, Div. 4 1970–71 87, Div. 3 1989–90	107, Div. 4 1959–60	15–0 v Rotherham Town FA Cup 1st Rd 24 October 1885	Les Bradd 124, 1967–78	Tom Keetley 39 Div. 3(S) 1930–31	Albert Iremonger 564, 1904–26	Harry Cursham 8, England 1880–84 Martin O'Neill 8, N. Ireland 1983–84

Ground	Capacity & record attendance	League career	Honours (domestic) League	Cup

OLDHAM ATHLETIC (1895) Blue, red trim/blue

Boundary Park Oldham 110 × 74 yd	19 432 47 671 v Sheffield W FA Cup 4th Rd 25 January 1930	1907 elected to Div. 2 1910–23 Div. 1 1923–35 Div. 2 1935–53 Div. 3(N) 1953–43 Div. 2	1954–58 Div. 3(N) 1958–63 Div. 4 1963–69 Div. 3 1969–71 Div. 4 1971–74 Div. 3 1974– Div. 2	Div. 1 runners-up 1915 Div. 2 runners-up 1910 Div. 3(N) Champions 1953 Div. 3 Champions 1974 Div. 4 runners-up 1963	FA Cup semi-finalists 1913, 1990 League Cup runners-up 1990

OXFORD UNITED (1893) Gold, blue trim/navy blue

Manor Ground Beech Road Headington Oxford OX3 7RS 110 × 75 yd	11 117 22 730 v Preston NE FA Cup 6th Rd 29 February 1964	1962 elected to Div. 4 1965–68 Div. 3	1968–76 Div. 2 1976–84 Div. 3 1984–85 Div. 2 1985–88 Div. 1 1988– Div. 2	Div. 2 Champions 1985 Div. 3 Champions 1968, 1984	FA Cup never past 6th Rd League Cup winners 1986

PETERBOROUGH UNITED (1923) Royal blue/white

London Road Ground Peterborough PE2 8AL 112 × 76 yd	16 414 30 096 v Swansea T FA Cup 5th Rd 20 February 1965	1960 elected to Div. 4 1961–68 Div. 3 1968 demoted for financial irregularities	1968–74 Div. 4 1974–79 Div. 3 1979– Div. 4	Div. 4 Champions 1961, 1974	FA Cup never past 6th Rd League Cup semi-finalists 1966

PLYMOUTH ARGYLE (1886) Green/black

Home Park Plymouth Devon PL2 1DQ 112 × 75 yd	26 000 43 596 v Aston Villa Div. 2 10 October 1936	1920 (founder member of Div. 3) 1921–30 Div. 3(S) 1930–50 Div. 2 1950–52 Div. 3(S) 1952–56 Div. 2 1956–58 Div. 3(S)	1958–59 Div. 3 1959–68 Div. 2 1968–75 Div. 3 1975–77 Div. 2 1977–86 Div. 3 1986– Div. 2	Div. 3(S) Champions 1930, 1952 Runners-up 1922, 1923, 1924 1925, 1926, 1927 Div. 3 Champions 1959 Runners-up 1975, 1986	FA Cup semi-finalists 1984 League Cup semi-finalists 1965, 1974

PORTSMOUTH (1898) Blue/white

Fratton Park Frogmore Road Portsmouth PO4 8RA 116 × 73 yd	23 000 51 385 v Derby Co FA Cup 6th Rd 26 February 1949	1920 (founder member of Div. 3) 1921–24 Div. 3(S) 1924–27 Div. 2 1927–59 Div. 1 1959–61 Div. 2 1961–62 Div. 3	1962–76 Div. 2 1976–78 Div. 3 1978–80 Div. 4 1980–83 Div. 3 1983–87 Div. 2 1987–88 Div. 1 1988– Div. 2	Div. 1 Champions 1949, 1950 Div. 2 runners-up 1927, 1987 Div. 3(S) Champions 1924 Div. 3 Champions 1962, 1983	FA Cup winners 1939 Runners-up 1929, 1934 League Cup never past 5th Rd

Most League points	goals	Record win	Highest number of League goals for club in total	in a season	Most League appearances for club	Most capped player

OLDHAM ATHLETIC

| 62, Div. 3 1973–74 75, Div. 2 1986–87 | 95, Div. 4 1962–63 | 11–0 v Southport Div. 4 26 December 1962 | Roger Palmer 129, 1980–90 | Tom Davis 33 Div. 3(N) 1936–37 | Ian Wood 525, 1966–80 | Albert Gray 9, Wales 1924–27 |

OXFORD UNITED

| 61, Div. 4 1964–65 95, Div. 3 1983–84 | 91, Div. 3 1983–84 | 7–0 v Barrow Div. 4 19 December 1964 | Graham Atkinson 73, 1962–73 | John Aldridge 30 Div. 2 1984–85 | John Shuker 478, 1962–77 | Ray Houghton 12, Eire 1986–87 Neil Slatter 12, Wales 1985–89 |

PETERBOROUGH UNITED

| 66, Div. 4 1960–61 82, Div. 4 1981–82 | 134, Div. 4 1960–61 | 8–1 v Oldham Athletic Div. 4 26 November 1969 | Jim Hall 122, 1967–75 | Terry Bly 52 Div. 4 1960–61 | Tommy Robson 482, 1968–81 | Tony Millington 8, Wales 1966–69 |

PLYMOUTH ARGYLE

| 68, Div. 3(S) 1929–30 87, Div. 3 1985–86 | 107, Div. 3(S) 1925–26, 1951–52 | 8–1 v Millwall Div. 2 16 January 1932 | Sammy Black 180, 1924–38 | Jack Cock 32 Div. 3(S) 1925–26 | Sammy Black 470, 1924–38 Kevin Hodges 470, 1978–90 | Moses Russell 20, Wales 1920–28 |

PORTSMOUTH

| 65, Div. 3 1961–62 91, Div. 3 1982–83 | 91, Div. 4 1979–80 | 9–1 v Notts County Div. 2 9 April 1927 | Peter Harris 194, 1946–60 | Billy Haines 40 Div. 2 1926–27 | Jimmy Dickinson 764, 1946–65 | Jimmy Dickinson 48, England 1949–56 |

Ground	Capacity & record attendance	League career		Honours (domestic) League	Cup

PORT VALE (1876) White/black

Ground	Capacity & record attendance	League career		League	Cup
Vale Park Burslem Stoke-on-Trent ST6 1AW 116×76 yd	20 950 50 000 v Aston Villa FA Cup 5th Rd 20 February 1960	1892 (founder member of Div. 2) 1896 failed re-election 1898 re-elected 1907 resigned 1919 returned in October and took over the fixtures of Leeds City 1929–30 Div. 3(N) 1930–36 Div. 2 1936–38 Div. 3(N)	1938–52 Div. 3(S) 1952–54 Div. 3(N) 1954–57 Div. 2 1957–58 Div. 3(S) 1958–59 Div. 4 1959–65 Div. 3 1965–70 Div. 4 1970–78 Div. 3 1978–83 Div. 4 1983–84 Div. 3 1984–86 Div. 4 1986–89 Div. 3 1989– Div. 2	Div. 3(N) Champions 1930, 1954 Runners-up 1953 Div. 4 Champions 1959	FA Cup semi-finalists 1954 League Cup never past 2nd Rd

PRESTON NORTH END (1881) White/navy blue

Ground	Capacity & record attendance	League career		League	Cup
Deepdale Preston PR1 6RU 112×78 yd	15 000 42 684 v Arsenal Div. 1 23 April 1938	1888 (founder member of League) 1901–04 Div. 2 1904–12 Div. 1 1912–13 Div. 2 1913–14 Div. 1 1914–15 Div. 2 1919–25 Div. 1 1925–34 Div. 2 1934–49 Div. 1	1949–51 Div. 2 1951–61 Div. 1 1961–70 Div. 2 1970–71 Div. 3 1971–74 Div. 2 1974–78 Div. 3 1978–81 Div. 2 1981–85 Div. 3 1985–87 Div. 4 1987– Div. 3	Div. 1 Champions 1889, 1890 Runners-up 1891, 1892, 1893, 1906, 1953, 1958 Div. 2 Champions 1904, 1913, 1951 Runners-up 1915, 1934 Div. 3 Champions 1971 Div. 4 Runners-up 1987	FA Cup winners 1889, 1938 Runners-up 1888, 1922, 1937, 1954, 1964 League Cup never past 4th Rd

QUEEN'S PARK RANGERS (1885/1886) Blue-white hoops/white

Ground	Capacity & record attendance	League career		League	Cup
South Africa Road London W12 7PA 112×72 yd	23 480 35 353 v Leeds U Div. 1 28 April 1974	1920 (founder member of Div. 3) 1921–48 Div. 3(S) 1948–52 Div. 2 1952–58 Div. 3(S) 1958–67 Div. 3	1967–68 Div. 2 1968–69 Div. 1 1969–73 Div. 2 1973–79 Div. 1 1979–83 Div. 2 1983– Div. 1	Div. 1 runners-up 1976 Div. 2 Champions 1983 Runners-up 1968, 1973 Div. 3(S) Champions 1948 Runners-up 1947 Div. 3 Champions 1967	FA Cup runners-up 1982 League Cup winners 1967 Runners-up 1986

READING (1871) Sky blue/navy blue

Ground	Capacity & record attendance	League career		League	Cup
Elm Park Norfolk Road Reading RG3 2EF 112×77 yd	12 500 33 042 v Brentford FA Cup 5th Rd 19 February 1927	1920 (founder member of Div. 3) 1921–26 Div. 3(S) 1926–31 Div. 2 1931–58 Div. 3(S) 1958–71 Div. 3 1971–76 Div. 4	1976–77 Div. 3 1977–79 Div. 4 1979–83 Div. 3 1983–84 Div. 4 1984–86 Div. 3 1986–88 Div. 2 1988– Div. 3	Div. 3 Champions 1986 Div. 3(S) Champions 1926 Runners-up 1932, 1935, 1949, 1952 Div. 4 Champions 1979	FA Cup semi-finalists 1927 League Cup never past 4th Rd

Most League points	goals	Record win	Highest number of League goals for club in total	in a season	Most League appearances for club .	Most capped player
						PORT VALE
69, Div. 3(N) 1953-54 88, Div. 4 1982-83	110, Div. 4 1958-59	9-1 v Chesterfield Div. 2 24 September 1932	Wilf Kirkham 154, 1923-29, 1931-33	Wilf Kirkham 38 Div. 2 1926-27	Roy Sproson 761, 1950-72	Sammy Morgan 7, N. Ireland 1972-73
						PRESTON NORTH END
61, Div. 3 1970-71 90, Div. 4 1986-87	100, Div. 2 1927-28 Div. 1 1957-58	26-0 v Hyde FA Cup 1st series 1st Rd 15 October 1887	Tom Finney 187, 1946-60	Ted Harper 37 Div. 2 1932-33	Alan Kelly 447, 1961-75	Tom Finney 76, England 1946-58
						QUEEN'S PARK RANGERS
67, Div. 3 1966-67 85, Div. 2 1982-83	111, Div. 3 1961-62	9-2 v Tranmere Rovers Div. 3 3 December 1960	George Goddard 172, 1926-34	George Goddard 37 Div. 3(S) 1929-30	Tony Ingham 519, 1950-63	Don Givens 26, Eire 1973-78
						READING
65, Div. 4 1978-79 94, Div. 3 1985-86	112, Div. 3(S) 1951-52	10-2 v Crystal Palace Div. 3(S) 4 September 1946	Ronnie Blackman 156, 1947-54	Ronnie Blackman 39 Div. 3(S) 1951-52	Steve Death 471, 1969-82	Billy McConnell 8, N. Ireland 1925-28

Ground	Capacity & record attendance	League career		Honours (domestic) League	Cup

ROCHDALE (1907) Royal blue/royal blue

Spotland	10 250	1921 elected to	1969–74 Div. 3	Div. 3(N)	FA Cup never
Sandy Lane	24 231 v	Div. 3(N)	1974– Div. 4	runners-up	past 5th Rd
Rochdale OL11 5DS	Notts Co	1958–59 Div. 3		1924, 1927	League Cup
113 × 75 yd	FA Cup 2nd Rd	1959–69 Div. 4			runners-up 1962
	10 December 1949				

ROTHERHAM UNITED (1884) Red/white

Millmoor Ground	15 736	1893 Rotherham	1951–68 Div. 2	Div. 3(N)	FA Cup never
Rotherham	25 000 v	Town elected to	1968–73 Div. 3	Champions 1951	past 5th Rd
115 × 75 yd	Sheffield U	Div. 2	1973–75 Div. 4	Runners-up 1947,	League Cup
	Div. 2	1896 failed	1975–81 Div. 3	1948, 1949	runners-up 1961
	13 December 1952	re-election	1981–83 Div. 2	Div. 3 Champions	
	and Sheffield W	1919 Rotherham	1983–88 Div. 3	1981	
	Div. 2	County elected to	1988–89 Div. 4		
	26 January 1952	Div. 2	1989– Div. 3		
		1923–51 Div. 3(N)			

SCARBOROUGH (1879) Red/red

The Athletic Ground	7 600	1987 elected to		Highest placing	FA Cup never
Seamer Road	11 130 v	Div. 4		5th 1988–89	past 3rd Rd
Scarborough	Luton T				League Cup never
YO12 4HF	FA Cup 3rd Rd				past 3rd Rd
120 × 75 yd	8 January 1938				

SCUNTHORPE UNITED (1899) Claret-blue stripes/blue

Old Show Ground	10 300	1950 elected to	1972–73 Div. 3	Div. 3(N)	FA Cup never
Scunthorpe	23 935 v	Div. 3(N)	1973–83 Div. 4	Champions 1958	past 5th Rd
South Humberside	Portsmouth	1958–64 Div. 2	1983–84 Div. 3		League Cup
DN15 7RH	FA Cup 4th Rd	1964–68 Div. 3	1984– Div. 4		never past
111 × 73 yd	30 January 1954	1968–72 Div. 4			3rd Rd

SHEFFIELD UNITED (1889) Red-white stripes/black

Bramall Lane Ground	35 618	1892 elected	1971–76 Div. 1	Div. 1 Champions	FA Cup winners
Sheffield	68 287 v	to Div. 2	1976–79 Div. 2	1898	1899, 1902, 1915,
S2 4SU	Leeds U	1893–1934 Div. 1	1979–81 Div. 3	Runners-up	1925
117 × 75 yd	FA Cup 5th Rd	1934–39 Div. 2	1981–82 Div. 4	1897, 1900	Runners-up
	15 February 1936	1946–49 Div. 1	1982–84 Div. 3	Div. 2 Champions	1901, 1936
		1949–53 Div. 2	1984–88 Div. 2	1953	League Cup
		1953–56 Div. 1	1988–89 Div. 3	Runners-up 1893	never past
		1956–61 Div. 2	1989–90 Div. 2	1939, 1961, 1971,	5th Rd
		1961–68 Div. 1	1990– Div. 1	1990	
		1968–71 Div. 2		Div. 4 Champions	
				1982	

Most League points	goals	Record win	Highest number of League goals for club in total	in a season	Most League appearances for club	Most capped player
ROCHDALE						
62, Div. 3(N) 1923-24 66, Div. 4 1989-90	105, Div. 3(N) 1926-27	8-1 v Chesterfield Div. 3(N) 18 December 1926	Reg Jenkins 119, 1964-73	Albert Whitehurst 44 Div. 3(N) 1926-27	Graham Smith 317, 1966-74	None
ROTHERHAM UNITED						
71, Div. 3(N) 1950-51 82, Div. 4 1988-89	114, Div. 3(N) 1946-47	8-0 v Oldham Athletic Div. 3(N) 26 May 1947	Gladstone Guest 130, 1946-56	Wally Ardron 38 Div. 3(N) 1946-47	Danny Williams 459, 1946-62	Harold Millership 6, Wales 1920-21
SCARBOROUGH						
77, Div. 4 1988-89	67, Div. 4 1988-89	6-0 v Rhyl Athletic FA Cup 1st Rd 29 November 1930	Paul Dobson 20, 1988-90	Paul Dobson 15 Div. 4, 1989-90	Steve Richards 119, 1987-90	None
SCUNTHORPE UNITED						
66, Div. 3(N) 1957-58 83, Div. 4 1982-83	88, Div. 3(N) 1957-58	9-0 v Boston United FA Cup 1st Rd 21 November 1953	Steve Cammack 110, 1979-81, 1981-86	Barrie Thomas 31 Div. 2 1961-62	Jack Brownsword 595, 1950-65	None
SHEFFIELD UNITED						
60, Div. 2 1952-53 96, Div. 4 1981-82	102, Div. 1 1925-26	10-0 v Burslem Port Vale Div. 2 10 December 1892	Harry Johnson 205, 1919-30	Jimmy Dunne 41 Div. 1 1930-31	Joe Shaw 629, 1948-66	Billy Gillespie 25, N. Ireland 1913-30

Ground	Capacity & record attendance	League career		Honours (domestic) League	Cup

SHEFFIELD WEDNESDAY (1867) Blue-white stripes/black

Ground	Capacity & record attendance	League career		League	Cup
Hillsborough	38 780	1892 elected	1955–56 Div. 2	Div. 1 Champions	FA Cup winners
Sheffield	72 841 v	to Div. 1	1956–58 Div. 1	1903, 1904, 1929,	1896, 1907, 1935
S61SW	Manchester C	1899–1900 Div. 2	1958–59 Div. 2	1930	Runners-up
115 × 75 yd	FA Cup 5th Rd	1900–20 Div. 1	1959–70 Div. 1	Runners-up 1961	1890, 1966
	17 February 1934	1920–26 Div. 2	1970–75 Div. 2	Div. 2 Champions	League Cup
		1926–37 Div. 1	1975–80 Div. 3	1900, 1926, 1952,	never past
		1937–50 Div. 2	1980–84 Div. 2	1956, 1959	5th Rd
		1950–51 Div. 1	1984–90 Div. 1	Runners-up 1950,	
		1951–52 Div. 2	1990– Div. 2	1984	
		1952–55 Div. 1			

SHREWSBURY TOWN (1886) White-blue trim/blue

Ground	Capacity & record attendance	League career		League	Cup
Gay Meadow	15 000	1950 elected	1974–75 Div. 4	Div. 3 Champions	FA Cup never
Shrewsbury	18 917 v	to Div. 3(N)	1975–79 Div. 3	1979	past 6th Rd
116 × 76 yd	Walsall Div. 3	1951–58 Div. 3(S)	1979–89 Div. 2	Div. 4 runners-up	League Cup
	26 April 1961	1958–59 Div. 4	1989– Div. 3	1975	semi-finalists
		1959–74 Div. 3			1961

SOUTHAMPTON (1885) Red-white stripes/black

Ground	Capacity & record attendance	League career		League	Cup
The Dell	21 900	1920 (founder	1958–60 Div. 3	Div. 1 runners-up	FA Cup winners
Milton Road	31 044 v	member of Div. 3)	1960–66 Div. 2	1984	1976
Southampton	Manchester U	1921–22 Div. 3(S)	1966–74 Div. 1	Div. 2 runners-up	Runners-up
SO9 4XX	Div. 1	1922–53 Div. 2	1974–78 Div. 2	1966, 1978	1900, 1902
110 × 72 yd	8 October 1969	1953–58 Div. 3(S)	1978– Div. 1	Div. 3(S)	League Cup
				Champions 1922	runners-up 1979
				Runners-up 1921	
				Div. 3 Champions	
				1960	

SOUTHEND UNITED (1906) Blue-yellow trim/yellow

Ground	Capacity & record attendance	League career		League	Cup
Roots Hall Ground	11 863	1920 (founder	1978–80 Div. 3	Div. 4 Champions	FA Cup never
Victoria Avenue	31 036 v	member of Div. 3)	1980–81 Div. 4	1981	past 5th Rd
Southend-on-Sea	Liverpool	1921–58 Div. 3(S)	1981–84 Div. 3	Runners-up	League Cup
SS2 6NQ	FA Cup 3rd Rd	1958–66 Div. 3	1984–87 Div. 4	1972, 1978	never past
110 × 74 yd	10 January 1979	1966–72 Div. 4	1987–89 Div. 3		3rd Rd
		1972–76 Div. 3	1989–90 Div. 4		
		1976–78 Div. 4	1990– Div. 3		

STOCKPORT COUNTY (1883) White/royal blue

Ground	Capacity & record attendance	League career		League	Cup
Edgeley Park	8 520	1900 elected	1922–26 Div. 2	Div. 3(N)	FA Cup never
Stockport	27 833 v	to Div. 2	1926–37 Div. 3(N)	Champions	past 5th Rd
Cheshire	Liverpool	1904 failed	1937–38 Div. 2	1922, 1937	League Cup
SK3 9DD	FA Cup 5th Rd	re-election	1938–58 Div. 3(N)	Runners-up	never past
110 × 71 yd	11 February 1950	1905 re-elected	1958–59 Div. 3	1929, 1930	4th Rd
		to Div. 2	1959–67 Div. 4	Div. 4 Champions	
		1905–21 Div. 2	1967–70 Div. 3	1967	
		1921–22 Div. 3(N)	1970– Div. 4		

Most League points	goals	Record win	Highest number of League goals for club in total	in a season	Most League appearances for club	Most capped player
SHEFFIELD WEDNESDAY						
62, Div. 2 1958–59 88, Div. 2 1983–84	106, Div. 2 1958–59	12–0 v Halliweil FA Cup 1st Rd 17 January 1891	Andy Wilson 199, 1900–20	Derek Dooley 46 Div. 2 1951–52	Andy Wilson 502, 1900–20	Ron Springett 33, England 1959–66
SHREWSBURY TOWN						
62, Div. 4 1974–75 70, Div. 2 1981–82	101, Div. 4 1958–59	7–0 v Swindon Town Div. 3(S) 6 May 1955	Arthur Rowley 152, 1958–65	Arthur Rowley 38 Div. 4 1958–59	Colin Griffin 406, 1975–89	Jimmy McLaughlin 5, N. Ireland 1961–63 Bernard McNally 5, N. Ireland 1986–88
SOUTHAMPTON						
61, Div. 3(S) 1921–22 Div. 3 1959–60 77, Div. 1 1983–84	112, Div. 3(S) 1957–58	9–3 v Wolverhampton W Div. 2 18 September 1965	Mike Channon 185, 1966–77 1979–82	Derek Reeves 39 Div. 3 1959–60	Terry Paine 713, 1956–74	Peter Shilton 49, England 1982–87
SOUTHEND UNITED						
67, Div. 4 1980–81 80, Div. 4 1986–87	92, Div. 3(S) 1950–51	10–1 v Golders Green FA Cup 1st Rd 24 November 1934 Brentwood FA Cup 2nd Rd 7 December 1968	Roy Hollis 122, 1953–60	Jim Shankly 31 Div. 3(S) 1928–29 Sammy McCrory 31 Div. 3(S) 1957–58	Sandy Anderson 451, 1950–63	George Mackenzie 9, Eire 1937–39
STOCKPORT COUNTY						
64, Div. 4 1966–67 74, Div. 4 1989–90	115, Div. 3(N) 1933–34	13–0 v Halifax Town Div. 3(N) 6 January 1934	Jackie Connor 132, 1951–56	Alf Lythgoe 46 Div. 3(N) 1933–34	Bob Murray 465, 1952–63	Harry Hardy 1, England 1924

Ground	Capacity & record attendance	League career		Honours (domestic) League	Cup

STOKE CITY (1863*) Red-white stripes/white

Victoria Ground	35 812	1888 (founder	1923–26 Div. 2	Div. 2 Champions	FA Cup
Stoke-on-Trent	51 380 v	member of	1926–27 Div. 3(N)	1933, 1963	semi-finalists
116 × 75 yd	Arsenal Div. 1	League)	1927–33 Div. 2	Runners-up 1922	1899, 1971, 1972
	29 March 1937	1890 not re-elected	1933–53 Div. 1	Div. 3(N)	League Cup
		1891 re-elected	1953–63 Div. 2	Champions 1927	winners 1972
		1907–08 Div. 2	1963–77 Div. 1		
		1908 resigned	1977–79 Div. 1		
		1919 re-elected	1979–85 Div. 1		
		to Div. 2	1985–90 Div. 2		
		1922–23 Div. 1	1990– Div. 3		
* more likely 1868					

SUNDERLAND (1879) Red-white stripes/black

Roker Park	31 887	1890 elected	1977–80 Div. 2	Div. 1 Champions	FA Cup winners
Sunderland	75 118 v	to Div. 1	1980–85 Div. 1	1892, 1893, 1895,	1937, 1973
Tyne & Wear	Derby Co	1958–64 Div. 2	1985–87 Div. 2	1902, 1913, 1936	Runners-up 1913
113 × 74 yd	FA Cup 6th Rd	1964–70 Div. 1	1987–88 Div. 3	Runners-up	League Cup
	replay	1970–76 Div. 2	1988–90 Div. 2	1894, 1898, 1901,	runners-up 1985
	8 March 1933	1976–77 Div. 1	1990– Div. 1	1923, 1935	
				Div. 2 Champions	
				1976	
				Runners-up 1964,	
				1980	
				Div. 3 Champions	
				1988	

SWANSEA CITY (1912) White/white

Vetch Field	16 098	1920 (founder	1973–78 Div. 4	Div. 3(S)	FA Cup
Swansea	32 796 v	member of Div. 3)	1978–79 Div. 3	Champions	semi-finalists
Glamorgan	Arsenal	1921–25 Div. 3(S)	1979–81 Div. 2	1925, 1949	1926, 1964
SA1 3SU	FA Cup 4th Rd	1925–47 Div. 2	1981–83 Div. 1		League Cup
112 × 74 yd	17 February 1968	1947–49 Div. 3(S)	1983–84 Div. 2		never past 4th Rd
		1949–65 Div. 2	1984–86 Div. 3		
		1965–67 Div. 3	1986–88 Div. 4		
		1967–70 Div. 4	1988– Div. 3		
		1970–73 Div. 3			

SWINDON TOWN (1881) Red/white

County Ground	16 153	1920 (founder	1965–69 Div. 3	Div. 3 runners-up	FA Cup
Swindon	32 000	member of Div. 3)	1969–74 Div. 2	1963, 1969	semi-finalists
Wiltshire SN1 2ED	Arsenal	1921–58 Div. 3(S)	1974–82 Div. 3	Div. 4 Champions	1910, 1912
114 × 72 yd	FA Cup 3rd Rd	1958–63 Div. 3	1982–86 Div. 4	1986	League Cup
	17 January 1972	1963–65 Div. 2	1986–87 Div. 3		winners 1969
			1987– Div. 2		

Most League points	goals	Record win	Highest number of League goals for club in total	in a season	Most League appearances for club	Most capped player
						STOKE CITY
63, Div. 3(N) 1926–27 62, Div. 2 1987–88	92, Div. 3(N) 1926–27	10–3 v West Bromwich Albion Div. 1 4 February 1937	Freddie Steele 142, 1934–49	Freddie Steele 33 Div. 1 1936–37	Eric Skeels 506, 1958–76	Gordon Banks 36, England 1967–72
						SUNDERLAND
61, Div. 2 1963–64 93, Div. 3 1987–88	109, Div. 1 1935–36	11–1 v Fairfield FA Cup 1st Rd 2 February 1895	Charlie Buchan 209, 1911–25	Dave Halliday 43 Div. 1 1928–29	Jim Montgomery 537, 1962–77	Martin Harvey 34, N. Ireland 1961–71
						SWANSEA CITY
62, Div. 3(S) 1948–49 70, Div. 4 1987–88	90, Div. 2 1956–57	12–0 v Sliema Wanderers Cup-Winners Cup 1st Rd 15 September 1982	Ivor Allchurch 166, 1949–58, 1965–68	Cyril Pearce 35 Div. 2 1931–32	Wilfred Milne 585, 1919–37	Ivor Allchurch 42, Wales 1950–58
						SWINDON TOWN
64, Div. 3 1968–69 102, Div. 4 1985–86	100, Div. 3(S) 1926–27	10–1 v Farnham United Breweries FA Cup 1st Rd 28 November 1925	Harry Morris 216, 1926–33	Harry Morris 47 Div. 3(S) 1926–27	John Trollope 770, 1960–80	Rod Thomas 30, Wales 1967–73

Ground	Capacity & record attendance	League career		Honours (domestic) League	Cup

TORQUAY UNITED (1898) Yellow/yellow

Plainmoor Ground Torquay Devon TQ1 3PS 112×74 yd	5 539 21 908 v Huddersfield T FA Cup 4th Rd 29 January 1955	1927 elected to Div. 3(S) 1958–60 Div. 4 1960–62 Div. 3	1962–66 Div. 4 1966–72 Div. 3 1972– Div. 4	Div. 3(S) runners-up 1957	FA Cup never past 4th Rd League Cup never past 3rd Rd

TOTTENHAM HOTSPUR (1882) White/navy blue

748 High Road Tottenham London N17 0AP 110×73 yd	29 700 75 038 v Sunderland FA Cup 6th Rd 5 March 1938	1908 elected to Div. 2 1909–15 Div. 1 1919–20 Div. 2 1920–28 Div. 1 1928–33 Div. 2	1933–35 Div. 1 1935–50 Div. 2 1950–77 Div. 1 1977–78 Div. 2 1978– Div. 1	Div. 1 Champions 1951, 1961 Runners-up 1922 1952, 1957, 1963 Div. 2 Champions 1920, 1950 Runners-up 1909, 1933	FA Cup winners 1901, 1921, 1961, 1962, 1967, 1981, 1982 (joint record) League Cup winners 1971, 1973 Runners-up 1982

TRANMERE ROVERS (1883) White/white

Prenton Park Prenton Road West Birkenhead 112×71 yd	14 200 24 424 v Stoke City FA Cup 4th Rd 5 February 1972	1921 (founder member of Div. 3(N) 1938–39 Div. 2 1946–58 Div. 3(N) 1958–61 Div. 3	1961–67 Div. 4 1967–75 Div. 3 1975–76 Div. 4 1976–79 Div. 3 1979–89 Div. 4 1989– Div. 3	Div. 3(N) Champions 1938 Div. 4 runners-up 1989	FA Cup never past 5th Rd League Cup never past 4th Rd

WALSALL (1888) Red/white

Bescot Stadium Bescot Crescent Walsall WS1 4SA 110 × 73 yd	12 000 25 453 v Newcastle U Div. 2 29 August 1961	1892 elected to Div. 2 1895 failed re-election 1896–1901 Div. 2 1901 failed re-election 1921 (founder member of Div.3(N)) 1927–31 Div. 3(S) 1931–36 Div. 3(N)	1936–58 Div. 3(S) 1958–60 Div. 4 1960–61 Div. 3 1961–63 Div. 2 1963–79 Div. 3 1979–80 Div. 4 1980–88 Div. 3 1988–89 Div. 2 1989–90 Div. 3 1990– Div. 4	Div. 4 Champions 1960 Runners-up 1980 Div. 3 runners-up 1961	FA Cup never past 5th Rd League Cup semi-finalists 1984

WATFORD (1891) Yellow with black-red trim/black

Vicarage Road Watford WD1 8ER 115×75 yd	23 000 34 099 v Manchester U FA Cup 4th Rd 3 February 1969	1920 (founder member of Div. 3) 1921–58 Div. 3(S) 1958–60 Div. 4 1960–69 Div. 3 1969–72 Div. 2	1972–75 Div. 3 1975–78 Div. 4 1978–79 Div. 3 1979–82 Div. 2 1982–88 Div. 1 1988– Div. 2	Div. 1 runners-up 1983 Div. 2 runners-up 1982 Div. 3 Champions 1969 Runners-up 1979 Div. 4 Champions 1978	FA Cup runners-up 1984 League Cup semi-finalists 1979

Most League points	goals	Record win	Highest number of League goals for club in total	in a season	Most League appearances for club	Most capped player
						TORQUAY UNITED
60, Div. 4 1959–60 77, Div. 4 1987–88	89, Div. 3(S) 1956–57	9–0 v Swindon Town Div. 3(S) 8 March 1952	Sammy Collins 204, 1948–58	Sammy Collins 40 Div. 3(S) 1955–56	Dennis Lewis 443, 1947–59	None
						TOTTENHAM HOTSPUR
70, Div. 2 1919–20 77, Div. 1 1984–85	115, Div. 1 1960–61	13–2 v Crewe Alexandra FA Cup 4th Rd replay 3 February 1960	Jimmy Greaves 220, 1961–70	Jimmy Greaves 37 Div. 1 1962–63	Steve Perryman 655, 1969–86	Pat Jennings 74, N. Ireland 1964–77, 1985–86
						TRANMERE ROVERS
60, Div. 4 1964–65 80, Div. 4 1988–89, 1989–90	111, Div. 3(N) 1930–31	13–4 v Oldham Athletic Div. 3(N) 26 December 1935	Ian Muir 105, 1985–90	Bunny Bell 35 Div. 3(N) 1933–34	Harold Bell 595, 1946–64	Albert Gray 3, Wales 1931
						WALSALL
65, Div. 4 1959–60 82, Div. 3 1987–88	102, Div. 4 1959–60	10–0 v Darwen Div. 2 4 March 1899	Tony Richards 184, 1954–63 Colin Taylor 184, 1958–63, 1964–68, 1969–73	Gilbert Alsop 40 Div. 3(N) 1933–34, 1934–35	Colin Harrison 467, 1964–82	Mick Kearns 15, Eire 1973–79
						WATFORD
71, Div. 4 1977–78 80, Div. 2 1981–82	92, Div. 4 1959–60	10–1 v Lowestoft Town FA Cup 1st Rd 27 November 1926	Tom Barnett 144, 1928–39	Cliff Holton 42 Div. 4 1959–60	Duncan Welbourne 411, 1963–74	John Barnes 31, England 1983–87 Kenny Jackett 31, Wales 1982–

Ground	Capacity & record attendance	League career		Honours (domestic) League	Cup

WEST BROMWICH ALBION (1879) Blue-white stripes/navy blue

Ground	Capacity & record attendance	League career		League	Cup
The Hawthorns West Bromwich B71 4LF 115 × 75 yd	26 159 64 815 v Arsenal FA Cup 6th Rd 6 March 1937	1888 (founder member of League) 1901–02 Div. 2 1902–04 Div. 1 1904–11 Div. 2 1911–27 Div. 1	1927–31 Div. 2 1931–38 Div. 1 1938–49 Div. 2 1949–73 Div. 1 1973–76 Div. 2 1976–86 Div. 1 1986– Div. 2	Div. 1 Champions 1920 Runners-up 1925, 1954 Div. 2 Champions 1902, 1911 Runners-up 1931, 1949	FA Cup winners 1888, 1892, 1931, 1954, 1968 Runners-up 1886, 1887, 1895, 1912, 1935 League Cup winners 1966 Runners-up 1967, 1970

WEST HAM UNITED (1895) Claret-blue/white

Ground	Capacity & record attendance	League career		League	Cup
Boleyn Ground Green Street Upton Park London E13 9AZ 112 × 72 yd	29 627 42 322 v Tottenham H Div. 1 17 October 1970	1919 elected to Div. 2 1923–32 Div. 1 1932–58 Div. 2	1958–78 Div. 1 1978–81 Div. 2 1981–89 Div. 1 1989– Div. 2	Div. 2 Champions 1958, 1981 Runners-up 1923	FA Cup winners 1964, 1975, 1980 Runners-up 1923 League Cup runners-up 1966, 1981

WIGAN ATHLETIC Blue/white

Ground	Capacity & record attendance	League career		League	Cup
Springfield Park Wigan 117 × 72 yd	11 434 27 500 v Hereford U FA Cup 2nd Rd 12 December 1953	1978 elected to Div. 4	1982– Div. 3	Highest placing 4th, Div. 3, 1986, 1987	FA Cup never past 4th Rd League Cup never past 4th Rd

WIMBLEDON (1889) Blue-yellow trim/blue

Ground	Capacity & record attendance	League career		League	Cup
Plough Lane Ground Durnsford Wimbledon London SW19 110 × 73 yd	13 806 18 000 v HMS Victory FA Amateur Cup 3rd Rd 23 February 1935	1977 elected to Div. 4 1979–80 Div. 3 1980–81 Div. 4 1981–82 Div. 3	1982–83 Div. 4 1983–84 Div. 3 1984–86 Div. 2 1986– Div. 1	Div. 3 runners-up 1984 Div. 4 Champions 1983	FA Cup winners 1988 League Cup never past 4th Rd

Most League points	goals	Record win	Highest number of League goals for club		Most League appearances for club	Most capped player
			in total	in a season		

WEST BROMWICH ALBION

60, Div. 1 1919–20 72, Div. 2 1988–89	105, Div. 2 1929–30	12–0 v Darwen Div. 1 4 April 1892	Tony Brown 218, 1963–79	William Richardson 39 Div. 1935–36	Tony Brown 574, 1963–80	Stuart Williams 33, Wales 1954–62

WEST HAM UNITED

66, Div. 2 1980–81 84, Div. 1 1985–86	101, Div. 2 1957–58	10–0 v Bury League Cup 2nd Rd 25 October 1980	Vic Watson 306, 1920–35	Vic Watson 41 Div. 1 1929–30	Billy Bonds 663, 1967–88	Bobby Moore 108, England 1962–73

WIGAN ATHLETIC

55, Div. 4 1978–79, 1979–80 91, Div. 4 1981–82	80, Div. 4 1981–82	6–0 v Carlisle United FA Cup 1st Rd 24 November 1934	Peter Houghton 62, 1978–84	Les Bradd 19 Div. 4 1981–82	Colin Methuen 296, 1979–86	None

WIMBLEDON

61, Div. 4 1978–79 98, Div. 4 1982–83	97, Div. 3 1983–84	6–0 v Newport County Div. 3 3 September 1983	Alan Cork 138, 1977–90	Alan Cork 29, 1983–84	Alan Cork 386, 1977–90	Glyn Hodges 5, Wales 1984–87

Ground	Capacity & record attendance	League career		Honours (domestic) League	Cup

WOLVERHAMPTON WANDERERS (1877*) Gold/black

Molineux Grounds	25 000	1888 (founder	1976–77 Div. 2	Div. 1 Champions	FA Cup winners
Wolverhampton	61 315 v	member of	1977–82 Div. 1	1954, 1958, 1959	1893, 1908, 1949,
WV1 4QR	Liverpool	League)	1982–83 Div. 2	Runners-up	1960
115 × 72 yd	FA Cup 5th Rd	1906–23 Div. 2	1983–84 Div. 1	1938, 1939, 1950,	Runners-up
	11 February 1939	1923–24 Div. 3(N)	1984–85 Div. 2	1955, 1960	1889, 1896, 1921,
		1924–32 Div. 2	1985–86 Div. 3	Div. 2 Champions	1939
		1932–65 Div. 1	1986–88 Div. 4	1932, 1977	League Cup
		1965–67 Div. 2	1988–89 Div. 3	Runners-up 1967,	winners 1974, 1980
		1967–76 Div. 1	1989– Div. 2	1983	
				Div. 3 (N)	
				Champions 1924	
				Div. 3 Champions	
				1989	
				Div. 4 Champions	
* firm basis from 1879				1988	

WREXHAM (1873) Red/white

Racecourse Ground	20 000	1921 (founder	1964–70 Div. 4	Div. 3 Champions	FA Cup never
Mold Road	34 445 v	member of	1970–78 Div. 3	1978	past 6th Rd
Wrexham	Manchester U	Div. 3(N)	1978–82 Div. 2	Div. 3(N)	League Cup
111 × 71 yd	FA Cup 4th Rd	1958–60 Div. 3	1982–83 Div. 3	runners-up 1933	never past
	26 January 1957	1960–62 Div. 4	1983– Div. 4	Div. 4 runners-up	5th Rd
		1962–64 Div. 3		1970	

YORK CITY (1922) Red/blue

Bootham Crescent	14 109	1929 elected	1971–74 Div. 3	Div. 4 Champions	FA Cup
York YO3 7AQ	28 123 v	to Div. 3(N)	1974–76 Div. 2	1984	semi-finalists
115 × 75 yd	Huddersfield T	1958–59 Div. 4	1976–77 Div. 3		1955
	FA Cup 5th Rd	1959–60 Div. 3	1977–84 Div. 4		League Cup
	5 March 1938	1960–65 Div. 4	1984–88 Div. 3		never past
		1965–66 Div. 3	1988– Div. 4		5th Rd
		1966–71 Div. 4			

Change of name

Clubs who have changed names since joining the Football League:

Club	Previous name(s)	Until
Aldershot	Aldershot Town	c. 1937
Arsenal	Woolwich Arsenal	1913
Birmingham City	Birmingham	1946
	Small Heath	1905
AFC Bournemouth	Bournemouth & Boscombe Athletic	1971
Burton United	Burton Swifts	1901
Gateshead	South Shields	1930
Hartlepool United	Hartlepool	1977
	Hartlepools United	1968

Most League points	goals	Record win	Highest number of League goals for club in total	in a season	Most League appearances for club	Most capped player

WOLVERHAMPTON WANDERERS

Most League points	goals	Record win	in total	in a season	Most League appearances	Most capped player
64, Div. 1 1957–58 92, Div. 4 1988–89	115, Div. 2 1931–32	14–0 v Crosswell's Brewery FA Cup 2nd Rd 13 November 1886	Bill Hartill 164, 1928–35	Dennis Westcott 37 Div. 1 1946–47	Derek Parkin 501, 1967–82	Billy Wright 105, England 1946–59

WREXHAM

61, Div. 4 1969–70 Div. 3 1977–78 71, Div. 4 1988–89	106, Div. 3(N) 1932–33	10–1 v Hartlepools United Div. 4 3 March 1962	Tom Bamford 175, 1928–34	Tom Bamford 44 Div. 3(N) 1933–34	Arfon Griffiths 592, 1959–61 1962–79	Dai Davies 28, Wales 1977–81

YORK CITY

62, Div. 4 1964–65 101, Div. 4 1983–84	96, Div. 4 1983–84	9–1 v Southport Div. 3(N) 2 February 1957	Norman Wilkinson 125, 1954–66	Bill Fenton 31 Div. 3(N) 1951–52 Arthur Bottom 31 Div. 3(N) 1954–55 and 1955–56	Barry Jackson 481, 1958–70	Peter Scott 7, N. Ireland 1976–78

Club	Previous name(s)	Until
Leicester City	Leicester Fosse	1919
Leyton Orient	Orient	1987
	Leyton Orient	1967
	Clapton Orient	1946
Manchester City	Ardwick	1894
Manchester United	Newton Heath	1902
Rotherham United	Rotherham County	1925
Sheffield Wednesday	The Wednesday	1929
Stoke City	Stoke	1925
Swansea City	Swansea Town	1970

League Champions 1889–1990

Season ending	Champions	Matches	Pts	Home						Away						Goal av.	No. of players	Ever present	Winning margin (pts)
				W	D	L	F	A	Pts	W	D	L	F	A	Pts				
1889	Preston North End	22	40	10	1	0	39	7	21	8	3	0	35	8	19	3.36	18	2	11
1890	Preston North End	22	33	8	1	2	41	12	17	7	2	2	30	18	16	3.23	19	3	2
1891	Everton	22	29	9	0	2	39	12	18	5	1	5	24	17	11	2.86	21	3	2
1892	Sunderland	26	42	13	0	0	55	11	26	8	0	5	38	25	16	3.57	15	2	5
1893	Sunderland	30	48	13	2	0	58	17	28	9	2	4	42	19	20	3.33	15	3	11
1894	Aston Villa	30	44	12	2	1	49	13	26	7	4	4	35	29	18	2.80	24	1	6
1895	Sunderland	30	47	13	2	0	51	14	28	8	3	4	29	23	19	2.66	16	2	5
1896	Aston Villa	30	45	14	1	0	47	17	29	6	4	5	31	28	16	2.60	17	2	4
1897	Aston Villa	30	47	10	3	2	36	16	23	11	2	2	37	22	24	2.43	17	4	11
1898	Sheffield United	30	42	9	4	2	27	14	22	8	4	3	29	17	20	1.86	23	1	5
1899	Aston Villa	34	45	15	2	0	58	13	32	4	5	8	18	27	13	2.23	24	1	2
1900	Aston Villa	34	50	12	4	1	45	18	28	10	2	5	32	17	22	2.26	21	2	2
1901	Liverpool	34	45	12	2	3	36	13	26	7	5	5	23	22	19	1.73	18	3	2
1902	Sunderland	34	44	12	3	2	32	14	27	7	3	7	18	21	17	1.47	19	1	3
1903	Sheffield Weds.	34	42	12	3	2	31	7	27	7	1	9	23	29	15	1.58	23	3	1
1904	Sheffield Weds.	34	47	14	3	0	34	10	31	6	4	7	14	18	16	1.41	22	2	3
1905	Newcastle United	34	48	14	1	2	41	12	29	9	1	7	31	21	19	2.11	21	0	1
1906	Liverpool	38	51	14	3	2	49	15	31	9	2	8	30	31	20	2.07	21	1	4
1907	Newcastle United	38	51	18	1	0	51	12	37	4	6	9	23	34	14	1.94	27	0	3
1908	Manchester United	38	52	15	1	3	43	19	31	8	5	6	38	29	21	2.13	25	0	9
1909	Newcastle United	38	53	14	1	4	32	20	29	10	4	5	33	21	24	1.71	25	1	7
1910	Aston Villa	38	53	17	2	0	62	19	36	6	5	8	22	23	17	2.21	18	0	5
1911	Manchester United	38	52	14	4	1	47	18	32	8	4	7	25	22	20	1.89	26	0	1
1912	Blackburn Rovers	38	49	13	6	0	35	10	32	7	3	9	25	33	17	1.57	21	0	3
1913	Sunderland	38	54	14	2	3	47	17	30	11	2	6	39	26	24	2.26	22	1	4
1914	Blackburn Rovers	38	51	14	4	1	51	15	32	6	7	6	27	27	19	2.05	21	1	7
1915	Everton	38	46	8	5	6	44	29	21	11	3	5	32	18	25	2.00	24	0	1

No national competition 1916–1919; regional leagues in operation

Season ending	Champions	Matches	Pts	Home						Away						Goal av.	No. of players	Ever present	Winning margin (pts)
1920	West Bromwich A.	42	60	17	1	3	65	21	35	11	3	7	39	26	25	2.47	18	1	9
1921	Burnley	42	59	17	3	1	56	16	37	6	10	5	23	20	22	1.88	23	1	5
1922	Liverpool	42	57	15	4	2	43	15	34	7	9	5	20	21	23	1.50	22	2	6
1923	Liverpool	42	60	17	3	1	50	13	37	9	5	7	20	18	23	1.66	19	3	6
1924	Huddersfield Town	42	57	15	5	1	35	9	35	8	6	7	25	24	22	1.42	22	1	gl av.
1925	Huddersfield Town	42	58	10	8	3	31	10	28	11	8	2	38	18	30	1.64	22	0	2
1926	Huddersfield Town	42	57	14	6	1	50	17	34	9	5	7	42	43	23	2.19	24	0	5
1927	Newcastle United	42	56	19	1	1	64	20	39	6	5	10	32	38	17	2.28	21	3	5
1928	Everton	42	53	11	8	2	60	28	30	9	5	7	42	38	23	2.42	24	2	2
1929	Sheffield Weds.	42	52	18	3	0	55	16	39	3	7	11	31	46	13	2.04	22	4	1
1930	Sheffield Weds.	42	60	15	4	2	56	20	34	11	4	6	49	37	26	2.50	22	1	10
1931	Arsenal	42	66	14	5	2	67	27	33	14	5	2	60	32	33	3.02	22	1	7
1932	Everton	42	56	18	0	3	84	30	36	8	4	9	32	34	20	2.76	20	0	2
1933	Arsenal	42	58	14	3	4	70	27	31	11	5	5	48	34	27	2.80	23	1	4
1934	Arsenal	42	59	15	4	2	45	19	34	10	5	6	30	28	25	1.78	23	1	3

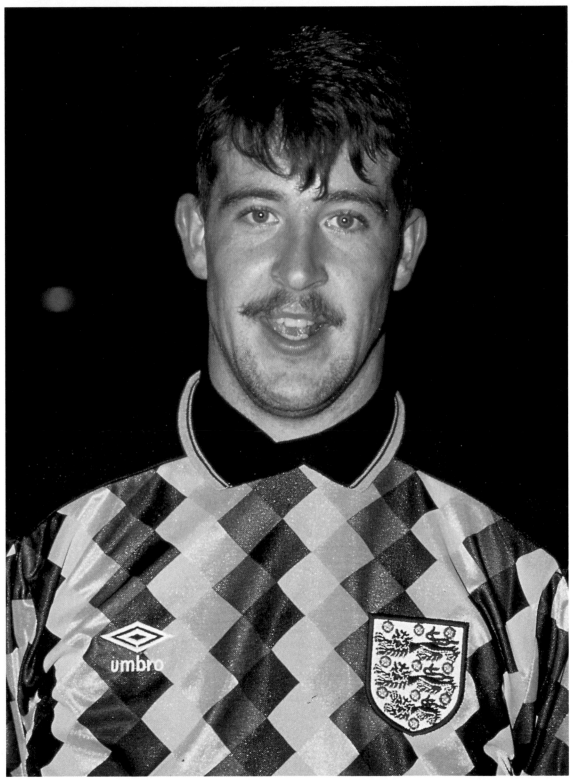

Nigel Martyn became the first £1 million goalkeeper when Crystal Palace signed him from Bristol Rovers in November 1989

(Allsport / Dan Smith)

Ally McCoist (blue shirt) fires wide for Rangers in the 1989 Scottish Cup Final. Celtic won 1–0 *(Action-Plus)*

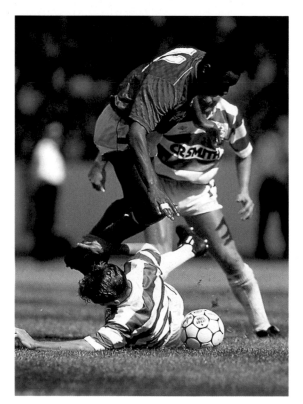

Rangers' Davie Cooper (above) leaves Celtic's Roy Aitken off balance as he prepares to cross the ball into the goalmouth *(Action-Plus)*

Mark Walters (left) tries a spot of hurdling to overcome Celtic opposition *(Action-Plus)*

Richard Gough (left) tries to get in his tackle before Mark McGhee can make ground towards goal for Celtic *(Action-Plus)*

Celtic skipper Aitken rises high to challenge Rangers striker Kevin Drinkell *(Action-Plus)*

Gary Pallister became the most expensive player to be transferred between English clubs when he joined Manchester United from Middlesbrough for £2.3 million in August 1989 *(Allsport / Ben Radford)*

Chris Waddle (above) moved from Tottenham Hotspur to Marseille in the 1989 close season for £4.5 million, a record fee for a player of British origin. Juventus agreed to pay £5.5 million to FC Cologne for West German midfield player Thomas Hassler (left) at the end of the 1989–90 season, then a record transfer for a German *(Allsport)*

Pat Nevin (blue shirt) and John Barnes
have a touchline tussle in the 1989 FA Cup Final,
eventually won 3–2 by Liverpool
(Allsport / Simon Bruty)

Ian Rush scores Liverpool's second goal in the all-Merseyside final at Wembley *(Allsport / Simon Bruty)*

Substitute Stuart McCall equalises for Everton in the dying moments of normal time *(Allsport / Simon Bruty)*

Opposing captains Kevin Ratcliffe (Everton, left) and Ronnie Whelan (Liverpool) pose for the cameras *(Allsport / Simon Bruty)*

Frank Bunn, seen here in action for Luton Town, created a record in the Littlewoods Cup when he scored six goals for Oldham Athletic against Scarborough in the 1989–90 season *(Allsport)*

Season ending	Champions	Matches	Pts	Home						Away						Goal av.	No. of players	Ever present	Winning margin (pts)
				W	D	L	F	A	Pts	W	D	L	F	A	Pts				
1935	Arsenal	42	58	15	4	2	74	17	34	8	8	5	41	29	24	2.73	25	0	4
1936	Sunderland	42	56	17	2	2	71	33	36	8	4	9	38	41	20	2.59	23	2	8
1937	Manchester City	42	57	15	5	1	56	22	35	7	8	6	51	39	22	2.54	22	4	3
1938	Arsenal	42	52	15	4	2	52	16	34	6	6	9	25	28	18	1.83	29	0	1
1939	Everton	42	59	17	3	1	60	18	37	10	2	9	28	34	22	2.09	22	1	4

No national competition 1940–1946; regional leagues were in operation

Season ending	Champions	Matches	Pts	Home						Away						Goal av.	No. of players	Ever present	Winning margin (pts)
1947	Liverpool	42	57	13	3	5	42	24	29	12	4	5	42	28	28	2.00	26	0	1
1948	Arsenal	42	52	15	3	3	56	15	33	8	10	3	25	17	26	1.92	19	2	7
1949	Portsmouth	42	58	18	3	0	52	12	39	7	5	9	32	30	19	2.00	18	2	5
1950	Portsmouth	42	56	12	7	2	44	15	31	10	2	9	30	23	22	1.76	25	2	gl av.
1951	Tottenham H.	42	60	17	2	2	54	21	36	8	8	5	28	23	24	1.95	19	2	4
1952	Manchester United	42	57	15	3	3	55	21	33	8	8	5	40	31	24	2.26	24	1	4
1953	Arsenal	42	54	15	3	3	60	30	33	6	9	6	37	34	21	2.30	21	0	gl av.
1954	Wolverhampton W.	42	57	16	1	4	61	25	33	9	6	6	35	31	24	2.28	22	1	4
1955	Chelsea	42	52	11	5	5	43	29	27	9	7	5	38	28	25	1.92	20	2	4
1956	Manchester United	42	60	18	3	0	51	20	39	7	7	7	32	31	21	1.97	24	1	11
1957	Manchester United	42	64	14	4	3	55	25	32	14	4	3	48	29	22	2.45	24	0	8
1958	Wolverhampton W.	42	64	17	3	1	60	21	37	11	5	5	43	26	27	2.45	21	0	5
1959	Wolverhampton W.	42	61	15	3	3	68	19	33	13	2	6	42	30	28	2.61	22	0	6
1960	Burnley	42	55	15	2	4	52	28	32	9	5	7	33	33	23	2.02	18	3	1
1961	Tottenham H.	42	66	15	3	3	65	28	33	16	1	4	50	27	33	2.73	17	4	8
1962	Ipswich Town	42	56	17	2	2	58	28	36	7	6	8	35	39	20	2.21	16	3	3
1963	Everton	42	61	14	7	0	48	17	35	11	4	6	36	25	26	2.00	20	2	6
1964	Liverpool	42	57	16	0	5	60	18	32	10	5	6	32	27	25	2.19	17	3	4
1965	Manchester United	42	61	16	4	1	52	13	36	10	5	6	37	26	25	2.11	18	4	gl av.
1966	Liverpool	42	61	17	2	2	52	15	36	9	7	5	27	19	25	1.88	14	5	6
1967	Manchester United	42	60	17	4	0	51	13	38	7	8	6	33	32	22	2.00	20	2	4
1968	Manchester City	42	58	17	2	2	52	16	36	9	4	8	34	27	22	2.04	21	1	2
1969	Leeds United	42	67	18	3	0	41	9	39	9	10	2	25	17	28	1.57	17	4	6
1970	Everton	42	66	17	3	1	46	19	37	12	5	4	26	15	29	1.71	17	4	9
1971	Arsenal	42	65	18	3	0	41	6	39	11	4	6	30	23	26	1.69	16	3	1
1972	Derby County	42	58	16	4	1	43	10	36	8	6	7	26	23	22	1.64	16	2	1
1973	Liverpool	42	60	17	3	1	45	19	37	8	7	6	27	23	23	1.71	16	3	3
1974	Leeds United	42	62	12	8	1	38	18	32	12	6	3	28	13	30	1.57	20	2	5
1975	Derby County	42	53	14	4	3	41	18	32	7	7	7	26	31	21	1.59	16	2	2
1976	Liverpool	42	60	14	5	2	41	21	33	9	9	3	25	10	27	1.57	19	2	1
1977	Liverpool	42	57	18	3	0	47	11	39	5	8	8	15	22	18	1.47	17	3	1
1978	Nottingham Forest	42	64	15	6	0	37	8	36	10	8	3	32	16	28	1.64	16	1	7
1979	Liverpool	42	68	19	2	0	51	4	40	11	6	4	34	12	28	2.02	15	4	8
1980	Liverpool	42	60	15	6	0	46	8	36	8	10	4	35	22	24	1.92	17	3	2
1981	Aston Villa	42	60	16	3	2	40	13	35	10	5	6	32	27	25	1.71	14	7	4
1982	Liverpool	42	87	14	3	4	39	14	45	12	6	3	41	18	42	1.90	16	3	4
1983	Liverpool	42	82	16	4	1	55	16	52	8	6	7	32	21	30	2.07	16	4	11

Season ending	Champions	Matches	Pts	Home						Away						Goal av.	No. of players	Ever present	Winning margin (pts)
				W	D	L	F	A	Pts	W	D	L	F	A	Pts				
1984	Liverpool	42	80	14	5	2	50	12	47	8	9	4	23	20	33	1.73	15	5	3
1985	Everton	42	90	16	3	2	58	17	51	12	3	6	30	26	42	2.09	25	1	13
1986	Liverpool	42	88	16	4	1	58	14	52	10	6	5	31	23	36	2.11	18	1	3
1987	Everton	42	86	16	4	1	49	11	52	10	4	7	27	20	34	1.80	23	1	9
1988	Liverpool	40	90	15	5	0	49	9	50	11	7	2	38	15	40	2.17	22	2	9
1989	Arsenal	38	76	10	6	3	35	19	36	12	4	3	38	17	40	1.92	17	3	gls
1990	Liverpool	38	79	13	5	1	38	15	44	10	5	4	40	22	35	2.05	21	2	9

CHAMPIONSHIP WINS

Liverpool 18
Aston Villa 7
Man United 7
Huddersfield T 3
Wolves 3
Man City 2
Burnley 2
Chelsea 1
Spurs 2
WBA 1
N Forest 1
Ipswich T 1
Sheff Utd 1
Derby Co 2
Portsmouth 2
Leeds United 2
Blackburn R 2
Preston NE 2
Sheff Wed 4
Sunderland 6
Newcastle U 4
Arsenal 9
Everton 9

League facts

Twenty-three different teams have won the Football League championship. Liverpool have been the most successful with 18 titles followed by Arsenal and Everton with nine, and Aston Villa and Manchester United with seven each.

The 12 original members of the Football League in 1888 were: Preston North End, Aston Villa, Wolverhampton Wanderers, Blackburn Rovers, Bolton Wanderers, West Bromwich Albion, Accrington, Everton, Burnley, Derby County, Notts County and Stoke, finishing the 1888–89 season in that order.

Accrington became the first permanent casualty among the dozen. After being relegated to Division Two in 1893 they left the Football League before the next season. Manchester United had actually finished five points below them at the bottom of the table.

Stoke had not been re-elected in 1890 but came back the following year, only to be relegated in 1907. After one season in Division Two, they resigned from the League for financial reasons, but were re-elected in 1919.

Notts County were the first team to reach 3000 League matches. They achieved this milestone in a Division Two game against Nottingham Forest on 25 March 1975 which ended in a 2–2 draw. Yet as one of four clubs who were forced to seek re-election to the League after its inaugural season in 1888–89, they had received seven votes, just two more than Birmingham St George's.

Notts County and Blackburn Rovers were the last two clubs to open their League programme in 1888. While the other ten began on 8 September, Notts and Rovers started a week later. Notts played at Everton, Blackburn at home to Accrington.

Aston Villa were the first to score 6000 goals in the Football League. They reached this milestone in a 1–1 draw against Bournemouth at Villa Park on 17 October 1987.

Everton hold the record for the largest championship-winning points margin in Division One, following the introduction of three points for a win. In 1984–85 they had a 13-point lead over the runners-up, Liverpool.

Under the two-points system, 11 points was the record, held jointly by Preston North End (1888–89),

Sunderland (1892–93), Aston Villa (1896–97) and Manchester United (1955–56).

Goal average was used to determine the League champions in 1923–24, 1949–50, 1952–53 and 1964–65. Goal difference had to be used in 1988–89, but as this was identical for both teams, Arsenal won the title by scoring more goals than Liverpool.

The highest-scoring championship winners in the post-war period were Tottenham Hotspur in 1960–61 with 115 goals at an average of 2.73 per game. Spurs were also the last team in Division One to score a century of goals, which they did in 1962–63 with 111 goals as runners-up.

Everton launched themselves into a highly successful season in 1984–85 by capturing the Charity Shield in August (Associated Sports Photography)

Between the wars, the highest-scoring winners were Arsenal in 1930–31 with 127 goals for an average of 3.02 per game. But the overall record is held by Sunderland, who in 1891–92 won the title with 93 goals at an average of 3.57 goals per game.

On 30 August 1986 only 12 goals were scored in 11 Division Two matches. No team scored more than once.

On 1 October 1983 there were 53 goals scored in 11 Division Two matches. The scores included a 7, two 5's, three 4's and three 3's.

On 26 December 1963 there were 66 goals scored in the ten Division One matches played.

On 1 February 1936 there were 209 goals scored in the 44 League matches played. It equalled the total achieved on 2 January 1932 from the same number of games.

On 6 September 1986 the Division One programme did not produce one home win. There were eight away wins and three draws. Similarly in Division Two there were seven away wins and four draws on 26 December 1987.

On 13 February 1926 all Division One clubs at home won their matches and it happened again on 10 December 1955. All 12 Division Two games were won by home teams on 26 November 1988.

Nine of 11 Division One games on 18 September 1948 were drawn.

Tottenham Hotspur's League and Cup double success in 1960–61 with a free-scoring attack which produced an average of 2.73 goals per game in the championship alone, gave them the chance to play an FA XI for the Charity Shield. Here Bobby Smith celebrates a goal by colleague Les Allen as Spurs won 3–2 (Associated Press)

Goal bonanzas

There have been only two drawn matches in Football League history in which each side scored as many as six goals – 6-6 draws between Leicester City and Arsenal in 1930 and Charlton Athletic and Middlesbrough in 1960. Below are the details of the matches in which each team scored five times or more:

F.Lge	Blackburn Rovers	5-5	Accrington Stanley	9 Sep 1888
Div.1	Derby County	8-5	Blackburn Rovers	6 Sep 1890
Div.2	Crewe Alexandra	5-6	Walsall Town S.	5 Nov 1892
Div.2	Burton Swifts	8-5	Walsall Town S.	24 Feb 1894
Div.2	Manchester United	5-5	Lincoln City	16 Nov 1895
Div.1	Derby County	5-5	Everton	15 Oct 1898
Div.1	Sheffield Wed.	5-5	Everton	12 Nov 1904
Div.1	Sunderland	5-5	Liverpool	19 Jan 1907
Div.1	Liverpool	6-5	Newcastle United	4 Dec 1909
Div.1	Middlesbrough	7-5	Tottenham Hotspur	13 Feb 1915
Div.1	Tottenham Hotspur	5-5	Huddersfield Town	19 Sep 1925
Div.3N	Wrexham	5-6	Accrington Stanley	24 Oct 1925
Div.3S	Crystal Palace	5-5	Plymouth Argyle	28 Nov 1925
Div.1	Bury	6-5	Manchester City	25 Dec 1925
Div.3S	Aberdare Athletic	5-6	Plymouth Argyle	2 Jan 1927
Div.1	Newcastle United	7-5	Aston Villa	10 Mar 1927
Div.3S	Northampton Town	6-5	Luton Town	26 Dec 1927
Div.2	Swansea Town	5-5	Blackpool	27 Aug 1928
Div.1	Blackburn Rovers	7-5	Birmingham City	28 Sep 1929
Div.1	Sheffield United	5-7	Blackburn Rovers	3 Mar 1930
Div.1	Leicester City	6-6	Arsenal	21 Apr 1930
Div.2	Millwall	5-7	Preston North End	4 Oct 1930
Div.1	Sunderland	6-5	Liverpool	6 Dec 1930
Div.1	West Ham United	5-5	Aston Villa	3 Jan 1931
Div.3S	Coventry City	5-5	Fulham	2 Jan 1932
Div.3N	Walsall	5-5	Accrington Stanley	2 Apr 1932
Div.1	W.B.A.	5-6	Grimsby Town	30 Apr 1932
Div.2	Grimsby Town	5-5	Port Vale	15 Oct 1932
Div.1	Blackburn Rovers	6-5	Blackpool	2 Jan 1933
Div.2	Grimsby Town	5-5	Charlton Athletic	7 Jan 1933
Div.3S	Luton Town	5-5	Brentford	1 Feb 1933
Div.3N	Stockport County	8-5	Chester	6 May 1933
Div.1	W.B.A.	6-5	Sunderland	24 Mar 1934
Div.3S	Bristol Rovers	5-5	Exeter City	10 Nov 1934
Div.3N	York City	7-5	Mansfield Town	16 Nov 1935
Div.3N	Crewe Alexandra	5-6	Chesterfield	1 Feb 1936
Div.1	Middlesbrough	5-5	Sunderland	17 Oct 1936
Div.3N	Darlington	5-5	Hartlepools United	21 Nov 1936
Div.1	Bolton Wanderers	5-5	Chelsea	30 Oct 1937
Div.3S	Walsall	5-6	Millwall	13 Nov 1948
Div.1	Derby County	6-5	Sunderland	16 Dec 1950
Div.2	Leicester City	5-5	Sheffield United	3 Nov 1951
Div.1	Chelsea	5-6	Manchester United	16 Oct 1954
Div.2	Charlton Athletic	7-6	Huddersfield Town	21 Dec 1957
Div.1	Chelsea	6-5	Newcastle United	10 Sep 1958
Div.2	Charlton Athletic	6-6	Middlesbrough	22 Oct 1960
Div.1	Newcastle United	5-5	West Ham United	10 Dec 1960
Div.1	Blackburn Rovers	5-5	Arsenal	3 Nov 1962
Div.1	Birmingham City	5-5	Blackburn Rovers	24 Apr 1965
Div.1	Tottenham Hotspur	5-5	Aston Villa	19 Mar 1966
Div.2	Birmingham City	5-5	Derby County	9 Apr 1966
Div.1	Chelsea	5-5	West Ham United	17 Dec 1966
Div.2	Bristol Rovers	5-5	Charlton Athletic	18 Nov 1978
Div.1	Southampton	5-5	Coventry City	4 May 1982
Div.3	Doncaster Rovers	7-5	Reading	25 Sep 1982
Div.1	Q.P.R.	5-5	Newcastle United	22 Sep 1984

Most wins in a season

Tottenham Hotspur won 31 of their 42 Division One matches in 1960–61. They finished eight points ahead of Sheffield Wednesday to win the championship with 66 points. Of their 115 goals, all but 24 were contributed by their most regular five forwards: Bobby Smith scored 28 goals, Les Allen 23, Cliff Jones 15, John White 13 and Terry Dyson 12. Only four other teams have scored more goals in Division One. Spurs achieved the League and Cup double that season, the third side to accomplish the feat at the time.

Tottenham Hotspur also won 32 of their 42 Division Two matches in 1919–20. Nineteen of these came from home wins but it was a 3–1 victory at Stoke on 10 April that clinched the championship. Up to then, they had failed to score just once in the League. Bert Bliss with 31 goals was their leading scorer.

Millwall won 30 of their 42 Division Three (South) matches in 1927–28. Nineteen of these came from wins at home where only two points were dropped in drawn matches.

Plymouth Argyle won 30 of their 42 Division Three (South) matches in 1929–30. They had finished as runners-up six times in succession during the previous eight seasons. They were undefeated until the 19th match and their total of 68 points was a club record.

Cardiff City won 30 of their 42 Division Three (South) matches in 1946–47. Eighteen of these came from wins at Ninian Park, where they dropped just three points in drawn games and conceded only 11 goals.

Nottingham Forest won 30 of their 46 Division Three (South) matches in 1950–51. Sixteen of these came from home wins. Only six matches were lost overall and ten drawn. The club also achieved a record 70 points and a record total of 110 goals. Thirty-two points were gained from away matches.

Bristol City won 30 of their 46 Division Three (South) matches in 1954–55. Thirteen came from away wins. The club also achieved a record 70 points.

Doncaster Rovers won 33 of their 42 Division Three (North) matches in 1946–47. They won 18 away games, taking 37 points, lost only three times overall and finished with a record 72 points.

Aston Villa won 32 of their 46 Division Three matches in 1971–72. Twenty matches were won at home, including 11 consecutively between October and March.

Football League attendances

Season	Matches	Total	Division 1	Division 2	Division 3S	Division 3N
1946–47	1 848	35 604 606	15 005 316	11 071 572	5 664 004	3 863 714
1947–48	1 848	40 259 130	16 732 341	12 286 350	6 653 610	4 586 829
1948–49	1 848	41 271 414	17 914 667	11 353 237	6 998 429	5 005 081
1949–50	1 848	40 517 865	17 278 625	11 694 158	7 104 155	4 440 927
1950–51	2 028	39 584 967	16 679 454	10 780 580	7 367 884	4 757 109
1951–52	2 028	39 015 866	16 110 322	11 066 189	6 958 927	4 880 428
1952–53	2 028	37 149 966	16 050 278	9 686 654	6 704 299	4 708 735
1953–54	2 028	36 174 590	16 154 915	9 510 053	6 311 508	4 198 114
1954–55	2 028	34 133 103	15 087 221	8 988 794	5 966 017	4 051 071
1955–56	2 028	33 150 809	14 108 961	9 080 002	5 692 479	4 269 367
1956–57	2 028	33 744 405	13 803 037	8 718 162	5 622 189	4 691 017
1957–58	2 028	33 562 208	14 468 652	8 663 712	6 097 183	4 332 661
					Division 3	Division 4
1958–59	2 028	33 610 985	14 727 691	8 641 997	5 946 600	4 276 697
1959–60	2 028	32 538 611	14 391 227	8 399 627	4 739 707	4 008 050
1960–61	2 028	28 619 754	12 926 948	7 033 936	4 784 256	3 874 614
1961–62	2 015	27 979 902	12 061 194	7 453 089	5 199 106	3 266 513
1962–63	2 028	28 885 852	12 490 239	7 792 770	5 341 362	3 261 481
1963–64	2 028	28 535 022	12 486 626	7 594 158	5 419 157	3 035 081
1964–65	2 028	27 641 168	12 708 752	6 984 104	4 436 245	3 512 067
1965–66	2 028	27 206 980	12 480 644	6 914 757	4 779 150	3 032 429
1966–67	2 028	28 902 596	14 242 957	7 253 819	4 421 172	2 984 648
1967–68	2 028	30 107 298	15 289 410	7 450 410	4 013 087	3 354 391
1968–69	2 028	29 382 172	14 584 851	7 382 390	4 339 656	3 075 275
1969–70	2 028	29 600 972	14 868 754	7 581 728	4 223 761	2 926 729
1970–71	2 028	28 194 146	13 954 337	7 098 265	4 377 213	2 764 331
1971–72	2 028	28 700 729	14 484 603	6 769 308	4 697 392	2 749 426
1972–73	2 028	25 448 642	13 998 154	5 631 730	3 737 252	2 081 506
1973–74	2 027	24 982 203	13 070 991	6 326 108	3 421 624	2 163 480
1974–75	2 028	25 577 977	12 613 178	6 955 970	4 086 145	1 992 684
1975–76	2 028	24 896 053	13 089 861	5 798 405	3 948 449	2 059 338
1976–77	2 028	26 182 800	13 647 585	6 250 597	4 152 218	2 132 400
1977–78	2 028	25 392 872	13 255 677	6 474 763	3 332 042	2 330 390
1978–79	2 028	24 450 627	12 704 549	6 153 223	3 374 558	2 308 297
1979–80	2 028	24 623 975	12 163 002	6 112 025	3 999 328	2 349 620
1980–81	2 028	21 907 569	11 392 894	5 175 442	3 637 854	1 701 379
1981–82	2 028	20 006 961	10 420 793	4 750 463	2 836 915	1 998 790
1982–83	2 028	18 766 158	9 295 613	4 974 937	2 943 568	1 552 040
1983–84	2 028	18 342 116	8 701 230	5 359 757	2 726 062	1 555 067
1984–85	2 028	17 849 835	9 761 404	4 030 823	2 667 008	1 390 600
1985–86	2 028	16 488 577	9 037 854	3 551 968	2 490 481	1 408 274
1986–87	2 028	17 379 218	9 144 676	4 168 131	2 350 970	1 715 441
1987–88	2 030	17 959 732	8 094 571	5 341 599	2 751 275	1 772 287
1988–89	2 036	18 464 192	7 809 993	5 887 805	3 035 327	1 791 067
1989–90	2 036	19 445 442	7 883 039	6 867 674	2 803 551	1 891 178

Lincoln City won 32 of their 46 Division Four matches in 1975–76. Twenty-one of these came from home wins. Only two points were dropped in drawn games on their own ground. The club also set records for the most wins, most points and fewest defeats in a season in the division.

Swindon Town won 32 of their 46 Division Four matches in 1985–86. Twenty of these came from home wins and only one game was lost at the County Ground. Yet overall they had won just two of their first eight games and were fourth from bottom on 28 September. However, they were undefeated in their last 21 matches.

Fewest wins in a season

Stoke achieved only three wins in 22 Division One matches in 1889–90. They finished bottom with 10 points, only two fewer than the previous season when they had won just four games. They failed to gain re-election but subsequently returned to the League in 1891 when it was extended to 14 clubs.

Woolwich Arsenal managed only three wins in 38 Division One matches in 1912–13. They amassed just 18 points, scoring 26 goals, finished bottom and were relegated to the Second Division.

Stoke City also achieved just three wins in 42 Division One matches in 1984–85. Their 17 points included just five from drawn games and ensured relegation. The club also set records for most defeats, fewest goals scored and fewest points in a season in the division.

Loughborough Town won only one match out of 34 Division Two games in 1899–1900. They drew six games but finished bottom, ten points behind their nearest rivals Luton Town. They scored 18 goals but conceded 100 and failed to gain re-election.

Queens Park Rangers achieved six wins in 42 Division Three (South) matches in 1925–26. They won one away game and drew nine overall but finished bottom, 14 points behind Charlton Athletic.

Merthyr Town also achieved six wins in 42 Division Three (South) matches in 1929–30. They too won one away game, drew nine overall, and finished bottom, nine points behind Gillingham.

Rochdale managed only four wins in 40 Division Three (North) matches in 1931–32. They suffered 33 defeats, including 17 in succession, as well as a record 13 consecutive home defeats.

Rochdale achieved just two wins in 46 Division Three matches in 1973–74. They completed their last 22 fixtures without a win and took only nine points from them in drawn games.

Southport achieved only three wins in 46 matches in Division Four in 1976–77. They failed to win away from home, but drew seven times. At home they drew another 12 and succeeded in finishing six points above the bottom club Workington, who failed to gain re-election.

Most drawn games in a season

Norwich City drew 23 of their 42 Division One matches in 1978–79. They finished 16th, drawing 10 times at home and 13 away in gaining 37 points under the two points for a win system.

Exeter City drew 23 of their 46 Division Four matches in 1986–87. They finished 14th, also drawing 10 times at home and 13 away in gaining 56 points under the three points for a win system.

In 1978–79 Carlisle United in Division Three equalled the record of 22 drawn games which had been held by three clubs: Tranmere Rovers in Division Three in 1970–71; Aldershot in Division Four in 1971–72 and Chester in Division Three in 1977–78. Carlisle finished sixth, with Tranmere 18th, Aldershot 17th and Chester fifth.

Most defeats in a season

Stoke City suffered 31 defeats in 42 Division One matches in 1984–85. Fifteen came from home matches and 16 away. They scored in just 17 games.

Tranmere Rovers suffered 31 defeats in 42 Division Two matches in 1938–39. They finished 14 points adrift of their nearest rivals and took just one point from away games.

Cambridge United suffered 33 defeats in 46 Division Three matches in 1984–85. Eighteen came from home matches and 15 away. Four matches were won, two at home and two away. They finished 25 points behind their nearest rivals.

Merthyr Town suffered 29 defeats in 42 Division Three (South) matches in 1924–25. Their 21 points was a record low for the division. They achieved only two points from away games, both of which were drawn.

Walsall suffered 29 defeats in 46 Division Three (South) matches in 1952–53. They won five times at home, twice away and achieved 24 points. They finished bottom, 12 points behind their nearest rivals.

Walsall also suffered 29 defeats in 46 Division Three (South) matches during the following 1953–54 season. They won eight times at home, once away and achieved 26 points. They finished bottom again but this time only four points adrift.

Rochdale suffered 33 defeats in 40 Division Three (North) matches in 1931–32. Only 11 points were taken, including just one away from home. A total of 135 goals were conceded and their nearest rivals were 13 points above them.

Newport County suffered 33 defeats in 46 Division Four matches in 1987–88. Four matches were won at home, two away. Fourteen defeats were inflicted at home and 19 away. Their total of 25 points was 19 fewer than their nearest rivals. They were relegated to the GM Vauxhall Conference.

Fewest defeats in a season

Preston North End went through 22 Division One matches in the inaugural 1888–89 season without defeat. Only four points were dropped, including just one at home, to Aston Villa on 10 November. Their opponents that day finished runners-up, 11 points behind them.

Leeds United suffered only two defeats in 42 Division One matches in 1968–69. These were on 28 September at Manchester City's Maine Road ground when they lost 3–1, and at Burnley's Turf Moor on 19 October where they were beaten 5–1. After this reverse, Leeds had a run of 28 undefeated matches until the end of the season.

Liverpool completed 28 Division Two matches without defeat in 1893–94. They won 22 and drew six. Liverpool then won their Test match for promotion and drew the first two games of the following season to establish a run of 31 consecutive matches without defeat.

Burnley suffered only two defeats in 30 Division Two matches in 1897–98. They won 20 and drew eight of their games. The 80 goals they scored included nine at home to Loughborough Town, and their heaviest defeat was 2–0 at Luton Town.

Bristol City suffered only two defeats in 38 Division Two matches in 1905–06. They won 30 and drew six of their games. Thirty-one of their points came from away fixtures which produced 13 wins and five

draws. They also won 14 consecutive League matches.

Leeds United suffered only three defeats in 42 Division Two matches in 1963–64. They won 24 games, which was one fewer than the runners-up, Sunderland, who finished two points below them.

Queens Park Rangers suffered five defeats in 46 Division Three matches in 1966–67. They won 26 and drew 15 of their games. They finished 12 points ahead of runners-up Middlesbrough and scored 103 goals, conceding only 38. That same season they won the League Cup.

Southampton suffered only four defeats in 42 Division Three (South) matches in 1921–22. They conceded just 21 goals, a record for the division. Their 61 points was also a club record. Among their wins was an 8–0 success over Northampton Town. They won 23 matches, two fewer than Plymouth Argyle who finished as runners-up on goal average behind them.

Plymouth Argyle suffered only four defeats in 42 Division Three (South) matches in 1929–30. Their 68 points was a club record. They conceded only 38 goals and won 30 of their matches.

Port Vale suffered only three defeats in 46 Division Three (North) matches in 1953–54. They won 26 games and drew 17. Both figures were better than those of any of their rivals and they finished 11 points ahead of Barnsley, the runners-up.

Doncaster Rovers suffered only three defeats in 42 Division Three (North) matches in 1946–47. Of their record 33 wins, 18 came away from home and they established a record points total of 72.

Wolverhampton Wanderers suffered only three defeats in 42 Division Three (North) matches in 1923–24. Twenty-four matches were won, one fewer than runners-up Rochdale, who finished a point behind. Fifteen games were drawn by Wolves and only 27 goals conceded, one more than by Rochdale.

Lincoln City suffered only four defeats in 46 Division Four matches in 1975–76. They won 32 games, achieved a record 74 points and scored 111 goals.

Bournemouth suffered only four defeats in 46 Division Four matches in 1981–82. They won only 23 games but drew 19 in finishing fourth and achieving promotion. After staying unbeaten in their opening nine matches, they lost twice in succession, but after their fourth defeat on February they remained unbeaten in the last 17 games.

Sheffield United also suffered only four defeats in 46 Division Four matches in 1981–82. They won 27 games and remained unbeaten at home, where they dropped eight points in draws. They finished with 96 points.

Winning sequences

Tottenham Hotspur won 11 successive Division One matches from the start of the 1960–61 season. They also achieved eight consecutive away wins and a total of 16 throughout the season, compared with 15 at home.

Manchester United won 14 successive Division Two matches in the 1904–05 season, an achievement which was equalled by Bristol City in 1905–06 and Preston North End in 1950–51.

Everton won the last four Division One matches of 1893–94 and the first eight of 1894–95 for a winning sequence of 12 games.

Unbeaten sequences

Nottingham Forest completed 42 Division One matches without defeat after losing 1–0 to Leeds United on 19 November 1977. The run ended in a 2–0 defeat against Liverpool on 9 December 1978. The sequence consisted of 21 wins and 21 draws. On 30 September 1978 their 2–1 win at Aston Villa had equalled Leeds United's record of 34 consecutive matches without defeat, established in the 1968–69 and 1969–70 seasons.

Burnley went 30 Division One matches without defeat after losing 2–0 to Bradford Park Avenue on 4 September 1920. The run ended in a 3–0 defeat against Manchester City on 26 March 1921.

Leeds United were undefeated in the first 29 matches of the 1973–74 season, before losing 3–2 at Stoke City on 23 February 1974. Liverpool equalled this performance in 1987–88. Their run of 29 games ended with a 1–0 defeat against Everton at Goodison Park on 20 March 1988.

Sequences without a win

Cambridge United completed 31 Division Two matches in 1983–84 without a win. After defeating Oldham Athletic 2–1 on 1 October 1983 they did not achieve another victory until 28 April 1984 when they beat Newcastle United 1–0. Cambridge finished bottom and were relegated.

Losing sequences

Rochdale lost 17 successive Division Three (North) matches in 1931–32. After defeating New Brighton 3–2 on 7 November 1931 they did not add to their points total until drawing 1–1 with the same opposition on 9 March 1932. Rochdale finished bottom with only eleven points from 40 matches, as Wigan Borough had resigned and had their record expunged.

Manchester United lost their first 12 matches in Division One during the 1930–31 season. Their first win was 2–0 against Birmingham at Old Trafford on 1 November 1930. They did not recover from this disastrous start and finished bottom with 22 points, nine behind their nearest rivals.

Nelson completed 24 away matches in Division Three (North) without gaining a point. Their 1–1 draw with Halifax Town on 29 March 1930 was in fact the last time they managed a league point away from home, because they failed to gain re-election at the end of the 1930–31 season.

Merthyr Town played 61 away matches in Division Three (South) without a win between September 1922 and September 1925. In the 1922–23 season they still finished 17th; they were 13th the following season, 1923–24, but in 1924–25 they finished bottom with 21 points.

Most goals in a season

Aston Villa scored 108 goals in 42 Division One matches during 1930–31. They scored in every home match and failed in only three away games. Eighty-six goals came at home and in 20 games four goals or more were recorded. At Villa Park, Middlesbrough were beaten 8–1, Manchester United 7–0, Huddersfield Town 6–1 and Arsenal 5–1. Villa also won 6–1 at Huddersfield and 4–0 at Birmingham. Top scorer was Pongo Waring with 49 goals while Eric Houghton had 30. Yet Villa could only finish as runners-up, seven points behind Arsenal.

Middlesbrough scored 122 goals in 42 Division Two matches during 1926–27. On three occasions they scored seven goals: against Portsmouth and Swansea Town at home and also at Grimsby, while they managed six on two other occasions. Portsmouth actually finished eight points behind them and were also promoted. Yet Middlesbrough had managed just one point and scored only one goal in their first four League matches. In the fourth they until the last match of the season, a 3–1 home win over South Shields. Top scorer Albert Whitehurst, signed from Liverpool in February 1929, was their leading marksman with 24 goals in 15 matches, including seven in succession against Tranmere Rovers on 6 March in an 8–0 win. Bradford City were unbeaten during this run after Whitehurst's appearance.

Queens Park Rangers scored 111 goals in 46 Division Three matches in 1961–62. On three occasions they scored six goals, but also lost 6–3 at home to Reading. They could finish no higher than fourth and Bournemouth, who were third, edged them out on goal average, despite scoring 42 fewer goals than Rangers.

Jack Lambert was Arsenal's leading scorer in 1930–31 with 38 goals despite playing in only 34 League games that season (Topical Press)

brought in George Camsell, who ended the season as their top scorer with 59 goals. His total included eight hat-tricks.

Millwall scored 127 goals in 42 Division Three (South) matches in 1927–28. Unbeaten at home where they dropped only two points, Millwall also won 11 times away and finished ten points ahead of second-placed Northampton Town. Millwall achieved 9–1 wins against Torquay United and Coventry City as well as scoring seven goals once and six on four occasions, including once away. However, they themselves also lost heavily, 5–0 and 6–1 at Bournemouth and Brentford respectively.

Bradford City scored 128 goals in 42 Division Three (North) matches in 1928–29. They managed double figures in their opening League game at home to Rotherham United, whom they defeated 11–1, the club's record victory. But promotion was not clinched

Albert Whitehurst's 44 League goals for Rochdale in 1926–27 is still a club record. He later played for Bradford City (Colorsport)

Peterborough United scored 134 goals in 46 Division Four matches in 1960–61. Seven goals were scored against Aldershot and Exeter City, and six on four occasions including once away at Stockport, who were ironically the only team to prevent Peterborough from scoring at home during the season. Terry Bly was top scorer with 52, a record for the division. The second best supported team in the division at home with an average attendance of 14 222, Peterborough also drew the crowds away from home with 12 182 on average in their first season in the Football League.

Most goals conceded in a season

Blackpool conceded 125 goals in 42 Division One matches during 1930–31. Their heaviest defeat, a club record 10–1, was suffered against Huddersfield Town on 13 December 1930. Seven goals were conceded on three occasions, including at home to Leeds United in a 7–3 defeat. But Blackpool escaped relegation by one point, finishing above Leeds. The previous season they had won promotion as Division Two champions with record points and goals.

Darwen conceded 141 goals in 34 Division Two matches during 1898–99. It proved to be the last of the club's eventful eight seasons in the League. They suffered three 10–0 reverses, away to Loughborough Town, Manchester City and Walsall, as well as losing 9–0 at Manchester United and 9–2 at Grimsby Town. They contrived just nine points, just one of them away in a 2–2 draw at Gainsborough Trinity. At the end of the season they were not re-elected.

Merthyr Town conceded 135 goals in 42 Division Three (South) matches in 1929–30. They finished bottom, nine points behind their nearest rivals Gillingham. Merthyr were not re-elected in what was their third application for re-admission. However, apart from losing 10–0 away to Newport County and 8–2 at home to Brighton & Hove Albion, Merthyr had not conceded more than six goals in any other game.

Nelson conceded 136 goals in 42 Division Three (North) matches in 1927–28. Their heaviest defeats were 9–1 at Bradford City, 8–0 at Stockport County and 7–1 at Accrington Stanley. Although they finished bottom, it was Durham City, who were three points above them, who failed to gain re-election.

Accrington Stanley conceded 123 goals in 46 Division Three matches in 1959–60. However, only twice did they let in as many as six goals, losing 6–1

at Southend United and Tranmere Rovers. They also had a 5–4 win of their own at Bradford City and took 14 points from seven away wins, more than they achieved at home. They were bottom with 27 points.

Hartlepools United conceded 109 goals in 46 Division Four matches in 1959–60. They lost 7–2 at Watford, but apart from a 6–2 defeat at Bradford Park Avenue and another at home to Doncaster Rovers, they did not let in more than five in any other games. They finished bottom, one point behind their nearest rivals Oldham Athletic.

Fewest goals scored in a season

Stoke City scored just 24 goals in 42 Division One matches in 1984–85. They did not score more than two goals in any one game and failed to score at all in 25. With 17 points they were 23 behind their nearest rivals Sunderland, and were relegated in last place.

Watford scored only 24 goals in 42 Division Two matches in 1971–72. They too failed to score more than two goals in any one match, and did not score at all in 23. In the second half of the season they scored only six goals in 21 matches.

Crystal Palace scored 33 goals in 42 Division Three (South) matches in 1950–51. Though they beat Gillingham 4–3 at home and Newport County 4–2 away, they failed to score at all in 24 games. They finished bottom with 27 points, two behind their nearest rivals Watford.

Stockport County scored only 27 goals in 46 Division Three matches in 1969–70. A 3–1 win over Doncaster Rovers at home was their best win and they failed to score at all in 25 games. They finished bottom, seven points adrift of their nearest rivals Barrow.

Crewe Alexandra scored only 32 goals in 42 Division Three (North) matches in 1923–24. They also failed to score more than two goals in any one game and did not score at all in 18. Although they managed just 27 points, it was two more than the bottom two clubs, Hartlepools United and Barrow, and they did not have to apply for re-election.

In 1981–82, Crewe Alexandra scored only 29 goals in Division Four. They beat Scunthorpe United 3–0 but failed to score more than two goals in any other game. In 23 matches they did not score at all. They finished bottom, 15 points behind their nearest rivals Scunthorpe.

Ray Clemence had an excellent season in goal for Liverpool during 1978–79. He conceded only 16 goals and kept his charge intact on 28 occasions. Here he shows firm handling of the ball against Southampton during a game in September 1970 (Associated Sports Photography)

Fewest goals conceded in a season

Liverpool conceded only 16 goals in 42 Division One matches in 1978–79. Goalkeeper Ray Clemence, who played in every match, was beaten three times on one occasion, away to Aston Villa on 16 April 1979 in a 3–1 defeat, but did not let more than one goal past him in any other game. On 28 occasions he kept a clean sheet, including 17 times at home where just four goals were conceded. Liverpool were champions eight points ahead of Nottingham Forest. Liverpool's 85 goals were the highest by the League champions since 1967–68. They conceded only seven goals in the last 21 games.

Manchester United conceded only 23 goals in 42 Division Two matches in 1924–25. Yet only a late revival, in which they took as many points in the last six matches as they had achieved in the previous eleven, enabled them to gain promotion in second place. Significantly they drew their last match at Barnsley 0–0.

Southampton conceded 21 goals in 42 Division Three (South) matches in 1921–22. They were champions and were promoted, though with two matches remaining Plymouth Argyle had led them by

four points. However, while Southampton won twice, Plymouth lost their last two games and were edged out on goal average.

Port Vale conceded 21 goals in 46 Division Three (North) matches in 1953–54. The three games they lost also established a record for fewest defeats. Five goals were conceded at home, over four matches. Port Vale kept a clean sheet in 30 games overall, and in winning the championship they had an 11-point lead over runners-up Barnsley.

Middlesbrough conceded only 30 goals in 46 Division Three matches in 1986–87. Three times they let in three goals, but on 27 occasions the defence did not concede. They were unbeaten in their last 13 games and finished second to achieve promotion.

Lincoln City conceded 25 goals in 46 Division Four matches in 1980–81. They were runners-up two points behind the champions Southend United, who conceded only 31 goals themselves. Two goals were the most City let in during any one match and this occurred just four times in the season. They kept their goal intact on 25 occasions. From December to mid-March they also completed 14 games without defeat.

Best Starters – season by season

Teams with the longest unbeaten runs in Football League matches from the start of each season:

Season	Team (Division)	Unbeaten in first	Season	Team (Division)	Unbeaten in first
1888–89	Preston North End (1)	all 22	1936–37	Chester (3N)	9
1889–90	Accrington Stanley (1)	3	1936–37	Hull City (3N)	9
1889–90	Aston Villa (1)	3	1937–38	Coventry City (2)	15
1890–91	Everton (1)	7	1938–39	Southport (3N)	9
1891–92	Aston Villa (1)	4	1946–47	Barnsley (2)	10
1891–92	Bolton Wanderers (1)	4	1947–48	Arsenal (1)	17
1892–93	Sunderland (1)	8	1948–49	Derby County (1)	16
1893–94	Liverpool (2)	all 28*	1949–50	Liverpool (1)	19
1894–95	Everton (1)	8	1950–51	Newcastle United (1)	11
1895–96	Liverpool (2)	5	1951–52	Oldham Athletic (3N)	9
1895–96	Newton Heath (2)	5	1952–53	Oldham Athletic (3N)	13
1896–97	Sheffield United (1)	8	1953–54	Norwich City (3S)	12
1897–98	Sheffield United (1)	14	1954–55	Bristol City (3S)	13
1898–99	Sheffield United (1)	11	1955–56	Blackpool (1)	8
1899–1900	Sheffield United (1)	22	1956–57	Manchester United (1)	12
1900–01	Small Heath (2)	14	1957–58	Scunthorpe United (3N)	8
1901–02	Lincoln City (2)	7	1958–59	Fulham (2)	12
1902–03	Blackpool (2)	6	1959–60	Millwall (4)	19
1903–04	Preston North End (2)	13	1960–61	Tottenham Hotspur (1)	16
1904–05	Liverpool (2)	13	1961–62	Bournemouth (3)	14
1905–06	Sheffield Wednesday (1)	7	1962–63	Huddersfield Town (2)	13
1905–06	Manchester United (2)	7	1963–64	Gillingham (4)	13
1906–07	Bolton Wanderers (1)	7	1964–65	Bradford Park Avenue (4)	12
1906–07	Hull City (2)	7	1965–66	Bristol City (2)	7
1907–08	Everton (1)	6	1966–67	Chelsea (1)	10
1908–09	Birmingham City (2)	8	1967–68	Torquay United (3)	10
1909–10	Sheffield United (1)	9	1968–69	Darlington (4)	14
1910–11	Sunderland (1)	14	1969–70	Port Vale (4)	18
1911–12	Clapton Orient (2)	7	1970–71	Notts County (4)	9
1912–13	Hull City (2)	8	1971–72	Norwich City (2)	13
1913–14	Blackburn Rovers (1)	10	1972–73	Burnley (2)	16
1914–15	Manchester City (1)	11	1973–74	Leeds United (1)	29
1919–20	Tottenham Hotspur (2)	12	1974–75	Manchester United (2)	9
1920–21	South Shields (2)	7	1975–76	Bury (3)	10
1921–22	Portsmouth (3S)	10	1976–77	Leicester City (1)	6
1922–23	Portsmouth (3S)	8	1976–77	Manchester City (1)	6
1923–24	Cardiff City (1)	11	1976–77	Wolverhampton Wanderers (2)	6
1924–25	Huddersfield Town (1)	10	1976–77	Stockport County (4)	6
1925–26	Chelsea (2)	14	1977–78	Manchester City (1)	8
1926–27	Stoke City (3N)	9	1977–78	Brighton & Hove Albion (2)	8
1927–28	Charlton Athletic (3S)	12	1977–78	Tottenham Hotspur (2)	8
1928–29	Luton Town (3S)	10	1977–78	Southend United (4)	8
1928–29	Wrexham (3N)	10	1978–79	Everton (1)	19
1929–30	Plymouth Argyle (3S)	18	1979–80	Walsall (4)	13
1930–31	Notts County (3S)	18	1980–81	Ipswich Town (1)	14
1931–32	Southend United (3S)	15	1981–82	Oldham Athletic (2)	9
1932–33	Brentford (3S)	14	1982–83	Wimbledon (4)	11
1933–34	Aldershot (3S)	8	1983–84	Sheffield Wednesday (2)	15
1934–35	Tranmere Rovers (3N)	8	1984–85	Portsmouth (2)	10
1935–36	Huddersfield Town (1)	9	1985–86	Reading (3)	14
1935–36	Chesterfield (3N)	9	1986–87	Exeter City (4)	13
1935–36	Tranmere Rovers (3N)	9	1987–88	Liverpool (1)	29
			1988–89	Millwall (1)	8
			1989–90	Blackburn Rovers (2)	10

* Liverpool also won one Test match and then began the next season with two games undefeated.

Football League leading goalscorers

The Football League 1888–1915

Season	Leading Scorer	Team	Goals	Season	Leading Scorer	Team	Goals
1888–89	John Goodall	Preston North End	21	1932–33	Jack Bowers	Derby County	35
1889–90	Jimmy Ross	Preston North End	24	1933–34	Jack Bowers	Derby County	34
1890–91	Jack Southworth	Blackburn Rovers	26	1934–35	Ted Drake	Arsenal	42
1891–92	John Campbell	Sunderland	32	1935–36	Ginger Richardson	West Bromwich Albion	39
1892–93	John Campbell	Sunderland	31				
1893–94	Jack Southworth	Everton	27	1936–37	Freddie Steele	Stoke City	33
1894–95	John Campbell	Sunderland	22	1937–38	Tommy Lawton	Everton	28
1895–96	Steve Bloomer	Derby County	22	1938–39	Tommy Lawton	Everton	34
1896–97	Steve Bloomer	Derby County	24				
1897–98	Fred Wheldon	Aston Villa	21	**Division 1 1946–90**			
1898–99	Steve Bloomer	Derby County	24	1946–47	Dennis Westcott	Wolverhampton Wanderers	38
1899–1900	Bill Garratt	Aston Villa	27				
1900–01	Steve Bloomer	Derby County	24	1947–48	Ronnie Rooke	Arsenal	33
1901–02	James Settle	Everton	18	1948–49	Willie Moir	Bolton Wanderers	25
	Fred Priest	Sheffield United	18	1949–50	Dickie Davis	Sunderland	25
1902–03	Alec Raybould	Liverpool	31	1950–51	Stan Mortensen	Blackpool	30
1903–04	Steve Bloomer	Derby County	20	1951–52	George Robledo	Newcastle United	33
1904–05	Arthur Brown	Sheffield United	23	1952–53	Charlie Wayman	Preston North End	24
1905–06	Bullet Jones	Birmingham City	26	1953–54	Jimmy Glazzard	Huddersfield Town	29
	Albert Shepherd	Bolton Wanderers	26		Johnny Nicholls	West Bromwich Albion	28
1906–07	Alec Young	Everton	28				
1907–08	Enoch West	Nottingham Forest	27	1954–55	Ronnie Allen	West Bromwich Albion	27
1908–09	Bert Freeman	Everton	36				
1909–10	John Parkinson	Liverpool	30	1955–56	Nat Lofthouse	Bolton Wanderers	33
1910–11	Albert Shepherd	Newcastle United	25	1956–57	John Charles	Leeds United	38
1911–12	Harold Hampton	Aston Villa	25	1957–58	Bobby Smith	Tottenham Hotspur	36
	Dave McLean	Sheffield Wednesday	25	1958–59	Jimmy Greaves	Chelsea	32
				1959–60	Dennis Viollet	Manchester United	32
	George Holley	Sunderland	35	1960–61	Jimmy Greaves	Chelsea	41
1912–13	Dave McLean	Sheffield Wednesday	30	1961–62	Ray Crawford	Ipswich Town	33
					Derek Kevan	West Bromwich Albion	33
1913–14	George Elliot	Middlesbrough	31				
1914–15	Bobby Parker	Everton	36	1962–63	Jimmy Greaves	Tottenham Hotspur	37
				1963–64	Jimmy Greaves	Tottenham Hotspur	35
Division 1 1919–39				1964–65	Jimmy Greaves	Tottenham Hotspur	29
1919–20	Fred Morris	West Bromwich Albion	37		Andy McEvoy	Blackburn Rovers	29
				1965–66	Roger Hunt	Liverpool	30
1920–21	Joe Smith	Bolton Wanderers	38	1966–67	Ron Davies	Southampton	37
1921–22	Andy Wilson	Middlesbrough	31	1967–68	George Best	Manchester United	28
1922–23	Charlie Buchan	Sunderland	30		Ron Davies	Southampton	28
1923–24	Wilf Chadwick	Everton	28	1968–69	Jimmy Greaves	Tottenham Hotspur	27
1924–25	Fred Roberts	Manchester City	31	1969–70	Jeff Astle	West Bromwich Albion	25
1925–26	Ted Harper	Blackburn Rovers	43				
1926–27	Jimmy Trotter	Sheffield Wednesday	37	1970–71	Tony Brown	West Bromwich Albion	28
1927–28	Dixie Dean	Everton	60	1971–72	Francis Lee	Manchester City	33
1928–29	Dave Halliday	Sunderland	43	1972–73	Bryan Robson	West Ham United	28
1929–30	Vic Watson	West Ham United	42	1973–74	Mick Channon	Southampton	21
1930–31	Pongo Waring	Aston Villa	49	1974–75	Malcolm Macdonald	Newcastle United	21
1931–32	Dixie Dean	Everton	45	1975–76	Ted MacDougall	Norwich City	23

Andy Gray (left) and Malcolm Macdonald shared the goalscoring honours in the First Division during 1976-77 for Aston Villa and Arsenal respectively (Associated Sports Photography)

Luther Blissett was Watford's top scorer in 1982-83 with 27 League goals (Associated Sports Photography)

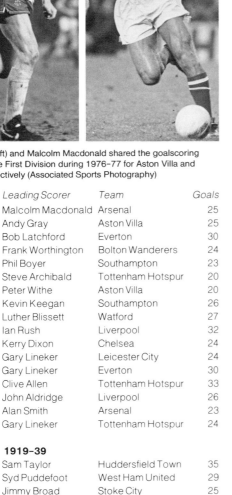

Season	Leading Scorer	Team	Goals
1976-77	Malcolm Macdonald	Arsenal	25
	Andy Gray	Aston Villa	25
1977-78	Bob Latchford	Everton	30
1978-79	Frank Worthington	Bolton Wanderers	24
1979-80	Phil Boyer	Southampton	23
1980-81	Steve Archibald	Tottenham Hotspur	20
	Peter Withe	Aston Villa	20
1981-82	Kevin Keegan	Southampton	26
1982-83	Luther Blissett	Watford	27
1983-84	Ian Rush	Liverpool	32
1984-85	Kerry Dixon	Chelsea	24
	Gary Lineker	Leicester City	24
1985-86	Gary Lineker	Everton	30
1986-87	Clive Allen	Tottenham Hotspur	33
1987-88	John Aldridge	Liverpool	26
1988-89	Alan Smith	Arsenal	23
1989-90	Gary Lineker	Tottenham Hotspur	24

John Aldridge (centre) is congratulated by his Liverpool colleagues after scoring his first goal of the 1987-88 season, against Arsenal at Highbury on the opening day. He finished the season with 26 league goals, including ten penalties (Sunday Telegraph)

Division 2   1919-39

1919-20	Sam Taylor	Huddersfield Town	35
1920-21	Syd Puddefoot	West Ham United	29
1921-22	Jimmy Broad	Stoke City	25
1922-23	Harry Bedford	Blackpool	32
1923-24	Harry Bedford	Blackpool	34
1924-25	Arthur Chandler	Leicester City	33
1925-26	Bob Turnbull	Chelsea	39
1926-27	George Camsell	Middlesbrough	59
1927-28	Jimmy Cookson	West Bromwich Albion	38
1928-29	Jimmy Hampson	Blackpool	40
1929-30	Jimmy Hampson	Blackpool	45
1930-31	Dixie Dean	Everton	39

Gary Lineker (10) was top scorer in Division One for the third time in 1989-90. He scored 24 League goals for Spurs, including one in this match against Crystal Palace at Selhurst Park (Allsport)

Season	Leading Scorer	Team	Goals
1931–32	Cyril Pearce	Swansea Town	35
1932–33	Ted Harper	Preston North End	37
1933–34	Pat Glover	Grimsby Town	42
1934–35	Jack Milsom	Bolton Wanderers	31
1935–36	Jack Dodds	Sheffield United	34
	Bob Finan	Blackpool	34
1936–37	Jack Bowers	Leicester City	33
1937–38	George Henson	Bradford Park Avenue	27
1938–39	Hugh Billington	Luton Town	28

Division 2   1946–90

Season	Leading Scorer	Team	Goals
1946–47	Charlie Wayman	Newcastle United	30
1947–48	Eddie Quigley	Sheffield Wednesday	22
1948–49	Charlie Wayman	Southampton	32
1949–50	Tommy Briggs	Grimsby Town	35
1950–51	Cecil McCormack	Barnsley	33
1951–52	Derek Dooley	Sheffield Wednesday	46
1952–53	Arthur Rowley	Leicester City	39
1953–54	John Charles	Leeds United	42
1954–55	Tommy Briggs	Blackburn Rovers	33
1955–56	Bill Gardiner	Leicester City	34
1956–57	Arthur Rowley	Leicester City	44
1957–58	Tom Johnston	Leyton Orient (35) and Blackburn Rovers (8)	43
1958–59	Brian Clough	Middlesbrough	42
1959–60	Brian Clough	Middlesbrough	39
1960–61	Ray Crawford	Ipswich Town	39
1961–62	Roger Hunt	Liverpool	41
	Barrie Thomas	Scunthorpe United (31) and Newcastle United (10)	41
1962–63	Bobby Tambling	Chelsea	35
1963–64	Ron Saunders	Portsmouth	33
1964–65	George O'Brien	Southampton	32
1965–66	Martin Chivers	Southampton	30
1966–67	Bobby Gould	Coventry City	24
1967–68	John Hickton	Middlesbrough	24
1968–69	John Toshack	Cardiff City	22
1969–70	John Hickton	Middlesbrough	24
1970–71	John Hickton	Middlesbrough	25
1971–72	Bob Latchford	Birmingham City	23
1972–73	Don Givens	Queen's Park Rangers	23
1973–74	Duncan McKenzie	Nottingham Forest	26
1974–75	Brian Little	Aston Villa	20
1975–76	Derek Hales	Charlton Athletic	28
1976–77	Mickey Walsh	Blackpool	26
1977–78	Bob Hatton	Blackpool	22
1978–79	Bryan Robson	West Ham United	24
1979–80	Clive Allen	Queen's Park Rangers	28
1980–81	David Cross	West Ham United	22
1981–82	Ronnie Moore	Rotherham United	22

Harry Morris was leading scorer two seasons in succession in the 1920s for Swindon Town in Division Three South (Colorsport)

Clarrie Bourton set up two goalscoring records for Coventry City in the 1930s: most goals in a season and most in aggregate career (Colorsport)

Season	Leading Scorer	Team	Goals
1982–83	Gary Lineker	Leicester City	26
1983–84	Kerry Dixon	Chelsea	28
1984–85	John Aldridge	Oxford United	30
1985–86	Kevin Drinkell	Norwich City	22
1986–87	Mick Quinn	Portsmouth	22
1987–88	Mark Bright	Crystal Palace	25
1988–89	Keith Edwards	Hull City	26
1989–90	Mick Quinn	Newcastle United	32

Division 3 (South)   1920–39

Season	Leading Scorer	Team	Goals
1920–21	John Connor	Crystal Palace	28
	Ernie Simms	Luton Town	28
	George Whitworth	Northampton Town	28
1921–22	Frank Richardson	Plymouth Argyle	31
1922–23	Fred Pagnam	Watford	30
1923–24	Billy Haines	Portsmouth	28
1924–25	Jack Fowler	Swansea Town	28
1925–26	Jack Cock	Plymouth Argyle	32
1926–27	Harry Morris	Swindon Town	47
1927–28	Harry Morris	Swindon Town	38
1928–29	Andrew Rennie	Luton Town	43
1929–30	George Goddard	Queen's Park Rangers	37

Season	Leading Scorer	Team	Goals
1930-31	Peter Simpson	Crystal Palace	46
1931-32	Clarrie Bourton	Coventry City	49
1932-33	Clarrie Bourton	Coventry City	40
1933-34	Albert Dawes	Northampton Town (11) and Crystal Palace (16)	27
1934-35	Ralph Allen	Charlton Athletic	32
1935-36	Albert Dawes	Crystal Palace	38
1936-37	Joe Payne	Luton Town	55
1937-38	Harry Crawshaw	Mansfield Town	25
1938-39	Ben Morton	Swindon Town	28

Division 3 (South)   1946-58

Season	Leading Scorer	Team	Goals
1946-47	Don Clark	Bristol City	36
1947-48	Len Townsend	Bristol City	31
1948-49	Don McGibbon	Bournemouth	30
1949-50	Tommy Lawton	Notts County	31
1950-51	Wally Ardron	Nottingham Forest	35
1951-52	Ronnie Blackman	Reading	39
1952-53	Geoff Bradford	Bristol Rovers	33
1953-54	Jack English	Northampton Town	28
1954-55	Ernie Morgan	Gillingham	31
1955-56	Sammy Collins	Torquay United	40
1956-57	Ted Phillips	Ipswich Town	41
1957-58	Sam McCrory	Southend United	31
	Derek Reeves	Southampton	31

Division 3 (North)   1921-39

Season	Leading Scorer	Team	Goals
1921-22	Jim Carmichael	Grimsby Town	37
1922-23	George Beel	Chesterfield	23
	Jim Carmichael	Grimsby Town	23
1923-24	David Brown	Darlington	27
1924-25	David Brown	Darlington	39
1925-26	Jimmy Cookson	Chesterfield	44
1926-27	Albert Whitehurst	Rochdale	44
1927-28	Joe Smith	Stockport County	38
1928-29	Jimmy McConnell	Carlisle United	43
1929-30	Frank Newton	Stockport County	36
1930-31	Jimmy McConnell	Carlisle United	37
1931-32	Alan Hall	Lincoln City	42
1932-33	Bill McNaughton	Hull City	39
1933-34	Alf Lythgoe	Stockport County	46
1934-35	Gilbert Alsop	Walsall	40
1935-36	Bunny Bell	Tranmere Rovers	33
1936-37	Ted Harston	Mansfield Town	55
1937-38	John Roberts	Port Vale	28
1938-39	Sam Hunt	Carlisle United	32

Division 3 (North)   1946-58

Season	Leading Scorer	Team	Goals
1946-47	Clarrie Jordan	Doncaster Rovers	42
1947-48	Jimmy Hutchinson	Lincoln City	32
1948-49	Wally Ardron	Rotherham United	29
1949-50	Peter Doherty	Doncaster Rovers	26
	Reg Phillips	Crewe Alexandra	26
1950-51	Jack Shaw	Rotherham United	37

Season	Leading Scorer	Team	Goals
1951-52	Andy Graver	Lincoln City	36
1952-53	Jimmy Whitehouse	Carlisle United	29
1953-54	Jack Connor	Stockport County	31
1954-55	Jack Connor	Stockport County	30
	Arthur Bottom	York City	30
	Don Travis	Oldham Athletic	30
1955-56	Bob Crosbie	Grimsby Town	36
1956-57	Ray Straw	Derby County	37
1957-58	Alf Ackerman	Carlisle United	35

Division 3   1958-90

Season	Leading Scorer	Team	Goals
1958-59	Jim Towers	Brentford	32
1959-60	Derek Reeves	Southampton	39
1960-61	Tony Richards	Walsall	36
1961-62	Cliff Holton	Northampton Town (36) and Walsall (1)	37
1962-63	George Hudson	Coventry City	30
1963-64	Alf Biggs	Bristol Rovers	30
1964-65	Ken Wagstaff	Mansfield Town (8) and Hull City (23)	31
1965-66	Les Allen	Queen's Park Rangers	30
1966-67	Rodney Marsh	Queen's Park Rangers	30
1967-68	Don Rogers	Swindon Town	25
	Bobby Owen	Bury	25
1968-69	Brian Lewis	Luton Town	22
	Don Rogers	Swindon Town	22
1969-70	George Jones	Bury	26
1970-71	Gerry Ingram	Preston North End	22
	Dudley Roberts	Mansfield Town	22
1971-72	Ted MacDougall	Bournemouth	35
	Alf Wood	Shrewsbury Town	35
1972-73	Bruce Bannister	Bristol Rovers	25
	Arthur Horsfield	Charlton Athletic	25
1973-74	Billy Jennings	Watford	26
1974-75	Dixie McNeil	Hereford United	31
1975-76	Dixie McNeil	Hereford United	35
1976-77	Peter Ward	Brighton & Hove Albion	32
1977-78	Alex Bruce	Preston North End	27
1978-79	Ross Jenkins	Watford	29
1979-80	Terry Curran	Sheffield Wednesday	22
1980-81	Tony Kellow	Exeter City	25
1981-82	Gordon Davies	Fulham	24
1982-83	Kerry Dixon	Reading	26
1983-84	Keith Edwards	Sheffield United	33
1984-85	Tommy Tynan	Plymouth Argyle	31
1985-86	Trevor Senior	Reading	27
1986-87	Andy Jones	Port Vale	29
1987-88	Steve Lovell	Gillingham	25
1988-89	Steve Bull	Wolverhampton Wanderers	37
1989-90	Bob Taylor	Bristol City	27

Keith Edwards ended the 1989-90 season as the most prolific goalscorer still active in the Football League. On loan to Huddersfield Town from Stockport County he scored his 249th League goal on 5 May 1990 in a Division Three match against Chester City. His goals had been achieved as follows: Sheffield United 29, Hull City 57, Sheffield United 114, Leeds United 6, Hull City 29, Stockport County 10 and Huddersfield Town 4. In addition he had scored two goals for Aberdeen (Allsport)

Richard Hill, top scorer in Division Four in 1986-87 with 29 goals for Northampton Town (Colorsport)

Season	Leading Scorer	Team	Goals
Division 4	**1958-90**		
1958-59	Arthur Rowley	Shrewsbury Town	37
1959-60	Cliff Holton	Watford	42
1960-61	Terry Bly	Peterborough United	52
1961-62	Bobby Hunt	Colchester United	41
1962-63	Ken Wagstaff	Mansfield Town	34
	Colin Booth	Doncaster Rovers	34
1963-64	Hugh McIlmoyle	Carlisle United	39
1964-65	Alick Jeffrey	Doncaster Rovers	36
1965-66	Kevin Hector	Bradford Park Avenue	44
1966-67	Ernie Phythian	Hartlepools United	23
1967-68	Roy Chapman	Port Vale	25
	Les Massie	Halifax Town	25
1968-69	Gary Talbot	Chester	22
1969-70	Albert Kinsey	Wrexham	27
1970-71	Ted MacDougall	Bournemouth	42
1971-72	Peter Price	Peterborough United	28
1972-73	Fred Binney	Exeter City	28
1973-74	Brian Yeo	Gillingham	31
1974-75	Ray Clarke	Mansfield Town	28
1975-76	Ronnie Moore	Tranmere Rovers	34
1976-77	Brian Joicey	Barnsley	25
1977-78	Steve Phillips	Brentford	32
	Alan Curtis	Swansea City	32
1978-79	John Dungworth	Aldershot	26

Alan Cork holds two Wimbledon records: most goals and most League appearances (Sporting Pictures)

Season	Leading Scorer	Team	Goals	Season	Leading Scorer	Team	Goals
1979-80	Colin Garwood	Portsmouth (17) and Aldershot (10)	27	1984-85	John Clayton	Tranmere Rovers	31
				1985-86	Richard Cadette	Southend United	25
1980-81	Alan Cork	Wimbledon	23	1985-86	Steve Taylor	Rochdale	25
1981-82	Keith Edwards	Sheffield United (35) and Hull City (1)	36	1986-87	Richard Hill	Northampton Town	29
				1987-88	Steve Bull	Wolverhampton Wanderers	34
1982-83	Steve Cammack	Scunthorpe United	25	1988-89	Phil Stant	Hereford United	28
1983-84	Trevor Senior	Reading	36	1989-90	Brett Angell	Stockport County	23

More than half

Players who, since the First World War, have scored as many as half their team's Football League goals in a completed season:

Player	Team	Division	Season	Goals	Out of
George Elliott	Middlesbrough	1	1919-20	31	61
Bob Blood	Port Vale	2	1919-20	24	42
Dave McLean	Bradford Park Avenue	1	1920-21	22	43
John McIntyre	Sheffield Wednesday	2	1920-21	27	48
Sid Puddefoot	West Ham United	2	1920-21	29	51
Jack Doran	Brighton & Hove Albion	3S	1920-21	22	42
Jack Doran	Brighton & Hove Albion	3S	1921-22	23	45
Jim Carmichael	Grimsby Town	3N	1921-22	37	72
Harry Bedford	Blackpool	2	1922-23	32	60
Fred Pagnam	Watford	3S	1922-23	30	57
Joe Bradford	Birmingham	1	1923-24	24	41
Tommy Roberts	Preston North End	1	1923-24	26	52
Hugh Davey	Bournemouth	3S	1923-24	20	40
Bertie Mills	Hull City	2	1924-25	25	50
Wilf Kirkham	Port Vale	2	1924-25	26	48
David Brown	Darlington	3N	1924-25	39	78
Tom Jennings	Leeds United	1	1926-27	35	69
Dixie Dean	Everton	1	1927-28	60	102
Tom Keetley	Doncaster Rovers	3N	1928-29	40	76
Jim McConnell	Carlisle United	3N	1928-29	43	86
Jimmy Dunne	Sheffield United	1	1930-31	41	78
Leopold Stevens	New Brighton	3N	1931-32	20	38
Ted Harper	Preston North End	2	1932-33	37	74
Jack Bowers	Derby County	1	1933-34	35	68
Albert Valentine	Halifax Town	3N	1935-36	29	57
Joe Payne	Luton Town	3S	1936-37	55	103
Ted Harston	Mansfield Town	3N	1936-37	55	91
John Charles	Leeds United	1	1956-57	38	72
Gordon Turner	Luton Town	1	1956-57	30	58
Colin Booth	Doncaster Rovers	4	1962-63	34	64
Ron Davies	Southampton	1	1966-67	37	74
Ted MacDougall	Bournemouth	4	1970-71	42	81

Note: Jack Doran, Irish International centre-forward, is the only player to have achieved this feat twice, and he did it in successive seasons.

In 1987-88 Stuart Rimmer had scored 24 of Chester City's 40 League goals when he was transferred to Notts County. Chester's final total was 51.

Derby Games

Everton v Liverpool

Everton were founded in 1878 as St Domingo Church Sunday School team, becoming Everton the following year. Liverpool came into being in 1892 following a split which led to the Everton club moving from Anfield to Goodison Park.

Of the 142 matches played between the sides in the League, Everton have won 48, Liverpool 51 and 43 have been drawn.

League results at Goodison Park (Everton's score first)

Season	Score	Season	Score
1894–95	3–0	1932–33	3–1
		1933–34	0–0
1896–97	2–1	1934–35	1–0
1897–98	3–0	1935–36	0–0
1898–99	1–2	1936–37	2–0
1899–1900	3–1	1937–38	1–3
1900–01	1–1	1938–39	2–1
1901–02	4–0		
1902–03	3–1	1946–47	1–0
1903–04	5–2	1947–48	0–3
		1948–49	1–1
1905–06	4–2	1949–50	0–0
1906–07	0–0	1950–51	1–3
1907–08	2–4		
1908–09	5–0	1962–63	2–2
1909–10	2–3	1963–64	3–1
1910–11	0–1	1964–65	2–1
1911–12	2–1	1965–66	0–0
1912–13	0–2	1966–67	3–1
1913–14	1–2	1967–68	1–0
1914–15	1–3	1968–69	0–0
		1969–70	0–3
1919–20	0–0	1970–71	0–0
1920–21	0–3	1971–72	1–0
1921–22	1–1	1972–73	0–2
1922–23	0–1	1973–74	0–1
1923–24	1–0	1974–75	0–0
1924–25	0–1	1975–76	0–0
1925–26	3–3	1976–77	0–0
1926–27	1–0	1977–78	0–1
1927–28	1–1	1978–79	1–0
1928–29	1–0	1979–80	1–2
1929–30	3–3	1980–81	2–2
		1981–82	1–3
1931–32	2–1		

Season	Score	Season	Score
1982–83	0–5	1986–87	0–0
1983–84	1–1	1987–88	1–0
1984–85	1–0	1988–89	0–0
1985–86	2–3	1989–90	1–3

League results at Anfield (Liverpool's score first)

Season	Score	Season	Score
1894–95	2–2	1936–37	3–2
		1937–38	1–2
1896–87	0–0	1938–39	0–3
1897–98	3–1		
1898–99	2–0	1946–47	0–0
1899–1900	1–2	1947–48	4–0
1900–01	1–2	1948–49	0–0
1901–02	2–2	1949–50	3–1
1902–03	0–0	1950–51	0–2
1903–04	2–2		
		1962–63	0–0
1905–06	1–1	1963–64	2–1
1906–07	1–2	1964–65	0–4
1907–08	0–0	1965–66	5–0
1908–09	0–1	1966–67	0–0
1909–10	0–1	1967–68	1–0
1910–11	0–2	1968–69	1–1
1911–12	1–3	1969–70	0–2
1912–13	0–2	1970–71	3–2
1913–14	1–2	1971–72	4–0
1914–15	0–5	1972–73	1–0
		1973–74	0–0
1919–20	3–1	1974–75	0–0
1920–21	1–0	1975–76	1–0
1921–22	1–1	1976–77	3–1
1922–23	5–1	1977–78	0–0
1923–24	1–2	1978–79	1–1
1924–25	3–1	1979–80	2–2
1925–26	5–1	1980–81	1–0
1926–27	1–0	1981–82	3–1
1927–28	3–3	1982–83	0–0
1928–29	1–2	1983–84	3–0
1929–30	0–3	1984–85	0–1
		1985–86	0–2
1931–32	1–3	1986–87	3–1
1932–33	7–4	1987–88	2–0
1933–34	3–2	1988–89	1–1
1934–35	2–1	1989–90	2–1
1935–36	6–0		

Manchester City v Manchester United

City were founded in 1887 as Ardwick FC and became Manchester City in 1894. United were formed a few years earlier in 1878 as Newton Heath and became Manchester United in 1902.

Of the 112 League matches played between the sides City have won 32 and United 40, with 40 draws.

League results at Maine Road (City's score first)

Season	Score	Season	Score
1894–95	2–5	1951–52	1–2
1895–96	2–1	1952–53	2–1
1896–97	0–0	1953–54	2–0
1897–98	0–1	1954–55	3–2
1898–99	4–0	1955–56	1–0
1902–03	0–2	1956–57	2–4
1906–07	3–0	1957–58	2–2
1907–08	0–0	1958–59	1–1
1908–09	1–2	1959–60	3–0
1910–11	1–1	1960–61	1–3
1911–12	0–0	1961–62	0–2
1912–13	0–2	1962–63	1–1
1913–14	0–2	1966–67	1–1
1914–15	1–1	1967–68	1–2
1919–20	3–3	1968–69	0–0
1920–21	3–0	1969–70	4–0
1921–22	4–1	1970–71	3–4
1925–26	1–1	1971–72	3–3
1928–29	2–2	1972–73	3–0
1929–30	0–1	1973–74	0–0
1930–31	4–1	1975–76	2–2
1936–37	1–0	1976–77	1–3
1947–48	0–0	1977–78	3–1
1948–49	0–0	1978–79	0–3
1949–50	1–2	1979–80	2–0
		1980–81	1–0
		1981–82	0–0
1982–83	1–2	1986–87	1–1
1985–86	0–3	1989–90	5–1

League results at Old Trafford (United's score first)

Season	Score	Season	Score
1894–95	4–1	1953–54	1–1
1895–96	1–1	1954–55	0–5
1896–97	2–1	1955–56	2–1
1897–98	1–1	1956–57	2–0
1898–99	3–0	1957–58	4–1
		1958–59	4–1
		1959–60	0–0
1902–03	1–1	1960–61	5–1
1906–07	1–1	1961–62	3–2
1907–08	3–1	1962–63	2–3
1908–09	3–1	1966–67	1–0
1910–11	2–1	1967–68	1–3
1911–12	0–0	1968–69	0–1
1912–13	0–1	1969–70	1–2
1913–14	0–1	1970–71	1–4
1914–15	0–0	1971–72	1–3
		1972–73	0–0
1919–20	1–0	1973–74	0–1
1920–21	1–1	1975–76	2–0
1921–22	3–1	1976–77	3–1
1925–26	1–6	1977–78	2–2
1928–29	1–2	1978–79	1–0
1929–30	1–3	1979–80	1–0
1930–31	1–3	1980–81	2–2
1936–37	3–2	1981–82	1–1
1947–48	1–1*	1982–83	2–2
1948–49	0–0*	1985–86	2–2
1949–50	2–1	1986–87	2–0
1951–52	1–1	1989–90	1–1
1952–53	1–1		

* Played at Maine Road

Manchester United striker Mark Hughes is shadowed by City's Brian Gayle (left). Despite a spectacular goal by Hughes, City won this 1989 derby at Maine Road 5–1 (Allsport)

Andy Hinchcliffe (second from left) is congratulated by jubilant team-mates after scoring City's fifth goal (Allsport)

Arsenal v Tottenham Hotspur

Arsenal were founded in 1886 as Royal Arsenal, becoming Woolwich Arsenal in 1891 and Arsenal from 1914. Tottenham Hotspur were founded four years earlier in 1882 and were known as the Hotspur Football Club before becoming Tottenham Hotspur in 1885.

Of the 106 League matches played between the two sides, Tottenham have won 40, Arsenal 45, and 21 have been drawn.

League results at Highbury (Arsenal's score first)

Season	Score	Season	Score
1909–10	1–0	1958–59	3–1
1910–11	2–0	1959–60	1–1
1911–12	3–1	1960–61	2–3
1912–13	0–3	1961–62	2–1
		1962–63	2–3
1920–21	3–2	1963–64	4–4
1921–22	1–0	1964–65	3–1
1922–23	0–2	1965–66	1–1
1923–24	1–1	1966–67	0–2
1924–25	1–0	1967–68	4–0
1925–26	0–1	1968–69	1–0
1926–27	2–4	1969–70	2–3
1927–28	1–1	1970–71	2–0
		1971–72	0–2
1933–34	1–3	1972–73	1–1
1934–35	5–1	1973–74	0–1
		1974–75	1–0
1950–51	2–2	1975–76	0–2
1951–52	1–1	1976–77	1–0
1952–53	4–0		
1953–54	0–3	1978–79	1–0
1954–55	2–0	1979–80	1–0
1955–56	0–1	1980–81	2–0
1956–57	3–1	1981–82	1–3
1957–58	4–4		

Season	Score	Season	Score
1982–83	2–0	1986–87	0–0
1983–84	3–2	1987–88	2–1
1984–85	1–2	1988–89	2–0
1985–86	0–0	1989–90	1–0

League results at White Hart Lane (Tottenham's score first)

Season	Score	Season	Score
1909–10	1–1	1962–63	4–4
1910–11	3–1	1963–64	3–1
1911–12	5–0	1964–65	3–1
1912–13	1–1	1965–66	2–2
		1966–67	3–1
1920–21	2–1	1967–68	1–0
1921–22	2–0	1968–69	1–2
1922–23	1–2	1969–70	1–0
1923–24	3–0	1970–71	0–1
1924–25	2–0	1971–72	1–1
1925–26	1–1	1972–73	1–2
1926–27	0–4	1973–74	2–0
1927–28	2–0	1974–75	2–0
		1975–76	0–0
1933–34	1–1	1976–77	2–2
1934–35	0–6		
		1978–79	0–5
1950–51	1–0	1979–80	1–2
1951–52	1–2	1980–81	2–0
1952–53	1–3	1981–82	2–2
1953–54	1–4	1982–83	5–0
1954–55	0–1	1983–84	2–4
1955–56	3–1	1984–85	0–2
1956–57	1–3	1985–86	1–0
1957–58	3–1	1986–87	1–2
1958–59	1–4	1987–88	1–2
1959–60	3–0	1988–89	2–3
1960–61	4–2	1989–90	2–1
1961–62	4–3		

Arsenal's David Rocastle (right) under pressure from Pat Van den Hauwe of Spurs at White Hart Lane in October 1989 (Syndication International)

Paul Walsh (white shirt) breaks into the Arsenal penalty area pursued by Siggi Jonsson. Walsh headed what proved to be the winning goal in a 2-1 victory for Spurs (Syndication International)

Aston Villa v Birmingham City

Aston Villa were founded in 1874. Birmingham were originally known as Small Heath Alliance from their formation in 1875 until 1888 when they dropped 'Alliance'. In 1905 they became Birmingham and added City in 1945.

Of the 96 League meetings between them, Villa have won 39 and Birmingham 32, with 25 drawn.

League results at Villa Park (Aston Villa's score first)

Season	Score	Season	Score
1894–95*	2–1	1949–50	1–1
1895–96*	7–3	1955–56	0–0
1901–02	1–0	1956–57	3–1
		1957–58	0–2
1903–04	1–1	1958–59	1–1
1904–05	2–1		
1905–06	1–3	1960–61	6–2
1906–07	4–1	1961–62	1–3
1907–08	2–3	1962–63	4–0
		1963–64	0–3
1921–22	1–1	1964–65	3–0
1922–23	3–0		
1923–24	0–0	1967–68	2–4
1924–25	1–0	1968–69	1–0
1925–26	3–3	1969–70	0–0
1926–27	4–2		
1927–28	1–1	1975–76	2–1
1928–29	1–2	1976–77	1–2
1929–30	2–1	1977–78	0–1
1930–31	1–1	1978–79	1–0
1931–32	3–2	1980–81	3–0
1932–33	1–0	1981–82	0–0
1933–34	1–1	1982–83	1–0
1934–35	2–2	1983–84	1–0
1935–36	2–1		
1938–39	5–1	1985–86	0–3
		1987–88	0–2
1948–49	0–3	* at Perry Barr	

League results at St Andrew's (Birmingham City's score first)

Season	Score	Season	Score
1894–95*	2–2	1921–22	1–0
1895–96*	1–4	1922–23	1–0
1901–02*	0–2	1923–24	3–0
		1924–25	1–0
1903–04*	2–2	1925–26	2–1
1904–05*	0–3	1926–27	1–2
1905–06*	2–0	1927–28	1–1
1906–07	3–2	1928–29	2–4
1907–08	2–3	1929–30	1–1

Season	Score	Season	Score
1930–31	0–4	1964–65	0–1
1931–32	1–1		
1932–33	3–2	1967–68	2–1
1933–34	0–0	1968–69	4–0
1934–35	2–1	1969–70	0–2
1935–36	2–2		
1938–39	3–0	1975–76	3–2
		1976–77	2–1
1948–49	0–1	1977–78	1–0
1949–50	2–2	1978–79	0–1
1955–56	2–2	1980–81	1–2
1956–57	1–2	1981–82	0–1
1957–58	3–1	1982–83	3–0
1958–59	4–1	1983–84	2–1
1960–61	1–1	1985–86	0–0
1961–62	0–2		
1962–63	3–2	1987–88	1–2
1963–64	3–3		
		* at Small Heath	

Sheffield United v Sheffield Wednesday

United were founded in 1889, Wednesday in 1867. Of the 92 matches played between the clubs United have won 35, Wednesday 30, and 27 have been drawn.

League results at Bramall Lane (United's score first)

Season	Score	Season	Score
1893–94	1–1	1914–15	0–1
1894–95	1–0		
1895–96	1–1	1919–20	3–0
1896–97	2–0	1926–27	2–0
1897–98	1–1	1927–28	1–1
1898–99	2–1	1928–29	1–1
		1929–30	2–2
1900–01	1–0	1930–31	1–1
1901–02	3–0	1931–32	1–1
1902–03	2–3	1932–33	2–3
1903–04	1–1	1933–34	5–1
1904–05	4–2		
1905–06	0–2	1937–38	2–1
1906–07	2–1	1938–39	0–0
1907–08	1–3		
1908–09	2–1	1949–50	2–0
1909–10	3–3	1951–52	7–3
1910–11	0–1		
1911–12	1–1	1953–54	2–0
1912–13	0–2	1954–55	1–0
1913–14	0–1	1958–59	1–0

Season	Score	Season	Score	Season	Score	Season	Score
1961–62	1–0	1966–67	1–0	1910–11	2–0	1949–50	2–1
1962–63	2–2	1967–68	0–1	1911–12	1–1		
1963–64	1–1			1912–13	1–0	1951–52	1–3
1964–65	2–3	1970–71	3–2	1913–14	2–1	1953–54	3–2
1965–66	1–0	1979–80	1–1	1914–15	1–1	1954–55	1–2

League results at Hillsborough (Wednesday's score first)

Season	Score	Season	Score	Season	Score	Season	Score
				1919–20	2–1	1958–59	2–0
				1926–27	2–3	1961–62	1–2
1893–94	1–2	1902–03	0–1	1927–28	3–3	1962–63	3–1
1894–95	2–3	1903–04	3–0	1928–29	5–2	1963–64	3–0
1895–96	1–0	1904–05	1–3	1929–30	1–1	1964–65	0–2
1896–97	1–1	1905–06	1–0	1930–31	1–3	1965–66	2–2
1897–98	0–1	1906–07	2–2	1931–32	2–1	1966–67	2–2
1898–99	1–1	1907–08	2–0	1932–33	3–3	1967–68	1–1
		1908–09	1–0	1933–34	0–1		
1900–01	1–0	1909–10	1–3	1937–38	0–1	1970–71	0–0
1901–02	1–0			1938–39	1–0	1979–80	4–0

Sheffield United line up before facing local rivals Wednesday at Hillsborough in 1955. The Blades won 2–1 (Hulton-Deutsch)

Newcastle United v Sunderland

Sunderland were founded in 1879 as Sunderland and District Teachers AFC and became known under their present title in 1881. Newcastle were founded in 1882 as Newcastle East End and changed to Newcastle United in 1892.

Of the 110 League matches played between the two sides, Sunderland have won 38, Newcastle 39 and 33 have been drawn.

League results at Roker Park (Sunderland's score first)

Season	Score	Season	Score
1898–99	2–3	1931–32	1–4
1899–1900	1–2	1932–33	0–2
1900–01	1–1	1933–34	2–0
1901–02	0–0		
1902–03	0–0	1948–49	1–1
1903–04	1–1	1949–50	2–2
1904–05	3–1	1950–51	2–1
1905–06	3–2	1951–52	1–4
1906–07	2–0	1952–53	0–2
1907–08	2–4	1953–54	1–1
1908–09	3–1	1954–55	4–2
1909–10	0–2	1955–56	1–6
1910–11	2–1	1956–57	1–2
1911–12	1–2	1957–58	2–0
1912–13	2–0	1961–62	3–0
1913–14	1–2	1962–63	0–0
1914–15	2–4	1963–64	2–1
1919–20	2–0	1965–66	2–0
1920–21	0–2	1966–67	3–0
1921–22	0–0	1967–68	3–3
1922–23	2–0	1968–69	1–1
1923–24	3–2	1969–70	1–1
1924–25	1–1		
1925–26	2–2	1976–77	2–2
1926–27	2–0	1978–79	1–1
1927–28	1–1	1979–80	1–0
1928–29	5–2		
1929–30	1–0	1984–85	0–0
1930–31	5–0	1989–90	0–0

League results at St James's Park (Newcastle's score first)

Season	Score	Season	Score
1898–99	0–1	1904–05	1–3
1899–1900	2–4	1905–06	1–1
1900–01	0–2	1906–07	4–2
1901–02	0–1	1907–08	1–3
1902–03	1–0	1908–09	1–9
1903–04	1–3	1909–10	1–0

Season	Score	Season	Score
1910–11	1–1	1951–52	2–2
1911–12	3–1	1952–53	2–2
1912–13	1–1	1953–54	2–1
1913–14	2–1	1954–55	1–2
1914–15	2–5	1955–56	3–1
		1956–57	6–2
1919–20	2–3	1957–58	2–2
1920–21	6–1		
1921–22	2–2	1961–62	2–2
1922–23	2–1	1962–63	1–1
1923–24	0–2	1963–64	1–0
1924–25	2–0		
1925–26	0–0	1965–66	2–0
1926–27	1–0	1966–67	0–3
1927–28	3–1	1967–68	2–1
1928–29	4–3	1968–69	1–1
1929–30	3–0	1969–70	3–0
1930–31	2–0		
1931–32	1–2	1976–77	2–0
1932–33	0–1		
1933–34	2–1	1978–79	1–4
		1979–80	3–1
1948–49	2–1		
1949–50	2–2	1984–85	3–1
1950–51	2–2	1989–90	1–1

Notts County v Nottingham Forest

Notts County were founded in 1862 and are the oldest club in the Football League. Nottingham Forest came into being in 1865, but did not enter the League until 1882, four years after Notts County had become a founder member.

Of the 82 League matches played between the two sides, Forest have won 33, County 27, and 22 have been drawn.

League results at Meadow Lane (Notts County's score first)

Season	Score	Season	Score
1892–93	3–0	1907–08	2–0
		1908–09	3–0
1897–98	1–3	1909–10	4–1
1898–99	2–2	1910–11	1–1
1899–1900	1–2		
1900–01	1–0	1913–14	2–2
1901–02	3–0		
1902–03	1–1	1920–21	2–0
1903–04	1–3	1921–22	1–1
1904–05	1–2		
1905–06	1–1	1923–24	2–1
		1924–25	0–0

Season	Score	Season	Score
1926-27	1-2	1953-54	1-1
1927-28	1-2	1954-55	4-1
1928-29	1-1	1955-56	1-3
1929-30	0-0	1956-57	1-2
1931-32	2-6	1973-74	0-1
1932-33	2-4	1974-75	2-2
1933-34	1-0	1975-76	0-0
1934-35	3-5	1976-77	1-1
1949-50	2-0	1981-82	1-2
1951-52	2-2	1982-83	3-2
1952-53	3-2	1983-84	0-0

League results at the City Ground (Forest's score first)

Season	Score	Season	Score
1892-93	3-1	1903-04	0-1
1897-98	1-1	1904-05	2-1
1898-99	0-0	1905-06	1-2
1899-1900	0-3	1907-08	2-0
1900-01	5-0	1908-09	1-0
1901-02	1-0	1909-10	2-1
1902-03	0-0	1910-11	0-2

Season	Score	Season	Score
1913-14	1-0	1949-50	1-2
1920-21	1-0	1951-52	3-2
1921-22	0-0	1952-53	1-0
1923-24	1-0	1953-54	5-0
1924-25	0-0	1954-55	0-1
1926-27	2-0	1955-56	0-2
1927-28	2-1	1956-57	2-4
1928-29	1-2	1973-74	0-0
1929-30	1-1	1974-75	0-2
1931-32	2-1	1975-76	0-1
1932-33	3-0	1976-77	1-2
1933-34	2-0	1981-82	0-2
1934-35	2-3	1982-83	2-1
		1983-84	3-1

High-flying action in the Nottingham derby between Notts County and Nottingham Forest in March 1982. Rachid Harkouk (stripes) is the highest for Notts above Ian Bowyer (Forest, right). Forest won 2-1 (Colorsport)

Bristol City v Bristol Rovers

Bristol City were founded in 1894 as Bristol South End and became known under their present title in 1897. Bristol Rovers were founded in 1883 as Black Arabs, changed to Eastville Rovers in 1884, Bristol Eastville Rovers in 1897 and became known as Bristol Rovers in 1898.

The 72 League meetings between the two clubs have resulted in Bristol City winning 26 matches and Rovers 19, with the other 27 drawn. Bristol Rovers moved to Bath City's ground in 1986.

League results at Ashton Gate (City's score first)

Season	Score	Season	Score
1922-23	0-1	1955-56	1-1
1924-25	2-0	1956-57	5-3
1925-26	0-0	1957-58	3-2
1926-27	3-1	1958-59	1-1
1932-33	3-1	1959-60	2-1
1933-34	0-3	1962-63	4-1
1934-35	1-1	1963-64	3-0
1935-36	0-2	1964-65	2-1
1936-37	4-1	1974-75	1-1
1937-38	0-0	1975-76	1-1
1938-39	2-1	1980-81	0-0
1946-47	4-0	1981-82	1-2
1947-48	5-2	1984-85	3-0
1948-49	1-1	1985-86	2-0
1949-50	1-2	1986-87	0-1
1950-51	1-0	1987-88	3-3
1951-52	1-1	1988-89	0-1
1952-53	0-0	1989-90	0-0

League results at Eastville and Twerton Park*
(Rovers' score first)

Season	Score	Season	Score
1922–23	1–2	1955–56	0–3
		1956–57	0–0
1924–25	0–0	1957–58	3–3
1925–26	0–1	1958–59	1–2
1926–27	0–5	1959–60	2–1
1932–33	1–1	1962–63	1–2
1933–34	5–1	1963–64	4–0
1934–35	2–2	1964–65	1–1
1935–36	1–1		
1936–37	3–1	1974–75	1–4
1937–38	1–0	1975–76	0–0
1938–39	1–1		
		1980–81	0–0
1946–47	0–3	1981–82	1–0
1947–48	0–2		
1948–49	3–1	1984–85	1–0
1949–50	2–3	1985–86	1–1
1950–51	2–1	1986–87*	0–0
1951–52	2–0	1987–88*	1–0
1952–53	0–0	1988–89*	1–1
		1989–90*	3–0

Crystal Palace v Charlton Athletic

Crystal Palace were founded in 1905, Charlton
Athletic in the same year. Of the 40 matches played
between the sides in the League, Crystal Palace
have won 21, Charlton Athletic 10 and nine have
been drawn.

League results at Selhurst Park (Palace's score first)

Season	Score	Season	Score
1925–26	4–1	1974–75	2–1
1926–27	2–1		
1927–28	5–0	1977–78	1–1
1928–29	0–2	1978–79	1–0
1933–34	1–0	1981–82	2–0
1934–35	1–2	1982–83	1–1
		1983–84	2–0
1964–65	3–1	1984–85	2–1
1965–66	2–0	1985–86	2–1
1966–67	1–0		
1967–68	3–0	1989–90	2–0
1968–69	3–3		

League results at The Valley (Charlton's score first)

Season	Score	Season	Score
1925–26	1–1	1928–29	1–3
1926–27	1–2		
1927–28	0–4	1933–34	4–2
		1934–35	2–2

Season	Score	Season	Score
1964–65	1–2	1978–79	1–1
1965–66	1–0		
1966–67	1–1	1981–82	2–1
1967–68	0–1	1982–83	2–1
1968–69	1–1	1983–84	1–0
		1984–85	1–1
1974–75	1–0	1985–86*	3–1
1977–78	1–0	1989–90*	1–2

at Selhurst Park

Chelsea v Fulham

Chelsea were founded in 1905 and Fulham in 1879
as Fulham St Andrew's, changing their name to
Fulham in 1888. Of the 44 matches played between
the sides in the League, Chelsea have won 26,
Fulham 6 and 12 have been drawn.

League results at Stamford Bridge (Chelsea's score
first)

Season	Score	Season	Score
1910–11	2–0	1963–64	1–2
1911–12	1–0	1964–65	1–0
		1965–66	2–1
1924–25	0–0	1966–67	0–0
1925–26	4–0	1967–68	1–1
1926–27	2–2		
1927–28	2–1	1975–76	0–0
		1976–77	2–0
1949–50	0–0		
1950–51	2–0	1979–80	0–2
1951–52	2–1		
		1982–83	0–0
1959–60	4–2	1983–84	4–0
1960–61	2–1		
1961–62	0–0		

League results at Craven Cottage (Fulham's score
first)

Season	Score	Season	Score
1910–11	1–0	1961–62	3–4
1911–12	0–1		
		1963–64	0–1
1924–15	1–2	1964–65	1–2
1925–26	0–3	1965–66	0–3
1926–27	1–2	1966–67	1–3
1927–28	1–1	1967–68	2–2
1949–50	1–1	1975–76	2–0
1950–51	1–2	1976–77	3–1
1951–52	1–2		
		1979–80	1–2
1959–60	1–3		
1960–61	3–2	1982–83	1–1
		1983–84	3–5

FA Cup Finals   1872–1990

Year	Date	Winners		Runners-up	Venue	Attendance
1872	16 March	Wanderers	1-0	Royal Engineers	Oval	2 000
1873	29 March	Wanderers	2-0	Oxford University	Lillie Bridge	3 000
1874	14 March	Oxford University	2-0	Royal Engineers	Oval	2 000
1875	13 March	Royal Engineers	1-1*	Old Etonians	Oval	3 000
Replay	16 March	Royal Engineers	2-0	Old Etonians	Oval	3 000
1876	11 March	Wanderers	1-1	Old Etonians	Oval	3 000
Replay	18 March	Wanderers	3-0	Old Etonians	Oval	3 500
1877	24 March	Wanderers	2-1*	Oxford University	Oval	3 000
1878	23 March	Wanderers	3-1	Royal Engineers	Oval	4 500
1879	29 March	Old Etonians	1-0	Clapham Rovers	Oval	5 000
1880	10 April	Clapham Rovers	1-0	Oxford University	Oval	6 000
1881	9 April	Old Carthusians	3-0	Old Etonians	Oval	4 500
1882	25 March	Old Etonians	1-0	Blackburn Rovers	Oval	6 500
1883	31 March	Blackburn Olympic	2-1*	Old Etonians	Oval	8 000
1884	29 March	Blackburn Rovers	2-1	Queen's Park	Oval	4 000
1885	4 April	Blackburn Rovers	2-0	Queen's Park	Oval	12 500
1886	3 April	Blackburn Rovers	0-0	West Bromwich Albion	Oval	15 000
Replay	10 April	Blackburn Rovers	2-0	West Bromwich Albion	Racecourse Ground	12 000
1887	2 April	Aston Villa	2-0	West Bromwich Albion	Oval	15 500
1888	24 March	West Bromwich Albion	2-1	Preston North End	Oval	19 000
1889	30 March	Preston North End	3-0	Wolverhampton Wanderers	Oval	22 000
1890	29 March	Blackburn Rovers	6-1	Sheffield Wednesday	Oval	20 000
1891	25 March	Blackburn Rovers	3-1	Notts County	Oval	23 000

* after extra time

Referee	Entries	Final facts
A Stair	15	First injury: Lt. Cresswell breaks his collar bone after ten minutes but carries on
A Stair	16	The Dark Blues dispense with their goalkeeper after the first goal by The Wanderers
A Stair	28	Conquerors of The Wanderers, Oxford had four England internationals in their side
C W Alcock C W Alcock	29	The Chatham Sappers thus completed 20 matches that season without losing one of them
W S Rawson W S Rawson	32	The Heron brothers become the only pair to win cup medals and international honours
S H Wright	37	More revenge for The Wanderers against their well-beaten undergraduate opposition
S R Bastard	43	C H R Wollaston wins his fifth medal; Wanderers return the trophy to the Association
C W Alcock	43	Despite a marathon quarter-final with Darwen, the Old Boys' stamina lasts out the better
Major Marindin	54	Lloyd Jones scores the only goal and Oxford play their last ever FA Cup tie
W Pierce Dix	63	Charterhouse has its finest moment and they are the first team to show any real teamwork
J C Clegg	73	Hon. A F Kinnaird achieves his fifth winners' medal but the era of the amateur is to pass
C Crump	84	The winners are the first team to train for the match; they go away to Blackpool
Major Marindin	100	Two goals disallowed upset the Scots who are used to a different 'offside' interpretation
Major Marindin	116	The first five-figure attendance and invasion of the South by fans travelling from the North
Major Marindin Major Marindin	130	Rovers receive a silver shield for their third consecutive victory in the final
Major Marindin	126	A disputed first goal, claimed to be offside, is the issue in the all-Midlands derby
Major Marindin	149	Albion become the first winners with an all-English side; Billy Bassett at 18 makes both goals
Major Marindin	149	The first League and Cup double. Preston do not concede a goal during their cup run
Major Marindin	132	William Townley is the first to record a hat-trick in the biggest final win to date
C J Hughes	161	James Forrest wins his fifth medal to emulate the feat of Wollaston and Hon. A F Kinnaird

Year	Date	Winners		Runners-up	Venue	Attendance
1892	19 March	West Bromwich Albion	3-0	Aston Villa	Oval	25 000
1893	26 March	Wolverhampton Wanderers	1-0	Everton	Fallowfield	45 000
1894	31 March	Notts County	4-1	Bolton Wanderers	Goodison Park	37 000
1895	20 April	Aston Villa	1-0	West Bromwich Albion	Crystal Palace	42 560
1896	18 April	Sheffield Wednesday	2-1	Wolverhampton Wanderers	Crystal Palace	48 836
1897	10 April	Aston Villa	3-2	Everton	Crystal Palace	65 891
1898	16 April	Nottingham Forest	3-1	Derby County	Crystal Palace	62 017
1899	15 April	Sheffield United	4-1	Derby County	Crystal Palace	73 833
1900	21 April	Bury	4-0	Southampton	Crystal Palace	68 945
1901	20 April	Tottenham Hotspur	2-2	Sheffield United	Crystal Palace	110 820
Replay	27 April	Tottenham Hotspur	3-1	Sheffield United	Burnden Park	20 470
1902	19 April	Sheffield United	1-1	Southampton	Crystal Palace	76 914
Replay	26 April	Sheffield United	2-1	Southampton	Crystal Palace	33 068
1903	18 April	Bury	6-0	Derby County	Crystal Palace	63 102
1904	23 April	Manchester City	1-0	Bolton Wanderers	Crystal Palace	61 374
1905	15 April	Aston Villa	2-0	Newcastle United	Crystal Palace	101 117
1906	21 April	Everton	1-0	Newcastle United	Crystal Palace	75 609
1907	20 April	Sheffield Wednesday	2-1	Everton	Crystal Palace	84 584
1908	25 April	Wolverhampton Wanderers	3-1	Newcastle United	Crystal Palace	74 967
1909	26 April	Manchester United	1-0	Bristol City	Crystal Palace	71 401
1910	23 April	Newcastle United	1-1	Barnsley	Crystal Palace	77 747
Replay	28 April	Newcastle United	2-0	Barnsley	Goodison Park	69 000
1911	22 April	Bradford City	0-0	Newcastle United	Crystal Palace	69 098
Replay	26 April	Bradford City	1-0	Newcastle United	Old Trafford	58 000
1912	20 April	Barnsley	0-0	West Bromwich Albion	Crystal Palace	54 556
Replay	24 April	Barnsley	1-0*	West Bromwich Albion	Bramall Lane	38 555
1913	19 April	Aston Villa	1-0	Sunderland	Crystal Palace	120 081

* after extra time

Referee	Entries	Final facts
J C Clegg	163	Crossbar and goal nets are featured for the first time in the second all-Midlands final
C J Hughes	183	Cup fever is reflected in the crowd bursting in and surrounding the touchlines in play
C J Hughes	155	The first winners from the Second Division and James Logan scores a hat-trick for them
J Lewis	179	John Devey gets a final touch in Villa's revenge and the goal comes in 40 seconds
Capt. W Simpson	210	Yorkshire's first taste of cup glory and a new cup; the first is stolen on 11 September 1895
J Lewis	244	Aston Villa become the second side in history to achieve the League and Cup double
J Lewis	213	Forest had lost 5–0 to Derby a week before winning this East Midlands derby
A Scragg	235	With broken ribs and a ruptured side, United back Harry Thickett plays in 50 yards of bandages
A G Kingscott	242	The Shakers on their way to living up to the nickname that has remained ever since
A G Kingscott A G Kingscott	220	Last non-league side to win the cup; Alex Brown scores in every round, 15 goals in all
T Kirkham T Kirkham	226	The goal area, penalty area and penalty spot were features to take a familiar place
J Adams	223	Bury concede no goals in their run and record the biggest margin of Cup final victory
A J Barker	252	A goal by Welshman Billy Meredith is enough to win this first all-Lancashire final
P R Harrower	274	Twenty-year-old 'Happy' Harry Hampton scores in the third minute and again after 75
T Kirkham	280	Newcastle field ten players with Cup final experience but their Palace hoodoo remains
N Whittaker	305	Everton have ten with similar experience but Wednesday win with four minutes remaining
T P Campbell	348	Second Division winners. The four 'H' men score: Rev. Hunt, Hedley, Harrison and Howie
J Mason	361	Meredith collects his second winner's medal – for the other Mancunian team
J T Ibbotson J T Ibbotson	424	Albert Shepherd scores twice in the replay, one of them from the first recorded final penalty
J H Pearson J H Pearson	403	City with a record eight Scots win a new trophy costing 50 guineas and made in Bradford
J R Schumacher J R Schumacher	410	Barnsley make it a record for a Second Division side; their second final in three years
A Adams	457	Record attendance for a match involving the chief League Championship challengers

Year	Date	Winners		Runners-up	Venue	Attendance
1914	25 April	Burnley	1-0	Liverpool	Crystal Palace	72 778
1915	24 April	Sheffield United	3-0	Chelsea	Old Trafford	49 557
1920	24 April	Aston Villa	1-0*	Huddersfield Town	Stamford Bridge	50 018
1921	23 April	Tottenham Hotspur	1-0	Wolverhampton Wanderers	Stamford Bridge	72 805
1922	29 April	Huddersfield Town	1-0	Preston North End	Stamford Bridge	53 000
1923	28 April	Bolton Wanderers	2-0	West Ham United	Wembley	126 047
1924	26 April	Newcastle United	2-0	Aston Villa	Wembley	91 695
1925	25 April	Sheffield United	1-0	Cardiff City	Wembley	91 763
1926	24 April	Bolton Wanderers	1-0	Manchester City	Wembley	91 447
1927	23 April	Cardiff City	1-0	Arsenal	Wembley	91 206
1928	21 April	Blackburn Rovers	3-1	Huddersfield Town	Wembley	92 041
1929	27 April	Bolton Wanderers	2-0	Portsmouth	Wembley	92 576
1930	26 April	Arsenal	2-0	Huddersfield Town	Wembley	92 488
1931	25 April	West Bromwich Albion	2-1	Birmingham	Wembley	92 406
1932	23 April	Newcastle United	2-1	Arsenal	Wembley	92 298
1933	29 April	Everton	3-0	Manchester City	Wembley	92 950
1934	28 April	Manchester City	2-1	Portsmouth	Wembley	93 258
1935	27 April	Sheffield Wednesday	4-1	West Bromwich Albion	Wembley	93 204
1936	25 April	Arsenal	1-0	Sheffield United	Wembley	93 384
1937	1 May	Sunderland	3-1	Preston North End	Wembley	93 495
1938	30 April	Preston North End	1-0*	Huddersfield Town	Wembley	93 497
1939	29 April	Portsmouth	4-1	Wolverhampton Wanderers	Wembley	99 370
1946	27 April	Derby County	4-1*	Charlton Athletic	Wembley	98 000
1947	26 April	Charlton Athletic	1-0*	Burnley	Wembley	99 000

* after extra time

Referee	Entries	Final facts
H S Bamlett	476	King George V becomes the first reigning monarch to attend the Cup final
H H Taylor	454	War-time game known as 'The Khaki Cup Final' with the crowd packed with servicemen
J T Howcroft	445	The only goal comes off the neck of Billy Kirton from a corner, but it is just as valid
J Davies	674	Cloudburst during the game turns the pitch into a quagmire but the classic Spurs win well
J W D Fowler	656	Billy Smith scores the winning goal from a penalty; the first decisive spot kick
D H Asson	548	Wembley's initial occasion and an invasion by a crowd estimated at around 200 000
W E Russell	555	Drama reserved for the last ninety seconds during which Newcastle score both goals
G N Watson	548	Keeping goal for Sheffield is Charlie Sutcliffe, youngest brother of Bolton's 1894 'keeper
I Baker	570	Bolton with ten men possessing previous final experience score through David Jack
W F Bunnell	552	The Cup goes out of England for the first and only time, a tragic mistake by goalkeeper Lewis
T G Bryan	544	First BBC final broadcast and a goal in under a minute; first loser's goal in 18 years
A Josephs	520	Bolton win again and a total of 17 different players used by them in 3 finals
T Crew	525	Manager Herbert Chapman of Arsenal wins at the expense of the club he formerly guided
A H Kingscott	526	A double of a rather different kind; Albion win the Cup and also win promotion
W P Harper	529	Arsenal become the first team to score first in the final and finish as the losers
E Wood	543	The players are numbered for the first time in the final but unusually, from 1 to 22
S F Rous	554	Fred Tilson, omitted from the City side in 1933, scores twice to ensure City's victory
A E Fogg	573	Two goals from Ellis Rimmer for Wednesday mean that the winger has scored in each round
H Nattrass	571	Despite the discomfiture of an injured knee, Ted Drake is the Arsenal goalscoring hero
R G Rudd	563	Frank O'Donnell scores in every round for Preston but to no final avail
A J Jewell	574	In the last minute of extra time, George Mutch hits a penalty in off the crossbar to seal it
T Thompson	556	The heavy favourites are beaten and Bert Barlow scores one of the goals against his old club
E D Smith	294	Charlton's John Oakes is the oldest ever Cup finalist at 42; Bert Turner scores for both sides
J M Wiltshire	438	The ball bursts for the second year but Chris Duffy scores with six minutes remaining

Year	Date	Winners		Runners-up	Venue	Attendance
1948	24 April	Manchester United	4-2	Blackpool	Wembley	99 000
1949	30 April	Wolverhampton Wanderers	3-1	Leicester City	Wembley	99 500
1950	29 April	Arsenal	2-0	Liverpool	Wembley	100 000
1951	28 April	Newcastle United	2-0	Blackpool	Wembley	100 000
1952	3 May	Newcastle United	1-0	Arsenal	Wembley	100 000
1953	2 May	Blackpool	4-3	Bolton Wanderers	Wembley	100 000
1954	1 May	West Bromwich Albion	3-2	Preston North End	Wembley	100 000
1955	7 May	Newcastle United	3-1	Manchester City	Wembley	100 000
1956	5 May	Manchester City	3-1	Birmingham City	Wembley	100 000
1957	4 May	Aston Villa	2-1	Manchester United	Wembley	100 000
1958	3 May	Bolton Wanderers	2-0	Manchester United	Wembley	100 000
1959	2 May	Nottingham Forest	2-1	Luton Town	Wembley	100 000
1960	7 May	Wolverhampton Wanderers	3-0	Blackburn Rovers	Wembley	100 000
1961	6 May	Tottenham Hotspur	2-0	Leicester City	Wembley	100 000
1962	5 May	Tottenham Hotspur	3-1	Burnley	Wembley	100 000
1963	25 May	Manchester United	3-1	Leicester City	Wembley	100 000
1964	2 May	West Ham United	3-2	Preston North End	Wembley	100 000
1965	1 May	Liverpool	2-1*	Leeds United	Wembley	100 000
1966	14 May	Everton	3-2	Sheffield Wednesday	Wembley	100 000
1967	20 May	Tottenham Hotspur	2-1	Chelsea	Wembley	100 000
1968	18 May	West Bromwich Albion	1-0*	Everton	Wembley	100 000
1969	26 April	Manchester City	1-0	Leicester City	Wembley	100 000

* after extra time

Referee	Entries	Final facts
C J Barrick	510	Eddie Shimwell becomes the first full-back to score at Wembley for Blackpool with a penalty
R A Mortimer	617	Don Revie misses the game for Leicester City because of an eve of the game nose bleed
H Pearce	617	Arsenal are the oldest team to play at Wembley but Reg Lewis scores twice for victory
W Ling	615	Jackie Milburn scores in every round and gets both goals in this final triumph
A Ellis	478	Arsenal lose Walley Barnes with a split cartilage; Chilean George Robledo scores
M Griffiths	477	Nat Lofthouse scores in every round but injury-hit Bolton lose to a Stan Mortensen hat-trick
A Luty	460	Charlie Wayman scores in every round for the losers; Ronnie Allen's two include one penalty
R Leafe	504	A Milburn goal in 45 seconds for Newcastle's fifth Wembley win; but City's Jimmy Meadows twists his knee
A Bond	460	Bert Trautmann plays the last 15 minutes in goal for Manchester City with a broken neck
F Coultas	438	Record seventh win for Villa but United goalkeeper Ray Wood suffers a broken collar-bone
J Sherlock	442	Stan Crowther, already cup-tied with Villa, plays for United in post-Munich patched side
J Clough	447	Roy Dwight scores for Forest, breaks his leg, then watches the game on a hospital TV set
K Howley	462	Kevin Howley at 35 is the youngest Wembley referee; Rovers' Dave Whelan breaks a leg
J Kelly	433	Tottenham achieve the first League Championship and Cup double of the present century
J Finney	414	Danny Blanchflower converts the fourth penalty awarded at Wembley nine minutes from the end
K Aston	411	Winter of postponements means that the final is put back to May 25 for first time
A Holland	400	Howard Kendall at 17 years 345 days becomes the youngest Cup finalist for Preston
W Clements	395	Gerry Byrne of Liverpool breaks his collar bone and extra time is played before victory
J K Taylor	403	Everton recover from a two-goal deficit to win and Wednesday do a losers' lap of honour
K Dagnall	406	The first all-London final and Spurs achieve their fifth win in five final appearances
L Callaghan	429	Jeff Astle manages to score in every round with the only goal in the third minute of extra time
G McCabe	438	Leicester suffer their fourth Wembley defeat and follow it with relegation to Division Two

Year	Date	Winners	Runners-up	Venue	Attendance
1970	11 April	Chelsea	2-2* Leeds United	Wembley	100 000
Replay	29 April	Chelsea	2-1* Leeds United	Old Trafford	62 078
1971	8 May	Arsenal	2-1* Liverpool	Wembley	100 000
1972	6 May	Leeds United	1-0 Arsenal	Wembley	100 000
1973	5 May	Sunderland	1-0 Leeds United	Wembley	100 000
1974	4 May	Liverpool	3-0 Newcastle United	Wembley	100 000
1975	3 May	West Ham United	2-0 Fulham	Wembley	100 000
1976	1 May	Southampton	1-0 Manchester United	Wembley	100 000
1977	21 May	Manchester United	2-1 Liverpool	Wembley	100 000
1978	6 May	Ipswich Town	1-0 Arsenal	Wembley	100 000
1979	12 May	Arsenal	3-2 Manchester United	Wembley	100 000
1980	10 May	West Ham United	1-0 Arsenal	Wembley	100 000
1981	9 May	Tottenham Hotspur	1-1* Manchester City	Wembley	100 000
Replay	14 May	Tottenham Hotspur	3-2 Manchester City	Wembley	100 000
1982	22 May	Tottenham Hotspur	1-1* Queens Park Rangers	Wembley	100 000
Replay	27 May	Tottenham Hotspur	1-0 Queens Park Rangers	Wembley	100 000
1983	21 May	Manchester United	2-2* Brighton & Hove Albion	Wembley	100 000
Replay	26 May	Manchester United	4-0 Brighton & Hove Albion	Wembley	100 000
1984	19 May	Everton	2-0 Watford	Wembley	100 000
1985	18 May	Manchester United	1-0* Everton	Wembley	100 000
1986	10 May	Liverpool	3-1 Everton	Wembley	98 000
1987	16 May	Coventry City	3-2* Tottenham Hotspur	Wembley	98 000
1988	14 May	Wimbledon	1-0 Liverpool	Wembley	98 000
1989	20 May	Liverpool	3-2* Everton	Wembley	82 800
1990	12 May	Manchester United	3-3* Crystal Palace	Wembley	80 000
Replay	17 May	Manchester United	1-0 Crystal Palace	Wembley	80 000

* after extra time

Referee	Entries	Final facts
E Jennings E Jennings	451	First ever replay for a Wembley final; Peter Osgood scores in every round
N Burtenshaw	464	Arsenal become the fourth side to achieve the double; Eddie Kelly the first substitute to score
D W Smith	471	Despite having ten players with previous cup final experience, Arsenal are the losers
K Burns	471	The first Second Division club to win the trophy in 42 years; Leeds' Johnny Giles' fifth final
G C Kew	468	A record 11th final for Newcastle but it coincides with their first Wembley reverse
P Partridge	453	The second all-London final and both goals are scored by Alan Taylor, signed in November
C Thomas	441	Another Second Division side are successful; it is Southampton's third time lucky
R Matthewson	454	United manager Tommy Docherty's eighth Wembley appearance as a player or manager but his first as a winner
D R G Nippard	469	A goal from Roger Osborne puts the 40th different name on the Cup, but he has to be taken off
R Challis	466	United score twice to level in 86 and 88 minutes but Alan Sunderland seals it 60 seconds later
G Courtney	475	Paul Allen at 17 years 256 days becomes the youngest FA Cup finalist in the first Cockney Cup Final
K Hackett K Hackett	480	The 100th final; Spurs make it six wins in six finals. Kevin Reeves' replay penalty is Wembley's fifth in five
C White C White	486	Spurs seventh in seven; Glenn Hoddle scores in the first game and clinches it with a replay penalty
A Grey A Grey	479	Underdogs Brighton miss their chance at the first attempt; Norman Whiteside is the youngest final scorer at 18 years 18 days in the replay
J Hunting	487	Graeme Sharp in-off-a-post and Andy Gray controversially with a header out of goalkeeper Steve Sherwood's hands are the scorers
P Willis	494	United's Kevin Moran becomes the first player sent off in a final but Whiteside drives in the only goal
A Robinson	496	Ian Rush scores twice in the first all-Merseyside final after Gary Lineker opens for Everton. Liverpool clinch fifth League and Cup double
N Midgley	504	Coventry end Spurs' invincibility in finals and take their first major honour in 104 years of existence
B Hill	516	John Aldridge becomes the first player to miss a penalty in a Wembley FA Cup final, Dave Beasant the first to save one, for Wimbledon
J Worrall	525	The second all-Merseyside final and substitutes Ian Rush and Stuart McCall make history by each scoring twice
A Gunn A Gunn	541	Six goals enliven an ordinary game; United's Les Sealey becomes the first on-loan finalist in the replay

FA Cup facts

Chester City, Hartlepool United, Southend United and Torquay United have never beaten a Division One team in the FA Cup. Gillingham have not done so since 1907–8 (Sunderland) when they were known as New Brompton; Reading since 1928–29 (Sheffield Wednesday); Brentford since 1948–49 (Burnley) and Chesterfield since 1949–50 (Middlesbrough).

Post-war cases of non-League teams avoiding defeat in FA Cup away ties against Division One opponents were:

1952–53	Manchester United	1–1	Walthamstow Ave. 3rd Rd
1953–54	Newcastle United	2–2	Wigan Athletic	3rd Rd
1955–56	Arsenal	2–2	Bedford Town	3rd Rd
1971–72	Newcastle United	2–2	Hereford United	3rd Rd
1974–75	Burnley	0–1	Wimbledon	3rd Rd
1974–75	Leeds United	0–0	Wimbledon	4th Rd

Newport County are the only Division One or Two club since the war to have played in the FA Cup before the third round. They operated in rounds one and two in season 1945–46 when in Division Two. Hull City (1945–46) and Shrewsbury Town (1950–51) are the only Football League clubs since the war to have missed a season in the FA Cup.

Southend United are the only team to have scored nine goals or more in the FA Cup three times since the last war and four times since the 1914–18 war: 10–1 v Golders Green in 1934–35; 9–2 v Barnet in 1946–47; 9–0 v King's Lynn and 10–1 v Brentwood in 1968–69.

Stoke City created an all-time record in 1954–55 in meeting Bury seven times in a season without being beaten. They defeated them in the fifth meeting of an FA Cup third round tie, won a Division Two home game by 3–2, and drew away 1–1.

Notts County won a Division One away match against Blackburn Rovers by 7–1 on 14 March 1891. On 25 March Rovers beat them in the Cup final 3–1!

Right-back Tom Smart made the quickest-ever rise from minor soccer to an FA Cup-winning team. Signed from Halesowen on 17 January 1920, he was in Aston Villa's side which defeated Huddersfield Town on 24 April.

The oldest known FA Cup final eleven of all time was the Arsenal side which defeated Liverpool in 1950. Its average age was slightly over 31.

JTIbbotson, living in Derby, was the appointed referee for the Newcastle United v Barnsley final in 1910. It transpired he had been born at Dodworth, just outside Barnsley. The South Yorkshire side vainly protested against his appointment, fearing that he might concentrate on avoiding 'favouritism', and would actually penalise Barnsley.

No player had ever been sent off in an FA Cup final before Kevin Moran (Manchester United) in 1985, but in 1913 there was such a stormy row between Aston Villa centre-forward Harry Hampton and Sunderland centre-half Charlie Thomson that both were suspended for a month.

Only three pairs of brothers have appeared in the same FA Cup-winning teams in this century: Denis and Leslie Compton (Arsenal, 1950); Ted and George Robledo (Newcastle United, 1952); and Brian and Jimmy Greenhoff (Manchester United, 1977).

Ted (right) and George Robledo played for Newcastle United in the 1952 FA Cup Final. They were born in Chile (Colorsport)

Only eight players have scored in all six rounds of the FA Cup (from 3rd round onwards) in one season: Ellis Rimmer (Sheffield Wednesday, 1935); Frank O'Donnell (Preston North End, 1937); Stan Mortensen (Blackpool, 1948); Jackie Milburn (Newcastle United, 1951); Nat Lofthouse (Bolton Wanderers, 1953); Charlie Wayman (Preston North End, 1954); Jeff Astle (West Bromwich Albion, 1968) and Peter Osgood (Chelsea, 1970).

Jackie Milburn scored in each round of the FA Cup in which Newcastle United played in the 1950-51 season (NSB)

In a third round tie in 1889–90, Sheffield Wednesday defeated Notts County twice and County beat Wednesday once. Each side had a protest upheld after being beaten.

Nottingham Forest's 14–0 win at Clapton in the first round (equivalent of the present-day third) in season 1890–91 ranks as the record away victory by any team in the competition proper since the Football League's 1888 formation.

The only instances of clubs having defeated opponents from five different grades in the FA Cup competition proper in the same season have been:
York City 1954–55 – Scarborough (Midland League), Dorchester (Western League), Blackpool (Division One), Bishop Auckland (Northern League), Tottenham Hotspur (Division One), Notts County (Division Two).
Oxford United 1963–64 – Folkestone (Southern League Two), Kettering (Southern League One), Chesterfield (Division Four), Brentford (Division Three), Blackburn Rovers (Division One).
Peterborough United 1964–65 – Salisbury (Western League), Queen's Park Rangers (Division Three), Chesterfield (Division Four), Arsenal (Division One), Swansea Town (Division Two).
Mansfield Town 1968–69 – Tow Law (Northern League), Rotherham United (Division Three), Sheffield United (Division Two), Southend United (Division Four), West Ham United (Division One).
Leeds United 1969–70 – Swansea Town (Division Four), Sutton United (non-League), Mansfield Town (Division Three), Swindon Town (Division Two), Manchester United (Division One).
Colchester United 1970–71 – Ringmer (Sussex), Cambridge United (Division Four), Barnet (Southern League), Rochdale (Division Three), Leeds United (Division One).
Plymouth Argyle 1983–84 – Southend United (Division Three), Barking (non-League), Newport County (Division Three), Darlington (Division Four), West Bromwich Albion (Division One), Derby County (Division Two).

The only Football League clubs to have defeated four teams in higher grades than their own in the FA Cup in the same season have been:
Notts County (Division Two) in 1893–94 – Burnley, Nottingham Forest, Blackburn Rovers and Bolton Wanderers (all Division One).
Millwall (Division Three Southern) in 1936–37 – Fulham (Division Two), Chelsea, Derby County and Manchester City (all Division One).
Norwich City (Division Three) in 1958–59 – Manchester United (Division One), Cardiff City (Division Two), Spurs (Division One) and Sheffield United (Division Two).
Bradford City (Division Four) in 1975–76 – Chesterfield, Rotherham United and Shrewsbury Town (all Division Three) and Norwich City (Division One).

Instances of teams below Division Two defeating three Division One sides in the FA Cup in the same season:
Charlton Athletic (Division Three Southern) in 1922–23 – Manchester City, Preston North End and West Bromwich Albion.
Millwall (Division Three Southern) in 1936–37 – Chelsea, Derby County and Manchester City.

Teams defeating opponents from all four Football League divisions in the FA Cup in the same season: Fulham 1961–62, Leeds United 1964–65 and 1969–70, Peterborough United 1964–65, Mansfield Town 1968–69. Sunderland 1972–73, Wrexham 1973–74, Southampton 1975–76, Shrewsbury Town 1978–79 and Plymouth Argyle 1983–84.

For more than 100 years it was wrongly reported that Wanderers had beaten Oxford University 2–0 in the 1877 FA Cup final at the Oval. But the *Football Calendar 1877* clearly stated that the Wanderers goalkeeper Kinnaird, after stopping the ball from one of his defenders, stepped back ball in hand between his posts and a goal was rightly given to the University. Thus after 90 minutes the score was 1–1 and extra time necessary. It appears that after the game Kinnaird pleaded that the ball did not cross the line and thus it was recorded as 2–0. In fact the Football Association still have it thus in their official records.

In 1890–91, Darwen beat Kidderminster 3–1 in the first round of the FA Cup but the match was replayed after a protest and Darwen won 13–0. In 1873–74 Sheffield and Shropshire Wanderers had completed two drawn games in the first round of the competition before the tie was decided on the toss of a coin, which Sheffield won.

In the FA Cup second round (first series) of the 1886–87 season there were three double figure scores recorded: Wolverhampton Wanderers 14 Crosswells Brewery 0; Cowlairs 10 Rossendale 2 and Aston Villa 14 Derby Midland 0. It was not for another 82 years that a side reached double figures at the same stage, when Southend United beat Brentwood 10–1.

Derby County hold the record for the highest number of wins in one season for the FA Cup proper. In 1945–46 they recorded nine, because for the only time in the history of the competition, ties were decided on a home and away basis. Derby also scored a record 37 goals and Raich Carter was their top scorer with 12. But he was not the leading marksman in the competition that season. Harry Brooks (Aldershot) scored 13 including five on two occasions.

On 7 March 1970 Manchester City, already holders of the FA Cup from the previous season, defeated West Bromwich Albion in the Football League Cup final. On 29 April they defeated Gornik Zabrze (Poland) in the Cup-Winners Cup final to make them, temporarily at least, holders of one European and two domestic

Harry Brooks (Aldershot) scored five goals in each of two FA Cup ties against Newport (Isle of Wight) and Reading during the 1945–46 season when he scored 13 in the competition (JR)

trophies. In fact their triple reign lasted just 90 minutes because later that same night Chelsea won the FA Cup after a replay to become the new holders of the trophy.

Halifax Town and Hartlepools United met each other in three successive seasons in the FA Cup, drawing 1–1 on each occasion at Halifax in 1933–34, 1934–35 and 1935–36. Leeds United were beaten 2–1 at home by Cardiff City in the same competition in seasons 1955–56, 1956–57 and 1957–58.

Everton and Sheffield Wednesday have been drawn together more times in the FA Cup than any other pair of clubs in history. They have clashed in 14 ties: 1892–93, 1894–95, 1895–96, 1905–06, 1906–07, 1920–21, 1936–37, 1946–47, 1953–54, 1964–65, 1965–66 (final), 1985–86, 1987–88 and 1989–90.

The 1886 FA Cup final was the first to be staged between professional teams. Blackburn Rovers and West Bromwich Albion drew 0–0 at Kennington Oval before Blackburn won the replay at the Racecourse Ground, Derby.

Brighton and Hove Albion and Watford were drawn together in the FA Cup for four consecutive seasons from 1924–28 as were Manchester City and Leicester City from 1965–69.

Nottingham Forest have been drawn to play FA Cup games in all four home countries. In 1885 they drew their semi-final with Queen's Park 1–1 at Derby and then lost the replay in Edinburgh 3–0. In 1888–89 they were drawn to play Linfield in Belfast only to discover on arrival that their opponents had scratched. However they did play a friendly and were beaten 3–1. In 1921–22 they lost 4–1 away to Cardiff City.

No non-league club has reached the last four of the FA Cup since Swindon Town in 1909–10 and again in 1911–12. In 1910 they lost 2–0 to Newcastle United, while in 1912 they drew 0–0 with Barnsley before losing the replay 1–0.

In 1927–28 Rochdale beat Crook Town 8–2 in a first round FA Cup tie. They did not win again in the competition until the same stage in 1945–46. They won 2–1 at Stockport County and drew 1–1 at home in the two-legged tie which was a feature of this season only. They achieved only one draw during this time, on 27 November 1937 against Lincoln City. On 25 November 1933 they were losing 2–1 to Sutton United with a few seconds remaining. Their centre-forward appeared to score only for the referee to disallow the goal, claiming he had blown for full-time.

In nine consecutive FA Cup competitions, from 1934–35 to 1948–49 inclusive, the team who defeated Preston North End either won the Cup or at least reached the final.

The lowest attendance for a third round FA Cup tie is 2 034. On 10 December 1986 Aldershot were forced to raise the prices of tickets for the game with Oxford United. Terrace prices were £9. Aldershot from Division Four beat Oxford of Division One 3–0.

The smallest sixth round crowd in post-war FA Cup history was 10 084 for the Cambridge United v Crystal Palace tie on 10 March 1990.

FA Cup attendances 1966–89

Season	1st Rd	2nd Rd	3rd Rd	4th Rd	5th Rd	6th Rd	SF+F	Total	Matches	Average
1966–67	390 292	295 112	1 288 341	921 303	602 111	252 672	217 378	3 967 209	169	23 475
1967–68	322 121	236 195	1 229 519	771 284	563 779	250 095	223 831	3 586 824	160	22 418
1968–69	331 858	252 710	1 094 043	883 675	464 915	188 121	216 232	3 431 554	157	21 857
1969–70	345 229	195 102	925 930	651 374	319 893	198 537	390 700	3 026 765	170	17 805
1970–71	329 687	230 942	956 683	757 852	360 687	304 937	279 644	3 220 432	162	19 879
1971–72	277 726	263 127	986 094	711 399	468 378	230 292	248 546	3 158 562	160	19 741
1972–73	259 432	169 114	938 741	735 825	357 386	241 934	226 543	2 928 975	160	18 306
1973–74	214 236	125 295	840 142	747 909	346 012	233 307	273 051	2 779 952	167	16 646
1974–75	283 956	170 466	914 994	646 434	393 323	268 361	291 369	2 968 903	172	17 261
1975–76	255 533	178 099	867 880	573 843	471 925	206 851	205 810	2 759 941	161	17 142
1976–77	379 230	192 159	942 523	631 265	373 330	205 379	258 216	2 982 102	174	17 139
1977–78	258 248	178 930	881 406	540 164	400 751	137 059	198 020	2 594 578	160	16 216
1978–79	243 773	185 343	880 345	537 748	243 683	263 213	249 897	2 604 002	166	15 687
1979–80	267 121	204 759	804 701	507 725	364 039	157 530	355 541	2 661 416	163	16 328
1980–81	246 824	194 502	832 578	534 402	320 530	288 714	339 250	2 756 800	169	16 312
1981–82	236 220	127 300	513 185	356 987	203 334	124 308	279 621	1 840 955	160	11 506
1982–83	191 312	150 046	670 503	452 688	260 069	193 845	291 162	2 209 625	159	13 897
1983–84	192 276	151 647	625 965	417 298	181 832	185 382	187 000	1 941 400	166	11 695
1984–85	174 604	137 078	616 229	320 772	269 232	148 690	242 754	1 909 359	157	12 162
1985–86	171 142	130 034	486 838	495 526	311 833	184 262	192 316	1 971 951	168	11 738
1986–87	209 290	146 769	593 520	349 342	263 550	119 396	195 533	1 877 400	165	11 378
1987–88	204 411	104 561	720 121	443 133	281 461	119 313	177 585	2 050 585	155	13 229
1988–89	212 775	121 326	690 199	421 255	206 781	176 629	167 353	1 966 318	164	12 173

League Cup Finals
Milk Cup 1982–86   Littlewoods Cup 1987–90

Year	Winners		Runners-up	Venue	Attendance	Referee
1961	Aston Villa	3-2	Rotherham United	(1) Millmoor	12 226	K A Collinge
				(2) Villa Park	31 202	C W Kingston
1962	Norwich City	4-0	Rochdale	(1) Spotland	11 123	A Holland
				(2) Carrow Road	19 708	R H Mann
1963	Birmingham City	3-1	Aston Villa	(1) St Andrew's	31 850	E Crawford
				(2) Villa Park	37 920	A W Starling
1964	Leicester City	4-3	Stoke City	(1) Victoria Ground	22 309	W Clements
				(2) Filbert Street	25 372	A Jobling
1965	Chelsea	3-2	Leicester City	(1) Stamford Bridge	20 690	J Finney
				(2) Filbert Street	26 958	K Howley
1966	West Bromwich Albion	5-3	West Ham United	(1) Upton Park	28 341	D W Smith
				(2) The Hawthorns	31 925	J Mitchell
1967	Queen's Park Rangers	3-2	West Bromwich Albion	Wembley	97 952	W Crossley
1968	Leeds United	1-0*	Arsenal	Wembley	97 887	L Hamer
1969	Swindon Town	3-1*	Arsenal	Wembley	98 189	W Handley
1970	Manchester City	2-1	West Bromwich Albion	Wembley	97 963	J James
1971	Tottenham Hotspur	2-0	Aston Villa	Wembley	100 000	J Finney
1972	Stoke City	2-1	Chelsea	Wembley	100 000	N C Burtenshaw
1973	Tottenham Hotspur	1-0	Norwich City	Wembley	100 000	D W Smith
1974	Wolverhampton Wanderers	2-1	Manchester City	Wembley	100 000	E D Wallace
1975	Aston Villa	1-0	Norwich City	Wembley	100 000	G W Hill
1976	Manchester City	2-1	Newcastle United	Wembley	100 000	J K Taylor
1977	Aston Villa	0-0	Everton	Wembley	100 000	G C Kew
	Aston Villa	1-1*	Everton	Hillsborough	55 000	G C Kew
	Aston Villa	3-2*	Everton	Old Trafford	54 749	G C Kew
1978	Nottingham Forest	0-0*	Liverpool	Wembley	100 000	P Partridge
	Nottingham Forest	1-0	Liverpool	Old Trafford	54 375	P Partridge
1979	Nottingham Forest	3-2	Southampton	Wembley	100 000	P G Reeves
1980	Wolverhampton Wanderers	1-0	Nottingham Forest	Wembley	100 000	D Richardson
1981	Liverpool	1-1*	West Ham United	Wembley	100 000	C Thomas
	Liverpool	2-1	West Ham United	Villa Park	36 693	C Thomas
1982	Liverpool	3-1*	Tottenham Hotspur	Wembley	100 000	P M Willis
1983	Liverpool	2-1*	Manchester United	Wembley	100 000	G Courtney
1984	Liverpool	0-0*	Everton	Wembley	100 000	A Robinson
	Liverpool	1-0	Everton	Maine Road	52 089	A Robinson
1985	Norwich City	1-0	Sunderland	Wembley	100 000†	N Midgley
1986	Oxford United	3-0	Queen's Park Rangers	Wembley	90 396	K Hackett
1987	Arsenal	2-1	Liverpool	Wembley	96 000	L Shapter
1988	Luton Town	3-2	Arsenal	Wembley	95 732	J Worrall
1989	Nottingham Forest	3-1	Luton Town	Wembley	76 130	R Milford
1990	Nottingham Forest	1-0	Oldham Athletic	Wembley	74 343	J Martin

after extra time   † unofficial figure

League Cup Facts

In every season since 1971–72 all the League clubs have played in the League Cup, but in all but one of the first eleven seasons of the competition there were the following instances of clubs not entering:

1960–61 – Arsenal, Sheffield Wednesday, Tottenham Hotspur, West Bromwich Albion, Wolverhampton Wanderers

1962–62 – Arsenal, Burnley, Chelsea, Everton, Liverpool, Manchester United, Sheffield Wednesday, Tottenham Hotspur, West Bromwich Albion, Wolverhampton Wanderers

1962–63 – Arsenal, Burnley, Chelsea, Everton, Liverpool, Manchester United, Ipswich Town, Nottingham Forest, Sheffield Wednesday, Tottenham Hotspur, West Bromwich Albion, Wolverhampton Wanderers

1963–64 – Arsenal, Burnley, Everton, Liverpool, Manchester United, Nottingham Forest, Sheffield Wednesday, Tottenham Hotspur, West Bromwich Albion, Wolverhampton Wanderers

1964–65 – Arsenal, Burnley, Everton, Liverpool, Manchester United, Nottingham Forest, Sheffield Wednesday, Tottenham Hotspur, West Bromwich Albion, Wolverhampton Wanderers

1965–66 – Arsenal, Chelsea, Everton, Liverpool, Manchester United, Nottingham Forest, Sheffield Wednesday, Tottenham Hotspur, Wolverhampton Wanderers

1966–67 – Everton, Liverpool

1967–68 – Manchester United, Tottenham Hotspur

1968–69 – Manchester United

1970–71 – Everton

There have been only two instances of teams below Division Two defeating three Division One sides in one season in the League Cup. Swindon Town did so against Coventry City, Burnley and Arsenal in 1968–69, and Plymouth Argyle against Burnley, Queen's Park Rangers and Birmingham City in 1973–74. The Plymouth case was the only one in which all three ties were won away from home.

The first League Cup goal was scored by Fulham centre-forward Maurice Cook 10 minutes after the start of an away tie in which they lost to Bristol Rovers by 2–1 on 26 September 1960.

When Norwich City won the League Cup in 1961–62 they figured in only six rounds, though the competition comprised seven: one to five inclusive, semi-final, and final. In the fourth round they drew . . . a bye. Ten clubs did not enter the competition that season.

Tranmere Rovers were drawn at home nine times in a row from season 1960–61 to 1964–65 inclusive, and Scunthorpe United eight times on the trot between 1967–68 and 1972–73 inclusive. Millwall were drawn away nine times in succession between 1967–68 and 1972–73 inclusive.

In 1964–65 Workington (Division Three), in 1966–67 Queen's Park Rangers (Division Three), in 1968–69 Swindon (Division Three) and in 1969–70 Oxford United (Division Two) all knocked out teams from all four divisions.

John Boyle (Chelsea in 1964–65), Danny Campbell (West Bromwich Albion, 1965–66), Jimmy Neighbour (Spurs, 1970–71) and Geoff Palmer (Wolves, 1973–74) all figured in League Cup-winning teams in the seasons of their Football League debuts.

Norwich City's manager when they won the trophy in season 1961–62 was Willie Reid, whose entire career in England lasted for only five months. He went to Norwich from St Mirren in December 1961, but left the club the following May and never had any other English service in any capacity, before or after.

Rochdale's Spotland is destined to remain as the only Division Four club ground on which a League Cup final has been played. The first leg of the 1962 final was played there, when they lost to Norwich City, watched by a crowd of 11 123.

The longest tie in the competition involved Swindon Town and Bolton Wanderers in the third round in 1989–90. It took three replays and 450 minutes in all before Swindon won 2–1.

Watford achieved the most impressive turnround of fortune over two legs of a Football League Cup tie in defeating Southampton in the second round in 1980–81. On 26 August they were beaten 4–0 by the Saints at The Dell, but recovered in the second leg on 2 September and were leading 5–1 at the end of 90 minutes. In extra time they added two more goals for a 7–1 win and an aggregate of 7–5.

Record individual performance: Frank Bunn, 6 goals for Oldham Athletic v Scarborough in a third round tie on 25 October 1989.

Record away win: Aldershot 0 Sheffield Wednesday 8 on 3 October 1989 in a second round second leg match. (The first leg had finished Sheffield Wednesday 0 Aldershot 0 and Wednesday had scored only two goals in eight League matches that season!)

League Cup: Gates and goals

Year	Entries	Aggregate attendances	Matches	Average attendance	Top Scorer	Goals
1961	87	1204580	112	10755	Gerry Hitchens (Aston Villa)	11
1962	82	1030534	104	9909	Ray Charnley (Blackpool)	6
1963	80	1029893	102	10097	Ken Leek (Birmingham City)	8
1964	82	945265	104	9089	John Ritchie (Stoke City)	10
1965	82	962802	98	9825	Tony Hateley (Aston Villa)	10
1966	83	1205876	106	11376	Tony Brown (West Bromwich Albion) } Geoff Hurst (West Ham United)	11
1967	90	1394553	118	11818	Rodney Marsh (Queen's Park Rangers)	11
1968	90	1671326	110	15194	John O'Hare (Derby County) } Jim Fryatt (Torquay United)	6
1969	91	2064647	118	17497	Don Rogers (Swindon Town)	7
1970	92	2299819	122	18851	Jeff Astle (West Bromwich Albion) John Byrom (Bolton Wanderers) Francis Lee (Manchester City) Rodney Marsh (Queen's Park Rangers)	5
1971	91	2038809	117	17425	Martin Chivers (Tottenham Hotspur)	7
1972	92	2397154	123	19489	Martin Chivers (Tottenham Hotspur)	7
1973	92	1935474	120	16129	Kevin Keegan (Liverpool) Graham Paddon (Norwich City) Martin Peters (Tottenham Hotspur)	5
1974	92	1722629	132	13050	Francis Lee (Manchester City)	8
1975	92	1901094	127	14969	Lou Macari (Manchester United)	7
1976	92	1841735	140	13155	Dennis Tueart (Manchester City)	8
1977	92	2236636	147	15215	Brian Little (Aston Villa)	10
1978	92	2038295	148	13722	Kenny Dalglish (Liverpool) } Ian Bowyer (Nottingham Forest)	6
1979	92	1827464	139	13148	Garry Birtles (Nottingham Forest) } Bob Latchford (Everton)	6
1980	92	2322866	169	13745	Alan Mayes (Swindon Town)	6
1981	92	2051576	161	12743	Kenny Dalglish (Liverpool)	7
1982	92	1880682	161	11681	Ian Rush (Liverpool)	8
1983	92	1679756	160	10498	Steve Coppell (Manchester United)	6
1984	92	1900491	168	11312	Ian Rush (Liverpool)	8
1985	92	1876429	167	11236	Kerry Dixon (Chelsea)	8
1986	92	1579243	163	9688	Simon Stainrod (Aston Villa)	9
1987	92	1534547	157	9774	Clive Allen (Tottenham Hotspur)	12
1988	92	1541786 †	158	9758 †	Jimmy Quinn (Swindon Town)	8
1989	92	1552780 †	162	9585 †	Nigel Clough (Nottingham Forest)	7
1990	92	1836916 †	168	10934 †	Andy Ritchie (Oldham Athletic)	10

† unofficial figure

Other domestic cup competitions

Associate Members Cup (1984)
Freight Rover Trophy (1985–86)
Sherpa Van Trophy (1986–89)
Leyland-DAF Cup (1990–   )

Year	Final			Attendance	Aggregate attendance	No. of matches	Average attendance
1984	Bournemouth	2–1	Hull City	6 514	135 813	51	2663
1985	Wigan Athletic	3–1	Brentford	34 932	210 279	75	2804
1986	Bristol City	3–0	Bolton Wanderers	55 330	212 114	67	3166
1987	Mansfield Town	1–1	Bristol City	60 050	279 594	81	3452
	(Mansfield Town won 5–4 on penalties)						
1988	Wolverhampton Wanderers	2–0	Burnley	80 841	359 787	82	4388
1989	Bolton Wanderers	4–1	Torquay United	46 513	320 775	81	3960
1990	Tranmere Rovers	2–1	Bristol Rovers	48 402	271 872 †	83	3275

Full Members Cup (1986–87)
Simod Cup (1988–89)
Zenith Data Systems Cup (1990–   )

Year	Final			Attendance	Aggregate attendance	No. of matches	Average attendance
1986	Chelsea	5–4	Manchester City	68 000	180 401	28	6443
1987	Blackburn Rovers	1–0	Charlton Athletic	40 000	218 506	35	6243
1988	Reading	4–1	Luton Town	61 740	293 834	39	7534
1989	Nottingham Forest	4–3	Everton	46 606	297 917	39	7638
1990	Chelsea	1–0	Middlesbrough	76 369	381 010	38	10 027

FA Charity Shield 1974–89 (at Wembley)

Year	Champions		Cup winners	Attendance	Scorers
1974	Leeds United	1–1	Liverpool	67 000	Cherry/Boersma
	(Liverpool won 6–5 on penalties)				
1975	Derby County	2–0	West Ham United	59 000	Hector, McFarland
1976	Liverpool	1–0	Southampton	76 500	Toshack
1977	Liverpool	0–0	Manchester United	82 000	
1978	Nottingham Forest	5–0	Ipswich Town	68 000	O'Neill 2, Withe, Lloyd, Robertson
1979	Liverpool	3–1	Arsenal	92 000	McDermott 2, Dalglish/Sunderland
1980	Liverpool	1–0	West Ham United	90 000	McDermott
1981	Aston Villa	2–2	Tottenham H	92 500	Withe 2/Falco 2
1982	Liverpool	1–0	Tottenham H	82 000	Rush
1983	Liverpool	0–2	Manchester United	92 000	Robson 2
1984	Liverpool	0–1	Everton	100 000	Grobbelaar (o.g.)
1985	Everton	2–0	Manchester United	82 000	Steven, Heath
1986	Liverpool	1–1	Everton	88 000	Rush/Heath
1987	Everton	1–0	Coventry City	88 000	Clarke
1988	Liverpool	2–1	Wimbledon	54 000	Aldridge 2/Fashanu
1989	Arsenal	0–1	Liverpool	64 000	Beardsley

Directory of Scottish League Clubs

Ground	Capacity & record attendance	League career		Honours (domestic) League	Cup

ABERDEEN (1903) Scarlet/scarlet

| Pittodrie Park
Aberdeen
AB2 1QH
110 × 72 yd | 22 568
45 061 v Heart of
Midlothian
Scottish Cup 4th rd
13 March 1954 | 1904–05 Div. 2
1905–17 Div. 1
1919–75 Div. 1.
1975– Prem. | | Premier Div.
Champions 1980,
1984, 1985
Runners-up 1978,
1981, 1982, 1989,
1990
Div. 1 Champions
1955
Runners-up 1911,
1937, 1956, 1971,
1972 | Scottish Cup
Winners 1947,
1970, 1982, 1983,
1984, 1986, 1990
Runners-up 1937,
1953, 1954, 1959,
1967, 1978
League Cup
Winners 1956, 1977,
1986, 1990
Runners-up 1979,
1980, 1988, 1989 |

AIRDRIEONIANS (1878) White/white

| Broomfield Park
Airdrie
Lanarkshire
ML6 9JL
112 × 67 yd | 11 830
24 000 v Heart of
Midlothian
Scottish Cup 4th rd
8 March 1952 | 1894–1903 Div. 2
1903–36 Div. 1
1936–47 Div. 2
1947–48 Div. 1
1948–50 Div. 2
1950–54 Div. 1
1954–55 Div. 2 | 1955–65 Div. 1
1965–66 Div. 2
1966–73 Div. 1
1973–74 Div. 2
1974–80 Div. 1
1980–82 Prem.
1982– Div. 1 | Div. 1 Runners-up
1923, 1924, 1925,
1926, 1980, 1990
Div. 2 Champions
1903, 1955, 1974
Runners-up 1901,
1947, 1950, 1966 | Scottish Cup
Winners 1924
Runners-up 1975 |

ALBION ROVERS (1822) Primrose/red

| Cliftonhill Park
Coatbridge
M15 9XX
100 × 70 yd | 878
27 381 v Rangers
Scottish Cup 2nd rd
8 February 1936 | 1903–15 Div. 2
1919–23 Div. 1
1923–34 Div. 2
1934–37 Div. 1
1937–38 Div. 2
1938–39 Div. 1 | 1946–48 Div. 2
1948–49 Div. 1
1949–89 Div. 2
1989–90 Div. 1
1990– Div. 2 | Div. 2 Champions
1934, 1989
Runners-up 1914,
1938, 1948 | Scottish Cup
Runners-up 1920 |

ALLOA (1883) Gold/black

| Recreation Ground
Alloa FK10
110 × 75 yd | 4 800
13 000 v
Dunfermline Athletic
Scottish Cup
3rd rd replay
26 February 1939 | 1921–22 Div. 2
1922–23 Div. 1
1923–77 Div. 2
1977–78 Div. 1
1978–82 Div. 2
1982–84 Div. 1 | 1984–85 Div. 2
1985–86 Div. 1
1986–89 Div. 2
1989–90 Div. 1
1990– Div. 2 | Div. 2 Champions
1922
Runners-up 1939,
1977, 1982, 1985,
1989 | |

ARBROATH (1878) Maroon/white

| Gayfield Park
Arbroath
DD11 12B
115 × 73 yd | 10 000
13 510 v Rangers
Scottish Cup 3rd rd
23 February 1952 | 1921–35 Div. 2
1935–39 Div. 1
1946–59 Div. 2
1959–60 Div. 1
1960–68 Div. 2 | 1968–69 Div. 1
1969–72 Div. 2
1972–80 Div. 1
1980– Div. 2 | Div. 2 Runners-up
1935, 1959, 1968,
1972 | |

Most League points	goals	Record win	Highest number of League goals for club in total	in a season	Most League appearances for club	Most capped player
						ABERDEEN
61, Div. 1 1935–36	96, Div. 1 1935–36	13–0 v Peterhead Scottish Cup 3rd rd 10 February 1923	Joe Harper 125, 1969–79	Benny Yorston 38, 1929–30	Willie Miller 556, 1973–90	Alex McLeish 72, Scotland
						AIRDRIEONIANS
60, Div. 2 1973–74	108, Div. 2 1961–62	15–1 v Dundee Wanderers Div. 2 1 December 1894		Bert Yarnall 39, 1916–17	Paul Jonquin 523, 1962–79	Jimmy Crapnell 9, Scotland
						ALBION ROVERS
54, Div. 2 1929–30	101, Div. 2 1929–30	12–0 v Airdriehill Scottish Cup 1st rd 3 September 1897	Bunty Weir 105, 1928–31	Jim Renwick 41, 1932–33	Murdy Walls 399, 1921–36	Jock White 1, Scotland
						ALLOA
60, Div. 2 1921–22	92, Div. 2 1961–62	9–2 v Forfar Div. 2 18 March 1933		Wee Crilley 49, 1921–22	Lawrence Haggart 237, 1980–88	Jock Hepburn 1, Scotland
						ARBROATH
57, Div. 2 1966–67	87, Div. 2 1967–68	36–0 v Bon Accord Scottish Cup 12 September 1885	Jimmy Jack 120, 1966–71	Dave Easson 45, 1958–59	Tom Cargill 445, 1966–81	Ned Doig 2, Scotland

Ground	Capacity & record attendance	League career		Honours (domestic) League	Cup

AYR UNITED (1910) White/black

| Somerset Park
Ayr KA8 9NB
111 × 72 yd | 18 500
25 225 v Rangers
Div. 1
13 September 1969 | 1897–1913 Div. 2
1913–25 Div. 1
1925–28 Div. 2
1928–36 Div. 1
1936–37 Div. 2
1937–39 Div. 1
1946–56 Div. 2
1956–57 Div. 1
1957–59 Div. 2 | 1959–61 Div. 1
1961–66 Div. 2
1966–67 Div. 1
1967–69 Div. 2
1969–75 Div. 1
1975–78 Prem.
1978–86 Div. 1
1986–88 Div. 2
1988– Div. 1 | Div. 2 Champions
1912, 1913, 1928,
1937, 1959, 1966,
1988
Runners-up 1911,
1956, 1969 | |

BERWICK RANGERS (1881) Black/gold

| Shielfield Park
Tweedmouth
Berwick-on-Tweed
TD15 2EF
112 × 76 yd | 10 673
13 365 v Rangers
Scottish Cup 1st rd
28 January 1967 | 1955–79 Div. 2
1979–81 Div. 1
1981– Div. 2 | | Div. 2 Champions
1979 | |

BRECHIN CITY (1906) Red/red

| Glebe Park
Brechin DD9 6BJ
110 × 67 yd | 3 491
8 122 v Aberdeen
Scottish Cup 3rd rd
3 February 1973 | 1929–39 Div. 2
1954–83 Div. 2
1983–87 Div. 1 | 1987–90 Div. 2
1990– Div. 1 | Div. 2 Champions
1983, 1990 | |

CELTIC (1888) Green, white/white

| Celtic Park
Parkhead
Glasgow G40 3RD
114 × 75 yd | 60 800
92 000 v Rangers
Div. 1
1 January 1938 | 1890–1975 Div. 1
1975– Premier | | Premier Div.
Champions 1977,
1979, 1981, 1982,
1986, 1988
Runners-up 1976,
1980, 1983, 1984,
1985, 1987
Div. 1 Champions
1893, 1894, 1896,
1898, 1905, 1906,
1907, 1908, 1909,
1910, 1914, 1915,
1916, 1917, 1919,
1922, 1926, 1936,
1938, 1954, 1966,
1967, 1968, 1969,
1970, 1971, 1972,
1973, 1974
Runners-up 16 times | Scottish Cup
Winners 1892, 1899,
1900, 1904, 1907,
1908, 1911, 1912,
1914, 1923, 1925,
1927, 1931, 1933,
1937, 1951, 1954,
1965, 1967, 1969,
1971, 1972, 1974,
1975, 1977, 1980,
1985, 1988, 1989
Runners-up 16 times
League Cup
Winners 1957, 1958,
1966, 1967, 1968,
1969, 1970, 1975,
1983
Runners-up 8 times |

Most League points	goals	Record win	Highest number of League goals for club in total	in a season	Most League appearances for club	Most capped player
						AYR UNITED
61, Div. 2 1987–88	122, Div. 2 1936–37	11–1 v Dumbarton League Cup 13 August 1952		Jimmy Smith 66, 1927–28	Ian McAllister 371, 1977–90	Jim Nisbet 3, Scotland
						BERWICK RANGERS
54, Div. 2 1978–79	83, Div. 2 1961–62	8–1 v Forfar Athletic Div. 2 25 December 1964 v Vale of Leithen Scottish Cup Pr. rd 30 September 1967	Eric Tait 115, 1970–87	Ken Bowron 38, 1963–64	Eric Tait 435, 1970–87	None
						BRECHIN CITY
55, Div. 2 1982–83	80, Div. 2 1957–58	12–1 v Thornhill Scottish Cup 1st rd 28 January 1926		Willie McIntosh 26, 1959–60	David Watt 451, 1975–88	None
						CELTIC
72, Prem. 1987–88	116, Div. 1 1916–17	11–0 v Dundee Div. 1 26 October 1895	Jimmy McGrory 397, 1922–23, 1924–38	Jimmy McGrory 50, 1935–36	Alec McNair 588, 1904–21	Danny McGrain 62, Scotland

Ground	Capacity & record attendance	League career		Honours (domestic) League	Cup

CLYDE (1878) White/black

| Firhill Park Glasgow G20 7AL 106 × 72 yd | 19 937 52 000 v Rangers Div. 1 21 November 1908 | 1891–93 Div. 1 1893–94 Div. 2 1894–1900 Div. 1 1900–1906 Div. 2 1906–24 Div. 1 1924–26 Div. 2 1926–51 Div. 1 1951–52 Div. 2 1952–56 Div. 1 1956–57 Div. 2 1957–61 Div. 1 | 1961–62 Div. 2 1962–63 Div. 1 1963–64 Div. 2 1964–72 Div. 1 1972–73 Div. 2 1973–76 Div. 1 1976–78 Div. 2 1978–80 Div. 1 1980–82 Div. 2 1982– Div. 1 | Div. 2 Champions 1905, 1952, 1957, 1962, 1973, 1978, 1982 Runners-up 1904, 1906, 1926, 1964 | Scottish Cup Winners 1939, 1955, 1958 Runners-up 1910, 1912, 1949 |

CLYDEBANK (1965) White/white

| Kilbowie Park Clydebank G81 2PB 110 × 68 yd | 9 950 14 900 v Hibernian Scottish Cup 1st rd 10 February 1965 | 1966–76 Div. 2 1976–77 Div. 1 1977–78 Prem. | 1978–85 Div. 1 1985–87 Prem. 1987– Div. 1 | Div. 1 Runners-up 1977, 1985 Div. 2 Champions 1976 | |

COWDENBEATH (1881) Blue/white

| Central Park Cowdenbeath KY4 9NP 110 × 70 yd | 4 810 25 586 v Rangers League Cup Quarter final 21 September 1949 | 1905–24 Div. 2 1924–34 Div. 1 1934–70 Div. 2 1970–71 Div. 1 1971– Div. 2 | | Div. 2 Champions 1914, 1915, 1939 Runners-up 1922, 1924, 1970 | |

DUMBARTON (1872) Amber/black

| Boghead Park Dumbarton G82 2JA 110 × 72 yd | 10 700 18 000 v Raith Rovers Scottish Cup 2nd rd 2 March 1957 | 1890–96 Div. 1 1896–97 Div. 2 1906–13 Div. 2 1913–22 Div. 1 1922–54 Div. 2 | 1955–72 Div. 2 1972–84 Div. 1 1984–85 Prem. 1985–88 Div. 1 1988– Div. 2 | Div. 1 Champions 1891 (shared), 1892 Runners-up 1984 Div. 2 Champions 1911, 1972 Runners-up 1908 | Scottish Cup Winners 1883 Runners-up 1881, 1882, 1887, 1891, 1897 |

DUNDEE (1893) Blue/white

| Dens Park Dundee DD1 1RQ 113 × 73 yd | 22 381 43 024 v Rangers Scottish Cup 2nd rd 7 February 1953 | 1893–1917 Div. 1 1919–38 Div. 1 1938–47 Div. 2 1947–75 Div. 1 1975–76 Prem. | 1976–79 Div. 1 1979–80 Prem. 1980–81 Div. 1 1981–90 Prem. 1990– Div. 1 | Div. 1 Champions 1962, 1979 Runners-up 1903, 1907, 1909, 1949, 1981 Div. 2 Champions 1947 | Scottish Cup Winners 1910 Runners-up 1925, 1952, 1964 League Cup Winners 1952, 1953, 1974 Runners-up 1968, 1981 |

Most League points	goals	Record win	Highest number of League goals for club in total	in a season	Most League appearances for club	Most capped player

CLYDE

| 64, Div. 2 1956–57 | 122, Div. 2 1956–57 | 11–1 v Cowdenbeath Div. 2 6 October 1951 | | Bill Boyd 32, 1932–33 | Brian Ahern 428, 1981–81, 1984–87 | Tommy Ring 12, Scotland |

CLYDEBANK

| 58, Div. 1 1976–77 | 89, Div. 1 1976–77 | 8–1 v Arbroath Div. 1 3 January 1977 | Blair Millar 84, 1977–83 | Blair Millar 28, 1978–79 | Jim Fallon 620, 1968–86 | None |

COWDENBEATH

| 60, Div. 2 1938–39 | 120, Div. 2 1938–39 | 12–0 v St Johnstone Scottish Cup 1st rd 21 January 1928 | | Willie Devlin 40, 1925–26 | | Jim Paterson 3, Scotland |

DUMBARTON

| 52, Div. 2 1971–72 | 101, Div. 2 1956–57 | 13–1 v Kirkintilloch Central Scottish Cup 1st rd 1 September 1888 | | Kenny Wilson 38, 1971–72 | | John Lindsay 8, Scotland James McAulay 8, Scotland |

DUNDEE

| 57, Div. 1 1977–78 | 113, Div. 2 1946–47 | 10–0 v Alloa Div. 2 8 March 1947 v Dunfermline Div. 2 22 March 1947 | Alan Gilzean 113, 1960–64 | Dave Halliday 38, 1923–24 | Doug Cowie 341, 1945–61 | Alex Hamilton 24, Scotland |

Ground	Capacity & record attendance	League career		Honours (domestic) League	Cup

DUNDEE UNITED (1910) Tangerine/black

| Tannadice Park Dundee DD3 7JW 109×70 yd | 22 316 28 000 v Barcelona Fairs Cup 2nd rd 16 November 1966 | 1910–15 Div. 2 1923–25 Div. 2 1925–27 Div. 1 1927–29 Div. 2 1929–30 Div. 1 | 1930–31 Div. 2 1931–32 Div. 1 1932–60 Div. 2 1960–75 Div. 1 1975– Prem. | Premier Div. Champions 1983 Div. 2 Champions 1925, 1929 Runners-up 1931, 1960 | Scottish Cup Runners-up 1974, 1981, 1985, 1987, 1988 League Cup Winners 1980, 1981 Runners-up 1982, 1985 |

DUNFERMLINE ATHLETIC (1885) Black, white/black

| East End Park Dunfermline Fife KY12 7RB 115×71 yd | 19 320 27 816 v Celtic Div. 1 30 April 1968 | 1912–15 Div. 2 1921–26 Div. 2 1926–28 Div. 1 1928–34 Div. 2 1934–37 Div. 1 1937–55 Div. 1 1955–57 Div. 1 1957–58 Div. 2 1958–72 Div. 1 | 1972–73 Div. 2 1973–76 Div. 1 1976–79 Div. 2 1979–83 Div. 1 1983–86 Div. 2 1986–87 Div. 1 1987–88 Prem. 1988–89 Div. 1 1989– Prem. | Div. 1 Champions 1989 Runners-up 1987 Div. 2 Champions 1926, 1986 Runners-up 1913, 1934, 1955, 1958, 1973, 1979 | Scottish Cup Winners 1961, 1968 Runners-up 1965 League Cup Runners-up 1950 |

EAST FIFE (1903) Black, gold/black

| Bayview Park Methil Fife KY8 3AG 110×71 yd | 5 150 22 515 v Raith Rovers Div. 1 2 January 1950 | 1921–30 Div. 2 1930–31 Div. 1 1931–48 Div. 2 1948–58 Div. 1 1958–71 Div. 2 1971–74 Div. 1 | 1974–75 Div. 2 1975–78 Div. 1 1978–84 Div. 2 1984–88 Div. 1 1988– Div. 2 | Div. 2 Champions 1948 Runners-up 1930, 1971, 1984 | Scottish Cup Winners 1938 Runners-up 1927, 1950 League Cup Winners 1948, 1950, 1954 |

EAST STIRLINGSHIRE (1881) Black, white/black

| Firs Park Falkirk FK2 7AY 110×75 yd | 6 000 11 500 v Hibernian Scottish Cup 2nd rd 10 February 1969 | 1900–15 Div. 2 1921–23 Div. 2 1924–39 Div. 2 1955–63 Div. 2 | 1963–64 Div. 1 1964–80 Div. 2 1980–82 Div. 1 1982– Div. 2 | Div. 2 Champions 1932 Runners-up 1963, 1980 | |

FALKIRK (1876) Blue/white

| Brockville Park Falkirk FK1 5AX 110×70 yd | 18 000 23 100 v Celtic Scottish Cup 3rd rd 21 February 1953 | 1902–05 Div. 2 1905–35 Div. 1 1935–36 Div. 2 1936–51 Div. 1 1951–52 Div. 2 1952–59 Div. 1 1959–61 Div. 2 1961–69 Div. 1 | 1969–70 Div. 2 1970–74 Div. 1 1974–75 Div. 2 1975–77 Div. 1 1977–80 Div. 2 1980–86 Div. 1 1986–88 Prem. 1988– Div. 1 | Div. 1 Runners-up 1908, 1910, 1986, 1989 Div. 2 Champions 1936, 1970, 1975, 1980 Runners-up 1905, 1952, 1961 | Scottish Cup Winners 1913, 1957 League Cup Runners-up 1948 |

Most League points	goals	Record win	Highest number of League goals for club in total	in a season	Most League appearances for club	Most capped player
						DUNDEE UNITED
60, Prem. 1986–87	105, Div. 2 1934–35	14–0 v Nithsdale Wanderers Scottish Cup 1st rd 17 January 1931	Peter McKay 158, 1947–54	John Coyle 41, 1955–56	Hamish McAlpine 625, 1969–85	Maurice Malpas 37, Scotland
						DUNFERMLINE ATHLETIC
59, Div. 2 1925–26	120, Div. 2 1957–58	11–2 v Stenhousemuir Div. 2 27 September 1930	Charles Dickson 154, 1955–64	Bobby Skinner 55, 1925–26	Bobby Robertson 360, 1977–88	Andy Wilson 6, Scotland
						EAST FIFE
57, Div. 2 1929–30	114, Div. 2 1929–30	13–2 v Edinburgh City Div. 2 11 December 1937		Jock Wood 41, 1926–27 Henry Morris 41, 1947–48	David Clarke 517, 1968–86	George Aitken 5, Scotland
						EAST STIRLINGSHIRE
55, Div. 2 1931–32	111, Div. 2 1931–32	10–1 v Stenhousemuir Scottish Cup 1st rd 1 September 1888		Malcolm Morrison 36, 1938–39		Humphrey Jones 5, Wales
						FALKIRK
59, Div. 2 1935–36	132, Div. 2 1935–36	12–1 v Laurieston Scottish Cup 2nd rd 23 March 1893		Evelyn Morrison 43, 1928–29		Alex Parker 14, Scotland

Ground	Capacity & record attendance	League career		Honours (domestic) League	Cup

FORFAR ATHLETIC (1884) Blue/white

| Station Park Forfar DD8 1DA 118 × 69 yd | 8 732 10 780 v Rangers Scottish Cup 2nd rd 2 February 1970 | 1921–25 Div. 2 1926–39 Div. 2 1949–84 Div. 2 1984– Div. 1 | | Div. 2 Champions 1984 | |

HAMILTON ACADEMICAL (1875) Red, white/white

| Douglas Park Hamilton ML3 0DF 110 × 70 yd | 10 500 28 690 v Heart of Midlothian Scottish Cup 3rd rd 3 March 1937 | 1897–1906 Div. 2 1906–47 Div. 1 1947–53 Div. 2 1953–54 Div. 1 1954–65 Div. 2 1965–66 Div. 1 | 1966–75 Div. 2 1975–86 Div. 1 1986–87 Prem. 1987–88 Div. 1 1988–89 Prem. 1989– Div. 1 | Div. 1 Champions 1986, 1988 Div. 2 Champions 1904 Runners-up 1953, 1965 | Scottish Cup Runners-up 1911, 1935 |

HEART OF MIDLOTHIAN (1874) Maroon/white

| Tynecastle Park Edinburgh EH11 2NL 110 × 74 yd | 29 000 53 496 v Rangers Scottish Cup 3rd rd 13 February 1932 | 1890–1975 Div. 1 1975–77 Prem. 1977–78 Div. 1 1978–79 Prem. | 1979–80 Div. 1 1980–81 Prem. 1981–83 Div. 1 1983– Prem. | Premier Div. Runners-up 1986, 1988 Div. 1 Champions 1895, 1897, 1958, 1960, 1980 Runners-up 1894, 1899, 1904, 1906, 1915, 1938, 1954, 1957, 1959, 1965, 1978, 1983 | Scottish Cup Winners 1891, 1896, 1901, 1906, 1956 Runners-up 1903, 1907, 1968, 1976, 1986 League Cup Winners 1955, 1959, 1960, 1963 Runners-up 1962 |

HIBERNIAN (1875) Green/white

| Easter Road Park Edinburgh EH7 5QG 112 × 74 yd | 27 156 65 860 v Heart of Midlothian Div. 1 2 January 1950 | 1893–95 Div. 2 1895–1931 Div. 1 1931–33 Div. 2 1933–75 Div. 1 | 1975–80 Prem. 1980–81 Div. 1 1981– Prem. | Div. 1 Champions 1903, 1948, 1951, 1952, 1981 Runners-up 1897, 1947, 1950, 1953, 1974, 1975 Div. 2 Champions 1894, 1895, 1933 | Scottish Cup Winners 1887, 1902 Runners-up 1896, 1914, 1923, 1924, 1947, 1958, 1972, 1979 League Cup Winners 1973 Runners-up 1951, 1969, 1975 |

KILMARNOCK (1869) Blue, white/blue

| Rugby Park Kilmarnock KA1 2DP 115 × 73 yd | 17 528 34 246 v Rangers League Cup Qualifying rd August 1963 | 1895–99 Div. 2 1899–1947 Div. 1 1947–54 Div. 2 1954–73 Div. 1 1973–74 Div. 2 1974–76 Div. 1 1976–77 Prem. | 1977–79 Div. 1 1979–81 Prem. 1981–82 Div. 1 1982–83 Prem. 1983–89 Div. 1 1989–90 Div. 2 1990– Div. 1 | Div. 1 Champions 1965 Runners-up 1960, 1961, 1963, 1964, 1976, 1979, 1982 Div. 2 Champions 1898, 1899 Runners-up 1954, 1974 | Scottish Cup Winners 1920, 1929 Runners-up 1898, 1932, 1938, 1957, 1960 League Cup Runners-up 1953, 1961, 1963 |

Most League points	goals	Record win	Highest number of League goals for club in total	in a season	Most League appearances for club	Most capped player

FORFAR ATHLETIC

Most League points	goals	Record win	Highest number of League goals for club in total	in a season	Most League appearances for club	Most capped player
63, Div. 2 1983-84	98, Div. 2 1929-30	14-1 v Lindertis Scottish Cup 1st rd 1 September 1888		Davie Kilgour 45, 1929-30	Alex Brash 376, 1974-86	None

HAMILTON ACADEMICAL

Most League points	goals	Record win	Highest number of League goals for club in total	in a season	Most League appearances for club	Most capped player
56, Div. 1 1985-86, 1987-88	91, Div. 1 1936-37 Div. 2 1959-60	10-2 v Cowdenbeath Div. 1 15 October 1932	David Wilson 246, 1928-39	David Wilson 34, 1936-37	Rikki Ferguson 447, 1974-88	Colin Miller 5, Canada

HEART OF MIDLOTHIAN

Most League points	goals	Record win	Highest number of League goals for club in total	in a season	Most League appearances for club	Most capped player
62, Div. 1 1957-58 Premier 1987-88	132, Div. 1 1957-58	15-0 v King's Park Scottish Cup 13 March 1937	Jimmy Wardhaugh 206, 1946-59	Barney Battles 44, 1930-31		Bobby Walker 29, Scotland

HIBERNIAN

Most League points	goals	Record win	Highest number of League goals for club in total	in a season	Most League appearances for club	Most capped player
57, Div. 1 1980-81	106, Div. 1 1959-60	15-1 v Peebles Rovers Scottish Cup 2nd rd 11 February 1961	Lawrie Reilly 185, 1946-58	Joe Baker 42, 1959-60	Arthur Duncan 446, 1970-84	Lawrie Reilly 38, Scotland

KILMARNOCK

Most League points	goals	Record win	Highest number of League goals for club in total	in a season	Most League appearances for club	Most capped player
58, Div. 2 1973-74	96, Div. 2 1973-74	13-2 v Saltcoats Victoria Scottish Cup 2nd rd 12 September 1896	Willie Culley 148, 1912-23	Peerie Cunningham 35, 1927-28	Alan Robertson 466, 1972-88	Joe Nibloe 11, Scotland

Ground	Capacity & record attendance	League career		Honours (domestic) League	Cup

MEADOWBANK THISTLE (1974) Amber/black

| Meadowbank Stadium Edinburgh EH7 6AE 105 × 72 yd | 16 500 4 000 v Albion Rovers League Cup Qualifying 9 September 1974 | 1974–83 Div. 2 1983–85 Div. 1 | 1985–87 Div. 2 1987–89 Div. 1 | Div. 1 Runners-up 1988 Div. 2 Champions 1987 Runners-up 1983 | |

MONTROSE (1879) White/white

| Links Park Montrose DD10 8QD 113 × 70 yd | 6 500 8 983 v Dundee Scottish Cup 3rd rd 17 March 1973 | 1929–39 Div. 2 1955–75 Div. 2 1975–79 Div. 1 | 1979–85 Div. 2 1985–87 Div. 1 1978– Div. 2 | Div. 2 Champions 1985 | |

MORTON (1874) Blue, white/white

| Cappielow Park Greenock PA15 2TY 110 × 71 yd | 16 577 23 500 v Rangers Scottish Cup 3rd rd 21 February 1953 | 1893–1900 Div. 2 1900–27 Div. 1 1927–29 Div. 2 1929–33 Div. 1 1933–37 Div. 2 1937–38 Div. 1 1938–39 Div. 2 1946–49 Div. 1 1949–50 Div. 2 1950–52 Div. 1 | 1952–64 Div. 2 1964–66 Div. 1 1966–67 Div. 2 1967–78 Div. 1 1978–83 Prem. 1983–84 Div. 1 1984–85 Prem. 1985–87 Div. 1 1987–88 Prem. 1988– Div. 1 | Div. 1 Champions 1978, 1984, 1987 Runners-up 1917 Div. 2 Champions 1950, 1964, 1967 | Scottish Cup Winners 1922 Runners-up 1948 League Cup Runners-up 1964 |

MOTHERWELL (1886) Amber, claret/amber

| Fir Park Motherwell ML1 2QN 110 × 75 yd | 22 400 35 632 v Rangers Scottish Cup 4th rd replay 12 March 1952 | 1893–1903 Div. 2 1903–53 Div. 1 1953–54 Div. 2 1954–68 Div. 1 1968–69 Div. 2 1969–75 Div. 1 | 1957–79 Prem. 1979–82 Div. 1 1982–84 Prem. 1984–85 Div. 1 1985– Prem. | Div. 1 Champions 1932, 1982, 1984 Runners-up 1927, 1930, 1933, 1934 Div. 2 Champions 1954, 1969 Runners-up 1895, 1903 | Scottish Cup Winners 1952 Runners-up 1931, 1933, 1939, 1951 League Cup Winners 1951 Runners-up 1955 |

PARTICK THISTLE (1876) Red, yellow/red

| Firhill Park Glasgow G20 7AL 106 × 72 yd | 19 937 49 838 v Rangers Div. 1 18 February 1922 | 1893–97 Div. 2 1897–99 Div. 1 1899–1900 Div. 2 1900–01 Div. 1 1901–02 Div. 2 | 1902–70 Div. 1 1970–71 Div. 2 1971–76 Div. 1 1976–82 Prem. 1982– Div. 1 | Div. 1 Champions 1976 Div. 2 Champions 1897, 1900, 1971 Runners-up 1902 | Scottish Cup Winners 1921 Runners-up 1930 League Cup Winners 1972 Runners-up 1954, 1957, 1959 |

Most League points	goals	Record win	Highest number of League goals for club in total	in a season	Most League appearances for club	Most capped player

MEADOWBANK THISTLE

| 55, Div. 2 1986–87 | 70, Div. 1 1987–88 | 6–1 v Stenhousemuir Div. 2 6 February 1982 | Adrian Sprott 63, 1980–85 | John McGachie 21, 1986–87 | Walter Boyd 408, 1979–88 | None |

MONTROSE

| 53, Div. 2 1974–75, 1984–85 | 82, Div. 2 1938–39, 1972–73 | 12–0 v Vale of Leithen Scottish Cup 2nd rd 4 January 1975 | | Brian Third 29, 1972–73 | | Alex Keillor 2, Scotland |

MORTON

| 69, Div. 2 1966–67 | 135, Div. 2 1963–64 | 11–0 v Carfin Shamrock Scottish Cup 1st rd 13 November 1886 | | Allan McGraw 41, 1963–64 | David Hayes 358, 1969–84 | Jimmy Cowan 25, Scotland |

MOTHERWELL

| 66, Div. 1 1931–32 | 119, Div. 1 1931–32 | 12–1 v Dundee United Div. 2 23 January 1954 | Hugh Ferguson 283, 1916–25 | Willie McFadyen 52, 1931–32 | Bobby Ferrier 626, 1918–37 | George Stevenson 12, Scotland |

PARTICK THISTLE

| 56, Div. 2 1970–71 | 91, Div. 1 1928–29 | 16–0 v Royal Albert Scottish Cup 17 January 1931 | | Alec Hair 41, 1926–27 | Alan Rough 410, 1969–82 | Alan Rough 51, Scotland |

Ground	Capacity & record attendance	League career		Honours (domestic) League	Cup

QUEEN OF THE SOUTH (1919) Blue/white

| Palmerston Park Dumfries DG2 9BA 112 × 72 yd | 12 000 24 500 v Heart of Midlothian Scottish Cup 3rd rd 23 February 1952 | 1925–33 Div. 2 1933–50 Div. 1 1950–51 Div. 2 1951–59 Div. 1 1959–62 Div. 2 1962–64 Div. 1 1964–75 Div. 2 | 1975–79 Div. 1 1979–81 Div. 2 1981–82 Div. 1 1982–86 Div. 2 1986–89 Div. 1 1989–   Div. 2 | Div. 2 Champions 1951 Runners-up 1933, 1962, 1975, 1981, 1986 | |

QUEEN'S PARK (1867) Black, white/white

| Hampden Park Glasgow G42 2BA 115 × 75 yd | 73 172 95 772 v Rangers Scottish Cup 1st rd 18 January 1930 | 1900–22 Div. 1 1922–23 Div. 2 1923–48 Div. 1 1948–56 Div. 2 | 1956–58 Div. 1 1958–81 Div. 2 1981–83 Div. 1 1983–   Div. 2 | Div. 2 Champions 1923, 1956, 1981 | Scottish Cup Winners 1874, 1875, 1876, 1880, 1881, 1882, 1884, 1886, 1890, 1893 Runners-up 1892, 1900 English FA Cup Runners-up 1884, 1885 |

RAITH ROVERS (1883) Blue/white

| Stark's Park Kirkcaldy KY1 1SA 113 × 67 yd | 9 500 31 306 v Heart of Midlothian Scottish Cup 2nd rd 7 February 1953 | 1902–10 Div. 2 1910–17 Div. 1 1919–26 Div. 1 1926–27 Div. 2 1927–29 Div. 1 1929–38 Div. 2 1938–39 Div. 1 1946–49 Div. 2 1949–63 Div. 1 | 1963–67 Div. 2 1967–70 Div. 1 1970–76 Div. 2 1976–77 Div. 1 1977–78 Div. 2 1978–84 Div. 1 1984–87 Div. 2 1987–   Div. 1 | Div. 2 Champions 1908, 1910 (shared), 1938, 1949 Runners-up 1909, 1927, 1967, 1976, 1978, 1987 | Scottish Cup Runners-up 1913 League Cup Runners-up 1949 |

RANGERS (1873) Blue/white

| Ibrox Stadium Glasgow G51 2XD 115 × 78 yd | 44 096 118 567 v Celtic Div 1 2 January 1939 | 1890–1975 Div. 1 1975–   Premier | | Premier Div. Champions 1976, 1978, 1987, 1989, 1990 Runners-up 1977, 1979 Div. 1 Champions 1891 (shared), 1899, 1900, 1901, 1902, 1911, 1912, 1913, 1918, 1920, 1921, 1923, 1924, 1925, 1927, 1928, 1929–31, 1933–35, 1937, 1939, 1947, 1949, 1950, 1953, 1956, 1957, 1959, 1961, 1963, 1964, 1975 Runners-up 21 times | Scottish Cup Winners 1894, 1897, 1898, 1903, 1928, 1930, 1932, 1934, 1935, 1936, 1948, 1949, 1950, 1953, 1960, 1962, 1963, 1964, 1966, 1973, 1976, 1978, 1979, 1981 Runners-up 15 times League Cup Winners 1947, 1949, 1961, 1962, 1964, 1965, 1971, 1976, 1978, 1979, 1982, 1984, 1985, 1987, 1988, 1989 Runners-up 7 times |

Most League points	goals	Record win	Highest number of League goals for club in total	in a season	Most League appearances for club	Most capped player
QUEEN OF THE SOUTH						
55, Div. 2 1985–86	99, Div. 2 1931–32	11–1 v Stranraer Scottish Cup 16 January 1932		Jimmy Gray 33, 1927–28	Allan Ball 619, 1963–82	Billy Houliston 3, Scotland
QUEEN'S PARK						
57, Div. 2 1922–23	100, Div. 1 1928–29	16–0 v St Peter's Scottish Cup 1st rd 12 September 1885	J. B. McAlpine 163, 1919–34	Willie Martin 30, 1937–38	J. B. McAlpine 473, 1919–34	Walter Arnott 14, Scotland
RAITH ROVERS						
59, Div. 2 1937–38	142, Div. 2 1937–38	10–1 v Coldstream Scottish Cup 2nd rd 13 March 1954		Norman Haywood 38, 1937–38		Dave Morris 6, Scotland
RANGERS						
76, Div. 1 1920–21	118, Div. 1 1931–32, 1933–34	14–2 v Whitehill Scottish Cup 2nd rd 33 September 1883; v Blairgowrie Scottish Cup 1st rd 20 January 1934	Bob McPhail 233, 1927–39	Sam English 44, 1931–32	John Greig 496, 1962–78	George Young 53, Scotland

Ground	Capacity & record attendance	League career		Honours (domestic) League	Cup

ST JOHNSTONE (1884) Blue/white

Ground	Capacity & record attendance	League career		Honours (domestic) League	Cup
McDiarmid Park Perth PH1 2SJ 115×75 yd	10 169 29 972 v Dundee Scottish Cup 2nd rd 10 February 1952	1911–15 Div. 2 1921–24 Div. 2 1924–30 Div. 1 1930–32 Div. 2 1932–39 Div. 1 1946–60 Div. 2 1960–62 Div. 1 1962–63 Div. 2	1963–75 Div. 1 1975–76 Prem. 1976–83 Div. 1 1983–84 Prem. 1984–85 Div. 1 1985–88 Div. 2 1988–90 Div. 1 1990– Prem.	Div. 1 Champions 1983 Div. 2 Champions 1924, 1960, 1963 Runners-up 1932, 1988	League Cup Runners-up 1970

ST MIRREN (1876) Black, white/black

Ground	Capacity & record attendance	League career		Honours (domestic) League	Cup
St Mirren Park Paisley PA3 2EJ 112×73 yd	25 241 47 438 v Celtic Scottish Cup 4th rd 7 March 1925	1890–1935 Div. 1 1935–36 Div. 2 1936–67 Div. 1 1967–68 Div. 2	1968–71 Div. 1 1971–75 Div. 2 1975–77 Div. 1 1977– Prem.	Div. 1 Champions 1977 Div. 2 Champions 1968 Runners-up 1936	Scottish Cup Winners 1926, 1959, 1987 Runners-up 1908, 1934, 1962 League Cup Runners-up 1956

STENHOUSEMUIR (1884) Maroon/white

Ground	Capacity & record attendance	League career		Honours (domestic) League	Cup
Ochilview Park Larbert FK5 4QL 113×78 yd	4 000 12 500 v East Fife Scottish Cup 4th rd 11 March 1950	1921– Div. 2		Highest League placing 3rd, Div. 2, 1959, 1961	

STIRLING ALBION (1945) Red/white

Ground	Capacity & record attendance	League career		Honours (domestic) League	Cup
Annfield Park Stirling S7K 83D 110×74 yd	12 000 26 400 v Celtic Scottish Cup 4th rd 14 March 1959	1947–49 Div. 2 1949–50 Div. 1 1950–51 Div. 2 1951–52 Div. 1 1952–53 Div. 2 1953–56 Div. 1 1956–58 Div. 2 1958–60 Div. 1	1960–61 Div. 2 1961–62 Div. 1 1962–65 Div. 2 1965–68 Div. 1 1968–77 Div. 2 1977–81 Div. 1 1981– Div. 2	Div. 2 Champions 1953, 1958, 1961, 1965, 1977 Runners-up 1949, 1951	

STRANRAER (1870) Blue/amber

Ground	Capacity & record attendance	League career		Honours (domestic) League	Cup
Stair Park Stranraer 110×70 yd	4 000 6 500 v Rangers Scottish Cup 1st rd 24 January 1948	1955– Div. 2		Highest League placing 4th, Div. 2, 1961, 1977	

Most League points	goals	Record win	Highest number of League goals for club in total	in a season	Most League appearances for club	Most capped player
						ST JOHNSTONE
59, Div. 2 1987–88	102, Div. 2 1931–32	8–1 v Partick Thistle League Cup 16 August 1969	John Brogan 114, 1977–83	Jimmy Benson 36, 1931–32		Sandy McLaren 5, Scotland
						ST MIRREN
62, Div. 2 1967–68 Div. 1 1976–77	114, Div. 2 1935–36	15–0 v Glasgow University Scottish Cup 1st rd 10 January 1960		Dunky Walker 45, 1921–22	Billy Abercromby 287, 1976–87	Iain Munro 7, Scotland Billy Thomson 7, Scotland
						STENHOUSEMUIR
50, Div. 2 1960–61	99, Div. 2 1960–61	9–2 v Dundee United Div. 2 17 April 1937		Evelyn Morrison 29, 1927–28 Bobby Murray 29, 1936–37		None
						STIRLING ALBION
59, Div. 2 1964–65	105, Div. 2 1957–58	20–0 v Selkirk Scottish Cup 1st rd 8 December 1984	Billy Steele 129, 1971–83	Joe Hughes 29, 1969–70	Matt McPhee 504, 1967–81	None
						STRANRAER
46, Div. 2 1976–77	83, Div. 2 1960–61	7–0 v Brechin City Div. 2 6 February 1965		Derek Frye 27, 1977–78	Dan McDonald 256, 1978–85	None

Scottish League Champions 1891–1990

Season	Champions	P	W	D	L	F	A	Pts	Margin
1890–91	Dumbarton	18	13	3	2	61	21	29	8
	Rangers	18	13	3	2	58	25	29	8
1891–92	Dumbarton	22	18	1	3	79	28	37	2
1892–93	Celtic	18	14	1	3	54	25	29	1
1893–94	Celtic	18	14	1	3	53	32	29	3
1894–95	Hearts	18	15	1	2	50	18	31	5
1895–96	Celtic	18	15	0	3	64	25	30	4
1896–97	Hearts	18	13	2	3	47	22	28	2
1897–98	Celtic	18	15	3	0	56	13	33	4
1898–99	Rangers	18	18	0	0	79	18	36	10
1899–1900	Rangers	18	15	2	1	69	27	32	7
1900–01	Rangers	20	17	1	2	60	25	35	6
1901–02	Rangers	18	13	2	3	43	29	28	2
1902–03	Hibernian	22	16	5	1	48	18	37	6
1903–04	Third Lanark	26	20	3	3	61	26	43	4
1904–05	Celtic	26	19	3	4	68	31	41	p-o
1905–06	Celtic	30	24	1	5	76	19	49	6
1906–07	Celtic	34	23	9	2	80	30	55	7
1907–08	Celtic	34	24	7	3	86	27	55	4
1908–09	Celtic	34	23	5	6	71	24	51	1
1909–10	Celtic	34	24	6	4	63	22	54	2
1910–11	Rangers	34	23	6	5	90	34	52	4
1911–12	Rangers	34	24	3	7	86	34	51	6
1912–13	Rangers	34	24	5	5	76	41	53	4
1913–14	Celtic	38	30	5	3	81	14	65	6
1914–15	Celtic	38	30	5	3	91	25	65	4
1915–16	Celtic	38	32	3	3	116	23	67	11
1916–17	Celtic	38	27	10	1	77	17	64	10
1917–18	Rangers	34	25	6	3	66	24	56	1
1918–19	Celtic	34	26	6	2	70	22	58	1
1919–20	Rangers	42	31	9	2	106	25	71	3
1920–21	Rangers	42	35	6	1	91	24	76	10
1921–22	Celtic	42	27	13	2	83	20	67	1
1922–23	Rangers	38	23	9	6	67	29	55	5
1923–24	Rangers	38	25	9	4	72	22	59	9
1924–25	Rangers	38	25	10	3	77	27	60	3
1925–26	Celtic	38	25	8	5	97	40	58	8
1926–27	Rangers	38	23	10	5	85	41	56	5
1927–28	Rangers	38	26	8	4	109	36	60	5
1928–29	Rangers	38	30	7	1	107	32	67	16
1929–30	Rangers	38	28	4	6	94	32	60	5
1930–31	Rangers	38	27	6	5	96	29	60	2
1931–32	Motherwell	38	30	6	2	119	31	66	5
1932–33	Rangers	38	26	10	2	113	43	62	3
1933–34	Rangers	38	30	6	2	118	41	66	4
1934–35	Rangers	38	25	5	8	96	46	55	3
1935–36	Celtic	38	32	2	4	115	33	66	5
1936–37	Rangers	38	26	9	3	88	32	61	7
1937–38	Celtic	38	27	7	4	114	42	61	3
1938–39	Rangers	38	25	9	4	112	55	59	11

1939–46 No national competition; regional leagues in operation

Season	Champions	P	W	D	L	F	A	Pts	Margin
1946–47	Rangers	30	21	4	5	76	26	46	2
1947–48	Hibernian	30	22	4	4	86	27	48	2
1948–49	Rangers	30	20	6	4	63	32	46	1

Season	Champions	P	W	D	L	F	A	Pts	Margin
1949–50	Rangers	30	22	6	2	58	26	50	1
1950–51	Hibernian	30	22	4	4	78	26	48	10
1951–52	Hibernian	30	20	5	5	92	36	45	4
1952–53	Rangers	30	18	7	5	80	39	43	gl.av.
1953–54	Celtic	30	20	3	7	72	29	43	5
1954–55	Aberdeen	30	24	1	5	73	26	49	3
1955–56	Rangers	34	22	8	4	85	27	52	6
1956–57	Rangers	34	26	3	5	96	48	55	2
1957–58	Hearts	34	29	4	1	132	29	62	13
1958–59	Rangers	34	21	8	5	92	51	50	2
1959–60	Hearts	34	23	8	3	102	51	54	4
1960–61	Rangers	34	23	5	6	88	46	51	1
1961–62	Dundee	34	25	4	5	80	46	54	3
1962–63	Rangers	34	25	7	2	94	28	57	9
1963–64	Rangers	34	25	5	4	85	31	55	6
1964–65	Kilmarnock	34	22	6	6	62	33	50	gl.av.
1965–66	Celtic	34	27	3	4	106	30	57	2
1966–67	Celtic	34	26	6	2	111	33	58	3
1967–68	Celtic	34	30	3	1	106	24	63	2
1968–69	Celtic	34	23	8	3	89	32	54	5
1969–70	Celtic	34	27	3	4	96	33	57	12
1970–71	Celtic	34	25	6	3	89	23	56	2
1971–72	Celtic	34	28	4	2	96	28	60	10
1972–73	Celtic	34	26	5	3	93	28	57	1
1973–74	Celtic	34	23	7	4	82	27	53	4
1974–75	Rangers	34	25	6	3	86	33	56	7
*1975–76	Rangers	36	23	8	5	60	24	54	6
1976–77	Celtic	36	23	9	4	79	39	55	9
1977–78	Rangers	36	24	7	5	76	39	55	2
1978–79	Celtic	36	21	6	9	61	37	48	3
1979–80	Aberdeen	36	19	10	7	68	36	48	1
1980–81	Celtic	36	26	4	6	84	37	56	7
1981–82	Celtic	36	24	7	5	79	33	55	2
1982–83	Dundee Utd	36	24	8	4	90	35	56	1
1983–84	Aberdeen	36	25	7	4	78	21	57	7
1984–85	Aberdeen	36	27	5	4	89	26	59	7
1985–86	Celtic	36	20	10	6	67	38	50	gl.dif.
1986–87	Rangers	44	31	7	6	85	23	69	6
1987–88	Celtic	44	31	10	3	79	23	72	10
1988–89	Rangers	36	26	4	6	62	26	56	6
1989–90	Rangers	36	20	11	5	48	19	51	7

* Premier Division introduced

Scottish League facts

Most wins in a season

Aberdeen won 27 of their 36 Premier Division matches in 1984–85. They won one more game away than at home and retained their championship title. Their worst spell came in December–January when in four games, they picked up just two points from draws. Overall they lost just four times.

Rangers won 31 of their 44 Premier Division matches in 1986–87. At the turn of the year they trailed Celtic by seven points but finished strongly to overtake their rivals and take the title. From the end of November until the end of March they were unbeaten in 19 games. During this period goalkeeper Chris Woods was unbeaten in 1095 minutes of League football.

Celtic won 31 of their 44 Premier Division matches in 1987–88. They lost just three times and dropped 16 points overall. From the middle of October until early April they went 26 games without defeat. They failed to score on only three occasions and were never headed in the table after the end of November.

Rangers' English international goalkeeper Chris Woods celebrates his side's 1986-7 Championship success, following a 1-1 draw at Aberdeen. Woods set a British goalkeeping record of 1196 minutes unbeaten in League and Cup games during this season (Allsport)

Rangers won 35 of their 42 Division One matches in 1920–21. They began with a 4–1 win over Airdrieonians and were undefeated in their first 23 games, dropping only two points (at Aberdeen and Ayr) before losing 2–0 at home to Celtic in their only defeat. From the end of September until mid-December they had a winning run of 12 matches.

Morton won 33 of their 38 Division Two matches in 1966–67. They finished as champions, having lost only two matches and conceded only 20 goals, the fewest on record in the division. Their 69 points was another Division Two record.

Fewest wins in a season

St Johnstone achieved only three wins in 36 Premier Division matches in 1975-76. From early October to mid-April they completed 27 games without a win. They scored just 29 goals, failed to score in 17 matches, and were relegated.

Kilmarnock achieved only three wins in 36 Premier Division matches in 1982–83. Only twice did they manage to score more than two goals in a game in a total of 28, and their defence conceded 91 goals including an 8–1 and a 7–0 defeat.

Vale of Leven failed to win any of their 22 Division One matches in 1891–92. They achieved only five points and were not re-elected.

Ayr United achieved only one win in 34 Division One matches in 1966–67. That solitary success came courtesy of a penalty scored by centre-half Eddie Monan at home to St Johnstone on 8 April.

East Stirling won only one of their 22 Division Two matches in 1905–06. They did manage to draw 10 times but finished bottom. Their only victory was achieved on 11 November when they won 4–2 at Ayr.

Forfar Athletic achieved only one win in 38 Division Two matches in 1974–75. They finished 12 points behind their nearest rivals at the bottom of the table. Only one point came from their last 15 games.

Most defeats in a single season

Morton suffered 29 defeats in 36 Premier Division matches in 1984–85. Unusually, their number of wins (five) outnumbered the drawn games (two) but they suffered 13 consecutive defeats and also conceded a record 100 goals. They first hit the bottom on 29 September and remained there for the rest of the season.

St Mirren suffered 31 defeats in 42 Division One matches in 1920–21. They did win seven games and for much of the season kept just ahead of Dumbarton until a slump in their last 15 games produced 13 defeats and they finished six points behind their nearest rivals. Their goals against total of 92 was the worst in either the Scottish or Football League that season. Fourteen of their defeats were at home.

Brechin City suffered 30 defeats in 36 Division Two matches in 1962–63. They finished bottom, 14 points behind their nearest rivals. Their nine points came from three wins and three draws and they lost 13 home games.

Lochgelly United suffered 30 defeats in 38 Division Two matches in 1923–24. They finished bottom, 20 points adrift of their nearest rivals. They won four and drew four other games but scored only 21 goals and conceded 86.

Fewest defeats in a season

Celtic suffered only three defeats in 44 Premier Division matches in 1987–88, and had a mid-season run of 26 games unbeaten. Their only defeats came at home to Dundee United and away at Dunfermline and Hearts.

Celtic went through 18 Division One matches in 1897–98 without a defeat. Only three points were dropped. In 1898–99 Rangers won all their Division One matches, while in the same season Kilmarnock were undefeated in Division Two, dropping only four points in 18 games.

Rangers suffered only one defeat in 42 Division One matches in 1920–21. Celtic beat them 2–0 on New Year's Day with inside-left Joe Cassidy scoring both goals. Heart of Midlothian suffered only one defeat in 34 Division One matches in 1957–58, as did both Rangers and Celtic in 1967–68. That season Celtic were champions, two points ahead of Rangers.

Clyde suffered only one defeat in 36 Division Two matches in 1956–57. They were not beaten until 20 April, losing 4–1 away to Forfar Athletic who finished fourth from bottom. Clyde scored 12 goals and finished as champions with 64 points, 13 ahead of their nearest rivals.

Morton suffered only one defeat in 36 Division Two matches in 1962–63. They were not beaten until 1 February when they lost 3–1 away to East Fife. Morton scored 135 goals and achieved 67 points to finish champions by a margin of 14 points.

St Mirren suffered only one defeat in 36 Division Two matches in 1967–68. They were beaten on 4 November, losing 2–1 away to East Fife. St Mirren scored exactly 100 goals for their 62 points, to finish champions, nine points ahead of their nearest rivals.

Most points in a season

Celtic achieved 72 points in 44 Premier Division matches in 1987–88. They finished ten points ahead of Hearts, the runners-up. They were beaten only once at home losing 2–1 to Dundee United on 24 October. Celtic did not suffer another defeat until losing 2–1 to Hearts at Tynecastle, on 16 April.

Rangers achieved 76 points in 42 Division One matches in 1920–21. They finished ten points ahead of Celtic, the runners-up, and 26 points in front of Hearts who were third. Rangers only defeat was 2–0 at home to Celtic on New Year's Day when they were weakened by injuries. The previous season they had established a new record with a total of 71 points. In these two seasons they lost only three of 84 League games played and enjoyed one spell of 56 consecutive games in which they were beaten only once, a 2–1 home defeat by Clydebank.

Morton achieved 69 points in 38 Division Two matches in 1966–67. They finished 11 points ahead of Raith Rovers, the runners-up. Morton suffered only two defeats and won 33 games, scoring 113 goals.

Most draws in a season

Hibernian drew 18 of their 36 Premier Division matches in 1976–77. They drew ten at home and eight away and had one run of eight games which produced seven draws. They scored 34 goals and conceded 35.

Sequences

After losing 2–0 at Tynecastle to Hearts on 13 November 1915, Celtic completed 62 Division One matches without defeat until losing 2–0 at home to Kilmarnock on 21 April 1917. They won 49 and drew 13 of their games. In 1915–16 they won the championship by a margin of 11 points and retained their title the following season by ten points.

Most goals scored in a season

Dundee United scored 90 goals in 36 Premier Division matches in 1982–83, their total being equalled by Celtic in the same season and again in 1986–87. Dundee United were champions in 1982–83 with 56 points, one ahead of Celtic. They were most consistent, losing only four times, including two defeats in succession in January. They clinched the title with a 2–1 win away to Tayside rivals Dundee on 14 May in the last game of the season. But they had virtually made certain of a first ever Championship with a 3–2 win at Celtic Park on 20 April. Celtic lost their next game 1–0 at Aberdeen, among six defeats. In 1986–87 Celtic surrendered a seven point lead over Rangers at the turn of the year and had to be content with being runners-up to their great rivals.

Heart of Midlothian scored 132 goals in 34 Division One matches during 1957–58. They were League champions by a margin of 13 points over runners-up Rangers. They suffered only one defeat, 2–1 away to Clyde, and collected a club record 62 points. Hearts beat East Fife 9–0, Falkirk 9–1 and Queen's Park 8–0.

Raith Rovers scored 142 goals in 34 Division Two matches during 1937–38. They never failed to score in any of their games and achieved five scores of six goals or more at home. They won 8–2 away at Brechin City, 8–1 at East Stirling and 8–3 at Alloa.

Most goals conceded in a season

Morton conceded 100 goals in 36 Premier Division matches in 1984–85 and the same total in 44 games in 1987–88. In 1984–85 they began well enough with two wins but won only three other matches and overall drew just twice. In one spell they were beaten on 13 consecutive occasions. They finished bottom and were relegated. In 1987–88 they won only three games and had a run of 28 without a win. They drew 10 times but finished bottom again.

Leith Athletic conceded 137 goals in 38 Division One matches during 1931–32. They were relegated having finished bottom, three points behind Dundee United. Leith won six and drew four of their matches.

Edinburgh City conceded 146 goals in 38 Division Two matches in 1931–32. They finished bottom, eight points below their nearest rivals. Though they scored as many as 78 goals themselves they managed to keep their goal intact only twice. Their heaviest defeats were 8–2 away to Alloa and 8–4 at home to Queen of the South.

Fewest goals scored in a season

Hamilton Academical scored only 19 goals in 36 Premier Division matches in 1988–89. They won six games but failed to score in 22, and did not score more than twice in any game. Although they won two of their first six matches and finished the season with two consecutive wins, this did not prevent them from being relegated. Their defence conceded eight goals to Celtic at Parkhead.

Morton scored only 18 goals in 18 Division One matches in 1901–02. They achieved seven points, won only one game and finished bottom, six points behind their nearest rivals.

Stirling Albion scored only 18 goals in 39 Division One matches in 1980–81. They achieved 23 points including six wins, two of which were away. Their highest win was 4–2 at home to East Stirling but overall they failed to score in 27 games. They were relegated but finished one point above Berwick Rangers.

Lochgelly United scored only 20 goals in 38 Division Two matches in 1923–24. They finished bottom with 12 points from four wins and four draws and were 19 points away from their nearest rivals.

Albion Rovers scored only 19 goals in 22 Division Two matches in 1911–12 while Johnstone (not to be confused with St Johnstone) scored 20 from 22 games in the same division in 1913–14.

Fewest goals conceded in a season

Rangers conceded only 19 goals in 36 Premier Division matches in 1989–90. In as many as 20 of these they were able to prevent the opposition from scoring. No team scored more than two goals against them in any game. They finished as champions seven points ahead of their nearest rivals.

Celtic conceded only 14 goals in 38 Division One matches in 1913–14. They kept their goal intact in 26 games and only Hearts were able to score more than a single goal against them, winning 2–0 at Tynecastle. Fourteen goals represent the lowest total of goals conceded in any Scottish League season irrespective of the number of games played.

Morton conceded only 20 goals in 38 Division Two matches in 1966–67. They lost just twice and were champions with 69 points. In 21 games they prevented the opposition from scoring. No team scored more than two goals against them in a match.

Scottish League attendances since 1961–62

Season	Matches	Division 1	Division 2			Total	Average
1961–62	648	3 411 129	576 659			3 987 788	6 153
1962–63	648	3 043 567	590 452			3 634 019	5 608
1963–64	648	2 962 114	498 309			3 460 423	5 340
1964–65	648	2 908 508	350 788			3 259 296	5 029
1965–66	648	2 667 380	346 432			3 013 812	4 650
1966–67	686	2 836 762	405 620			3 242 382	4 726
1967–68	648	2 869 815	345 280			3 215 095	4 961
1968–69	648	3 060 783	334 747			3 395 530	5 240
1969–70	648	3 045 994	371 919			3 417 913	5 274
1970–71	648	2 893 652	412 566			3 306 218	5 102
1971–72	648	3 132 141	484 241			3 616 382	5 580
1972–73	648	2 816 106	467 763			3 283 869	5 067
1973–74	648	2 452 562	451 107			2 903 669	4 480
1974–75	648	2 673 655	445 656			3 119 311	4 813
		Premier	Division 1	Division 2			
1975–76	544	2 411 833	451 153	140 391		3 014 377	5 541
1976–77	726	2 131 848	636 410	208 861		2 977 119	4 100
1977–78	726	2 356 440	790 111	268 830		3 415 381	4 704
1978–79	726	2 324 799	538 735	249 791		3 113 325	4 288
1979–80	726	2 225 650	599 958	205 452		3 031 060	4 175
1980–81	726	1 759 856	601 152	166 175		2 527 183	3 480
1981–82	726	1 704 140	512 242	151 675		2 368 057	3 261
1982–83	726	1 859 856	474 859	140 709		2 475 444	3 409
1983–84	726	2 019 949	321 749	156 078		2 497 776	3 440
1984–85	726	1 949 788	366 785	188 283		2 504 856	3 450
1985–86	726	2 260 411	351 610	255 831		2 837 852	3 908
1986–87	801	3 094 224	402 236	180 733		3 677 193	4 590
1987–88	801	3 682 604	353 578	203 481		4 239 663	5 292
1988–89	726	2 827 519	670 158	137 522		3 635 199	5 007

Change of name

Clubs who have changed names since joining the Scottish League:

Club	Previous name(s)	Until
Alloa	Alloa Athletic	c. 1980
Ayr United	Ayr, Ayr Parkhouse	1910
Dundee United	Dundee Hibs	1923
East Stirlingshire	ES Clydebank for one season (1964–65)	
Hamilton Academical	Hamilton Academicals Football and Athletic Club	1965

Derby Games

Rangers v Celtic

Rangers were founded in 1873, Celtic in 1888. Of the 216 Scottish League matches played between the clubs, Rangers have won 84, Celtic 68 and 64 have been drawn.

League results at Ibrox Park (Rangers' score first)

Season	Score	Season	Score
1890-91	1-2	1930-31	1-0
1891-92	1-1	1931-32	0-0
1892-93	2-2	1932-33	0-0
1893-94	5-0	1933-34	2-2
1894-95	1-1	1934-35	2-1
1895-96	2-4	1935-36	1-2
1896-97	2-0	1936-37	1-0
1897-98	0-4	1937-38	3-1
1898-99	4-1	1938-39	2-1
1899-1900	3-3		
1900-01	2-1	1946-47	1-1
1901-02	2-2	1947-48	2-0
1902-03	3-3	1948-49	4-0
1903-04	0-0	1949-50	4-0
1904-05	1-4	1950-51	1-0
1905-06	3-2	1951-52	1-1
1906-07	2-1	1952-53	1-0
1907-08	0-1	1953-54	1-1
1908-09	1-3	1954-55	4-1
1909-10	0-0	1955-56	0-0
1910-11	1-1	1956-57	2-0
1911-12	3-1	1957-58	2-3
1912-13	0-1	1958-59	2-1
1913-14	0-2	1959-60	3-1
1914-15	2-1	1960-61	2-1
1915-16	3-0	1961-62	2-2
1916-17	0-0	1962-63	4-0
1917-18	1-2	1963-64	2-1
1918-19	1-1	1964-65	1-0
1919-20	3-0	1965-66	2-1
1920-21	0-2	1966-67	2-2
1921-22	1-1	1967-68	1-0
1922-23	2-0	1968-69	1-0
1923-24	0-0	1969-70	0-1
1924-25	4-1	1970-71	1-1
1925-26	1-0	1971-72	2-3
1926-27	2-1	1972-73	2-1
1927-28	1-0	1973-74	0-1
1928-29	3-0	1974-75	3-0
1929-30	1-0	1975-76	2-1
			1-0

Season	Score	Season	Score
1976-77	0-1	1983-84	1-2
	2-2		1-0
1977-78	3-2	1984-85	0-0
	3-1		1-2
1978-79	1-1	1985-86	3-0
	1-0		4-4
1979-80	2-2	1986-87	1-0
	1-1		2-0
1980-81	3-0	1987-88	2-2
	0-1		1-2
1981-82	0-2	1988-89	5-1
	1-0		4-1
1982-83	1-2	1989-90	1-0
	2-4		3-0

League results at Parkhead (Celtic's score first)

Season	Score	Season	Score
1890-91	2-2	1920-21	1-2
1891-92	3-0	1921-22	0-0
1892-93	3-0	1922-23	1-3
1893-94	3-2	1923-24	2-2
1894-95	5-3	1924-25	0-1
1895-96	6-2	1925-26	2-2
1896-97	1-1	1926-27	0-1
1897-98	0-0	1927-28	1-0
1898-99	0-4	1928-29	1-2
1899-1900	3-2	1929-30	1-2
1900-01	2-1	1930-31	2-0
1901-02	2-4	1931-32	1-2
1902-03	1-1	1932-33	1-1
1903-04	2-2	1933-34	2-2
1904-05	2-2	1934-35	1-1
1905-06	1-0	1935-36	3-4
1906-07	2-1	1936-37	1-1
1907-08	2-1	1937-38	3-0
1908-09	2-3	1938-39	6-2
1909-10	1-1		
1910-11	0-1	1946-47	2-3
1911-12	3-0	1947-48	0-4
1912-13	3-2	1948-49	0-1
1913-14	4-0	1949-50	1-1
1914-15	2-1	1950-51	3-2
1915-16	2-2	1951-52	1-4
1916-17	0-0	1952-53	2-1
1917-18	0-0	1953-54	1-0
1918-19	0-3	1954-55	2-0
1919-20	1-1	1955-56	0-1
		1956-57	0-2

Season	Score	Season	Score	Season	Score	Season	Score
1957-58	0-1	1978-79	3-1	1905-06	1-0	1955-56	0-1
1958-59	2-2		4-2	1906-07	4-1	1956-57	0-2
1959-60	0-1	1979-80	1-0	1907-08	1-2	1957-58	3-1
1960-61	1-5		1-0	1908-09	1-1	1958-59	1-3
1961-62	1-1	1980-81	1-2	1909-10	1-0	1959-60	2-2
1962-63	0-1		3-1	1910-11	2-0	1960-61	1-2
1963-64	0-1	1981-82	3-3	1911-12	3-0	1961-62	4-2
1964-65	3-1		2-1	1912-13	1-0	1962-63	3-3
1965-66	5-1	1982-83	3-2	1913-14	3-1	1963-64	4-2
1966-67	2-0		0-0	1914-15	3-1	1964-65	0-1
1967-68	2-2	1983-84	2-1	1915-16	1-3	1965-66	0-4
1968-69	2-4		3-0	1916-17	2-1	1966-67	0-0
1969-70	0-0	1984-85	1-1	1917-18	1-0	1967-68	1-4
1970-71	2-0		1-1	1918-19	3-1	1968-69	0-0
1971-72	2-1	1985-86	1-1	1919-20	1-3	1969-70	0-2
1972-73	3-1		2-0	1920-21	5-1	1970-71	0-0
1973-74	1-0	1986-87	1-1	1921-22	0-2	1971-72	0-2
1974-75	1-2		3-1	1922-23	2-2	1972-73	0-7
1975-76	1-1	1987-88	1-0	1923-24	1-1	1973-74	4-1
	0-0		2-0	1924-25	2-0	1974-75	0-0
1976-77	2-2	1988-89	3-1	1925-26	1-4	1975-76	1-1
	1-0		1-2	1926-27	2-2		0-1
1977-78	1-1	1989-90	1-1	1927-28	2-2	1976-77	0-1
	2-0		0-1	1928-29	1-1		2-2
				1929-30	1-1		
				1930-31	4-1	1978-79	1-1
							1-2
				1933-34	0-0		
				1934-35	5-2	1983-84	3-2
				1935-36	8-3		1-1
				1936-37	3-2	1984-85	0-0
				1937-38	3-2		2-2
				1938-39	0-1	1985-86	2-1
							3-1
				1946-47	2-3	1986-87	1-1
				1947-48	2-1		2-1
				1948-49	3-2	1987-88	1-0
				1949-50	5-2		0-0
				1950-51	2-1	1988-89	1-2
				1951-52	1-1		2-1
				1952-53	1-2	1989-90	1-0
				1953-54	4-0		2-0
				1954-55	5-1		

Old Firm action from Parkhead in 1989 (Action-Plus)

Heart of Midlothian v Hibernian

Heart of Midlothian were founded in 1874 and Hibernian in 1875. The two clubs have played each other 182 times in the League; Hearts have won 79 matches, Hibs 52 and 51 have been drawn.

League results at Tynecastle (Hearts' score first)

Season	Score	Season	Score
1895-96	4-3	1900-01	0-3
1896-97	1-0	1901-02	2-1
1897-98	3-2	1902-03	1-1
1898-99	4-0	1903-04	2-0
1899-1900	1-3	1904-05	1-0

League results at Easter Road (Hibs' score first)

Season	Score	Season	Score
1895-96	3-2	1902-03	0-0
1896-97	2-0	1903-04	4-2
1897-98	1-1	1904-05	3-0
1898-99	5-1	1905-06	0-3
1899-1900	1-0	1906-07	0-0
1900-01	0-0	1907-08	2-3
1901-02	1-2	1908-09	0-1

Season	Score	Season	Score
1909-10	1-4	1957-58	0-2
1910-11	1-0	1958-59	0-4
1911-12	0-4	1959-60	1-5
1912-13	0-3	1960-61	1-4
1913-14	1-2	1961-62	1-4
1914-15	2-2	1962-63	0-4
1915-16	1-2	1963-64	1-1
1916-17	0-2	1964-65	3-5
1917-18	1-3	1965-66	2-3
1918-19	1-3	1966-67	3-1
1919-20	2-4	1967-68	1-0
1920-21	3-0	1968-69	1-3
1921-22	2-1	1969-70	0-0
1922-23	2-1	1970-71	0-0
1923-24	1-1	1971-72	0-0
1924-25	2-1	1972-73	2-0
1925-26	0-0	1973-74	3-1
1926-27	2-2	1974-75	2-1
1927-28	2-1	1975-76	3-0
1928-29	1-0		1-0
1929-30	1-1	1976-77	3-1
1930-31	2-2		1-1
1933-34	1-4	1978-79	1-1
1934-35	1-0		1-2
1935-36	1-1	1983-84	1-1
1936-37	3-3		0-0
1937-38	2-2	1984-85	1-2
1938-39	4-0		1-2
1946-47	0-1	1985-86	0-0
1947-48	3-1		1-2
1948-49	3-1	1986-87	1-3
1949-50	1-2		2-2
1950-51	0-1	1987-88	2-1
1951-52	2-3		0-0
1952-53	3-1	1988-89	0-0
1953-54	1-2		1-0
1954-55	2-3	1989-90	1-1
1955-56	2-2		1-2
1956-57	2-3		

Season	Score	Season	Score
1938-39	2-0	1979-80	1-0
1946-47	2-0		1-1
1960-61	3-0	1981-82	1-3
1961-62	4-1		0-2
1962-63	1-2	1982-83	0-2
1963-64	1-1		1-2
1964-65	2-4	1983-84	1-4
1965-66	0-5		2-5
1966-67	2-3	1984-85	0-2
1967-68	2-2		1-0
1968-69	1-2	1985-86	0-3
1969-70	1-2		0-1
1970-71	2-3	1986-87	0-2
1971-72	6-4		1-1
1972-73	3-0	1987-88	1-1
1973-74	0-1		0-2
1974-75	2-0	1988-89	0-3
1975-76	0-0		0-1
	2-1	1989-90	4-3
			1-1

League results at Tannadice Park (Dundee United's score first)

Season	Score	Season	Score
1925-26	0-1	1975-76	1-2
1926-27	1-0		1-0
1929-30	0-1	1979-80	3-0
1931-32	0-3		2-0
1938-39	3-0	1981-82	5-2
1946-47	1-2		1-1
1960-61	3-1	1982-83	1-0
1961-62	1-2		5-3
1962-63	1-1	1983-84	0-1
1963-64	2-1		1-1
1964-65	1-4	1984-85	3-4
1965-66	2-1		4-0
1966-67	1-4	1985-86	2-0
1967-68	0-0		0-0
1968-69	3-1	1986-87	0-3
1969-70	4-1		1-1
1970-71	3-2	1987-88	1-3
1971-72	1-1		1-0
1972-73	2-1	1988-89	2-0
1973-74	1-2		2-1
1974-75	3-0	1989-90	0-0
			1-2

Dundee v Dundee United

Dundee were founded in 1893 while United were formed in 1909 as Dundee Hibernians; they became known as Dundee United in 1923.

The 86 League meetings between the two clubs have resulted in Dundee United winning 42 times to Dundee's 27 with 17 drawn matches.

League results at Dens Park (Dundee's score first)

Season	Score	Season	Score
1925-26	0-0	1929-30	1-0
1926-27	5-0	1931-32	1-1

Scottish Cup Finals 1874–1990

Year	Date	Winners		Runners-up	Venue	Attendance
1874	21 Mar	Queen's Park	2–0	Clydesdale	First Hampden	3 500
1875	10 Apr	Queen's Park	3–0	Renton	First Hampden	7 000
1876	11 Mar	Queen's Park	1–1	3rd Lanark Rifles	Hamilton Crescent	10 000
Replay	18 Mar	Queen's Park	2–0	3rd Lanark Rifles	Hamilton Crescent	6 000
1877	17 Mar	Vale of Leven	1–1	Rangers	Hamilton Crescent	10 000
Replay	7 Apr	Vale of Leven	1–1	Rangers	Hamilton Crescent	15 000
2nd replay	13 Apr	Vale of Leven	3–2	Rangers	First Hampden	12 000
1878	30 Mar	Vale of Leven	1–0	3rd Lanark Rifles	First Hampden	5 000
1879	19 Apr	Vale of Leven[1]	1–1	Rangers	First Hampden	9 000
1880	21 Feb	Queen's Park	3–0	Thornliebank	First Cathkin	4 000
1881	26 Mar	Queen's Park	2–1	Dumbarton	Kinning Park	15 000
Replay	9 Apr	Queen's Park	3–1[2]	Dumbarton	Kinning Park	7 000
1882	18 Mar	Queen's Park	2–2	Dumbarton	First Cathkin	12 500
Replay	1 Apr	Queen's Park	4–1	Dumbarton	First Cathkin	14 000
1883	31 Mar	Dumbarton	2–2	Vale of Leven	First Hampden	9 000
Replay	7 Apr	Dumbarton	2–1	Vale of Leven	First Hampden	12 000
1884		Queen's Park[3]	w.o.	Vale of Leven		
1885	21 Feb	Renton	0–0	Vale of Leven	Second Hampden	2 500
Replay	28 Feb	Renton	3–1	Vale of Leven	Second Hampden	3 500
1886	13 Feb	Queen's Park	3–1	Renton	First Cathkin	7 000
1887	12 Feb	Hibernian	2–1	Dumbarton	Second Hampden	12 000
1888	4 Feb	Renton	6–1	Cambuslang	Second Hampden	11 000
1889	2 Feb	Third Lanark	3–0	Celtic	Second Hampden	18 000
Replay[4]	9 Feb	Third Lanark	2–1	Celtic	Second Hampden	13 000
1890	15 Feb	Queen's Park	1–1	Vale of Leven	Ibrox	11 000
Replay	22 Feb	Queen's Park	2–1	Vale of Leven	Ibrox	14 000
1891	7 Feb	Heart of Midlothian	1–0	Dumbarton	Second Hampden	10 836
1892	12 Mar	Celtic	1–0	Queen's Park	Ibrox	40 000
Replay[5]	9 Apr	Celtic	5–1	Queen's Park	Ibrox	26 000
1893	25 Feb	Queen's Park	0–0	Celtic	Ibrox	18 771
Replay	11 Mar	Queen's Park	2–1	Celtic	Ibrox	13 239
1894	17 Feb	Rangers	3–1	Celtic	Second Hampden	17 000
1895	20 Apr	St Bernard's	2–1	Renton	Ibrox	15 000
1896	14 Mar	Heart of Midlothian	3–1	Hibernian	Logie Green	17 034
1897	20 Mar	Rangers	5–1	Dumbarton	Second Hampden	14 000
1898	26 Mar	Rangers	2–0	Kilmarnock	Second Hampden	13 000
1899	22 Apr	Celtic	2–0	Rangers	Second Hampden	25 000
1900	14 Apr	Celtic	4–3	Queen's Park	Ibrox	15 000
1901	6 Apr	Heart of Midlothian	4–3	Celtic	Ibrox	12 000
1902	26 Apr	Hibernian	1–0	Celtic	Celtic Park	16 000
1903	11 Apr	Rangers	1–1	Heart of Midlothian	Celtic Park	40 000
Replay	18 Apr	Rangers	0–0	Heart of Midlothian	Celtic Park	35 000
2nd replay	25 Apr	Rangers	2–0	Heart of Midlothian	Celtic Park	32 000
1904	16 Apr	Celtic	3–2	Rangers	Hampden Park	65 000
1905	8 Apr	Third Lanark	0–0	Rangers	Hampden Park	54 000
Replay	15 Apr	Third Lanark	3–1	Rangers	Hampden Park	55 000
1906	28 Apr	Heart of Midlothian	1–0	Third Lanark	Ibrox	25 000

Year	Date	Winners		Runners-up	Venue	Attendance
1907	20 Apr	Celtic	3-0	Heart of Midlothian	Hampden Park	50 000
1908	18 Apr	Celtic	5-1	St Mirren	Hampden Park	55 000
1909	10 Apr	Celtic	2-2	Rangers	Hampden Park	70 000
Replay	17 Apr	Celtic	1-1[6]	Rangers	Hampden Park	61 000
1910	9 Apr	Dundee	2-2	Clyde	Ibrox	62 300
Replay	16 Apr	Dundee	0-0	Clyde	Ibrox	24 500
2nd replay	8 Apr	Dundee	2-1	Clyde	Ibrox	25 400
1911	8 Apr	Celtic	0-0	Hamilton Academical	Ibrox	45 000
Replay	15 Apr	Celtic	2-0	Hamilton Academical	Ibrox	24 700
1912	6 Apr	Celtic	2-0	Clyde	Ibrox	46 000
1913	12 Apr	Falkirk	2-0	Raith Rovers	Celtic Park	45 000
1914	11 Apr	Celtic	0-0	Hibernian	Ibrox	56 000
Replay	16 Apr	Celtic	4-1	Hibernian	Ibrox	40 000
1920	17 Apr	Kilmarnock	3-2	Albion Rovers	Hampden Park	95 000
1921	16 Apr	Partick Thistle	1-0	Rangers	Celtic Park	28 300
1922	15 Apr	Morton	1-0	Rangers	Hampden Park	75 000
1923	31 Mar	Celtic	1-0	Hibernian	Hampden Park	80 100
1924	19 Apr	Airdrieonians	2-0	Hibernian	Ibrox	59 218
1925	11 Apr	Celtic	2-1	Dundee	Hampden Park	75 137
1926	10 Apr	St Mirren	2-0	Celtic	Hampden Park	98 620
1927	16 Apr	Celtic	3-1	East Fife	Hampden Park	80 070
1928	14 Apr	Rangers	4-0	Celtic	Hampden Park	118 115
1929	6 Apr	Kilmarnock	2-0	Rangers	Hampden Park	114 708
1930	12 Apr	Rangers	0-0	Partick Thistle	Hampden Park	107 475
Replay	16 Apr	Rangers	2-1	Partick Thistle	Hampden Park	103 686
1931	11 Apr	Celtic	2-2	Motherwell	Hampden Park	105 000
Replay	15 Apr	Celtic	4-2	Motherwell	Hampden Park	98 579
1932	16 Apr	Rangers	1-1	Kilmarnock	Hampden Park	111 982
Replay	2 Apr	Rangers	3-0	Kilmarnock	Hampden Park	104 965
1933	15 Apr	Celtic	1-0	Motherwell	Hampden Park	102 339
1934	21 Apr	Rangers	5-0	St Mirren	Hampden Park	113 403
1935	20 Apr	Rangers	2-1	Hamilton Academical	Hampden Park	87 286
1936	18 Apr	Rangers	1-0	Third Lanark	Hampden Park	88 859
1937	24 Apr	Celtic	2-1	Aberdeen	Hampden Park	147 365
1938	23 Apr	East Fife	1-1	Kilmarnock	Hampden Park	80 091
Replay	27 Apr	East Fife	4-2	Kilmarnock	Hampden Park	92 716
1939	22 Apr	Clyde	4-0	Motherwell	Hampden Park	94 799
1947	19 Apr	Aberdeen	2-1	Hibernian	Hampden Park	82 140
1948	17 Apr	Rangers	1-1*	Morton	Hampden Park	129 176
Replay	21 Apr	Rangers	1-0*	Morton	Hampden Park	133,570
1949	23 Apr	Rangers	4-1	Clyde	Hampden Park	108 435
1950	22 Apr	Rangers	3-0	East Fife	Hampden Park	118 262
1951	21 Apr	Celtic	1-0	Motherwell	Hampden Park	131 943
1952	19 Apr	Motherwell	4-0	Dundee	Hampden Park	136 274
1953	25 Apr	Rangers	1-1	Aberdeen	Hampden Park	129 681
Replay	29 Apr	Rangers	1-0	Aberdeen	Hampden Park	112 619
1954	24 Apr	Celtic	2-1	Aberdeen	Hampden Park	129 926
1955	23 Aor	Clyde	1-1	Celtic	Hampden Park	106 111
Replay	27 Apr	Clyde	1-0	Celtic	Hampden Park	68 735
1956	21 Apr	Heart of Midlothian	3-1	Celtic	Hampden Park	133 339
1957	20 Apr	Falkirk	1-1	Kilmarnock	Hampden Park	83 000
Replay	24 Apr	Falkirk	2-1*	Kilmarnock	Hampden Park	79 785

Year	Date	Winners		Runners-up	Venue	Attendance
1958	26 Apr	Clyde	1-0	Hibernian	Hampden Park	95 124
1959	25 Apr	St Mirren	3-1	Aberdeen	Hampden Park	108 591
1960	23 Apr	Rangers	2-0	Kilmarnock	Hampden Park	108 017
1961	22 Apr	Dunfermline Athletic	0-0	Celtic	Hampden Park	113 618
Replay	26 Apr	Dunfermline Athletic	2-0	Celtic	Hampden Park	87 866
1962	21 Apr	Rangers	2-0	St Mirren	Hampden Park	126 930
1963	4 May	Rangers	1-1	Celtic	Hampden Park	129 527
Replay	15 May	Rangers	3-0	Celtic	Hampden Park	120 263
1964	25 Apr	Rangers	3-1	Dundee	Hampden Park	120 982
1965	24 Apr	Celtic	3-2	Dunfermline Athletic	Hampden Park	108 800
1966	23 Apr	Rangers	0-0	Celtic	Hampden Park	126 552
Replay	27 Apr	Rangers	1-0	Celtic	Hampden Park	98 202
1967	29 Apr	Celtic	2-0	Aberdeen	Hampden Park	127 117
1968	27 Apr	Dunfermline Athletic	3-1	Heart of Midlothian	Hampden Park	56 366
1969	26 Apr	Celtic	4-0	Rangers	Hampden Park	138 874
1970	11 Apr	Aberdeen	3-1	Celtic	Hampden Park	108 434
1971	9 May	Celtic	1-1	Rangers	Hampden Park	120 092
Replay	12 May	Celtic	2-1	Rangers	Hampden Park	103 332
1972	6 May	Celtic	6-1	Hibernian	Hampden Park	106 102
1973	5 May	Rangers	3-2	Celtic	Hampden Park	122 714
1974	4 May	Celtic	3-0	Dundee United	Hampden Park	75 959
1975	3 May	Celtic	3-1	Airdrieonians	Hampden Park	75 457
1976	1 May	Rangers	3-1	Heart of Midlothian	Hampden Park	85 354
1977	7 May	Celtic	1-0	Rangers	Hampden Park	54 252
1978	6 May	Rangers	2-1	Aberdeen	Hampden Park	61 563
1979	12 May	Rangers	0-0	Hibernian	Hampden Park	50 610
Replay	16 May	Rangers	0-0*	Hibernian	Hampden Park	33 506
2nd replay	28 May	Rangers	3-2*	Hibernian	Hampden Park	30 602
1980	10 May	Celtic	1-0*	Rangers	Hampden Park	70 303
1981	9 May	Rangers	0-0*	Dundee United	Hampden Park	55 000
Replay	12 May	Rangers	4-1	Dundee United	Hampden Park	43 009
1982	22 May	Aberdeen	4-1*	Rangers	Hampden Park	53 788
1983	21 May	Aberdeen	1-0*	Rangers	Hampden Park	62 070
1984	19 May	Aberdeen	2-1*	Celtic	Hampden Park	58 900
1985	18 May	Celtic	2-1	Dundee United	Hampden Park	60 346
1986	10 May	Aberdeen	3-0	Heart of Midlothian	Hampden Park	62 841
1987	16 May	St Mirren	1-0*	Dundee United	Hampden Park	51 782
1988	14 May	Celtic	2-1	Dundee United	Hampden Park	74 000
1989	20 May	Celtic	1-0	Rangers	Hampden Park	72 069
1990	12 May	Aberdeen	0-0*	Celtic	Hampden Park	60 493

(Aberdeen won 9-8 on penalties)

* after extra time

[1] Vale of Leven awarded cup; Rangers failed to appear for replay

[2] After Dumbarton protested the first game

[3] Queen's Park awarded cup, Vale of Leven failing to appear

[4] Replay by order of Scottish FA because of playing conditions in first match

[5] After mutually protested first game

[6] Declared a friendly due to fog and frost

[7] Owing to riot, the cup was withheld after two drawn games

Scottish League Cup Finals 1947–90
Bell's Cup 1979–84
Skol Cup 1985–90

Season	Date	Winners		Runners-up	Venue	Attendance
1946–47	5 Apr	Rangers	4–0	Aberdeen	Hampden Park	82 584
1947–48	1 Nov	East Fife[1]	4–1	Falkirk	Hampden Park	30 664
1948–49	12 Mar	Rangers	2–0	Raith Rovers	Hampden Park	53 359
1949–50	29 Oct	East Fife	3–0	Dunfermline Athletic	Hampden Park	38 897
1950–51	28 Oct	Motherwell	3–0	Hibernian	Hampden Park	63 074
1951–52	27 Oct	Dundee	3–2	Rangers	Hampden Park	91 075
1952–53	25 Oct	Dundee	2–0	Kilmarnock	Hampden Park	51 830
1953–54	24 Oct	East Fife	3–2	Partick Thistle	Hampden Park	38 529
1954–55	23 Oct	Heart of Midlothian	4–2	Motherwell	Hampden Park	55 640
1955–56	22 Oct	Aberdeen	2–1	St Mirren	Hampden Park	44 103
1956–57	31 Oct	Celtic[2]	3–0	Partick Thistle	Hampden Park	31 126
1957–58	19 Oct	Celtic	7–1	Rangers	Hampden Park	82 293
1958–59	25 Oct	Heart of Midlothian	5–1	Partick Thistle	Hampden Park	59 960
1959–60	24 Oct	Heart of Midlothian	2–1	Third Lanark	Hampden Park	57 974
1960–61	29 Oct	Rangers	2–0	Kilmarnock	Hampden Park	82 063
1961–62	18 Dec	Rangers[3]	3–1	Heart of Midlothian	Hampden Park	47 552
1962–63	27 Oct	Heart of Midlothian	1–0	Kilmarnock	Hampden Park	51 280
1963–64	26 Oct	Rangers	5–0	Morton	Hampden Park	105 907
1964–65	24 Oct	Rangers	2–1	Celtic	Hampden Park	91 000
1965–66	23 Oct	Celtic	2–1	Rangers	Hampden Park	107 609
1966–67	29 Oct	Celtic	1–0	Rangers	Hampden Park	94 532
1967–68	28 Oct	Celtic	5–3	Dundee	Hampden Park	66 660
1968–69	5 Apr	Celtic	6–2	Hibernian	Hampden Park	74 000
1969–70	25 Oct	Celtic	1–0	St Johnstone	Hampden Park	73 067
1970–71	24 Oct	Rangers	1–0	Celtic	Hampden Park	106 263
1971–72	23 Oct	Partick Thistle	4–1	Celtic	Hampden Park	62 740
1972–73	9 Dec	Hibernian	2–1	Celtic	Hampden Park	71 696
1973–74	15 Dec	Dundee	1–0	Celtic	Hampden Park	27 974
1974–75	26 Oct	Celtic	6–3	Hibernian	Hampden Park	53 848
1975–76	25 Oct	Rangers	1–0	Celtic	Hampden Park	58 806
1976–77	6 Nov	Aberdeen	2–1*	Celtic	Hampden Park	69 268
1977–78	18 Mar	Rangers	2–1*	Celtic	Hampden Park	60 168
1978–79	31 Mar	Rangers	2–1	Aberdeen	Hampden Park	54 000
1979–80	12 Dec	Dundee United[4]	3–0	Aberdeen	Hampden Park	28 984
1980–81	6 Dec	Dundee United	3–0	Dundee	Hampden Park	24 466
1981–82	28 Nov	Rangers	2–1	Dundee United	Hampden Park	53 795
1982–83	4 Dec	Celtic	2–1	Rangers	Hampden Park	55 372
1983–84	25 Mar	Rangers	3–2*	Celtic	Hampden Park	66 369
1984–85	28 Oct	Rangers	1–0	Dundee United	Hampden Park	44 698
1985–86	27 Oct	Aberdeen	3–0	Hibernian	Hampden Park	40 065
1986–87	26 Oct	Rangers	2–1	Celtic	Hampden Park	74 219
1987–88	25 Oct	Rangers[5]	3–3*	Aberdeen	Hampden Park	71 961
1988–89	23 Oct	Rangers	3–2	Aberdeen	Hampden Park	72 122
1989–90	22 Oct	Aberdeen	2–1	Rangers	Hampden Park	61 190

*After extra time   [1] after 0–0 draw (aet)   [2] after 0–0 draw   [3] after 1–1 draw   [4] after 0–0 draw (aet)   [5] won 5–3 on penalties

Goalscoring Facts

The highest number of goals scored in one season of first-class football in the British Isles is 96. This was achieved by Fred Roberts (Glentoran) in 1930–31: Irish League 55, Irish Cup 4, City Cup 28, Antrim Shield 7 and Belfast Charity Cup 2. Joe Bambrick (Linfield) had scored 94 in 1929–30: Irish League 50, Irish Cup 7, City Cup 10, Antrim Shield 5, Belfast Charity Cup 9, Inter-League 5, Gold Cup 1, Conder Cup 1, Internationals 6.

Jimmy Smith scored 66 League goals for Ayr United in 1927–28. His sequence was: 3 0 2 0 5 0 3 3 0 0 1 1 2 0 0 3 3 1 2 2 4 2 0 3 5 2 1 1 0 4 2 1 0 1 2 2 4 1. Dumbarton was the only team he did not score against. In addition to these Division Two goals he scored two Scottish Cup goals, one in the Ayr Charity Cup and 15 in friendly and tour games for a total of 84.

William Ralph Dean, known as 'Dixie', scored 60 League goals in 39 games for Everton in 1927–28. He dominated the club's goalscoring to such an extent that season that the other players managed only 42 between them. Dean hit one 5, one 4, five hat-tricks, fourteen 2's and eight singles. His prolific season produced an aggregate of 82 goals. In addition to his 60 in the League, there were three in the FA Cup, six in Inter-League, eight in international trials and five in Internationals.

He began his career with Tranmere Rovers in January 1924 and scored 27 goals in as many games before joining Everton. At Goodison Park he scored 349 goals in 399 League games before finishing his Football League career with Notts County, whom he joined in 1938. After three goals in nine games he signed for the League of Ireland club Sligo Rovers and added 11 goals, again in as many games, for them.

During the 1939–45 war Dean served in the King's (Liverpool) Regiment and later transferred to the Royal Tank Regiment where he became a Corporal mechanical instructor. He rarely played, but during basic training at Formby he was asked to pick a team to play against the PT Instructors and his team of 'unknowns' won 8–3. He also once guested for Cambridge Town in a 15–1 win over an RAF XI. Dean's contribution was eight goals, including six in 39 minutes. Most of his other games were in unit football, but on 13 September 1941 he scored three in a 5–2 win for an Army team against Southampton at Warminster. However, he did turn out for York City against Gateshead two months later on 22 November and scored a goal in a 4–3 defeat.

He played only 16 games for England but scored 18 times. His nickname of 'Dixie' was considered to have come directly form his crinkly hair, but subsequent research has revealed that it might well have been a corruption from 'Digsy'. Dean disliked being called 'Dixie', and preferred friends to call him Bill.

As a schoolboy he had gained a reputation for playfully putting his fist into friends' backs when playing 'tag'. He once scored 18 goals in a day, in three games with six goals in each. In the morning he played in a Birkenhead Schoolboys trial, in the afternoon for Laird Street School and in the evening for Moreton Bible Class. Dean scored 37 hat-tricks during his Football League career of 16 seasons.

Dean's 60 League goals sequence was: 1 1 1 2 1 2 2 2 5 0 3 3 2 0 2 0 3 0 1 2 0 2 2 2 0 1 0 3 0 0 0 2 2 1 2 1 2 4 3. He missed three matches.

George Camsell scored 59 goals in Division Two during 1926–27. His total was all the more remarkable because he did not figure in the side until the fifth game. He scored one 5, three 4's and five 3's and missed five games altogether. His nine hat-tricks in one seasons are a record. His total of League goals for Middlesbrough was 325 in 418 appearances. He had made his debut as an outside-left and began his League career with Durham City in Division Three (North), scoring 20 goals in 21 appearances. Despite winning only nine England caps he scored in every game and totalled 18 goals.

Camsell's sequence for his 59 goals was: 0 2 1 1 3 0 1 1 1 4 1 4 1 2 4 5 2 3 0 1 2 3 1 2 2 0 0 3 1 1 1 0 1 0 1 3 1. He missed five matches.

Camsell was the first player to score a century of League and Cup goals over two consecutive seasons. In 1926–27 he added five FA Cup goals to his 59 in the League for Middlesbrough and in 1927–28, he scored 33 League and four FA Cup goals. Steve Bull scored 34 League and 18 cup goals in 1987–88 for Wolverhampton Wanderers, followed by 37 League and 13 cup goals in 1988–89. Bull's

Steve Bull (Wolverhampton Wanderers) became the first player in post-war football to aggregate a century of League and Cup goals in two consecutive season (Sporting Pictures)

1987–88 cup goals consisted of 12 in the Sherpa Van Trophy, three Littlewoods Cup and three FA Cup; in 1988–89 there were 11 Sherpa Van Trophy and two Littlewoods Cup goals.

The record for the most successive seasons in which a player scored 20 or more Football League goals was set up by Arthur Rowley with Leicester City and Shrewsbury Town, over a period of 13 seasons ending in 1962–63.

League Career Figures

George Arthur Rowley's goalscoring record in League matches

1946–47	West Bromwich Albion	–
1947–48		4
1948–49		–
1948–49	Fulham	19
1949–50		8
1950–51	Leicester City	28
1951–52		38
1952–53		39
1953–54		30
1954–55		23
1955–56		29
1956–57		44
1957–58		20
1958–59	Shrewsbury Town	38
1959–60		32
1960–61		28
1961–62		23
1962–63		24
1963–64		5
1964–65		2
		434

Jimmy McGrory's goalscoring record in League matches

1922–23	Celtic	1
1923–24	Clydebank (loan)	13
1924–25	Celtic	17
1925–26		35
1926–27		49
1927–28		47
1928–29		20
1929–30		32
1930–31		37
1931–32		28
1932–33		22
1933–34		17
1934–35		18
1935–36		50
1936–37		19
1937–38		5
		410

Dixie Dean's goalscoring record in League matches

1923–24	Tranmere Rovers	–
1924–25		27
1924–25	Everton	2
1925–26		32
1926–27		21
1927–28		60

1928–29	26
1929–30	23
1930–31	39
1931–32	45
1932–33	24
1933–34	9
1934–35	26
1935–36	17
1936–37	24
1937–38	1
1937–38 Notts County	–
1938–39	3
	379

Hugh Kilpatrick (Hughie) Gallacher scored 387 League goals in 543 matches between 1921 and 1939. He is the highest goalscorer among players who have played in both English and Scottish football. He was with Airdrieonians, Newcastle United, Chelsea, Derby County, Notts County, Grimsby Town and Gateshead. The highest Scottish League scorer was Hugh Ferguson for Motherwell, Cardiff City and Dundee. His Scottish total alone was 284.

Notts County could claim to have had three of the most prolific goalscorers of the inter-war period on their staff in three seasons late in the 1930s. In 1936–37 Gallacher scored 25 goals in 32 appearances for County, while Jimmy Smith, who had set up the Scottish League record of 66 goals for Ayr United in 1927–28 in Division Two, scored once in four games for them. In 1937–38 County had Gallacher scoring seven goals in 13 games and Dixie Dean making three appearances without a goal. In 1938–39 Dean scored three times in six games.

After the war, Notts paid a record fee for a Division Three club of £20 000 for Tommy Lawton of Chelsea. In three seasons as a schoolboy he had scored 570 goals. He scored a hat-trick on his debut for Burnley and was still only 17 when Everton paid £6500 for him in March 1937. He scored 231 goals in 390 League games in a career which ended with Brentford and Arsenal, but with his wartime games his scoring rate doubled. He scored 22 goals in 23 England internationals and with wartime and Victory internationals had 46 goals in 45 games overall.

Goalscoring has proved to be one of the most erroneous areas of football statistics over the years. It was long considered that Arthur Chandler of Leicester City had established the record for the longest sequence of consecutive scoring, in an

The Greatest Haul

Paul Moulden scored 289 goals in League and Cup games for Bolton Lads Club in 1981–82. He achieved this total in 40 matches.

Opponents	Venue	Score	Moulden
All Saints	H	12–0	8
St Williams	H	16–0	11
Farnworth Boys	A	12–1	8
Christ Church	H	13–0	5
Sharples	H	28–0	16
Brenshaw	A	18–0	8
Moss Bank	A	15–0	6
Turton	A	14–0	8
Sutton	H	15–0	9
Marauders	H	14–1	9
St Peters	H	18–1	9
Marauders	H	5–1	4
Atherton RR	A	18–0	10
St Williams	A	14–2	8
Park Lane	H	11–0	8
Rose Lea	A	11–0	6
Farnworth Boys	H	14–1	8
St Judes	H	13–0	10
Atherton RR	A	1–0	1
Pegasus	H	6–2	3
Brenshaw	H	8–1	6
Marauders	H	13–0	7
Blackpool R	N	2–0	2
Atherton RR	H	25–0	15
Farnworth Boys	N	9–0	6
High Lawn	A	8–0	5
Rose Lea	A	9–2	4
Christ Church	A	7–0	6
Sharples	A	11–0	8
Sutton	A	9–0	6
Smithills	A	10–0	9
Turton	H	11–0	9
Smithills	H	13–0	7
Moss Bank	H	10–0	8
St Peters	A	7–0	6
Rose Lea	H	11–0	8
Moss Bank	N	11–0	5
All Saints	A	17–0	10
High Lawn	H	8–2	3
Marauders	A	14–0	4

Played 40, Won 40, Goals for 481, Goals against 14, Moulden 289

Kenny Dalglish achieved a century of goals in Scotland and then in England. Here in Celtic's hoops he watches Rangers John Greig clear the ball in a rainy Glasgow Cup encounter in 1975 (Colorsport)

unbroken spell of 16 Division Two matches in 1924–25. Although Leicester had one run of 19 games in which they scored in every match, Chandler was on target in only 13 and just seven in a row. He was leading scorer that season, though, with 32 League goals and remains overall the club's all-time top marksman with 259 League goals.

Scoring 100 goals for two separate Football League clubs is a comparatively rare feat but scoring a century of goals for clubs in Scotland and England is even more uncommon. However Kenny Dalglish achieved it for Celtic (112) and Liverpool (118).

There was something special about Boxing Day when Tranmere Rovers were playing in the 1930s. In addition to the League record 13–4 score in their club record win in 1935 against Oldham Athletic, they also suffered a 9–3 defeat in 1938 at the hands of Manchester City, during their season in Division Two. On 25 December 1931 Tranmere had beaten Rochdale 9–1 and the following day won 6–3 at Rochdale in Division Three (North).

There has only been one instance in the Football League of a match finishing 12–2. Aston Villa beat Accrington by that score in Division One on 12 March 1892. There have been two 13–0 wins: Stockport County against Halifax Town in Division Three (North) on 6 January 1934 and Newcastle United against Newport County on 5 October 1946 in Division Two. There was one score of 12–1 when Barrow beat Gateshead on 5 May 1934 in Division Three (North). It is interesting to note that Accrington, Newport County, Barrow and Gateshead have all subsequently lost their League status.

On 16 April 1900 West Bromwich Albion beat Nottingham Forest 8–0, having lost 6–1 away to Forest on 6 October 1899, in Division One. On 20 October 1900 Albion lost 6–1 at home to Forest.

The man who scored the highest number of goals for Everton in a League match was Jack Southworth. He hit six in a 7–1 win over West Bromwich Albion on 30 December 1893. A week earlier he had scored four times in an 8–1 win over Sheffield Wednesday, and between 9 December and 13 January he registered 16 goals. Southworth played 31 times for Everton and scored 36 goals.

George Hilsdon scored five goals on his debut for Chelsea in a Division Two match on 1 September 1906 against Glossop. The game ended in a 9–2 win. He later scored six times in an FA Cup tie against Worksop on 11 January 1908 in a 9–1 win.

On 26 September 1947 Chris Marron scored ten goals for South Shields against Radcliffe in an FA Cup preliminary round tie. Ted MacDougall scored nine times in an FA Cup first round tie on 20 November 1971 for Bournemouth against Margate.

Since the Second World War, Tottenham Hotspur have been involved in both the FA Cup tie and the Football League match which produced the highest aggregate of goals in those competitions. On 11 October 1958 they beat Everton 10–4 in a Division One match and the following season on 3 February 1960 in a fourth round Cup replay they defeated Crewe Alexandra 13–2.

When Sheffield Wednesday won the Second Division championship in the 1925–26 season, Jimmy Trotter scored 37 goals in 41 matches. In Division One a year later he again finished with 37 in 41.

On 10 September 1983 Simon Garner scored all five goals, including a penalty, for Blackburn Rovers against Derby County in a 5–1 win in Division Two, while Tony Caldwell scored five for Bolton Wanderers in an 8–1 win over Walsall in Division Three. On 29 October 1983 Tony Woodcock scored five goals for Arsenal in their 6–2 win at Aston Villa in Division One and Ian Rush five for Liverpool in their 6–0 success over Luton Town at Anfield, also in Division One.

Only Darwen, who subsequently disappeared from the League, and Rotherham United have suffered as many as four double-figure defeats. These include two such results in 1896 involving the old Rotherham Town club, which amalgamated with Rotherham County to form the present United in 1925. In 1898–99 Darwen conceded 109 goals in their 17 away fixtures in Division Two. They included three 10–0 defeats against Loughborough Town, Manchester City and Walsall. They were not re-elected.

In the 1933–34 season, four teams in the Third Division (North) scored more than a century of goals: Barnsley 118, Stockport County 115, Wrexham 102 and Barrow 116, who finished respectively 1st, 3rd, 6th and 8th. Darlington, who were 16th, conceded

Bob Gurney was a prolific scorer for Sunderland with more than 200 goals for the club after signing from Bishop Auckland in 1925 (Sunderland FC)

101, Gateshead (19th) 110, Accrington Stanley (20th) 101 and Rochdale (22nd) 103. The 462 games in the division yielded 1800 goals.

Bob Gurney scored 228 League and Cup goals for Sunderland after starting his career with Hetton Juniors and Bishop Auckland. He arrived at Roker Park in 1925 and in his first competitive game scored nine goals for Sunderland reserves against Hartlepool. His first-team debut came in April 1926 but he was kept out of a regular place by Dave Halliday until 1929–30 when he finished as leading scorer. He was also top scorer in the next six seasons. Gurney helped Sunderland to win the First Division title in 1936 and the FA Cup in the following year, when his 51st minute equaliser proved the turning point of the final with Preston North End. Sunderland won 3–1. He made one appearance for England but in 1939 his career ended when he broke his leg after just two minutes of a cup-tie with Blackburn Rovers. Gurney actually hobbled back onto the pitch before the full extent of the injury was diagnosed.

Bunny Bell was the only player to average more than a goal per game in both Divisions One and Three in the same season. In 1935–36 in Division Three (North) he scored 33 goals in 28 matches before a transfer to Everton for whom he added three goals in two games before the end of the season.

The first three Football League goals scored by John King were for different clubs in different divisions in different seasons: Everton (Division One in 1958–59), Bournemouth (Division Three in 1960–61) and Tranmere Rovers (Division Four in 1961–62). David Helliwell scored his first four in different divisions in different seasons: for Luton Town (Division Four 1965–66), for Middlesbrough (Division Three 1966–67 and Division Two 1967–68) and Coventry City (Division One 1969–70). Bill Horton's first three appearances in first class football were made in three different national competitions for Aldershot in the FA Cup (1961–62), Football League Cup and Football League (1962–63) in that order.

Trevor Francis scored all four goals for Birmingham City against Bolton Wanderers on 20 February 1971 in a 4–0 win to become the first under-17 player in history to score as many times in a Football League match. He was not 17 until the following April.

William Pendergast scored in 12 successive Division Three (North) matches for Chester in the 1938–39 season. He finished with 26 goals in 34 games. Dixie Dean had scored in 12 successive Division Two games in 1930–31. He finished with 39 goals from 37 games. John Aldridge scored in ten successive Division One matches for Liverpool, the last game in 1986–87 and the first nine in 1987–88.

Bill Hartill was born in Wolverhampton and developed locally, playing as a centre-forward for Wolverhampton Schools. He joined the Royal Horse Artillery and represented the Army against France and Belgium in the Kentish Cup, the oldest cup competition in Europe, which had launched after the First World War. Eventually he joined Wolves and led them to promotion to the First Division in 1931–32 when the club scored a record 115 goals. Hartill contributed 30 of them and between 1928 and 1935 he registered 164 League goals. Appropriately enough he was nicknamed 'Hartillery'.

Hat-tricks

Jimmy Greaves scored five Division One goals for Chelsea on three occasions: against Wolverhampton Wanderers in August 1958, Preston in December 1959 and West Bromwich Albion in December 1960. No other player since the war has scored five or more, more than once, in matches in any division. Greaves, born in March 1940, also became the youngest-ever player to score five times in a First Division match.

Nottingham Forest have gone longest of all the 92 League clubs since a hat-trick was scored against them in a League game. The last was scored by Mel Machin for Norwich City on 2 October 1974.

On 10 December 1983 Terry Gibson scored a hat-trick for Coventry City in a 4–0 win over Liverpool in Division One at Highfield Road. It was the first time a player had scored a hat-trick against Liverpool since Keith Weller did so for Leicester City in a 3–2 success in Division One on 30 August 1972.

The most hat-tricks by one player in any Football League division in one season since the war came from Terry Bly with seven for Peterborough United in Division Four in 1960–61 against Crystal Palace, Exeter City (twice), Darlington, Carlisle United, Chester and Barrow.

Bill Hartill the Wolves striker who still holds the club record for aggregate scoring (Colorsport)

Denis Law, seen here in the not-so-long ago days before designer-shirts and advertising motifs, was a prolific marksman for Scotland (Associated Sports Photography)

Maurice Edelston scored three goals in two consecutive home games in 1946–47: a 10–2 win over Crystal Palace and a 7–2 success against Southend United while an amateur (David Downs)

Arthur Rowley was the only player who ever scored two League hat-tricks in the same season when appearing against his former club. In Division Two matches in season 1952–53 he achieved the feat for Leicester City against Fulham at Filbert Street and Craven Cottage.

Playing for Reading against Crystal Palace on 4 September 1946, and Southend United on 7 September, Maurice Edelston became the only amateur ever to score two Football League hat-tricks in successive matches within four days.

John McClelland achieved an away hat-trick in his home town on 27 October 1962. He claimed all three Queen's Park Rangers goals in a 3–0 win at Bradford.

Only two players in history scored Football League hat-tricks on their wedding day: Bill Poyntz (Leeds United) against Leicester City on 20 February 1922, and Bill Holmes (Southport) against Carlisle United on 30 October 1954.

Playing for Middlesbrough in Division Two in 1958–59, Brian Clough became the only player who ever 'did the double' in hat-tricks against the same club in the same season. He scored a hat-trick in both games against Brighton and Hove Albion and also twice against Scunthorpe United. Clough also scored four times in Middlesbrough's 6–2 win over Swansea Town on 21 March 1959, his 24th birthday.

South African-born England international Colin Viljoen was the last player to record a hat-trick on his Football League debut, for Ipswich Town against Portsmouth on 25 March 1967.

David Gwyther scored four goals, all headed, for Swansea Town against Oxford City in an FA Cup second round tie on 6 December 1969, his 21st birthday.

Cliff Holton ranks as the only player since the war to have scored hat-tricks on successive days – for Watford in Division Four against Chester on Good Friday, 15 April 1960 and Gateshead a day later.

John Goodchild claimed three of Sunderland's goals in a 4–2 away win against Leeds United in Division Two on 25 February 1961. It was the only Football League match in which he appeared in that season.

Since substitutes were introduced in August 1965, three players have hit hat-tricks after coming off the bench: Geoffrey Vowden (Birmingham City) against Huddersfield Town in Division Two on 7 September 1968; Keith Allen (Luton Town) against Ware in the FA Cup first round on 16 November 1968; and Steve Staunton (Liverpool) against Wigan Athletic in the second leg of the Littlewoods Cup second round tie on 4 October 1989.

All five goals scored by the late Johnny Summer in Charlton Athletic's 7–6 defeat of Huddersfield Town, on 21 December 1957, were obtained with his 'wrong' foot. He said: 'I'm a natural left-footer, but I scored them all with my right.'

The only case of two players of the same side both scoring hat-tricks in successive rounds in the FA Cup competition proper came in season 1968–69. For Southend United Billy Best and Gary Moore each scored three times in the 9–0 first round defeat of King's Lynn; then Best scored five and Moore four in the 10–0 second round win against Brentwood.

Ted Drake scored four goals in the last Football League peace-time match of his career, for Arsenal against Sunderland on 2 September 1939. Ray Bowden scored three in the last League game of his career – for Newcastle United against Swansea Town on the same day.

John Galley ranks as the only player in history to have achieved hat-tricks when making his Football League debut with two clubs – and in an away match in each case. He did it for Rotherham United at Coventry in December 1964 and Bristol City at Huddersfield in December 1967.

Division One hat-tricks scored by Derek Dougan (Leicester City) and Harry Burrows (Stoke City) in September and December respectively in 1966 were

both obtained against Aston Villa, with whom both had previously played.

Of the eight hat-tricks claimed for Chelsea by former England international forward Bobby Tambling in League games, five came from away matches.

Jimmy Greaves scored six First Division hat-tricks for Chelsea in season 1960–61 and four hat-tricks for Spurs in both 1962–63 and 1963–64. No other player claims more than four such feats in Division One in any post-war season.

Denis Law claims the existing record for the most hat-tricks to have been scored in European cup competitions by anyone for a Football League club. With Manchester United he recorded five: two each in the European Cup and Cup-Winners Cup and one in the Fairs Cup.

Law also scored four times for Manchester United against Ipswich Town on 3 November 1962, and four times for Scotland against Norway four days later, on 7 November. Ian Edwards scored three times for Wales against Malta on 25 October 1978 and three for Chester v Brentford on 28 October.

Geoff Hurst (West Ham United) and Malcolm Macdonald (Newcastle United and Arsenal) both scored hat-tricks for England in full international matches, in FA Cup and League Cup ties, and in Football League games.

In a Division Four match on 31 March 1973, John Murray of Bury, playing against Doncaster Rovers, became the first player in history to score a Football League hat-trick and then be sent off.

Playing for Scotland at Hampden Park, Denis Law scored four goals against Northern Ireland on 7 November 1962, and four against Norway on 7 November 1963. Playing for Newcastle United in League Cup ties, Malcolm Macdonald scored three against Doncaster Rovers on 8 October 1973, and three against Queen's Park Rangers on 8 October 1974.

Playing for Rotherham United in the Third Division (North), Walter Ardron scored four against Carlisle United on 13 September 1947, and four against Hartlepools United on 13 September 1948.

Playing for Luton Town at centre-forward in an emergency in a Division Four game on 20 November 1965, Tony Read became the only recognised goalkeeper who ever scored a Football League hat-trick.

Left to right: Tony Adcock, Paul Stewart and David White share the ball after each had scored a hat-trick for Manchester City in the 10–1 win over Huddersfield Town in November 1987 (Manchester City FC)

Ken Barnes scored three times for Manchester City against Everton on 7 December 1957 and Peter Barnes did so for West Bromwich Albion against Bolton Wanderers on 18 March 1980 – the only case of father and son both achieving Division One hat-tricks.

Manchester City defeated Huddersfield Town 10–1 in a Division Two match at Maine Road on 7 November 1987. Three City players scored hat-tricks: Paul Stewart, Tony Adcock and David White. It was the fifth time in Football League history that three players had scored as many goals for one team, following West, Souncer and Hooper for Nottingham Forest against Leicester Fosse in in Division One on 21 April 1909; Loasby, Smith and Wells for Northampton Town against Walsall in Division Three (South) on 5 November 1927; Bowater, Hoyland and Readman for Mansfield Town against Rotherham United in Division Three (North) on 27 December 1932; and Davies, Barnes, and Ambler for Wrexham against Hartlepool United in Division Four on 5 March 1962.

During the last 50 peace-time seasons of League football, only two players have achieved hat-tricks in three successive matches. Frank Wrightson did it with Chester in February 1936 and Jack Balmer with Liverpool in November 1946. Wrightson actually scored four in the first game of his series.

Twenty-four hours after signing for Airdrie from Clydebank in a £175 000 transfer, Owen Coyle scored a hat-trick against Ayr United in a Division One match on 10 February 1990. His goals came in a nine-minute spell, after 57, 62 and 66 minutes.

Managers

England

Before World War Two there was, with one exception, no England team-manager. That exception was a last-minute decision to allow a manager travelling unofficially with the FA party to take charge of the team shortly before their match. This was when the Arsenal manager, Herbert Chapman, travelled to Rome with the England team which drew 1–1 with Italy on 13 May 1933. Chapman denied that he had been asked to take charge, though it was assumed that he was on hand for the second game of the tour in Berne, a 4–0 win over Switzerland. However his appointment, if it existed at all, was so informal that it can be practically dismissed from any list of England team managers.

Before the war, and indeed for several years afterwards, England teams were selected by an International Committee and if anyone could be said to have been in charge of the England team it was a member of the International Committee, although he, of course, did not discuss tactics but merely concerned himself with arrangements off the field.

The first time the FA actually appointed a team manager – and advised him of their decision well in advance of the game for which he was to be in charge – was in April 1946, when they informed Tom Whittaker, the Arsenal trainer, that they would require his services as manager of the England team to meet Switzerland at Stamford Bridge on 11 May 1946 and France in Paris eight days later. These were Victory Internationals; England won the first game 4–1 but lost the second 2–1.

However, even this appointment was only a temporary one, for the FA were, somewhat reluctantly it seemed, considering the appointment of a full-time manager. The man pressing for such an appointment to be made was the FA's secretary, Stanley Rous, and he had his way in the summer of 1946 when former Manchester United half-back Walter Winterbottom was appointed director of coaching and England team manager. The first official England international game for which Winterbottom actually took charge of the team was against Ireland in Belfast on 28 September 1946. England won 7–2. He had, however, been present a month earlier when England met Scotland at Maine Road, Manchester, in aid of the Bolton Disaster Fund.

Surprisingly enough there was considerable resistance to the appointment of an England team-manager both inside and outside the FA, and it is true to say that during his appointment, which lasted until August 1962 when he resigned to become general secretary of the Central Council of Physical Education, Winterbottom never had the power that one would expect a man in this position to be given.

The first man to be given this power was Alf Ramsey, appointed in October 1962 and officially operating from May 1963, though he had been in charge of the team which lost 5–2 to France in February 1963 in a Nations Cup match in Paris. Ramsey was manager of championship teams from Divisions One, Two and Three. He led Ipswich Town to the Division Three title in the 1956–57 season, Division Two in 1960–61 and the League Championship itself in 1961–62.

The most extensive family in football management was the Maley dynasty. Tom Maley, born in Scotland, managed Manchester City and Bradford Park Avenue; Willie, his brother, born in Ireland, managed Celtic; and Alec, born in England, managed Hibernian. Charlie Maley, son of Tom, was secretary of both Bradford clubs and also of Leicester City.

Player-managers in Division One of the Football League have been: Andy Cunningham (Newcastle United) prior to the Second World War, in 1930; Les Allen (Queens Park Rangers) 1968–69; Johnny Giles (West Bromwich Albion) 1976–77; Howard Kendall (Everton) 1981–82; Kenny Dalglish (Liverpool) 1985–89; and Trevor Francis (Queens Park Rangers) 1988–89.

When David Steele, as Bradford Park Avenue manager, turned out in an emergency in a wartime match against Sheffield Wednesday in October 1942, his age exceeded the combined ages of three other members of the team: Billy Elliott, Johnny Downie and Geoff Walker. Steele was 49 at the time and the three youngsters were 16-year-olds. The match ended in a 3–3 draw.

Steve Murray was appointed manager of Forfar Athletic on 18 August 1980 and informed the club's board of directors that he was resigning on

21 August, though the news was withheld from the playing staff until 23 August.

Harold Wightman was with four different clubs in different divisions over a period of 12 months during 1935–36. He was assistant manager to George Jobey at Derby when the 1934–35 season ended and during the summer he was appointed secretary-manager of Luton Town. He became manager of Mansfield Town in January 1936 and manager of Nottingham Forest in May 1936. Derby were in Division One, Forest in Division Two, Luton in Division Three (South) and Mansfield in Division Three (North).

Bill Lambton was appointed manager of Scunthorpe United on 21 April 1959 but the appointment, a verbal one, was cancelled three days later. Jimmy McIlroy was team manager of Bolton Wanderers for 18 days during November 1970 before resigning, but Johnny Cochrane was manager of Reading for just 13 days from 31 March 1939 to 13 April 1939.

Tim Ward was appointed manager of Exeter City in March 1953 but became manager of his former club Barnsley 25 days later. His actual stay at Exeter was only seven days because he was recalled by Barnsley who still held his registration as a player.

Bobby Flavell spent 17 days as manager of Ayr United in December 1961 before returning in a similar capacity to St Mirren where he had previously been coach.

In May 1984 Dave Bassett was named as Crystal Palace manager but changed his mind four days later without signing hist contract and returned to Wimbledon.

Charles Foweraker (Bolton Wanderers) was the only man to manage the same Football League club for 20 years between the wars.

Eric Taylor was with Sheffield Wednesday from August 1929 to June 1974, graduating on the administrative staff from junior to assistant secretary and secretary before the war. He became manager in 1942, secretary-manager in 1945 and general-manager and secretary from September 1958.

Eddie Davison was manager of Sheffield United for 20 years from June 1932 to the summer of 1952. He had served Sheffield Wednesday as a goalkeeper from 1908 to 1926 after joining them from Gateshead Town. He made one appearance for England. Before taking over as United's manager he had been in charge of Chesterfield, where he later returned.

Billy Walker was appointed manager of Sheffield Wednesday in December 1933 and took up a similar position with Nottingham Forest in March 1939 after being in charge of Chelmsford for a time. He remained at Forest for 21 years until 1960 when he retired to be appointed a manager member of the Club Committee. His aggregate of 213 goals in the League between 1919 and 1934 had been a joint Aston Villa record and he also once held the appearance record with 480 games over the same period. While at Villa he made 18 appearances for England.

Joe Smith became manager of Blackpool in 1935 after four seasons in charge of Reading. Over the next 23 years the club won promotion to Division One in 1937, were FA Cup runners-up in 1948 and 1951, winners in 1953 and Division One runners-up in 1955–56. As an inside-forward he had had a career of more than 20 years with Bolton Wanderers and Stockport County as well as appearing for England five times.

Jimmy Seed had just over 23 years in charge of Charlton Athletic from May 1933 to September 1956. He had also been an inside-forward with Tottenham Hotspur and Sheffield Wednesday and similarly made five appearances for England. Under his guidance Charlton won promotion in successive seasons from Division Three (South) to Division One and in 1936–37, their first season in that division, they were runners-up. They also won the FA Cup in 1947 after finishing runners-up the previous season.

Billy McCandless managed three Welsh teams who acheived promotion from the Third Division: Newport County 1938–39, Cardiff City 1946–47 and Swansea Town 1948–49. He was an Irishman from Ballymena.

Herbert Chapman, a Yorkshireman born at Kiveton Park, had a modest playing career with Grimsby, Swindon, Northampton, Sheffield United, Notts County and Tottenham Hotspur, then a successful one as a manager:
1907 Northampton Town – Midland Southern League champions 1908–09
1912 Leeds City – Midland Section champions (wartime regional league) 1916–17 and 1917–18
1920 Huddersfield Town – FA Cup winners 1921–22, League champions 1923–24, 1924–25
1925 Arsenal – FA Cup winners 1929–30, League champions 1930–31, 1932–33
But investigations into financial irregularities in administration at Leeds City resulted in the club being expelled in 1919 and the directors suspended,

along with Chapman. He was pardoned a year later to continue a successful career, ended by his death in January 1934 when Arsenal were in the middle of emulating Huddersfield's three successive League Championship wins.

Ten England international players who played in the 1948–49 side – Laurie Scott, Alf Ramsey, Tim Ward, Neil Franklin, Billy Wright, Stanley Matthews, Stan Mortensen, Jackie Milburn, Roy Bentley and Stan Pearson – all subsequently became either managers or player-managers of Football League clubs.

Several members of England's successful World Cup-winning team of 1966 had spells as Football League managers, two of them with the same club. Nobby Stiles became manager of Preston North End in 1977–78, where Bobby Charlton had previously acted as player-manager. Bobby's elder brother Jack Charlton took over as manager of Sheffield Wednesday after holding a similar position with Middlesbrough. He later led Newcastle United and finally became the Republic of Ireland manager in February 1986. Bobby Moore had a brief spell in charge of Southend United from 1984–86, and Alan Ball was player-manager of Blackpool, then manager of Portsmouth in the 1980s before taking charge at Stoke City. Geoff Hurst was the Chelsea manager from 1979–81.

Bobby Charlton (top left, leading Manchester United out at Crystal Palace), his brother Jack, Geoff Hurst (bottom left) and Nobby Stiles all had varying experiences at the managerial role after playing together in England's 1966 World Cup squad (Associated Sports Photography)

Player and Manager of League Championship winning teams

Ted Drake	*Player:* Arsenal 1934, 1935, 1938
	Manager: Chelsea 1955
Bill Nicholson	*Player:* Tottenham Hotspur 1951
	Manager: Tottenham Hotspur 1961
Alf Ramsey	*Player:* Tottenham Hotspur 1951
	Manager: Ipswich Town 1962
Joe Mercer	*Player:* Everton 1939, Arsenal 1948, 1953
	Manager: Manchester City 1968
Dave Mackay	*Player:* Tottenham Hotspur 1961
	Manager: Derby County 1975
Bob Paisley	*Player:* Liverpool 1947
	Manager: Liverpool 1976, 1977, 1979, 1980, 1982, 1983
Howard Kendall	*Player:* Everton 1970
	Manager: Everton 1985, 1987
Kenny Dalglish	*Player:* Liverpool 1979, 1980, 1982, 1983, 1984
	Manager: Liverpool 1986, 1988, 1990
George Graham	*Player:* Arsenal 1971
	Manager: Arsenal 1989

Only two managers have won the League Championship with different clubs: Herbert Chapman, Huddersfield Town (1923–24, 1924–25) and Arsenal (1930–31, 1932–33) and Brian Clough, Derby County (1971–72) and Nottingham Forest (1977–78).

Since the Second World War, two players appeared in and later managed both FA Cup and League Championship-winning teams. Joe Mercer played for Arsenal in their 1948 and 1953 League successes and 1950 FA Cup and later managed Manchester City when they won the championship in 1968 and the FA Cup the following year. Kenny Dalglish played for Liverpool in the 1979, 1980, 1982, 1983 and 1984 Championship successes and, as player-manager, guided them to the League and FA Cup double in 1986. Since then, as a manager, Dalglish has won the League title twice, in 1988 and 1990, and the FA Cup in 1989.

West Ham United have had only seven managers in their history: Syd King, Charlie Paynter, Ted Fenton, Ron Greenwood, John Lyall, Lou Macari and Billy Bonds.

Sir Matt Busby was in charge of Manchester United from October 1945 to June 1971, his last two years as General Manager and team manager.

At the end of the 1989–90 season, Brian Clough of Nottingham Forest was the longest serving one-club manager in the Football League, having taken up his post in January 1975. He completed 1 000 matches as a manager (with Hartlepool United, Derby County, Brighton & Hove Albion and Nottingham Forest) when Forest won 3–2 at Tottenham on 30 December 1989.

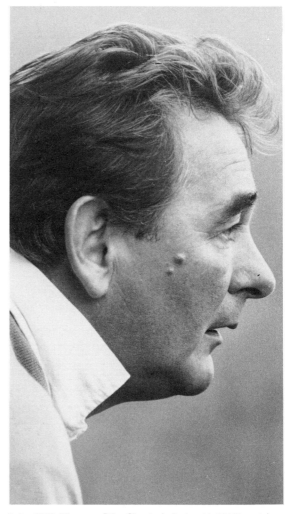

In the 1989–90 season Brian Clough clocked up his 1000tn match as a manager. He had also completed 15 years in charge of Nottingham Forest (Sporting Pictures)

Home Countries' Full International Records

England

	P	W	D	L	F	A
Albania	2	2	0	0	7	0
Argentina	9	4	3	2	13	9
Australia	4	2	2	0	4	2
Austria	15	8	3	4	54	25
Belgium	18	13	4	1	67	24
Bohemia	1	1	0	0	4	0
Brazil	14	2	5	7	12	20
Bulgaria	5	3	2	0	7	1
Cameroon	1	1	0	0	3	2
Canada	1	1	0	0	1	0
Chile	4	2	2	0	4	1
Colombia	2	1	1	0	5	1
Cyprus	2	2	0	0	6	0
Czechoslovakia	11	7	2	2	23	15
Denmark	12	8	3	1	26	11
Ecuador	1	1	0	0	2	0
Egypt	2	2	0	0	5	0
FIFA (Rest of the World)	3	2	1	0	9	5
Finland	8	7	1	0	32	5
France	20	14	2	4	60	27
Germany	3	2	1	0	12	6
East Germany	4	3	1	0	7	3
West Germany	16	7	3	6	24	19
Greece	5	4	1	0	10	1
Holland	10	4	4	2	16	10
Hungary	16	10	1	5	45	27
Iceland	1	0	1	0	1	1
Northern Ireland	96	74	6	16	319	80
Republic of Ireland	11	5	4	2	17	10
Israel	2	1	1	0	2	1
Italy	17	6	5	6	25	22
Kuwait	1	1	0	0	1	0
Luxembourg	7	7	0	0	38	3
Malta	2	2	0	0	6	0
Mexico	6	3	1	2	14	3
Morocco	1	0	1	0	0	0
Norway	6	5	0	1	25	4
Paraguay	1	1	0	0	3	0
Peru	2	1	0	1	5	4
Poland	7	3	3	1	9	4
Portugal	15	8	5	2	35	17
Romania	8	2	5	1	6	4
Saudi Arabia	1	0	1	0	1	1
Scotland	107	43	24	40	188	168
Spain	16	10	2	4	35	19
Sweden	13	6	4	3	23	14
Switzerland	15	10	2	3	37	12
Tunisia	1	0	1	0	1	1
Turkey	4	3	1	0	21	0
USA	5	4	0	1	29	5
Uruguay	8	2	2	4	8	11
USSR	10	4	3	3	16	12
Wales	97	62	21	14	239	90
Yugoslavia	14	5	5	4	23	20

Scotland

	P	W	D	L	F	A
Argentina	3	1	1	1	3	4
Austria	14	3	4	7	18	28
Australia	2	1	1	0	2	0
Belgium	12	4	1	7	17	20
Brazil	8	0	2	6	2	12
Bulgaria	3	2	1	0	3	1
Canada	3	3	0	0	7	0
Chile	2	2	0	0	6	2
Colombia	1	0	1	0	0	0
Costa Rica	1	0	0	1	0	1
Cyprus	4	4	0	0	18	3
Czechoslovakia	10	5	1	4	18	16
Denmark	10	8	0	2	17	6
Egypt	1	0	0	1	1	3
England	107	40	24	43	168	188
Finland	4	4	0	0	13	3
France	10	6	0	4	12	11
Germany	2	1	1	0	3	1
East Germany	6	2	1	3	6	4
West Germany	8	2	3	3	14	14
Holland	9	5	2	2	13	10
Hungary	7	2	2	3	13	15
Iceland	2	2	0	0	4	0
Iran	1	0	1	0	1	1
Northern Ireland	91	60	16	15	253	81
Republic of Ireland	6	2	2	2	8	4
Israel	3	3	0	0	5	1
Italy	4	1	0	3	1	8
Luxembourg	3	2	1	0	9	0
Malta	2	1	1	0	3	2
New Zealand	1	1	0	0	5	2
Norway	10	7	2	1	30	14
Paraguay	1	0	0	1	2	3

	P	W	D	L	F	A
Peru	3	1	1	1	4	4
Poland	6	1	2	3	7	9
Portugal	11	4	2	5	13	11
Romania	3	1	2	0	5	2
Saudi Arabia	1	0	1	0	2	2
Spain	10	3	3	4	16	16
Sweden	7	4	1	2	11	8
Switzerland	9	5	1	3	15	13
Turkey	1	0	0	1	2	4
Uruguay	4	1	1	2	4	10
USA	1	1	0	0	6	0
USSR	3	0	1	2	2	5
Wales	101	60	23	18	238	111
Yugoslavia	8	2	5	1	16	11
Zaire	1	1	0	0	2	0

Wales

	P	W	D	L	F	A
Austria	4	1	0	3	3	6
Belgium	2	1	0	1	6	4
Bulgaria	2	1	0	1	1	1
Brazil	6	0	1	5	4	12
Canada	2	1	0	1	3	2
Chile	1	0	0	1	0	2
Costa Rica	1	1	0	0	1	0
Czechoslovakia	10	3	1	6	7	12
Denmark	4	2	0	2	5	4
England	97	14	21	62	90	239
Finland	6	3	2	1	11	4
France	4	1	1	2	4	9
East Germany	4	1	0	3	7	8
West Germany	8	0	4	4	5	14
Greece	2	1	0	1	4	3
Holland	2	0	0	2	1	3
Hungary	8	3	2	3	11	13
Iceland	4	2	1	1	8	4
Iran	1	1	0	0	1	0
Northern Ireland	90	42	21	27	181	126
Republic of Ireland	4	4	0	0	9	4
Israel	4	2	2	0	7	3
Italy	4	1	0	3	3	9
Kuwait	2	0	2	0	0	0
Luxembourg	2	2	0	0	8	1
Malta	3	3	0	0	12	2
Mexico	2	0	1	1	2	3
Norway	5	1	2	2	4	6
Poland	2	1	0	1	2	3
Portugal	2	1	0	1	4	4
Romania	3	1	1	1	5	2
Saudi Arabia	1	1	0	0	2	1
Scotland	101	18	23	60	111	238

	P	W	D	L	F	A
Spain	5	1	2	2	6	7
Sweden	3	0	1	2	1	6
Switzerland	2	1	0	1	3	6
Turkey	4	3	0	1	6	1
Rest of UK	2	1	0	1	3	3
Uruguay	1	0	1	0	0	0
USSR	5	1	2	2	3	6
Yugoslavia	7	0	3	4	10	18

Northern Ireland

	P	W	D	L	F	A
Albania	4	2	2	0	6	2
Algeria	1	0	1	0	1	1
Argentina	1	0	0	1	1	3
Austria	3	1	1	1	5	5
Australia	3	2	1	0	5	3
Belgium	2	1	0	1	3	2
Brazil	1	0	0	1	0	3
Bulgaria	4	2	1	1	4	3
Chile	1	0	0	1	0	1
Cyprus	4	3	0	1	11	1
Czechoslovakia	2	2	0	0	3	1
Denmark	3	1	1	1	3	6
England	96	6	16	74	80	319
Finland	2	1	0	1	2	2
France	7	0	3	4	4	17
West Germany	7	2	1	4	8	15
Greece	3	1	0	2	5	5
Holland	5	1	2	2	4	8
Honduras	1	0	1	0	1	1
Hungary	2	0	0	2	1	3
Iceland	2	1	0	1	2	1
Republic of Ireland	4	1	2	1	1	3
Israel	6	3	3	0	9	4
Italy	4	1	1	2	6	7
Malta	2	2	0	0	5	0
Mexico	1	1	0	0	4	1
Morocco	1	1	0	0	2	1
Norway	2	1	0	1	4	2
Poland	3	2	1	0	5	1
Portugal	6	2	3	1	7	4
Romania	2	2	0	0	4	2
Scotland	91	15	16	60	81	253
Spain	10	1	3	6	6	20
Sweden	4	2	0	2	6	3
Switzerland	2	1	0	1	2	2
Turkey	8	5	2	1	12	3
Uruguay	2	2	0	0	4	0
USSR	4	0	2	2	1	4
Wales	90	27	21	42	126	181
Yugoslavia	5	1	1	3	2	6

Republic of Ireland

	P	W	D	L	F	A		P	W	D	L	F	A
Algeria	1	0	0	1	0	2	Israel	3	1	1	1	5	3
Argentina*	3	0	1	2	0	2	Italy	6	0	0	6	3	13
Austria	10	2	2	6	13	27	Luxembourg	5	5	0	0	14	2
Belgium	12	4	4	4	22	22	Malta	5	5	0	0	16	0
Brazil	3	1	0	2	2	9	Mexico	1	0	1	0	0	0
Bulgaria	6	2	1	3	7	5	Norway	14	6	6	2	26	16
Chile	4	2	0	2	5	4	Poland	19	5	5	9	20	34
Cyprus	2	2	0	0	9	2	Portugal	5	1	0	4	3	9
Czechoslovakia	12	4	1	7	14	29	Romania	2	1	1	0	2	0
Denmark	9	3	3	3	12	15	Scotland	6	2	2	2	4	8
Ecuador	1	1	0	0	3	2	Spain	21	4	5	12	16	44
England	11	2	4	5	10	17	Sweden	6	1	1	4	7	14
Egypt	1	0	1	0	0	0	Switzerland	10	6	1	3	13	4
Finland	2	1	1	0	4	1	Trinidad & Tobago	1	0	0	1	1	2
France	11	4	3	4	13	15	Tunisia	1	1	0	0	4	0
Germany	3	1	1	1	7	6	Turkey	7	3	3	1	15	9
West Germany	11	4	1	6	12	20	Uruguay	2	0	1	1	1	3
Holland	11	4	2	5	20	21	USA	1	1	0	0	3	2
Hungary	9	1	3	5	14	22	USSR	7	2	1	4	7	8
Iceland	5	4	1	0	12	4	Wales	4	0	0	4	4	9
Iran	1	1	0	0	2	1	Yugoslavia	2	1	0	1	3	4
Northern Ireland	4	1	2	1	3	1	* Includes 0–0 draw in 1979 not considered a full international.						

International Facts

Billy Wright established a record of 70 consecutive international appearances for England up to 1959 when he retired (GSL)

Although Danny Blanchflower holds the record for consecutive appearances in the British International Championship – 33 for Northern Ireland between 1952 and 1962 – two other players appeared in more games overall in the competition. Billy Wright played in 38 including an English record of 25 successive appearances from 14 April 1951 to April 1959. However, Billy Meredith (Manchester City and Manchester United), capped on 48 occasions by Wales between 1895 and 1920, made all his appearances in the International Championship in the years before Wales met foreign opposition for the first time, against France in Paris on 25 May 1933.

Wright set up a world record of 70 consecutive appearances which began against France on 3 October 1951 and ended against the USA on 28 May 1959. He captained England for the first time against Northern Ireland in October 1948 and remained as skipper until his last game against the USA. He played in all but three of England's first 108 international matches after the Second World War. Moving from his original position of wing-half to centre-half for the game with Switzerland in June 1954, he played in that position thereafter.

Before 1971 there were few instances of players being born in one country and playing for another. But since then the international qualification rules have been altered to allow a player to represent not only the country of the father's birth but also the mother's birth.

An early example was Stuart Macrae, born in Port Bannantyne, Bute, Scotland who made six appearances for England at wing-half in 1883–84. Macrae was a Corinthians player at the time he appeared for England. Another Scot, Bob Milne, played 27 times for Ireland between 1894 and 1906. He had come to the attention of Linfield after he played for the Gordon Highlanders when they won the 1890 Irish Cup.

Several players have appeared for more than one of the countries in the British Isles. John Hawley Edwards played for England against Scotland in 1874 despite being born in Wales and later turned out for Wales against Scotland. He was with Shropshire Wanderers while playing for England. His appearance for Wales came when he was Clerk to Shrewsbury magistrates.

John Reynolds had already played five times for Ireland in 1890–91 when he moved from Distillery to West Bromwich, where it was discovered that he had been born in England. He subsequently played eight times for the country of his birth. Robert Ernest Evans played for Wales against England four times and also for England against Wales twice in the years before the First World War.

Manchester United had 18 full international players on their staff in the 1977–78 season: six from Scotland, five from England, five from Northern Ireland and two from the Republic of Ireland. They also hold the record for providing most players to an association other than their own for a single game: on 14 February 1973 when Scotland had five United men – Alex Forsyth, Martin Buchan, Lou Macari, George Graham and Willie Morgan – playing against England in the Scottish FA Centenary match at Hampden Park. Scotland lost 5–0!

In December 1976 United fielded eight full international players in a reserve Central League game, and in a period of just over seven years in the 1970s, they could claim 38 full international players: ten from England, eleven from Scotland, three from Wales, eight from Northern Ireland and six from the Republic of Ireland.

Cardiff City had 17 players on their staff towards the end of the 1925–26 season, all of whom had been capped: nine for Wales, four for Scotland and four for Northern Ireland.

In May 1971 Leeds United supplied eight players for two British International Championship matches: Paul Madeley, Terry Cooper and Allan Clarke for England v Northern Ireland; Peter Lorimer, Billy Bremner and Eddie Gray for Scotland v Wales and Gary Sprake and Terry Yorath for Wales in the same fixture.

Leeds also achieved a remarkable feat on 20 November 1974 by providing ten of their players for full international matches on the same day. Madeley, Cooper and Clarke for England v Portugal; David Harvey, Bremner, Gordon McQueen, Lorimer and Joe Jordan for Scotland v Spain; Yorath for Wales v Luxembourgh and Johnny Giles for the Republic of Ireland v Turkey.

In 1973 Leeds had 14 international players on their staff. In addition to those mentioned previously, they had Jack Charlton, Norman Hunter, Paul Reaney and Mick Jones, all capped by England.

Linfield supplied seven of the players in the Ireland team against Scotland on 25 March 1893 in Glasgow, but the Scots won 6–1.

Although Arsenal supplied seven players for the England team against Italy at Highbury on 14 November 1934, only five had originally been selected. George Male came in for the injured Tom Cooper (Derby County), who had been chosen to captain the team, at right-back. At centre-forward Fred Tilson (Manchester City) was the first choice but also had to drop out with injury. His replacement was George Hunt (Tottenham Hotspur), but he, too, was forced to withdraw for a similar reason. The reserves selected were a right-half, Tom Gardner (Aston Villa), and an inside-forward, Raich Carter (Sunderland). Both Male and Hunt appeared on the official programme but it was Ted Drake who played at centre-forward, following the late withdrawal of Hunt. The other five Arsenal players were Frank Moss, Eddie Hapgood, Wilf Coping, Ray Bowden and Cliff Bastin. England's trainer was Tom Whittaker of Arsenal. England won 3–2 against the World Cup holders.

During 1936–37 Arsenal had 14 international players on their books. In addition to the seven mentioned previously, Jack Crayston, Joe Hulme, Bernard Joy, Alf Kirchen and Herbie Roberts (all England), Alex James (Scotland) and Bob John (Wales) completed the set.

Harry Hibbs tips the ball over the bar for Birmingham in a match at Stamford Bridge against Chelsea in February 1936 (Hulton-Deutsch)

In the 1933–34 season Aston Villa had 15 internationals on their staff. There were ten who played for England: Joe Beresford, George Brown, Arthur Cunliffe, Tommy Gardner, Eric Houghton, Tommy Mort, Joe Tate, Tommy Smart, Billy Walker and Pongo Waring; three Scots, Danny Blair, Jimmy Gibson and Joe Nibloe and a Welshman, Dai Astley.

Birmingham had four international goalkeepers on their staff simultaneously in 1929. Dan Tremelling and Harry Hibbs were full England internationals, Kenneth Tewkesbury an amateur international and Arthur Slater a junior international.

Hibbs won 25 caps for England between November 1929 and February 1936 at a time when the international fixture list was limited. A goalkeeper of exceptional ability and temperament, he had started his career as a centre-forward but switched to goal in 1922 when with Tamworth Castle. He joined Birmingham in May 1924 and retired in 1940. He managed Walsall for a time up to 1951 but remarkably was reinstated as a permit player for De Havilands FC in 1953 when in his 48th year!

Northern Ireland is the only home country to have included a non-British player in a British International Championship match. He was Willie Andrews, a half-back who played for Glentoran and Grimsby Town. He was born in Kansas City, USA and played against Scotland (twice) and England between 1908 and 1913.

There have been only two occasions this century when Scotland have not included a player from a Glasgow club in a full international match against England. It happened at Newcastle in April 1907 when they drew 1–1 and at Wembley in May 1979 when they lost 3–1.

On only one other occasion since the Second World War have Scotland fielded a team in a British International Championship match that did not include a player from either Celtic or Rangers. On 2 April 1955 they lost 7–2 to England at Wembley, but they did have two players each from Glasgow clubs Clyde and Partick Thistle in their side.

Prior to the war, the Scots' side fielded no Glasgow-based players in October 1933, when they lost 3–2 to Wales. They had been unable to field a number of regular players owing to injuries and other causes.

The Scottish team which played Norway at Hampden Park on 25 October 1978 was composed entirely of Anglo-Scots. Scotland won 3–2. The Scottish team which played Holland at the same venue on 11 May 1966 was made up entirely of players with Scottish League teams. Holland won 3–0.

The Scots included ten Anglos in their team which started the match against East Germany in East Berlin on 7 September 1977. Later they brought on two more Anglos as substitutes. The only Scottish League player in the side was Danny McGrain, the Celtic full-back.

Arguably the shortest international career of any player was the 50 seconds in which Tommy Bogan of Hibernian made his debut for Scotland against England in a wartime international at Hampden Park on 14 April 1945. He was injured in a collision with the England goalkeeper Frank Swift, who carried him off the field unaided. He was not selected again.

Jim Barrett of West Ham United had the shortest full international career in peacetime. He was carried off injured in the eighth minute of his England debut against Ireland on 22 October 1928 and was not selected again.

When Celtic and former Liverpool forward Frank McGarvey made his full international debut, as a Liverpool player, on 2 May 1979, he came on as a sustitute for the last 90 seconds for Scotland against Northern Ireland and had not touched the ball at the end of the game. He went on to win seven caps.

The only hat-trick to have been achieved for Northern Ireland in a British International Championship match in the present century was a double one: six goals for Joe Bambrick in a 7–0 win over Wales in Belfast on 1 February 1930.

Only four players in this century have achieved hat-tricks when making their debuts for England in full international matches: George Mills (Chelsea) against Northern Ireland in October 1937; Wilf Mannion (Middlesbrough) against Northern Ireland in September 1946; Stan Mortensen (Blackpool) against

Frank McGarvey's debut for Scotland was brief but not an isolated appearance (Allsport)

Portugal in May 1947 and Fred Pickering (Everton) against the USA in May 1964.

A post-war record was established by Jimmy Greaves who achieved six hat-tricks for England in full international matches while with Chelsea and Tottenham Hotspur. They were against Luxembourg in October 1960, Scotland in April 1961, Peru in May 1962, Northern Ireland in November 1963 (when he scored four goals), Northern Ireland in October 1964 and Norway in June 1966 (four goals).

England scored seven goals in each of two successive games against Northern Ireland although they had to wait eight years between the matches. On 16 November 1938 England won 7–0 at Old Trafford and on 28 September 1946 they beat the Irish 7–2 at Windsor Park, Belfast.

Billy Foulkes of Newcastle United scored with his first kick on his international debut for Wales against England at Ninian Park, Cardiff on 20 October 1951. The game ended in a 1–1 draw.

In the 1946–47 season, Chelsea's Tommy Lawton scored four goals against both Holland and Portugal and one against Northern Ireland and Wales. He added two for Great Britain against the Rest of Europe for a total of twelve goals.

After scoring a hat-trick for England against Poland in the World Cup in Mexico on 11 June 1986, Gary Lineker's scoring in the following ten matches was thus: 2, 1, 2, 0, 4, 0, 0, 1, 1, 3 for a total of 17 goals.

For many years the three goals scored by Fulham's Johnny Haynes against the USSR at Wembley on 22 October 1958 ranked as the only hat-trick ever achieved by England against any of the Eastern European countries. But Gary Lineker matched this when he scored three for England v Poland in the 1986 World Cup.

Ireland had played fifty international matches before including a player from a Football League club in their side. It was their 51st game on 4 March 1899 against Wales in Belfast when Archie Goodall (Derby County), Bill Taggart (Walsall) and Tom Morrison (Burnley) played in a 1–0 win.

Johnny Haynes who holds the Fulham record for the highest aggregate of League goals scored and also contrived a rare hat-trick against Eastern European opposition for England (Allsport)

Scotland first used a player from the Football League in their 59th international match on 4 April 1894 against England at Celtic Park. They had five Anglo-Scots in their side, and won 2–1.

The last non-league amateur to appear for England in a full international was inside-forward Edgar Kail of Dulwich Hamlet. He had been reserve for the team against Ireland, Scotland and Wales before he was finally rewarded with a full cap by playing inside-right in three of England's games on their 1929 continental tour. He scored two goals in the 4–1 win over France, helped the team beat Belgium 5–1 and was on the losing side when they lost 4–3 to Spain in Madrid.

Bernard Joy (Arsenal and Corinthian Casuals) was the last amateur to play for England in a full international. He played against Belgium in Brussels on 9 May 1936.

Between 1946 and 1948, Kevin O'Flanagan and his brother Michael played for Ireland at soccer and Rugby Union. It was the only instance of brothers both becoming internationals in two football codes. Kevin played for Ireland against France at rugby on 27 January 1946 in Dublin, against Scotland at soccer the following week in Dublin and was chosen for Ireland v England at rugby again seven days after that. However, his train was late at Liverpool, he missed the boat to Dublin and unable to travel by air, he missed a unique hat-trick. Michael played centre-forward with Kevin at outside-right for the Republic of Ireland against England in Dublin on 30 September 1946. Kevin, who played for London Irish, was first capped for the Republic in pre-war days while playing for Bohemians, his brother's club. In 1946–47 he was with Arsenal.

When Nigel Clough was capped by England against Chile on 23 May 1989 at Wembley he emulated the achievement of George Eastham junior by following in his father's footsteps. Brian Clough had been capped twice in the 1959–60 season. George Eastham senior played once pre-war for England, his son 19 times afterwards.

At Wrexham on 17 March 1937 in the Wales v Northern Ireland match, all the players from the Welsh team were drawn from clubs outside the country and all but two of the Irish team, Fulton and Banks, both amateurs, were similarly taken from outside their country. Wales won 4–1.

In November 1959, Johnny Crossan was chosen for Northern Ireland against England at Wembley, yet at the time he was banned from playing with any Irish or

Brian Clough's son Nigel followed in his father's footsteps by playing for England. He was the first to so do since George Eastham junior had emulated his father George senior in 1962–63 (Paul Clarke)

English club. Then in Dutch soccer, with Sparta Rotterdam, he was under 'permanent suspension' by both the Football League and the Irish League.

After the Second World War it was not unusual for Irish players to play for both the Republic and Northern Ireland. For example Johnny Carey, when a Manchester United player, turned out against England in two full international matches within three days and for different countries. He appeared for Northern Ireland in Belfast on 28 September 1946 and for the Republic of Ireland in Dublin on 30 September.

Later, in the same season, he played in four countries in eight days. The sequence began with a Division One match for Manchester United at Liverpool on Saturday 3 May 1947 and was followed by playing for the Republic of Ireland against Portugal in Dublin the next day. He then played in a Dutch trial match at The Hague on 6 May and for the Rest of Europe against Great Britain at Hampden Park on 10 May.

Far more rare have been instances of players turning out for three different countries. Joe Kennaway, the Celtic goalkeeper, is supposed to have played for both the USA and Canada (his birthplace) and later for Scotland in 1934 on two occasions.

However, Ladislav Kubala certainly played for Hungary on three occasions followed by six games for Czechoslovakia. He was later naturalised by Spain and made 19 appearances for them in the 1950s and 1960s.

Wartime emergencies caused other cases of dual nationality. When Germany overran Austria in 1938 they co-opted a number of leading Austrian internationals into their national team. Hans Pesser was just one who played for both countries in the 1930s and 1940s. In addition Ernst Willimowski, who scored four goals for Poland against Brazil in the 1938 World Cup, later played for Germany following the invasion of his country.

Tommy Pearson (Newcastle United), born in Scotland, played for England against the Scots in a wartime Red Cross international at Newcastle on 2 December 1939 when he was pressed into service as a replacement for Eric Brook (Manchester City) who had been injured in a road accident on the way to the game. Brook actually had to retire following this mishap.

Stan Mortensen (Blackpool) made his international debut for Wales in wartime against his own country, at Wembley on 25 September 1943. He was reserve for England, but when Wales lost their left-half Ivor Powell with injury it was agreed that Mortensen should take his place. Mortensen subsequently played for England.

The lowest attendance for a British International Championship match since before the First World War was at Wrexham on 27 May 1982 when Wales and Northern Ireland played before a crowd of 2315. On the same day there was live television coverage of the FA Cup Final replay.

The highest attendance for a British International Championship match was at Hampden Park on 17 April 1937 when Scotland and England played before a crowd of 149 547.

Hungary are the only continental side to have scored as many as six and seven goals in full international matches against England. They won 6–3 at Wembley on 25 November 1953 and 7–1 in Budapest on 23 May 1954.

During the 1980–81 season England had a run of six matches without a win, losing four times. Between March and May 1981 they had five successive games at Wembley losing three, drawing the other two and scoring just one goal, in the first game of the sequence. In the period May to October 1958 they had seven without a win, drawing five and losing two.

Scotland's most successful run came in the 1880s when they had 13 wins in a row, beating Wales six times, England five and Ireland twice. They actually completed 22 games without defeat from beating Wales 3-0 on 7 April 1879 until a 5-1 win over Wales on 10 March 1888.

England's most successful run came in the following decade. It began when they beat Wales 3-1 on 15 March 1890 and ended after they again defeated the Welsh 9-1 on 16 March 1896. A sequence of 20 matches, it comprised 16 wins and four draws and at one time produced nine successive wins.

Northern Ireland's best sequence of results began on 1 May 1957 against Portugal in a 3-0 win and ended after a 1-0 win against Czechoslovakia in the World Cup on 8 June 1958. It produced four wins and three draws.

Wales' best sequence of results began with a 1-1 draw against Scotland on 13 November 1957 and ended after a 2-1 win over Hungary on 17 June 1958 in the World Cup. It produced three wins and five draws.

In the 1890s there were three occasions when England were engaged in two international fixtures on the same day. The dates were: 15 March 1890, 7 March 1891 and 5 March 1892. England met Ireland and Wales on each day and won all six games. But the total number of internationals played by England during this period was only eight.

Jack Charlton appeared in 35 international matches for England between 1965 and 1970 at centre-half and was only on the losing side on two occasions. In 23 of the games England did not concede a goal.

Joe Davies won 11 caps for Wales over a period of 11 years from 1889 to 1900 and did so with seven different clubs: Everton, Chirk, Ardwick, Sheffield United, Manchester City, Millwall and Reading. However Ardwick subsequently changed their name to Manchester City, making the total really only six.

John Parris, a left-winger with Bradford Park Avenue, Luton Town, Bournemouth and Northampton Town from 1928 to 1939, was the first coloured player to appear in a Home International match. He played for Wales against Northern Ireland in December 1931. England's first coloured player was Viv Anderson, the Nottingham Forest full-back who made his debut against Czechoslovakia in November 1978.

At Blackburn on 6 April 1891 thousands of spectators stayed away from the England v Scotland match as there was no Blackburn Rovers player in the side. England won 2-1 and the second goal was scored by Everton's Edgar Chadwick, a native of Blackburn.

On 31 October 1974 all five countries in the British Isles won full international matches without a goal being scored against any of them. Results were: England 3 Czechoslovakia 0, Wales 2 Hungary 0, Scotland 3 East Germany 0, Sweden 0 Northern Ireland 2, Republic of Ireland 3 USSR 0. All the losers except Sweden were Eastern Europeans.

Kevin Keegan's first three international appearances for England were all made against Wales: at Cardiff on 15 November 1972, Wembley on 24 January 1973 and Cardiff on 11 May 1974.

England's first substitute in a full international match was Jimmy Mullen (Wolverhampton Wanderers) who took over from the injured Jackie Milburn after ten minutes of the game against Belgium in Brussels on 18 May 1950. Mullen then became the first substitute to score.

When Norman Hunter came on as a substitute for Joe Baker after 35 minutes of England's match in Madrid against Spain on 8 December 1965, he became the first England player to win his first cap as a substitute.

On 22 June 1966 Northern Ireland brought on Billy Johnston (Oldham Athletic) as substitute for Willie Irvine (Burnley) against Mexico in Belfast. Northern Ireland won 4-1 and Johnston was one of the scorers.

On 29 May 1960 Scotland brought on Alex Young (Hearts) as substitute for Denis Law (Manchester City) against Austria in Vienna. Austria won 4-1.

Major British records

Highest scores

First class match
This century: Stirling Albion 20 Selkirk 0, Scottish Cup
Overall: Arbroath 36 Bon Accord 0, Scottish Cup 1st
Round, 12 Sep 1885

International
England 13 Northern Ireland 0, 18 Feb 1882

FA Cup
Preston North End 26 Hyde 0, 1st Round, 15 Oct
1897

League Cup
West Ham United 10 Bury 0, 2nd Round, 2nd leg,
25 Oct 1983
Liverpool 10 Fulham 0, 2nd Round, 1st leg,
23 Sep 1986

Football League
Division 1
Home: West Bromwich Albion 12 Darwen 0, 4 Apr
1892
Nottingham Forest 12 Leicester Fosse 0, 21 Apr
1909
Away: Newcastle United 1 Sunderland 9, 5 Dec 1908
Cardiff City 1 Wolverhampton Wanderers 9, 3 Sep
1955
Division 2
Home: Newcastle United 13 Newport County 0, 5 Oct
1946
Away: Burslem Port Vale 0 Sheffield United 10,
10 Dec 1892
Division 3
Home: Tranmere Rovers 9 Accrington Stanley 0,
18 Apr 1959
Brentford 9 Wrexham 0, 15 Oct 1963
Away: Halifax Town 0 Fulham 8, 16 Sep 1969
Brighton & Hove Albion 2 Bristol Rovers 8, 1 Dec
1973
Division 3 (South)
Home: Luton Town 12 Bristol Rovers 0, 13 Apr 1936
Away: Northampton Town 0 Walsall 8, 2 Feb 1947
Division 3 (North)
Home: Stockport County 13 Halifax Town 0, 6 Jan
1934
Away: Accrington Stanley 0 Barnsley 9, 3 Feb 1934
Division 4
Home: Oldham Athletic 11 Southport 0, 26 Dec 1962
Away: Crewe Alexandra 1 Rotherham United 8, 8 Sep
1973

Aggregate
Tranmere Rovers 13 Oldham Athletic 4, Div 3N, 26
Dec 1935

Scottish League
Premier Division
Home: Aberdeen 8 Motherwell 0, 26 Mar 1979
Away: Kilmarnock 1 Rangers 8, 20 Sep 1980
Division 1
Home: Celtic 11 Dundee 0, 26 Oct 1895
Away: Airdrieonians 1 Hibernian 11, 24 Oct 1950
Division 2
Home: East Fife 13 Edinburgh City 2, 11 Dec 1937
Away: Alloa Athletic 0 Dundee 0, 8 Mar 1947

Most goals in one match (individual)

Football League
10 goals, Joe Payne, Luton Town v Bristol Rovers,
Division 3S, 13 Apr 1936

Division 1
7 goals, Ted Drake, Arsenal v Aston Villa, 14 Dec
1935; and James Ross, Preston North End v Stoke
City, 6 Oct 1888

FA Cup
9 goals, Ted MacDougall, Bournemouth v Margate,
20 Nov 1971

Preliminary rounds
10 goals, Chris Marron, South Shields v Radcliffe, 20
Sep 1947

League Cup
6 goals, Frankie Bunn, Oldham Athletic v
Scarborough, 25 Oct 1989

Scottish League
8 goals, Jimmy McGrory, Celtic v Dunfermline
Athletic, 14 Jan 1928

Scottish Cup
13 goals, John Petrie, Arbroath v Bon Accord, 5 Sep
1885

British International Championship
6 goals, Joe Bambrick, Ireland v Wales, 1 Feb 1930

Highest career goalscoring totals

Football League
434 goals, Arthur Rowley, West Bromwich Albion,
Fulham, Leicester City and Shrewsbury Town,
1946–65

Scottish League
410 goals, Jimmy McGrory, Celtic and Clydebank,
1922–1938

David O'Leary created a club record in the last match of the 1989–90 season when he came on as substitute for Arsenal against Norwich City to make his 501st League appearance. He had already set a new League and Cup appearance record of 622 games for the Gunners earlier in the season against the same opponents *(Allsport)*

Tommy Hutchison became the oldest player to make his debut in a European cup competition when he was in his 42nd year, appearing in the Cup-Winners' Cup for Swansea City in September 1989 *(Allsport / Ben Radford)*

Before the ban was imposed, the last matches in European club competition to involve an English side were two finals in May 1985. Juventus forward Zbigniew Boniek (above, stripes) finds himself harrassed by John Wark and Ian Rush (9) of Liverpool during the Italian club's 1–0 win in the ill-fated European Cup Final *(Allsport / David Cannon)*

Trevor Steven (blue shirt) gets underneath this drive for Everton in the 1985 Cup-Winners' Cup Final against Rapid Vienna. Steven was among the scorers as Everton won 3–1 *(Allsport / David Cannon)*

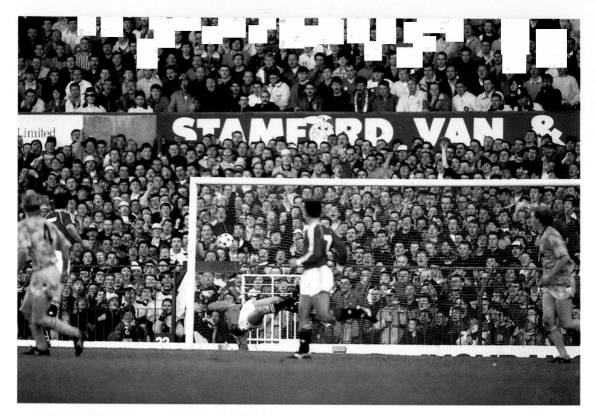

A spectacular long-range effort from Ian Brightwell (above, 4) beats Jim Leighton in the United goal, and the delighted City players celebrate this equalising strike (left) in the Manchester derby at Old Trafford on 3 February 1990. The teams drew 1–1 *(Sporting Pictures (UK) Ltd)*

Danny Wallace (11) moves forward leaving two City defenders in his wake *(Sporting Pictures (UK) Ltd)*

Manchester United striker Mark Hughes (10) prepares to shield the ball as he is challenged by City's Colin Hendry *(Sporting Pictures (UK) Ltd)*

Alan Smith (left) of Arsenal and Tottenham skipper Gary Mabbutt tussle for possession in the North London derby at Highbury on 20 January 1990 *(Allsport / Dan Smith)*

All eyes on Steve Sedgley and Perry Groves (centre, facing camera) as they battle it out *(Syndication International)*

Tottenham's Gary Lineker (below, white shirt) hit the post in this match but it was Tony Adams who scored (right) to give Arsenal a 1–0 win *(Allsport / Dan Smith – Syndication International)*

A South London derby game with added significance in 1989–90 saw Crystal Palace take on Charlton Athletic on 21 April at the Selhurst Park ground the two clubs share. Tommy Caton (left, yellow shirt) just beats Garry Thompson in the air, but Palace won 2–0 with Thompson, recruited from Watford, scoring one of their goals *(Allsport)*

Nigel Martyn (below) saves in the Palace goal from Charlton's Joe McLoughlin (yellow shirt, facing camera) *(Sporting Pictures (UK) Ltd)*

Quickest goals

6 seconds, Albert Mundy, Aldershot v Hartlepool
United, Division 4, 25 Oct 1958
6 seconds, Barrie Jones, Notts County v Torquay
United, Division 3, 31 Mar 1962
6 seconds, Keith Smith, Crystal Palace v Derby
County, Division 2, 12 Dec 1964

Fastest hat-tricks

3 goals in 2½ minutes, Ephraim 'Jock' Dodds,
Blackpool v Tranmere Rovers, Wartime Regional
League, 28 February 1943
Jimmy Scarth, Gillingham v Leyton Orient, Division 3S,
1 Nov 1952
4 goals in 5 minutes, John McIntyre, Blackburn
Rovers v Everton, 16 Sep 1922
Billy 'Ginger' Richardson, West Bromwich Albion v
West Ham United, 7 Nov 1931 (from the start of the
game including three in 3 minutes)
6 goals in 21 minutes, Frank Keetley, Lincoln City v
Halifax Town, Division 3N, 16 Jan 1932
In internationals
3 goals in 3½ minutes, Willie Hall, England v Ireland,
16 Nov 1938

Fastest own goal

6 seconds, Pat Kruse, Torquay United v Cambridge
United, 3 Jan 1977

Goalkeeping records

British record (all competitive games)
Chris Woods, Rangers, 1196 minutes from 26
November 1986 to 31 January 1987
Football League
Steve Death, Reading, 1103 minutes from 24 March
to 18 August 1979
International
Dino Zoff, Italy, unbeaten in 1142 minutes from
September 1972 to June 1974

Most cup-winners medals

FA Cup
5 James Forrest (Blackburn Rovers) 1884–86,
1890–91
The Hon. Sir Arthur Fitzgerald Kinnaird, Kt
(Wanderers) 1873, 1877–78, (Old Etonians) 1879,
1882
Charles H R Wollaston (Wanderers) 1872–73, 1876–
78
Scottish Cup
8 Charles Campbell (Queen's Park), 1874–76, 1880–
82, 1884 and 1886

Of all the players who have made 750 or more League appearances,
Frank Worthington has done so with more clubs than most. Here he
celebrates with a goal for Bolton Wanderers. He almost joined
Liverpool in the 1970s but failed their medical test (Associated Sports
Photography)

Most League appearances

Football League
*899 Peter Shilton (286 Leicester City, 110 Stoke City,
202 Nottingham Forest, 188 Southampton, 113 Derby
County) 1966–
824 Terry Paine (713 Southampton, 111 Hereford
United) 1957–77
*786 Tommy Hutchison (165 Blackpool, 314
Coventry City, 46 Manchester City, 92 Burnley, 169
Swansea City) 1968– ; also 68 Alloa 1965–68
777 Alan Oakes (565 Manchester City, 211 Chester
City, 1 Port Vale) 1959–84
770 John Trollope (all for Swindon Town) 1960–80
764 Jimmy Dickinson (all for Portsmouth) 1946–65
761 Roy Sproson (all for Port Vale) 1950–72
758 Billy Bonds (95 Charlton Athletic, 663 West Ham
United)
758 Ray Clemence (48 Scunthorpe United, 470
Liverpool, 240 Tottenham Hotspur) 1966–87
757 Pat Jennings (48 Watford, 472 Tottenham
Hotspur, 237 Arsenal) 1963–86
757 Frank Worthington (171 Huddersfield Town, 210
Leicester City, 84 Bolton Wanderers, 75 Birmingham
City, 32 Leeds United, 19 Sunderland,
34 Southampton, 31 Brighton & Hove Albion,
59 Tranmere Rovers, 23 Preston North End,
19 Stockport County) 1966–88
Scottish League
Division 1
626 Bob Ferrier (Motherwell) 1918–37

Peter Shilton has played in more internationals for England and more first-class games than any other player in the country (Sporting Pictures)

Most first-class appearances

*1263 Peter Shilton (899 League, 125 internationals, 90 League Cup, 81 FA Cup, 13 Under-23, four Football League, 51 others – European Cup, UEFA Cup, World Club Championship, Charity Shield, European Super Cup, Full Members Cup, Screen Sport Super Cup, Anglo-Italian Cup, Texaco Cup, Simod Cup and Zenith Data Systems Cup

Youngest players

Football League debut
Albert Geldard, 15 years 158 days, Bradford Park Avenue v Millwall, Division 2, 16 Sep 1929
Ken Roberts, 15 years 158 days, Wrexham v Bradford Park Avenue, Division 3N, 1 Sep 1951

Football League scorer
Ronnie Dix, 15 years 180 days, Bristol Rovers v Norwich City, Division 3S, 3 Mar 1928

Division 1 debut
Derek Forster, 15 years 185 days, Sunderland v Leicester City, 22 Aug 1984

Division 1 scorer
Jason Dozzell, 16 years 57 days, as substitute for Ipswich Town v Coventry City, 4 Feb 1984

FA Cup
Andy Awford, 15 years 88 days as substitute for Worcester City v Borehamwood, 3rd Qualifying Round, 10 Oct 1987

FA Cup proper
Scott Endersby, 15 years 288 days, Kettering v Tilbury, 1st Round, 26 Nov 1977

FA Cup Final
Paul Allen, 17 years 256 days, West Ham United v Arsenal, 1980

FA Cup Final scorer
Norman Whiteside, 18 years 18 days, Manchester

United v Brighton & Hove Albion, 1983

FA Cup Final captain
David Nish, 21 years 212 days, Leicester City v Manchester City, 1969

Internationals
England
Pre-war: James Prinsep (Clapham Rovers) 17 years 252 days, 5 Apr 1879
Post-war: Duncan Edwards (Manchester United), 18 years 183 days, v Scotland, 2 Apr 1955

Northern Ireland
Norman Whiteside (Manchester United), 17 years 42 days, v Yugoslavia, 17 Jun 1982

Scotland
Johnny Lambie (Queen's Park), 17 years 92 days, v Ireland, 20 Mar 1886

Wales
John Charles (Leeds United), 18 years 71 days, v Ireland, 8 Mar 1950

Republic of Ireland
Jimmy Holmes, 17 years 200 days, v Austria, 30 May 1971

Oldest players

Football League
Neil McBain, 52 years 4 months, New Brighton v Hartlepools United, Div 3N, 15 Mar 1957 (McBain was New Brighton's manager and had to play in an emergency)

Division 1
Stanley Matthews, 50 years 5 days, Stoke City v Fulham, 6 Feb 1965

FA Cup Final
Walter Hampson, 41 years 8 months, Newcastle United v Aston Villa, 1924

FA Cup
Billy Meredith, 49 years 8 months, Manchester City v Newcastle United, 29 Mar 1924

International debut
Leslie Compton, 38 years 2 months, England v Wales, 15 Nov 1950

International
Billy Meredith, 45 years 229 days, Wales v England, 15 Mar 1920

Highest attendances

International
149 547 Scotland v England, Hampden Park, Glasgow, 17 Apr 1937

European Cup
136 505, Celtic v Leeds United, semi-final, Hampden Park, Glasgow, 15 Apr 1970

FA Cup Final
160 000 (126 047 counted admissions) West Ham
United v Bolton Wanderers, Wembley, 28 Apr 1923

Scottish Cup Final
146 433, Celtic v Aberdeen, Hampden Park, Glasgow,
24 Apr 1937

Football League

Division 1
83 260, Manchester United v Arsenal, Maine Road,
17 Jan 1948

Division 2
68 029, Aston Villa v Coventry City, Villa Park, 30 Oct
1937

Division 3
49 309, Sheffield Wednesday v Sheffield United,
Hillsborough, 26 Dec 1979

Division 3S
51 621, Cardiff City v Bristol City, Ninian Park, 7 Apr
1947

Division 3N
49 655, Hull City v Rotherham United, Boothferry
Park, 25 Dec 1948

Division 4
37 774, Crystal Palace v Millwall, Selhurst Park, 31
Mar 1961

Scottish League
118 567, Rangers v Celtic, Ibrox Park, 2 Jan 1939

Non League
FA Amateur Cup Finals
100 000, Pegasus v Harwich and Parkeston,
Wembley Stadium, 11 Apr 1953

GM Vauxhall Conference
9432, Lincoln City v Wycombe Wanderers, 2 May
1988

Southern League
29 786, Queen's Park Rangers v Plymouth Argyle,
Park Royal, 25 Dec 1907

Lowest attendances

British International
2315, Wales v Northern Ireland, Racecourse Ground,
Wrexham, 27 May 1982

Football League (under 500)
484, Gateshead v Accrington Stanley, Div 3N, 26 Mar
1952
469, Thames v Luton Town, Div 3S, 6 Dec 1930
450, Rochdale v Cambridge United, Div 3, 5 Feb
1974

Division 1
3496, Wimbledon v Luton Town, 14 Feb 1990

NB Although the Stockport County v Leicester City Division 2 game at
Old Trafford on 7 May 1921 was reported to have had an official
attendance of only 13, contemporary reports estimated the crowd at
2000. Similarly, for the FA Cup third round second replay between
Bradford City and Norwich City at Lincoln in 1915 the official
attendance was nil, but although it was played behind closed doors
so as not to interfere with war work in nearby factories, several
hundred spectators gained admittance without paying.

Scottish League
80, Meadowbank Thistle v Stenhousemuir, Div 2,
22 Dec 1979 at Meadowbank

Transfers (highest figures)

(involving British players)

Chris Waddle	Tottenham Hotspur to Marseille	July 1989	£4.5 million
Ian Rush	Liverpool to Juventus	June 1987	£3.2 m
Ian Rush	Juventus to Liverpool	August 1988	£2.8 m
Gary Lineker	Everton to Barcelona	June 1986	£2.75 m
Mark Hughes	Manchester United to Barcelona	May 1986	£2.3 m
*Gary Pallister	Middlesbrough to Manchester United	August 1989	£2.3 m
Tony Cottee	West Ham United to Everton	July 1988	£2.2 m
Paul Gascoigne	Newcastle United to Tottenham Hotspur	July 1988	£2 m

* record between English clubs

(Major foreign)

Roberto Baggio	Fiorentina to Juventus	June 1990	£7.7m
Diego Maradona	Barcelona to Napoli	June 1984	£6.9 m
Ruud Gullit	PSV Eindhoven to AC Milan	June 1987	£5.5 m
Karl-Heinz Riedle	Werder Bremen to Lazio	June 1990	£5.5m
Thomas Hassler	Cologne to Juventus	June 1990	£5.5 m
Dragan Stojkovic	Red Star Belgrade to Marseille	June 1990	£4.8m
Diego Maradona	Boca Juniors to Barcelona	June 1982	£4.8 m
Lajos Detari	Eintracht Frankfurt to Olympiakos	July 1988	£4.8 m
Rui Barros	Porto to Juventus	July 1988	£4 m
Ronald Koeman	PSV Eindhoven to Barcelona	July 1989	£4 m

EUROPEAN FOOTBALL

European Cup Finals 1956–1990

Year	Winners		Runners-up	Venue	Attendance	Referee
1956	Real Madrid	4–3	Stade de Reims	Paris, France	38 000	Ellis (England)
1957	Real Madrid	2–0	Fiorentina	Madrid, Spain	124 000	Horn (Holland)
1958	Real Madrid	3–2	AC Milan	Brussels, Belgium	67 000	Alsteen (Belgium)
1959	Real Madrid	2–0	Stade de Reims	Stuttgart, West Germany	80 000	Dutsch (West Germany)
1960	Real Madrid	7–3	Eintracht Frankfurt	Glasgow, Scotland	135 000	Mowat (Scotland)
1961	Benfica	3–2	Barcelona	Berne, Switzerland	28 000	Dienst (Switzerland)
1962	Benfica	5–3	Real Madrid	Amsterdam, Holland	65 000	Horn (Holland)
1963	AC Milan	2–1	Benfica	Wembley, England	45 000	Holland (England)
1964	Internazionale	3–1	Real Madrid	Vienna, Austria	74 000	Stoll (Austria)
1965	Internazionale	1–0	Benfica	Milan, Italy	80 000	Dienst (Switzerland)
1966	Real Madrid	2–1	Partizan Belgrade	Brussels, Belgium	55 000	Kreitlein (West Germany)
1967	Celtic	2–1	Internazionale	Lisbon, Portugal	56 000	Tschenscher (West Germany)
1968	Manchester United	4–1*	Benfica	Wembley, England	100 000	Lo Bello (Italy)
1969	AC Milan	4–1	Ajax	Madrid, Spain	50 000	Ortiz de Mendibil (Spain)
1970	Feyenoord	2–1	Celtic	Milan, Italy	50 000	Lo Bello (Italy)
1971	Ajax	2–0	Panathinaikos	Wembley, England	90 000	Taylor (England)
1972	Ajax	2–0	Internazionale	Rotterdam, Holland	67 000	Helies (France)
1973	Ajax	1–0	Juventus	Belgrade, Yugoslavia	93 500	Guglovic (Yugoslavia)
1974	Bayern Munich	1–1*	Atletico Madrid	Brussels, Belgium	65 000	Loraux (Belgium)
Replay	Bayern Munich	4–0	Atletico Madrid	Brussels, Belgium	65 000	Delcourt (Belgium)
1975	Bayern Munich	2–0	Leeds United	Paris, France	50 000	Kitabdjian (France)
1976	Bayern Munich	1–0	St Etienne	Glasgow, Scotland	54 864	Palotai (Hungary)

Year	Winners		Runners-up	Venue	Attendance	Referee
1977	Liverpool	3-1	Borussia Moenchengladbach	Rome, Italy	57 000	Wurtz (France)
1978	Liverpool	1-0	FC Bruges	Wembley, England	92 000	Corver (Holland)
1979	Nottingham Forest	1-0	Malmo	Munich, West Germany	57 500	Linemayr (Austria)
1980	Nottingham Forest	1-0	Hamburg	Madrid, Spain	50 000	Garrido (Portugal)
1981	Liverpool	1-0	Real Madrid	Paris, France	48 360	Palotai (Hungary)
1982	Aston Villa	1-0	Bayern Munich	Rotterdam, Holland	46 000	Konrath (France)
1983	Hamburg	1-0	Juventus	Athens, Greece	75 000	Rainea (Romania)
1984	Liverpool (Liverpool won 4-2 on penalties)	1-1*	Roma	Rome, Italy	69 693	Fredriksson (Sweden)
1985	Juventus	1-0	Liverpool	Brussels, Belgium	58 000	Daina (Switzerland)
1986	Steaua Bucharest (Steaua won 2-0 on penalties)	0-0*	Barcelona	Seville, Spain	70 000	Vautrot (France)
1987	Porto	2-1	Bayern Munich	Vienna, Austria	59 000	Ponnet (Belgium)
1988	PSV Eindhoven (PSV won 6-5 on penalties)	0-0*	Benfica	Stuttgart, West Germany	70 000	Agnolin (Italy)
1989	AC Milan	4-0	Steaua Bucharest	Barcelona, Spain	97 000	Tritschler (West Germany)
1990	AC Milan	1-0	Benfica	Vienna, Austria	57 500	Kohl (Austria)

European Cup: Gates and goals

Year	Games	Goals	Aggregate attendance	Average attendance	Top scorer	Goals
1955-56	29	127	912 000	31 450	Milutinovic (Partizan Belgrade)	7
1956-57	44	170	1 786 000	40 590	Viollet (Manchester United)	9
1957-58	48	189	1 790 000	37 290	Di Stefano (Real Madrid)	10
1958-59	55	199	2 010 000	36 545	Fontaine (Stade de Reims)	10
1959-60	52	218	2 780 000	50 545	Puskas (Real Madrid)	12
1960-61	51	166	1 850 000	36 274	Jose Aguas (Benfica)	11
1961-62	55	221	2 135 000	45 727	Di Stefano, Puskas and Tejada (Real Madrid)	7
1962-63	59	214	2 158 000	36 593	Altafini (AC Milan)	14
1963-64	61	212	2 180 000	35 737	Mazzola (Internazionale), Puskas (Real Madrid), Kovacevic (Partizan)	7
1964-65	62	215	2 577 000	41 564	Eusebio and Torres (Benfica)	9

Year	Games	Goals	Aggregate attendance	Average attendance	Top scorer	Goals
1965–66	58	234	2 112 000	36 431	Albert (Ferencvaros) and Eusebio (Benfica)	7
1966–67	65	211	2 248 000	34 584	Van Himst (Anderlecht), Pipenburg (Vorwarts)	6
1967–68	60	162	2 544 000	42 500	Eusebio (Benfica)	6
1968–69	52	176	2 056 000	39 540	Law (Manchester United)	9
1969–70	63	202	2 345 000	37 222	Jones (Leeds United)	8
1970–71	63	210	2 124 000	33 714	Antoniadis (Panathinaikos)	10
1971–72	64	175	2 066 976	32 280	Cruyff (Ajax), Macari (Celtic), Takac (Standard)	5
1972–73	58	160	1 712 277	30 000	Muller (Bayern Munich)	12
1973–74	60	180	1 586 852	26 448	Muller (Bayern Munich)	9
1974–75	55	174	1 380 254	25 096	Muller (Bayern Munich)	6
1975–76	61	202	1 736 087	28 460	Heynckes (Moenchengladbach), Santillana (Real Madrid)	6
1976–77	61	155	2 010 000	34 325	Cucinotta (Zurich), Muller (Bayern Munich)	5
1977–78	59	172	1 509 471	25 584	Simonsen (Moenchengladbach)	5
1978–79	63	185	1 511 291	23 988	Sulser (Grasshoppers)	11
1979–80	63	185	1 729 415	27 451	Lerby (Ajax)	10
1980–81	63	166	1 166 593	26 374	Rummenigge (Bayern Munich), McDermott and Souness (Liverpool)	6
1981–82	63	170	1 530 082	24 287	Hoeness (Bayern Munich), Geurts (Anderlecht)	7
1982–83	61	180	1 718 075	28 165	Rossi (Juventus)	6
1983–84	59	165	1 601 065	27 137	Sokol (Dynamo Minsk)	6
1984–85	61	186	1 475 740	24 192	Platini (Juventus), Nilsson (Gothenburg)	7
1985–86	59	167	1 493 117	25 307	Nilsson (Gothenburg)	6
1986–87	57	163	1 829 442	32 095	Cvetkovic (Red Star Belgrade)	7
1987–88	60	140	1 563 497	26 058	Ferreri (Bordeaux), Hagi (Steaua), Madjer (Porto), Rui Aguas (Benfica)	4
1988–89	59	170	1 575 703	26 706	Van Basten (AC Milan)	10

European Cup-Winners' Cup Finals 1961–1990

Year	Winners		Runners-up	Venue	Attendance	Referee
1961	(1) Fiorentina	2-0	Rangers	Glasgow, Scotland	80 000	Steiner (Austria)
	(2) Fiorentina	2-1	Rangers	Florence, Italy	50 000	Hernadi (Hungary)
1962	(1) Atletico Madrid	1-1	Fiorentina	Glasgow, Scotland	27 389	Wharton (Scotland)
	(2) Atletico Madrid	3-0	Fiorentina	Stuttgart, West Germany	45 000	Tschenscher (West Germany)
1963	Tottenham Hotspur	5-1	Atletico Madrid	Rotterdam, Holland	25 000	Van Leuwen (Holland)
1964	Sporting Lisbon	3-3	MTK Budapest	Brussels, Belgium	9 000	Van Nuffel (Belgium)
1964	Sporting Lisbon	1-0	MTK Budapest	Antwerp, Belgium	18 000	Versyp (Belgium)
1965	West Ham United	2-0	Munich 1860	Wembley, England	100 000	Szolt (Hungary)
1966	Borussia Dortmund	2-1*	Liverpool	Glasgow, Scotland	41 657	Schwinte (France)
1967	Bayern Munich	1-0*	Rangers	Nuremberg, West Germany	69 480	Lo Bello (Italy)
1968	AC Milan	2-0	Hamburg	Rotterdam, Holland	60 000	Ortiz de Mendibil (Spain)
1969	Slovan Bratislava	3-2	Barcelona	Basle, Switzerland	40 000	Van Ravens (Holland)
1970	Manchester City	2-1	Gornik Zabrze	Vienna, Austria	10 000	Schiller (Austria)
1971	Chelsea	1-1*	Real Madrid	Athens, Greece	42 000	Scheurer (Switzerland)
Replay	Chelsea	2-1	Real Madrid	Athens, Greece	24 000	Bucheli (Switzerland)
1972	Rangers	3-2	Moscow Dynamo	Barcelona, Spain	35 000	Ortiz de Mendibil (Spain)
1973	AC Milan	1-0	Leeds United	Salonika, Greece	45 000	Mihas (Greece)
1974	Magdeburg	2-0	AC Milan	Rotterdam, Holland	5 000	Van Gemert (Holland)
1975	Dynamo Kiev	3-0	Ferencvaros	Basle, Switzerland	13 000	Davidson (Scotland)
1976	Anderlecht	4-2	West Ham United	Brussels, Belgium	58 000	Wurtz (France)
1977	Hamburg	2-0	Anderlecht	Amsterdam, Holland	65 000	Partridge (England)
1978	Anderlecht	4-0	Austria/WAC	Amsterdam, Holland	48 679	Adlinger (West Germany)
1979	Barcelona	4-3*	Fortuna Dusseldorf	Basle, Switzerland	58 000	Palotai (Hungary)
1980	Valencia	0-0*	Arsenal	Brussels, Belgium	40 000	Christov (Czechoslovakia)
	(Valencia won 5-4 on penalties)					
1981	Dynamo Tbilisi	2-1	Carl Zeiss Jena	Dusseldorf, West Germany	9 000	Lattanzi (Italy)
1982	Barcelona	2-1	Standard Liege	Barcelona, Spain	100 000	Eschweiler (West Germany)
1983	Aberdeen	2-1*	Real Madrid	Gothenburg, Sweden	17 804	Menegali (Italy)
1984	Juventus	2-1	Porto	Basle, Switzerland	60 000	Prokop (East Germany)
1985	Everton	3-1	Rapid Vienna	Rotterdam, Holland	30 000	Casarin (Italy)
1986	Dynamo Kiev	3-0	Atletico Madrid	Lyon, France	39 300	Wohrer (Austria)

Year	Winners		Runners-up	Venue	Attendance	Referee
1987	Ajax	1-0	Lokomotive Leipzig	Athens, Greece	35 000	Agnolin (Italy)
1988	Mechelen	1-0	Ajax	Strasbourg, France	39 446	Pauly (West Germany)
1989	Barcelona	2-0	Sampdoria	Berne, Switzerland	45 000	Courtney (England)
1990	Sampadoria	2-0*	Anderlecht	Gothenburg, Sweden	20 103	Galler (Switzerland)

Cup-Winners Cup: Gates and goals

Season	Games	Goals	Aggregate attendance	Average attendance	Top scorer	Goals
1960–61	18	60	290 000	16 111	Hamrin (Fiorentina)	6
1961–62	44	174	650 000	14 733	Gorocs (Ujpest Dosza)	8
1962–63	48	169	1 100 000	22 916	Asparoukhov (Botev)	6
1963–64	62	202	1 300 000	20 967	Mascarenhas (Sporting)	11
1964–65	61	163	1 100 000	18 032	Masek and Mraz (Sparta)	6
1965–66	59	188	1 546 000	26 203	Emmerich (Dortmund)	14
1966–67	61	170	1 556 000	25 508	Claessen (Standard Liege)	10
1967–68	64	200	1 683 000	26 269	Seeler (Hamburg)	6
1968–69	51	157	957 000	18 765	Ruhl (Cologne)	6
1969–70	64	179	1 675 000	25 890	Lubanski (Gornik)	8
1970–71	67	203	1 570 000	23 582	Lubanski (Gornik)	8
1971–72	65	186	1 145 211	17 615	Osgood (Chelsea)	8
1972–73	61	174	908 564	15 000	Chiarugi (AC Milan)	7
1973–74	61	169	1 105 494	18 123	Heynckes (Moenchengladbach)	10
1974–75	59	177	1 298 850	22 014	Van der Kuylen (PSV Eindhoven)	7
1975–76	61	189	1 128 962	18 508	Rensenbrink (Anderlecht)	8
1976–77	63	198	1 537 000	24 400	Milanov (Levski)	13
1977–78	63	179	1 161 383	18 434	Keller (Hamburg), Van der Elst (Anderlecht)	6
1978–79	59	160	1 041 135	17 646	Altobelli (Internazionale)	7
1979–80	63	176	1 193 682	18 947	Kempes (Valencia)	9
1980–81	65	176	1 239 795	19 074	Cross (West Ham United)	6
1981–82	63	176	1 504 023	23 873	Shengelia (Tbilisi), Voordeckers (Standard Liege)	6
1982–83	65	198	1 424 104	21 909	Santillana (Real Madrid)	8
1983–84	63	198	1 451 136	23 034	McGhee (Aberdeen), Morozov (Donetn)	5
1984–85	62	156	1 152 605	18 590	Gazayev (Dynamo Moscow), Panenka (Rapid Vienna), Gray (Everton)	5
1985–86	59	191	1 330 286	22 547	Yaremchuk (Dynamo Kiev), Funkel (Bayer Uerdingen)	6
1986–87	61	172	1 139 609	18 682	Bosman (Ajax)	8
1987–88	63	126	930 858	14 775	Cascavel (Sporting)	6
1988–89	63	152	887 748	14 091	Stoichkov (Sredets)	7

UEFA Cup Finals
Fairs Cup 1955–71

Year	Winners		Runners-up	Venue	Attendance
1955–58	(1) Barcelona	2–2	London	Stamford Bridge, England	45 466
	(2) Barcelona	6–0	London	Barcelona, Spain	62 000
1958–60	(1) Barcelona	0–0	Birmingham City	Birmingham, England	40 500
	(2) Barcelona	4–1	Birmingham City	Barcelona, Spain	70 000
1960–61	(1) Roma	2–2	Birmingham City	Birmingham, England	21 005
	(2) Roma	2–0	Birmingham City	Rome, Italy	60 000
1961–62	(1) Valencia	6–2	Barcelona	Valencia, Spain	65 000
	(2) Valencia	1–1	Barcelona	Barcelona, Spain	60 000
1962–63	(1) Valencia	2–1	Dynamo Zagreb	Zagreb, Yugoslavia	40 000
	(2) Valencia	2–0	Dynamo Zagreb	Valencia, Spain	55 000
1963–64	Zaragoza	2–1	Valencia	Barcelona, Spain	50 000
1964–65	Ferencvaros	1–0	Juventus	Turin, Italy	25 000
1965–66	(1) Barcelona	0–1	Zaragoza	Barcelona, Spain	70 000
	(2) Barcelona	4–2	Zaragoza	Zaragoza, Spain	70 000
1966–67	(1) Dynamo Zagreb	2–0	Leeds United	Zagreb, Yugoslavia	40 000
	(2) Dynamo Zagreb	0–0	Leeds United	Leeds, England	35 604
1967–68	(1) Leeds United	1–0	Ferencvaros	Leeds, England	25 368
	(2) Leeds United	0–0	Ferencvaros	Budapest, Hungary	70 000
1968–69	(1) Newcastle United	3–0	Ujpest Dozsa	Newcastle, England	60 000
	(2) Newcastle United	3–2	Ujpest Dozsa	Budapest, Hungary	37 000
1969–70	(1) Arsenal	1–3	Anderlecht	Brussels, Belgium	37 000
	(2) Arsenal	3–0	Anderlecht	Highbury, England	51 612
1970–71	(1) Leeds United	0–0	Juventus	Turin, Italy	65 000
	(abandoned 51 minutes)				
	(1) Leeds United	2–2	Juventus	Turin, Italy	65 000
	(2) Leeds United	1–1	Juventus	Leeds, England	42 483
	(Leeds won on away goals)				
1971–72	(1) Tottenham Hotspur	2–1	Wolverhampton Wanderers	Wolverhampton, England	45 000
	(2) Tottenham Hotspur	1–1	Wolverhampton Wanderers	White Hart Lane, England	48 000
1972–73	(1) Liverpool	3–0	Moenchengladbach	Anfield, England	41 169
	(2) Liverpool	2–0	Moenchengladbach	Moenchengladbach, West Germany	35 000
1973–74	(1) Feyenoord	2–2	Tottenham Hotspur	White Hart Lane, England	46 281
	(2) Feyenoord	2–0	Tottenham Hotspur	Rotterdam, Holland	68 000
1974–75	(1) Moenchengladbach	0–0	Twente	Dusseldorf, West Germany	45 000
	(2) Moenchengladbach	5–1	Twente	Enschede, Holland	24 500
1975–76	(1) Liverpool	3–2	FC Bruges	Anfield, England	56 000
	(2) Liverpool	1–1	FC Bruges	Bruges, Belgium	32 000
1976–77	(1) Juventus	1–0	Athletic Bilbao	Turin, Italy	75 000
	(2) Juventus	1–2	Athletic Bilbao	Bilbao, Spain	43 000
1977–78	(1) PSV Eindhoven	0–0	Bastia	Bastia, Corsica	15 000
	(2) PSV Eindhoven	3–0	Bastia	Eindhoven, Holland	27 000
1978–79	(1) Moenchengladbach	1–1	Red Star Belgrade	Belgrade, Yugoslavia	87 500
	(2) Moenchengladbach	1–0	Red Star Belgrade	Dusseldorf, West Germany	45 000
1979–80	(1) Eintracht Frankfurt	2–3	Moenchengladbach	Moenchengladbach, West Germany	25 000
	(2) Eintracht Frankfurt	1–0	Moenchengladbach	Frankfurt, West Germany	60 000
	(Eintracht won on away goals)				

Year		Winners		Runners-up	Venue	Attendance
1980–81	(1)	Ipswich Town	3–0	AZ '67	Ipswich, England	27 532
	(2)	Ipswich Town	2–4	AZ '67	Amsterdam, Holland	28 500
1981–82	(1)	Gothenburg	1–0	Hamburg	Gothenburg, Sweden	42 548
	(2)	Gothenburg	3–0	Hamburg	Hamburg, West Germany	60 000
1982–83	(1)	Anderlecht	1–0	Benfica	Brussels, Belgium	45 000
	(2)	Anderlecht	1–1	Benfica	Lisbon, Portugal	80 000
1983–84	(1)	Tottenham Hotspur	1–1	Anderlecht	Brussels, Belgium	40 000
	(2)	Tottenham Hotspur	1–1	Anderlecht	White Hart Lane, England	46 258
		(Tottenham won 4–3 on penalties)				
1984–85	(1)	Real Madrid	3–0	Videoton	Szekesfehervar, Hungary	30 000
	(2)	Real Madrid	0–1	Videoton	Madrid, Spain	98 300
1985–86	(1)	Real Madrid	5–1	Cologne	Madrid, Spain	80 000
	(2)	Real Madrid	0–2	Cologne	West Berlin, West Germany	15 000
1986–87	(1)	Gothenburg	1–0	Dundee United	Gothenburg, Sweden	50 023
	(2)	Gothenburg	1–1	Dundee United	Tannadice Park, Scotland	20 911
1987–88	(1)	Bayer Leverkusen	0–3	Espanol	Barcelona, Spain	42 000
	(2)	Bayer Leverkusen	3–0	Espanol	Leverkusen, West Germany	22 000
		(Leverkusen won 3–2 on penalties)				
1988–89	(1)	Napoli	2–1	Stuttgart	Naples, Italy	83 000
	(2)	Napoli	3–3	Stuttgart	Stuttgart, West Germany	67 000
1989–90	(1)	Juventus	3–1	Fiorentina	Turin, Italy	45 000
	(2)	Juventus	0–0	Fiorentina	Avellino, Italy	32 000

European Super Cup 1972–89

Contested by the winners of the Champions' Cup and Cup-Winners Cup, played the following season.

Year	Winners	Runners-up	Scores
1972	Ajax	Rangers	3–1, 3–2
1973	Ajax	AC Milan	0–1, 6–0
1974	Not contested		
1975	Dynamo Kiev	Bayern Munich	1–0, 2–0
1976	Anderlecht	Bayern Munich	4–1, 1–2
1977	Liverpool	Hamburg	1–1, 6–0
1978	Anderlecht	Liverpool	3–1, 1–2
1979	Nottingham Forest	Barcelona	1–0, 1–1
1980	Valencia*	Nottingham Forest	1–2, 1–0

Year	Winners	Runners-up	Scores
1981	Not contested		
1982	Aston Villa	Barcelona	0–1, 3–0
1983	Aberdeen	Hamburg	0–0, 2–0
1984	Juventus	Liverpool	2–0 (in Turin)
1985	Not contested		
1986	Steaua Bucharest	Dynamo Kiev	1–0 (in Monaco)
1987	Porto	Ajax	1–0, 1–0
1988	Mechelen	PSV Eindhoven	3–0, 0–1
1989	AC Milan	Barcelona	1–1, 1–0

* won on away goals

British Clubs in Europe: Complete Record

* won on away goals counting double
† won on penalties
‡ won on the toss of a coin

Football League Clubs

Season	Competition	Round	Date	Opponents (Country)	Venue	Result	Scorers
ARSENAL							
1963-64	Fairs Cup	1	25 Sep 63	Staevnet (Denmark)	A	W 7-1	Strong 3, Baker 3, MacLeod
			22 Oct 63		H	L 2-3	Skirton, Barnwell
		2	13 Nov 63	Liege (Belgium)	H	D 1-1	Anderson
			18 Dec 63		A	L 1-3	McCullough
1969-70	Fairs Cup	1	9 Sep 69	Glentoran (Northern	H	W 3-0	Graham 2, Gould
			29 Sep 69	Ireland)	A	L 0-1	
		2	29 Oct 69	Sporting Lisbon	A	D 0-0	
			26 Nov 69	(Portugal)	H	W 3-0	Radford, Graham 2
		3	17 Dec 69	Rouen (France)	A	D 0-0	
			13 Jan 70		H	W 1-0	Sammels
		QF	11 Mar 70	Dynamo Bacau	A	W 2-0	Sammels, Radford
			18 Mar 70	(Romania)	H	W 7-1	George 2, Sammels 2, Radford 2, Graham
		SF	8 Apr 70	Ajax (Holland)	H	W 3-0	George 2 (1 pen), Sammels
			15 Apr 70		A	L 0-1	
		F	22 Apr 70	Anderlecht (Belgium)	A	L 1-3	Kennedy
			28 Apr 70		H	W 3-0	Kelly, Radford, Sammels
1970-71	Fairs Cup	1	16 Sep 70	Lazio (Italy)	A	D 2-2	Radford 2
			23 Sep 70		H	W 2-0	Radford, Armstrong
		2	21 Oct 70	Sturm Graz (Austria)	A	L 0-1	
			4 Nov 70		H	W 2-0	Storey (pen), Kennedy
		3	2 Dec 70	Beveren (Belgium)	H	W 4-0	Graham, Kennedy 2, Sammels
			16 Dec 70		A	D 0-0	
		QF	9 Mar 71	FC Cologne*	H	W 2-1	McLintock, Storey
			23 Mar 71	(West Germany)	A	L 0-1	
1971-72	European Cup	1	15 Sep 71	Stromsgodset	A	W 3-1	Simpson, Marinello, Kelly*
			29 Sep 71	(Norway)	H	W 4-0	Kennedy, Radford 2, Armstrong
		2	20 Oct 71	Grasshoppers	A	W 2-0	Kennedy, Graham
			3 Nov 71	(Switzerland)	H	W 3-0	Kennedy, George, Radford
		QF	8 Mar 72	Ajax (Holland)	A	L 1-2	Kennedy
			22 Mar 72		H	L 0-1	
1978-79	UEFA Cup	1	13 Sep 78	Lokomotive Leipzig	H	W 3-0	Stapleton 2, Sunderland
			27 Sep 78	(East Germany)	A	W 4-1	Brady (pen), Stapleton 2, Sunderland
		2	18 Oct 78	Hajduk Split	A	L 1-2	O'Leary
			1 Nov 78	(Yugoslavia)	H	W 1-0	Young

	3	22 Nov 78	Red Star Belgrade	A	L	0–1	
		6 Dec 78	(Yugoslavia)	H	D	1–1	Sunderland
1979–80 Cup-Winners'	1	19 Sep 79	Fenerbahce (Turkey)	H	W	2–0	Sunderland, Young
Cup		3 Oct 79		A	D	0–0	
	2	24 Oct 79	Magdeburg	H	W	2–1	Young, Sunderland
		7 Nov 79	(East Germany)	A	D	2–2	Price, Brady
	QF	5 Mar 80	Gothenburg (Sweden)	H	W	5–1	Sunderland 2, Price, Brady, Young
		19 Mar 80		A	D	0–0	
	SF	9 Apr 80	Juventus (Italy)	H	D	1–1	own goal
		23 Apr 80		A	W	1–0	Vaessen
	F	14 May 80	Valencia (Spain) †	N	D	0–0	
1981–82 UEFA Cup	1	16 Sep 81	Panathinaikos	A	W	2–0	McDermott, Meade
		30 Sep 81	(Greece)	H	W	1–0	Talbot
	2	20 Oct 81	Winterslag (Belgium)*	A	L	0–1	
		3 Nov 81		H	W	2–1	Hollins, Rix
1982–83 UEFA Cup	1	14 Sep 82	Moscow Spartak	A	L	2–3	Robson, Chapman
		29 Sep 82	(USSR)	H	L	2–5	Chapman, own goal

ASTON VILLA

1975–76 UEFA Cup	1	17 Sep 75	Antwerp (Belgium)	A	L	1–4	Graydon
		1 Oct 75		H	L	0–1	
1977–78 UEFA Cup	1	14 Sep 77	Fenerbahce (Turkey)	H	W	4–0	Gray, Deehan 2, Little
		28 Sep 77		A	W	2–0	Deehan, Little
	2	19 Oct 77	Gornik Zabrze	H	W	2–0	McNaught 2
		2 Nov 77	(Poland)	A	D	1–1	Gray
	3	23 Nov 77	Athletic Bilbao	H	W	2–0	own goal, Deehan
		7 Dec 77	(Spain)	A	D	1–1	Mortimer
	QF	1 Mar 78	Barcelona (Spain)	H	D	2–2	McNaught, Deehan
		15 Mar 78		A	L	1–2	Little
1981–82 European Cup	1	16 Sep 81	Valur (Iceland)	H	W	5–0	Morley, Withe 2, Donovan 2
		30 Sep 81		A	W	2–0	Shaw 2
	2	21 Oct 81	Dynamo Berlin	A	W	2–1	Morley 2
		4 Nov 81	(East Germany)	H	L	0–1	
	QF	3 Mar 82	Dynamo Kiev	A	D	0–0	
		17 Mar 82	(USSR)	H	W	2–0	Shaw, McNaught
	SF	7 Apr 82	Anderlecht (Belgium)	H	W	1–0	Morley
		21 Apr 82		A	D	0–0	
	F	26 May 82	Bayern Munich (West Germany)	N	W	1–0	Withe
1982–83 European Cup	1	15 Sep 82	Besiktas (Turkey)	H	W	3–1	Withe, Morley, Mortimer
		29 Sep 82		A	D	0–0	
	2	20 Oct 82	Dinamo Bucharest	A	W	2–0	Shaw 2
		3 Nov 82	(Romania)	H	W	4–2	Shaw 3, Walters
	QF	2 Mar 83	Juventus (Italy)	H	L	1–2	Cowans
		16 Mar 83		A	L	1–3	Withe
1982–83 Super Cup	F	19 Jan 83	Barcelona (Spain)	A	L	0–1	
		26 Jan 83		H	W	3–0	Shaw, Cowans, McNaught
1983–84 UEFA Cup	1	14 Sep 83	Vitoria Guimaraes	A	L	0–1	
		28 Sep 83	(Portugal)	H	W	5–0	Withe 3, Ormsby, Gibson

2	19 Oct 83	Moscow Spartak	A	D	2-2	Gibson, Walters
	2 Nov 83	(USSR)	H	L	1-2	Withe

BIRMINGHAM CITY

1955-58	Fairs Cup	Gp.D	15 May 56	Inter Milan (Italy)	A	D	0-0	
			17 Apr 57		H	W	2-1	Govan 2
			22 May 56	Zagreb (Yugoslavia)	A	W	1-0	Brown
			3 Dec 56		H	W	3-0	Orritt, Brown, Murphy
		SF	23 Oct 57	Barcelona (Spain)	H	W	4-3	Murphy 2, Brown, Orritt
			13 Nov 57		A	L	0-1	
			26 Nov 57		N	L	1-2	Murphy
1958-60	Fairs Cup	1	14 Oct 58	FC Cologne	A	D	2-2	Neal, Hooper
			11 Nov 58	(West Germany)	H	W	2-0	Larkin, Taylor
		QF	6 May 59	Zagreb (Yugoslavia)	H	W	1-0	Larkin
			25 May 59		A	D	3-3	Larkin 2, Hooper
		SF	7 Oct 59	Union St Gilloise (Belgium)	A	W	4-2	Hooper, Gordon, Barrett, Taylor
			11 Nov 59		H	W	4-2	Gordon 2, Larkin, Hooper
		F	29 Mar 60	Barcelona (Spain)	H	D	0-0	
			4 May 60		A	L	1-4	Hooper
1960-61	Fairs Cup	1	19 Oct 60	Ujpest Dozsa	H	W	3-2	Gordon 2, Astall
			26 Oct 60	(Hungary)	A	W	2-1	Rudd, Singer
		QF	23 Nov 60	Copenhagen	A	D	4-4	Gordon 2, Singer 2
			7 Dec 60	(Denmark)	H	W	5-0	Stubbs 2, Harris, Hellawell, own goal
		SF	19 Apr 61	Inter Milan (Italy)	A	W	2-1	Harris, own goal
			3 May 61		H	W	2-1	Harris 2
		F	27 Sep 61	AS Roma (Italy)	H	D	2-2	Hellawell, Orritt
			11 Oct 61		A	L	0-2	
1961-62	Fairs Cup	1		bye				
		2	15 Nov 61	Espanol (Spain)	A	L	2-5	Bloomfield, Harris (pen)
			7 Dec 61		H	W	1-0	Auld

BURNLEY

1960-61	European Cup	Pr		bye				
		1	16 Nov 60	Reims (France)	H	W	2-0	Robson, McIlroy
			30 Nov 60		A	L	2-3	Robson, Connelly
		QF	18 Jan 61	SV Hamburg	H	W	3-1	Pilkington 2, Robson
			15 Mar 61	(West Germany)	A	L	1-4	Harris
1966-67	Fairs Cup	1	20 Sep 66	Stuttgart	A	D	1-1	Irvine
			27 Sep 66	(West Germany)	H	W	2-0	Coates, Lochhead
		2	10 Oct 66	Lausanne	A	W	3-1	Coates, Harris, Lochhead
			25 Oct 66	(Switzerland)	H	W	5-0	Lochhead 3, O'Neill, Irvine
		3	18 Jan 67	Napoli (Italy)	H	W	3-0	Coates, Latcham, Lochhead
			8 Feb 67		A	D	0-0	
		QF	4 Apr 67	Eintracht Frankfurt	A	D	1-1	Miller
			18 Apr 67	(West Germany)	H	L	1-2	Miller

CARDIFF CITY

1964–65	Cup-Winners' Cup	1	9 Sep 64	Esbjerg (Denmark)	A	D 0–0	
			13 Oct 64		H	W 1–0	King
		2	16 Dec 64	Sporting Lisbon	A	W 2–1	Farrell, Tapscott
			23 Dec 64	(Portugal)	H	D 0–0	
		QF	20 Jan 65	Real Zaragoza (Spain)	A	D 2–2	Williams, King
			3 Feb 65		H	L 0–1	
1965–66	Cup-Winners' Cup	1	8 Sep 65	Standard Liege	H	L 1–2	Johnston
			20 Oct 65	(Belgium)	A	L 0–1	
1967–68	Cup-Winners' Cup	1	20 Sep 67	Shamrock Rovers	A	D 1–1	King
			4 Oct 67	(Eire)	H	W 2–0	Toshack, Brown (pen)
		2	15 Nov 67	NAC Breda	A	D 1–1	King
			29 Nov 67	(Holland)	H	W 4–1	Brown, Barrie Jones, Clark, Toshack
		QF	6 Mar 68	Moscow Torpedo	H	W 1–0	Barrie Jones
			19 Mar 68	(USSR)	A	L 0–1	
			3 Apr 68		H	W 1–0	Dean
		SF	24 Apr 68	SV Hamburg	A	D 1–1	Dean
			1 May 68	(West Germany)	H	L 2–3	Dean, Harris
1968–69	Cup-Winners' Cup	1	18 Sep 68	Porto (Portugal)	H	D 2–2	Toshack, Bird (pen)
			2 Oct 68		A	L 1–2	Toshack
1969–70	Cup-Winners'	1	17 Sep 69	Mjondalen (Norway)	A	W 7–1	Clark 2, Toshack 2, Lea, Sutton, King
			1 Oct 69		H	W 5–1	King 2, Allan 3
		2	12 Nov 69	Goztepe Izmir	A	L 0–3	
			16 Nov 69	(Turkey)	H	W 1–0	Bird
1970–71	Cup-Winners'	1	16 Sep 70	Pezoporikos (Cyprus)	H	W 8–0	Toshack 2, Clark 2, Sutton, Gibson, King, Woodruff
			30 Sep 70		A	D 0–0	
		2	21 Oct 70	Nantes (France)	H	W 5–1	Toshack 2, Gibson, King, Phillips
			4 Nov 70		A	W 2–1	Toshack, Clark
		QF	10 Mar 70	Real Madrid (Spain)	H	W 1–0	Clark
			24 Mar 70		A	L 0–2	
1971–72	Cup-Winners' Cup	1	15 Sep 71	Dynamo Berlin	A	D 1–1	Gibson
			29 Sep 71	(East Germany) †	H	D 1–1	Clark
1973–74	Cup-Winners' Cup	1	19 Sep 73	Sporting Lisbon	H	D 0–0	
			3 Oct 73	(Portugal)	A	L 1–2	Vincent
1974–75	Cup-Winners' Cup	1	18 Sep 74	Ferencvaros	A	L 0–2	
			2 Oct 74	(Hungary)	H	L 1–4	Dwyer
1976–77	Cup-Winners' Cup	Pr	4 Aug 76	Servette (Switzerland)	H	W 1–0	Evans
			11 Aug 76		A	L 1–2	*Showers
		1	15 Sep 76	Dynamo Tbilisi	H	W 1–0	Alston
			29 Sep 76	(USSR)	A	L 0–3	
1977–78	Cup-Winners' Cup	1	14 Sep 77	Austria/WAC	H	D 0–0	
			28 Sep 77	(Austria)	A	L 0–1	
1988–89	Cup-Winners' Cup	1	7 Sep 88	Derry City (Eire)	A	D 0–0	
			5 Oct 88		H	W 4–0	McDermott, Gilligan 3
		2	26 Sep 88	Aarhus (Denmark)	H	L 1–2	Gilligan
			2 Nov 88		A	L 0–4	

CHELSEA

1958–59	Fairs Cup	1	30 Sep 58	Frem Copenhagen (Denmark)	A	W 3–1	Harrison, Greaves, Nicholas
			4 Nov 58		H	W 4–1	Greaves 2, Sillett (P), own goal
		QF	29 Apr 59	Belgrade	H	W 1–0	Brabrook
			13 May 59	(Yugoslavia)	H	L 1–4	Brabrook
1965–66	Fairs Cup	1	22 Sep 65	AS Roma (Italy)	H	W 4–1	Venables 3, Graham
			6 Oct 65		A	D 0–0	
		2	17 Nov 65	Wiener SK (Austria)	A	L 0–1	
			1 Dec 65		H	W 2–0	Murray, Osgood
		3	9 Feb 66	AC Milan (Italy)	A	L 1–2	Graham
			16 Feb 66		H	W 2–1	Graham, Osgood
			2 Mar 66		A	D 1–1‡	Bridges
		QF	15 Mar 66	Munich 1860	A	D 2–2	Tambling 2
			29 Mar 66	(West Germany)	H	W 1–0	Osgood
		SF	27 Apr 66	Barcelona (Spain)	A	L 0–2	
			11 May 66		H	W 2–0	own goals 2
			25 May 66		A	L 0–5	
1968–69	Fairs Cup	1	18 Sep 68	Morton (Scotland)	H	W 5–0	Osgood, Birchenall, Cooke, Boyle, Hollins
			30 Sep 68		A	W 4–3	Baldwin, Birchenall, Houseman, Tambling
		2	23 Oct 68	DWS Amsterdam	H	D 0–0	
			30 Oct 68	(Holland) ‡	A	D 0–0	
1970–71	Cup-Winners' Cup	1	16 Sep 70	Aris Salonika	A	D 1–1	Hutchinson
			30 Sep 70	(Greece)	H	W 5–1	Hutchinson 2, Hollins 2, Hinton
		2	21 Oct 70	CSKA Sofia	A	W 1–0	Baldwin
			4 Nov 70	(Bulgaria)	H	W 1–0	Webb
		QF	10 Mar 71	FC Bruges	A	L 0–2	
			24 Mar 71	(Belgium)	H	W 4–0	Houseman, Osgood 2, Baldwin
		SF	14 Apr 71	Manchester City	H	W 1–0	Smethurst
			28 Apr 71	(England)	A	W 1–0	Weller
		F	19 May 71	Real Madrid (Spain)	N	D 1–1	Osgood
			21 May 71		N	W 2–1	Dempsey, Osgood
1971–72	Cup-Winners'	1	15 Sep 71	Jeunesse Hautcharage (Luxembourg)	A	W 8–0	Osgood 3, Houseman 2, Hollins, Webb, Baldwin
			29 Sep 71		H	W 13–0	Osgood 5, Baldwin 3, Hollins (pen), Hudson, Webb, Houseman, Harris
		2	20 Oct 71	Atvidaberg (Sweden)*	A	D 0–0	
			3 Nov 71		H	D 1–1	Hudson

COVENTRY CITY

1970–71	Fairs Cup	1	16 Sep 70	Trakia Plovdiv	A	W 4–1	O'Rourke 3, Martin
			30 Sep 70	(Bulgaria)	H	W 2–0	Joicey, Blockley
		2	20 Oct 70	Bayern Munich	A	L 1–6	Hunt
			3 Nov 70	(West Germany)	H	W 2–1	Martin, O'Rourke

DERBY COUNTY

1972–73	European Cup	1	13 Sep 72	Zeljeznicar	H	W	2–0	McFarland, Gemmill
			27 Sep 72	(Yugoslavia)	A	W	2–1	Hinton, O'Hare
		2	25 Oct 72	Benfica (Portugal)	H	W	3–0	McFarland, Hector, McGovern
			8 Nov 72		A	D	0–0	
		QF	7 Mar 73	Spartak Trnava	A	D	0–0	
			21 Mar 73	(Czechoslovakia)	H	W	2–0	Hector 2
		SF	11 Apr 73	Juventus (Italy)	A	L	1–3	Hector
			25 Apr 73		H	D	0–0	
1974–75	UEFA Cup	1	18 Sep 74	Servette (Switzerland)	H	W	4–1	Hector 2, Daniel, Lee
			2 Oct 74		A	W	2–1	Lee, Hector
		2	23 Oct 74	Atletico Madrid	H	D	2–2	Nish, Rioch (pen)
			6 Nov 74	(Spain)	A	D	2–2†	Rioch, Hector
		3	27 Nov 74	Velez Mostar	H	W	3–1	Bourne 2, Hinton
			11 Dec 74	(Yugoslavia)	A	L	1–4	Hector
1975–76	European Cup	1	17 Sep 75	Slovan Bratislava	A	L	0–1	
			1 Oct 75	(Czechoslovakia)	H	W	3–0	Bourne, Lee 2
		2	22 Oct 75	Real Madrid (Spain)	H	W	4–1	George 3 (2 pen), Nish
			5 Nov 75		A	L	1–5	George
1976–77	UEFA Cup	1	15 Sep 76	Finn Harps (Eire)	H	W	12–0	Hector 5, James 3, George 3, Rioch
			29 Sep 76		A	W	4–1	Hector 2, George 2
		2	20 Oct 76	AEK Athens (Greece)	A	L	9–2	
			3 Nov 76		H	L	2–3	George, Rioch

EVERTON

1962–63	Fairs Cup	1	24 Oct 62	Dunfermline Athletic	H	W	1–0	Stevens
			31 Oct 62	(Scotland)	A	L	0–2	
1963–64	European Cup	1	18 Sep 63	Inter Milan (Italy)	H	D	0–0	
			25 Sep 63		A	L	0–1	
1964–65	Fairs Cup	1	23 Sep 64	Valerengen (Norway)	A	W	5–2	Pickering 2, Harvey, Temple 2
			14 Oct 64		H	W	4–2	Young 2, Vernon, own goal
		2	11 Nov 64	Kilmarnock (Scotland)	A	W	2–0	Temple, Morrissey
			23 Nov 64		H	W	4–1	Harvey, Pickering 2, Young
		3	20 Jan 65	Manchester United	A	D	1–1	Pickering
			9 Feb 65	(England)	H	L	1–2	Pickering
1965–66	Fairs Cup	1	28 Sep 65	FC Nuremberg	A	D	1–1	Harris
			12 Oct 65	(West Germany)	H	W	1–0	Gabriel
		2	3 Nov 65	Ujpest Dosza	A	L	0–3	
			16 Nov 65	(Hungary)	H	W	2–1	Harris, own goal
1966–67	Cup-Winners' Cup	1	28 Sep 66	Aalborg (Denmark)	A	D	0–0	
			11 Oct 66		H	W	2–1	Morrissey, Ball
		2	9 Nov 66	Real Zaragoza	A	L	0–2	
			23 Nov 66	(Spain)	H	W	1–0	Brown
1970–71	European Cup	1	16 Sep 70	Keflavik (Iceland)	H	W	6–2	Ball 3, Royel 2, Kendall
			30 Sep 70		A	W	3–0	Royle 2, Whittle
		2	21 Oct 70	Borussia	A	D	1–1	Kendall
			4 Nov 70	Moenchengladbach (West Germany)	H	D	1–1†	Morrissey

		QF	9 Mar 71	Panathinaikos		H	D	1-1	Johnson
			24 Mar 71	(Greece)		A	D	0-0	
1975-76	UEFA Cup	1	17 Sep 75	AC Milan (Italy)		H	D	0-0	
			1 Oct 75			A	L	0-1	
1978-79	UEFA Cup	1	12 Sep 78	Finn Harps (Eire)		A	W	5-0	Thomas, King 2, Latchford, Walsh
			26 Sep 78			H	W	5-0	King, Latchford, Walsh, Ross, Dobson
		2	18 Oct 78	Dukla Prague		H	W	2-1	Latchford, King
			1 Nov 78	(Czechoslovakia)		A	L	0-1	
1979-80	UEFA Cup	1	19 Sep 79	Feyenoord (Holland)		A	L	0-1	
			3 Sep 79			H	L	0-1	
1984-85	Cup-Winners' Cup	1	19 Sep 84	UCD (Eire)		A	D	0-0	
			2 Oct 84			H	W	1-0	Sharp
		2	24 Oct 84	Inter Bratislava		A	W	1-0	Bracewell
			7 Nov 84	(Czechoslovakia)		H	W	3-0	Heath, Sharp, Sheedy
		QF	6 Mar 85	Fortuna Sittard		H	W	3-0	Gray 3
			20 Mar 85	(Holland)		A	W	2-0	Reid, Sharp
		SF	10 Apr 85	Bayern Munich		A	D	0-0	
			24 Apr 85	(West Germany)		H	W	3-1	Gray, Sharp, Steven
		F	15 May 85	Rapid Vienna (Austria)		N	W	3-1	Gray, Sheedy, Steven

IPSWICH TOWN

1962-63	European Cup	Pr	18 Sep 62	Floriana (Malta)		A	W	4-1	Crawford 2, Phillips 2
			25 Sep 62			H	W	10-0	Crawford 5, Moran 2, Phillips 2, Elsworthy
		1	14 Nov 62	AC Milan (Italy)		A	L	0-3	
			28 Nov 62			H	W	2-1	Crawford, Blackwood
1973-74	UEFA Cup	1	19 Sep 73	Real Madrid (Spain)		H	W	1-0	own goal
			3 Oct 73			A	D	0-0	
		2	24 Oct 73	Lazio (Italy)		H	W	4-0	Whymark 4
			7 Nov 73			A	L	2-4	Viljoen (pen), Johnson
		3	28 Nov 73	Twente Enschede		H	W	1-0	Whymark
			12 Dec 73	(Holland)		A	W	2-1	Morris, Hamilton
		QF	6 Mar 74	Lokomotive Leipzig		H	W	1-0	Beattie
			20 Mar 74	(East Germany)†		H	L	0-1	
1974-75	UEFA Cup	1	18 Sep 74	Twente Enschede		H	D	2-2	Hamilton, Talbot
			2 Oct 74	(Holland)*		A	D	1-1	Hamilton
1975-76	UEFA Cup	1	17 Sep 75	Feyenoord (Holland)		A	W	2-1	Whymark, Johnson
			1 Oct 75			H	W	2-0	Woods, Whymark
		2	22 Oct 75	FC Bruges (Belgium)		H	W	3-0	Gates, Peddelty, Austin
			5 Nov 75			A	L	0-4	
1977-78	UEFA Cup	1	14 Sep 77	Landskrona (Sweden)		A	W	1-0	Whymark
			28 Sep 77			H	W	5-0	Whymark 4 (1 pen), Mariner
		2	19 Oct 77	Las Palmas (Spain)		H	W	1-0	Gates
			2 Nov 77			A	D	3-3	Mariner 2, Talbot
		3	23 Nov 77	Barcelona (Spain)†		H	W	3-0	Gates, Whymark, Talbot
			7 Dec 77			A	L	0-3	
1978-79	Cup-Winners' Cup	1	13 Sep 78	AZ 67 (Holland)		A	D	0-0	
			27 Sep 78			H	W	2-0	Mariner, Wark (pen)

	2	18 Oct 78	SW Innsbruck (Austria)	H	W	1–0	Wark (pen)
		1 Nov 78		A	D	1–1	Burley
	QF	7 Mar 79	Barcelona (Spain)	H	W	2–1	Gates 2
		21 Mar 79		A	L	0–1	
1979–80 UEFA Cup	1	19 Sep 79	Skeid Oslo (Norway)	A	W	3–1	Mills, Turner, Mariner
		3 Oct 79		H	W	7–0	Muhren 2, McCall 2, Wark, Thijssen, Mariner
	2	24 Oct 79	Grasshoppers*	A	D	0–0	
		7 Nov 79	(Switzerland)	H	D	1–1	Beattie
1980–81 UEFA Cup	1	17 Sep 80	Aris Salonika	H	W	5–1	Wark 4 (3 pens), Mariner
		1 Oct 80	(Greece)	A	L	1–3	Gates
	2	22 Oct 80	Bohemians	H	W	3–0	Wark 2, Beattie
		5 Nov 80	(Czechoslovakia)	A	L	0–2	
	3	26 Nov 80	Widzew Lodz	H	W	5–0	Wark 3, Brazil, Mariner
		10 Dec 80	(Poland)	A	L	0–1	
	QF	4 Mar 81	St Etienne	A	W	4–1	Mariner 2, Wark, Brazil
		18 Mar 81	(France)	H	W	3–1	Butcher, Wark (pen), Mariner
	SF	8 Apr 81	FC Cologne	H	W	1–0	Wark
		22 Apr 81	(West Germany)	A	W	1–0	Butcher
	F	6 May 81	AZ 67 (Holland)	H	W	3–0	Wark (pen), Thijssen, Mariner
		20 May 81		A	L	2–4	Thijssen, Wark
1981–82 UEFA Cup	1	16 Sep 81	Aberdeen (Scotland)	H	D	1–1	Thijssen
		30 Sep 81		A	L	1–3	Wark (pen)
1982–83 UEFA Cup	1	15 Sep 82	AS Roma (Italy)	A	L	0–3	
		29 Sep 82		H	W	3–1	Gates, McCall, Butcher

LEEDS UNITED

1965–66 Fairs Cup	1	29 Sep 65	Torino (Italy)	H	W	2–1	Bremner, Peacock
		6 Oct 65		A	D	0–0	
	2	24 Nov 65	Lokomotive Leipzig	A	W	2–1	Lorimer, Bremner
		1 Dec 65	(East Germany)	H	D	0–0	
	3	2 Feb 66	Valencia (Spain)	H	D	1–1	Lorimer
		16 Feb 66		A	W	1–0	O'Grady
	QF	2 Mar 66	Ujpest Dosza	H	W	4–1	Cooper, Bell, Storrie, Bremner
			(Hungary)				
		9 Mar 66		A	D	1–1	Lorimer
	SF	20 Apr 66	Real Zaragoza	A	L	0–1	
		27 Apr 66	(Spain)	H	W	2–1	Johanneson, Charlton
		11 Mar 66		N	L	1–3	Charlton
1966–67 Fairs Cup	1		bye				
	2	18 Oct 66	DWS Amsterdam	A	W	3–1	Bremner, Johanneson, Greenhoff
			(Holland)				
		26 Oct 66		H	W	5–1	Johanneson 3, Giles, Madeley
	3	18 Jan 67	Valencia (Spain)	H	D	1–1	Greenhoff
		8 Feb 67		A	W	2–0	Giles, Lorimer
	QF	22 Mar 67	Bologna (Italy)	A	L	0–1	
		19 Apr 67		H	W	1–0†	Giles (pen)
	SF	19 May 67	Kilmarnock	H	W	4–2	Belfitt 3, Giles (pen)
		24 May 67	(Scotland)	A	D	0–0	

	F	30 Aug 67	Dynamo Zagreb	A	L	0-2	
		6 Sep 67	(Yugoslavia)	H	D	0-0	
1967–68 Fairs Cup	1	3 Oct 67	Spora Luxembourg	A	W	9-0	Lorimer 4, Greenhoff 2,
			(Luxembourg)				Madeley, Jones, Bremner
		17 Oct 67		H	W	7-0	Johanneson 3,
							Greenhoff 2, Cooper,
							Lorimer
	2	29 Nov 67	Partizan Belgrade	A	W	2-1	Lorimer, Belfitt
		6 Dec 67	(Yugoslavia)	H	D	1-1	Lorimer
	3	20 Dec 67	Hibernian (Scotland)	H	W	1-0	Gray (E)
		10 Jan 68		A	D	0-0	
	QF	26 Mar 68	Rangers (Scotland)	A	D	0-0	
		9 Apr 68		H	W	2-0	Lorimer, Giles (pen)
	SF	1 May 68	Dundee (Scotland)	A	D	1-1	Madeley
		15 May 68		H	W	1-0	Gray (E)
	F	7 Aug 68	Ferencvaros	H	W	1-0	Charlton
		11 Sep 68	(Hungary)	A	D	0-0	
1968–69 Fairs Cup	1	18 Sep 68	Standard Liege	A	D	0-0	
		23 Oct 68	(Belgium)	H	W	3-2	Charlton, Lorimer,
							Bremner
	2	13 Nov 68	Napoli (Italy)	H	W	2-0	Charlton 2
		27 Nov 68		A	L	0-2 ‡	
	3	18 Dec 68	Hanover 96	H	W	5-1	O'Grady, Hunter,
			(West Germany)				Lorimer 2, Charlton
		4 Feb 69		A	W	2-1	Belfitt, Jones
	QF	5 Mar 69	Ujpest Dozsa	A	L	0-1	
		19 Mar 69	(Hungary)	H	L	0-2	
1969–70 European Cup	1	17 Sep 69	Lyn Oslo (Norway)	H	W	10-0	Jones 3, Clarke 2, Giles 2,
							Bremner 2, O'Grady
		1 Oct 69		A	W	6-0	Belfitt 2, Hibbitt 2,
							Jones, Lorimer
	2	12 Nov 69	Ferencvaros	H	W	3-0	Giles, Jones 2
		26 Nov 69	(Hungary)	A	W	3-0	Jones 2, Lorimer
	QF	4 Mar 70	Standard Liege	A	W	1-0	Lorimer
		18 Mar 70	(Belgium)	H	W	1-0	Giles (pen)
	SF	1 Apr 70	Celtic (Scotland)	H	L	0-1	
		15 Apr 70		A	L	1-2	Bremner
1970–71 Fairs Cup	1	15 Sep 70	Sarpsborg (Norway)	H	W	1-0	Lorimer
		29 Sep 70		H	W	5-0	Charlton 2, Bremner 2,
							Lorimer
	2	21 Oct 70	Dynamo Dresden	A	W	1-0	Lorimer
		4 Nov 70	(East Germany)	A	L	1-2*	Jones
	3	2 Dec 70	Sparta Prague	H	W	6-0	Clarke, Bremner,
			(Czechoslovakia)				Grey (E) 2, Cherlton,
							own goal
		9 Dec 70		A	W	3-2	Gray (E), Clarke, Belfitt
	QF	10 Mar 71	Setubal (Portugal)	H	W	2-1	Lorimer, Giles (pen)
		24 Mar 71		A	D	1-1	Lorimer
	SF	14 Apr 71	Liverpool (England)	A	W	1-0	Bremner
		28 Apr 71		H	D	0-0	
	F	28 May 71	Juventus (Italy)	A	D	2-2	Madeley, Bates
		3 Jun 71		H	D	1-1*	Clarke

1971–72	UEFA Cup	1	15 Sep 71	Lierse (Belgium)	A	W	2–0	Galvin, Lorimer
			29 Sep 71		H	L	0–4	
1972–73	Cup-Winners' Cup	1	13 Sep 72	Ankaragucu (Turkey)	A	D	1–1	Jordan
			28 Sep 72		H	W	1–0	Jones
		2	25 Oct 72	Carl Zeiss Jena	A	D	0–0	
			8 Nov 72	(East Germany)	H	W	2–0	Cherry, Jones
		QF	7 Mar 73	Rapid Bucharest (Romania)	H	W	5–0	Giles, Clarke, Lorimer 2, Jordan
			23 Mar 73		A	W	3–1	Jones, Jordan, Bates
		SF	11 Apr 73	Hajduk Split	H	W	1–0	Clarke
			25 Apr 73	(Yugoslavia)	A	D	0–0	
		F	16 May 73	AC Milan (Italy)	N	L	0–1	
1973–74	UEFA Cup	1	19 Sep 73	Stromsgodset	A	D	1–1	Clarke
			3 Oct 73	(Norway)	H	W	6–1	Clarke 2, Jones 2, Gray (F), Bates
		2	24 Oct 73	Hibernian (Scotland)	H	D	0–0	
			7 Nov 73		A	D	0–0†	
		3	28 Nov 73	Setubal (Portugal)	H	W	1–0	Cherry
			12 Dec 73		A	L	1–3	Liddell
1974–75	European Cup	1	28 Sep 74	FC Zurich (Switzerland)	H	W	4–1	Clarke 2, Lorimer (pen), Jordan
			2 Oct 74		A	L	1–2	Clarke
		2	23 Oct 74	Ujpest Dozsa	A	W	2–1	Lorimer, McQueen
			6 Nov 74	(Hungary)	H	W	3–0	McQueen, Bremner, Yorath
		QF	5 Mar 75	Anderlecht (Belgium)	H	W	3–0	Jordan, McQueen, Lorimer
			19 Mar 75		A	W	1–0	Bremner
		SF	9 Apr 75	Barcelona (Spain)	H	W	2–1	Bremner, Clarke
			24 Apr 75		A	D	1–1	Lorimer
		F	28 May 75	Bayern Munich (West Germany)	N	L	0–2	
1979–80	UEFA Cup	1	19 Sep 79	Valletta (Malta)	A	W	4–0	Graham 3, Hart
			3 Oct 79		H	W	3–0	Curtis, Hankin, Hart
		2	24 Oct 79	Uni. Craiova	A	L	0–2	
			7 Nov 79	(Romania)	H	L	0–2	

N.B. Leeds met Barcelona in Spain on 22 Sep 71 in a match to determine who should hold the Fairs Cup trophy permanently. Barcelona, the first winners beat Leeds, the holders 2–1 (Jordan was the United scorer).

LEICESTER CITY

1961–62	Cup-Winners' Cup	1	13 Sep 61	Glenavon (Northern Ireland)	A	W	4–1	Walsh 2, Appleton, Keyworth
			27 Sep 61		H	W	3–1	Wills, Keyworth, McIlmoyle
		2	25 Oct 61	Atletico Madrid	H	D	1–1	Keyworth
			15 Nov 61	(Spain)	A	L	0–2	

LIVERPOOL

Season	Competition	Round	Date	Opponent	Venue	Result	Scorers
1964–65	European Cup	Pr	17 Aug 64	KR Reykjavik (Iceland)	A	W 5–0	Wallace 2, Hunt 2, Chisnall
			14 Sep 64		H	W 6–1	Byrne, St John 2, Graham, Hunt, Stevenson
		1	25 Nov 64	Anderlecht	H	W 3–0	St John, Hunt, Yeats
			16 Dec 64	(Belgium)	A	W 1–0	Hunt
		QF	10 Feb 65	FC Cologne	A	D 0–0	
			17 Mar 65	(West Germany)	H	D 0–0	
			24 Mar 65		N	D 2–2 ‡	St John, Hunt
		SF	4 May 65	Inter Milan (Italy)	H	W 3–1	Hunt, Callaghan, St John
			12 May 65		A	L 0–3	
1965–66	Cup-Winners' Cup	1	29 Sep 65	Juventus (Italy)	A	L 0–1	
			13 Oct 65		H	W 2–0	Lawler, Strong
		2	1 Dec 65	Standard Liege	H	W 3–1	Lawler 2, Thompson (P)
			15 Dec 65	(Belgium)	A	W 2–1	Hunt, St John
		QF	1 Mar 66	Honved (Hungary)	A	D 0–0	
			8 Mar 66		H	W 2–0	Lawler, St John
		SF	14 Apr 66	Celtic (Scotland)	A	L 0–1	
			19 Apr 66		H	W 2–0	Smith, Strong
		F	5 May 66	Borussia Dortmund (West Germany)	N	L 1–2	Hunt
1966–67	European Cup	1	28 Sep 66	Petrolul Ploesti	H	W 2–0	St John, Callaghan
			12 Oct 66	(Romania)	A	L 1–3	Hunt
			19 Oct 66		N	W 2–0	St John, Thompson (P)
		2	7 Dec 66	Ajax (Holland)	A	L 1–5	Lawler
			14 Dec 66		H	D 2–2	Hunt 2
1967–68	Fairs Cup	1	19 Sep 67	Malmo FF (Sweden)	A	W 2–0	Hateley 2
			4 Oct 67		H	W 2–1	Yeats, Hunt
		2	7 Nov 67	Munich 1860 (West Germany)	H	W 8–0	St John, Hateley, Thompson (P), Smith (pen), Hunt 2, Callaghan 2
			14 Nov 67		A	L 1–2	Callaghan
		3	28 Nov 67	Ferencvaros	A	L 0–1	
			9 Jan 68	(Hungary)	H	L 0–1	
1968–69	Fairs Cup	1	18 Sep 68	Athletic Bilbao	A	L 1–2	Hunt
			2 Oct 68	(Spain) ‡	H	W 2–1	Lawler, Hughes
1969–70	Fairs Cup	1	16 Sep 69	Dundalk (Eire)	H	W 10–0	Evans 2, Smith 2, Graham 2, Lawler, Lindsay, Thompson (P), Callaghan
			30 Sep 69		A	W 4–0	Thompson (P) 2, Graham, Callaghan
		3	11 Nov 69	Setubal (Portugal)*	A	L 0–1	
			26 Nov 69		H	W 3–2	Smith (pen), Evans, Hunt
1970–71	Fairs Cup	1	15 Sep 70	Ferencvaros	H	W 1–0	Graham
			29 Sep 70	(Hungary)	A	D 1–1	Hughes
		2	21 Oct 70	Dinamo Bucharest	H	W 3–0	Lindsay, Lawler, Hughes
			4 Nov 70	(Romania)	A	D 1–1	Boersma
		3	9 Dec 70	Hibernian (Scotland)	A	W 1–0	Toshack
			22 Dec 70		H	W 2–0	Heighway, Boersma

Season	Competition	Round	Date	Opponent (Country)	H/A	Result	Scorers
		QF	10 Mar 71	Bayern Munich	H	W 3–0	Evans 3
			24 Mar 71	(West Germany)	A	D 1–1	Ross
		SF	14 Apr 71	Leeds United	H	L 0–1	
			28 Apr 71	(England)	A	D 0–0	
1971–72	Cup-Winners' Cup	1	15 Sep 71	Servette	A	L 1–2	Lawler
			29 Sep 71	(Switzerland)	H	W 2–0	Hughes, Heighway
		2	20 Oct 71	Bayern Munich	H	D 0–0	
			3 Nov 71	(West Germany)	A	L 1–3	Evans
1972–73	UEFA Cup	1	12 Sep 72	Eintracht Frankfurt	H	W 2–0	Keegan, Hughes
			26 Sep 72	(West Germany)	A	D 0–0	
		2	24 Oct 72	AEK Athens (Greece)	H	W 3–0	Boersma, Cormack, Smith (pen)
			7 Nov 72		A	W 3–1	Hughes 2, Boersma
		3	29 Nov 72	Dynamo Berlin	A	D 0–0	
			12 Dec 72	(East Germany)	H	W 3–1	Boersma, Heighway, Toshack
		QF	7 Mar 73	Dynamo Dresden	H	W 2–0	Hall, Boersma
			21 Mar 73	(East Germany)	A	W 1–0	Keegan
		SF	10 Apr 73	Tottenham Hotspur	H	W 1–0	Lindsay
			25 Apr 73	(England)	A	L 1–2*	Heighway
		F	10 May 73	Borussia	H	W 3–0	Keegan 2, Lloyd
			23 May 73	Moenchengladbach (West Germany)	A	L 0–2	
1973–74	European Cup	1	19 Sep 73	Jeunesse D'Esch	A	D 1–1	Hall
			3 Oct 73	(Luxembourg)	H	W 2–0	Toshack, own goal
		2	24 Oct 73	Red Star Belgrade	A	L 1–2	Lawler
			6 Nov 73	(Yugoslavia)	H	L 1–2	Lawler
1974–75	Cup-Winners'	1	17 Sep 74	Stromsgodset (Norway)	H	W 11–0	Lindsay (pen), Boersma 2, Heighway, Thompson (P B) 2, Smith, Cormack, Hughes, Callaghan, Kennedy
			1 Oct 74		A	W 1–0	Kennedy
		2	23 Oct 74	Ferencvaros	H	D 1–1	Keegan
			5 Nov 74	(Hungary)*	A	D 0–0	
1975–76	UEFA Cup	1	17 Sep 75	Hibernian (Scotland)	A	L 0–1	
			30 Sep 75		H	W 3–1	Toshack 3
		2	22 Oct 75	Real Sociedad (Spain)	A	W 3–1	Heighway, Callaghan, Thompson (P B)
			4 Nov 75		H	W 6–0	Toshack, Kennedy 2, Fairclough, Heighway, Neal
		3	26 Nov 75	Slask Wroclaw	A	W 2–1	Kennedy, Toshack
			10 Dec 75	(Poland)	H	W 3–0	Case 3
		QF	3 Mar 76	Dynamo Dresden	A	D 0–0	
			17 Mar 76	(East Germany)	H	W 2–1	Case, Keegan
		SF	30 Mar 76	Barcelona (Spain)	A	W 1–0	Toshack
			14 Apr 76		H	D 1–1	Thompson (P B)
		F	28 Apr 76	FC Bruges (Belgium)	H	W 3–2	Kennedy, Case, Keegan (pen)
			19 May 76		A	D 1–1	Keegan
1976–77	European Cup	1	14 Sep 76	Crusaders	H	W 2–0	Neal (pen), Toshack
			28 Sep 76	(Northern Ireland)	A	W 5–0	Johnson 2, Keegan, McDermott, Heighway

		2	20 Oct 76	Trabzonspor (Turkey)	A	L	0-1	
			3 Nov 76		H	W	3-0	Heighway, Johnson, Keegan
		QF	2 Mar 77	St Etienne (France)	A	L	0-1	
			16 Mar 77		H	W	3-1	Keegan, Kennedy, Fairclough
		SF	6 Apr 77	FC Zurich	A	W	3-1	Neal 2 (1 pen), Heighway
			20 Apr 77	(Switzerland)	H	W	3-0	Case 2, Keegan
		F	25 May 77	Borussia Moenchengladbach (West Germany)	N	W	3-1	McDermott, Smith, Neal (pen)
1977-78	Super Cup	F	22 Nov 77	SV Hamburg	A	D	1-1	Fairclough
			6 Dec 77	(West Germany)	H	W	6-0	Thompson, McDermott 3, Fairclough, Dalglish
1977-78	European Cup	1		bye				
		2	19 Oct 77	Dynamo Dresden (East Germany)	H	W	5-1	Hansen, Case 2, Neal (pen), Kennedy
			2 Nov 77		A	L	1-2	Heighway
		QF	1 Mar 78	Benfica (Portugal)	A	W	2-1	Case, Hughes
			15 Mar 78		H	W	4-1	Callaghan, Dalglish, McDermott, Neal
		SF	29 Mar 78	Borussia Moenchengladbach (West Germany)	A	L	1-2	Johnson
			12 Apr 78		H	W	3-0	Kennedy, Dalglish, Case
		F	10 May 78	FC Bruges (Belgium)	N	W	1-0	Dalglish
1978-79	Super Cup	F	4 Dec 78	Anderlecht (Belgium)	A	L	1-3	Case
			19 Dec 78		H	W	2-1	Hughes, Fairclough
1978-79	European Cup	1	13 Sep 78	Nottingham Forest (England)	A	L	0-2	
			27 Sep 78		H	D	0-0	
1979-80	European Cup	1	19 Sep 79	Dynamo Tbilisi (USSR)	H	W	2-1	Johnson, Case
			3 Oct 79		A	L	0-3	
1980-81	European Cup	1	17 Sep 80	Oulun Palloseura (Finland)	A	D	1-1	McDermott
			1 Oct 80		H	W	10-1	Souness 3 (1 pen), Fairclough 2, McDermott 2, Dalglish, Lee, Kennedy (R)
		2	22 Oct 80	Aberdeen (Scotland)	A	W	1-0	McDermott
			5 Nov 80		H	W	4-0	Neal, Dalglish, Hansen, own goal
		QF	4 Mar 81	CSKA Sofia (Bulgaria)	H	W	5-1	Souness 3, Lee, McDermott
			18 Mar 81		A	W	1-0	Johnson
		SF	8 Apr 81	Bayern Munich (West Germany)	H	D	0-0	
			22 Apr 81		A	D	1-1*	Kennedy (R)
		F	27 May 81	Real Madrid (Spain)	N	W	1-0	Kennedy (A)
1981-82	European Cup	1	16 Sep 81	Oulun Palloseura (Finland)	A	W	1-0	Dalglish
			30 Sep 81		H	W	7-0	Dalglish, McDermott 2, Kennedy (R), Johnson, Rush, Lawrenson
		2	21 Oct 81	AZ 67 (Holland)	A	D	2-2	Johnson, Lee
			4 Nov 81		H	W	3-2	McDermott (pen), Rush, Hansen

	QF	3 Mar 82	CSKA Sofia	H	W	1–0	Whelan
		17 Mar 82	(Bulgaria)	A	L	0–2	
1982–83 European Cup	1	14 Sep 82	Dundalk (Eire)	A	W	4–1	Whelan 2, Rush, Hodgson
		28 Sep 82		H	W	1–0	Whelan
	2	19 Oct 82	HJK Helsinki	A	L	0–1	
		2 Nov 82	(Finland)	H	W	5–0	Dalglish, Johnston, Neal, Kennedy (A) 2
	QF	2 Mar 83	Widzew Lodz	A	L	0–2	
		16 Mar 83	(Poland)	H	W	3–2	Neal (pen), Rush, Hodgson
1983–84 European Cup	1	14 Sep 83	BK Odense (Denmark)	A	W	1–0	Dalglish
		28 Sep 83		H	W	5–0	Robinson 2, Dalglish 2, own goal
	2	19 Oct 83	Athletic Bilbao	H	D	0–0	
		2 Nov 83	(Spain)	A	W	1–0	Rush
	QF	7 Mar 84	Benfica (Portugal)	H	W	1–0	Rush
		21 Mar 84		A	W	4–1	Whelan 2, Johnston, Rush
	SF	11 Apr 84	Dinamo Bucharest	H	W	1–0	Lee
		25 Apr 84	(Rumania)	A	W	2–1	Rush 2
	F	30 May 84	AS Roma (Italy)	N	D	1–1†	Neal
1984–85 Super Cup	F	16 Jan 85	Juventus (Italy)	A	L	0–2	
1984–85 European Cup	1	19 Sep 84	Lech Poznan (Poland)	A	W	1–0	Wark
		3 Oct 84		H	W	4–0	Wark 3, Walsh
	2	24 Oct 84	Benfica (Portugal)	H	W	3–1	Rush 3
		7 Nov 84		A	L	0–1	
	QF	6 Mar 85	FK Austria (Austria)	A	D	1–1	Nicol
		20 Mar 85		H	W	4–1	Walsh 2, Nicol, own goal
	SF	10 Apr 85	Panathinaikos	H	W	4–0	Wark, Rush 2, Beglin
		24 Apr 85	(Greece)	A	W	1–0	Lawrenson
	F	29 May 85	Juventus (Italy)	N	L	0–1	

MANCHESTER CITY

1968–69 European Cup	1	18 Sep 68	Fenerbahce (Turkey)	H	D	0–0	
		2 Oct 68		A	L	1–2	Coleman
1969–70 Cup-Winners' Cup	1	17 Sep 69	Athletic Bilbao	A	D	3–3	Young, Booth, own goal
		1 Oct 69	(Spain)	H	W	3–0	Oakes, Bell, Bowyer
	2	12 Nov 69	Lierse (Belgium)	A	W	3–0	Lee 2, Bell
		26 Nov 69		H	W	5–0	Bell 2, Lee 2, Summerbee
	QF	4 Mar 70	Academica Coimbra	A	D	0–0	
		18 Mar 70	(Portugal)	H	W	1–0	Towers
	SF	1 Apr 70	Schalke 04	A	L	0–1	
		15 Apr 70	(West Germany)	H	W	5–1	Young 2, Doyle, Lee, Bell
	F	29 Apr 70	Gornik Zabrze (Poland)	N	W	2–1	Young, Lee (pen)
1970–71 Cup-Winners' Cup	1	16 Sep 70	Linfield	H	W	1–0	Bell
		30 Sep 70	(Northern Ireland)	A	L	1–2*	Lee
	2	21 Oct 70	Honved (Hungary)	A	W	1–0	Lee
		4 Nov 70		H	W	2–0	Bell, Lee
	QF	10 Mar 71	Gornik Zabrze	A	L	0–2	
		24 Mar 71	(Poland)	H	W	2–0	Mellor, Doyle
		31 Mar 71		N	W	3–1	Young, Booth, Lee
	SF	14 Apr 71	Chelsea (England)	A	L	0–1	
		28 Apr 71		H	L	0–1	

1972–73	UEFA Cup	1	13 Sep 72	Valencia (Spain)	H	D	2–2	Mellor, Marsh
			27 Sep 72		A	L	1–2	Marsh
1976–77	UEFA Cup	1	15 Sep 76	Juventus (Italy)	H	W	1–0	Kidd
			29 Sep 76		A	L	0–2	
1977–78	UEFA Cup	1	14 Sep 77	Widzew Lodz	H	D	2–2	Barnes, Channon
			28 Sep 77	(Poland)*	A	D	0–0	
1978–79	UEFA Cup	1	13 Sep 78	Twente Enschede	A	D	1–1	Watson
			27 Sep 78	(Holland)	H	W	3–2	Kidd, Bell, own goal
		2	18 Oct 78	Standard Liege	H	W	4–0	Hartford, Kidd 2 (1 pen),
				(Belgium)				Palmer
			1 Nov 78		A	L	0–2	
		3	23 Nov 78	AC Milan (Italy)	A	D	2–2	Kidd, Power
			6 Dec 78		H	W	3–0	Booth, Hartford, Kidd
		QF	7 Mar 79	Borussia	H	D	1–1	Channon
			21 Mar 79	Moenchengladbach	A	L	1–3	Deyna
				(West Germany)				

MANCHESTER UNITED

1956–57	European Cup	Pr	12 Sep 56	Anderlecht (Belgium)	A	W	2–0	Viollet, Taylor (T)
			29 Sep 56		H	W	10–0	Viollet 4, Taylor (T) 3,
								Whelan 2, Berry
		1	17 Oct 56	Borussia Dortmund	H	W	3–2	Viollet 2, Pegg
			21 Nov 56	(West Germany)	A	D	0–0	
		QF	16 Jan 57	Athletic Bilbao	A	L	3–5	Taylor (T), Viollet, Whelan
			6 Feb 57	(Spain)	H	W	3–0	Viollet, Taylor (T), Berry
		SF	11 Apr 57	Real Madrid (Spain)	A	L	1–3	Taylor (T)
			24 Apr 57		H	D	2–2	Taylor (T), Charlton
1957–58	European Cup	Pr	25 Sep 57	Shamrock Rovers	A	W	6–0	Whelan 2, Taylor (T) 2,
				(Eire)				Berry, Pegg
			2 Oct 57		H	W	3–2	Viollet 2, Pegg
		1	20 Nov 57	Dukla Prague	H	W	3–0	Webster, Taylor (T), Pegg
			4 Dec 57	(Czechoslovakia)	A	L	0–1	
		QF	14 Jan 58	Red Star Belgrade	H	W	2–1	Charlton, Colman
			5 Feb 58	(Yugoslavia)	A	D	3–3	Viollet, Charlton 2
		SF	8 May 58	AC Milan (Italy)	H	W	2–1	Viollet, Taylor (E) (pen)
			14 May 58		A	L	0–4	
1963–64	Cup Winners' Cup	1	25 Sep 63	Tilburg Willem II	A	D	1–1	Herd
			15 Oct 63	(Holland)	H	W	6–1	Setters, Law 3, Charlton,
								Chisnall
		2	3 Dec 63	Tottenham Hotspur	A	L	0–2	
			10 Dec 63	(England)	H	W	4–1	Herd 2, Charlton 2
		QF	26 Feb 64	Sporting Lisbon	H	W	4–1	Law 3 (2 pens), Charlton
			18 Mar 65	(Portugal)	A	L	0–5	
1964–65	Fairs Cup	1	23 Sep 64	Djurgaarden (Sweden)	A	D	1–1	Herd
			27 Oct 64		H	W	6–1	Law 3 (1 pen), Charlton 2,
								Best
		2	11 Nov 64	Borussia Dortmund	A	W	6–1	Herd, Charlton 3, Best,
				(West Germany)				Law
			2 Dec 64		H	W	4–0	Charlton 2, Law, Connelly
		3	20 Jan 65	Everton (England)	H	D	1–1	Connelly
			9 Feb 65		A	W	2–1	Connelly, Herd

Season	Competition	Round	Date	Opponent	H/A/N	Result	Scorers
		QF	12 May 65	Strasbourg (France)	A	W 5–0	Connelly, Herd, Law 2, Charlton
			19 May 65		H	D 0–0	
		SF	31 May 65	Ferencvaros	H	W 3–2	Law (pen), Herd 2
			6 Jun 65	(Hungary)	A	L 0–1	
			16 Jun 65		A	L 1–2	Connelly
1965–66	European Cup	Pr	22 Sep 65	HJK Helsinki	A	W 3–2	Herd, Connelly, Law
			6 Oct 65	(Finland)	H	W 6–0	Connelly 3, Best 2, Charlton
		1	17 Nov 65	Vorwaerts Berlin	A	W 2–0	Law, Connelly
			1 Dec 65	(East Germany)	H	W 3–1	Herd 3
		QF	2 Feb 66	Benfica (Portugal)	H	W 3–2	Herd, Law, Foulkes
			9 Mar 66		A	W 5–1	Best 2, Connelly, Crerand, Charlton
		SF	13 Apr 66	Partizan Belgrade	A	L 0–2	
			20 Apr 66	(Yugoslavia)	H	W 1–0	own goal
1967–68	European Cup	1	20 Sep 67	Hibernians (Malta)	H	W 4–0	Sadler 2, Law 2
			27 Sep 67		A	D 0–0	
		2	15 Nov 67	Sarajevo (Yugoslavia)	A	D 0–0	
			29 Nov 67		H	W 2–1	Aston, Best
		QF	28 Feb 68	Gornik Zabrze	H	W 2–0	Kidd, own goal
			13 Mar 68	(Poland)	A	L 0–1	
		SF	24 Apr 68	Real Madrid (Spain)	H	W 1–0	Best
			15 May 68		A	D 3–3	Sadler, Kidd, Foulkes
		F	29 Apr 68	Benfica (Portugal)	N	W 4–1	Charlton 2, Best, Kidd
1968–69	European Cup	1	18 Sep 68	Waterford (Eire)	A	W 3–1	Law 3
			2 Oct 68		H	W 7–1	Stiles, Law 4, Burns, Charlton
		2	13 Nov 68	Anderlecht (Belgium)	H	W 3–0	Kidd, Law 2
			27 Nov 68		A	L 1–3	Sartori
		QF	26 Feb 69	Rapid Vienna (Austria)	H	W 3–0	Best 2, Morgan
			5 Mar 69		A	D 0–0	
		SF	23 Apr 69	AC Milan (Italy)	A	L 0–2	
			15 Apr 69		H	W 1–0	Charlton
1976–77	UEFA Cup	1	15 Sep 76	Ajax (Holland)	A	L 0–1	
			29 Sep 76		H	W 2–0	Macari, McIlroy
		2	20 Oct 76	Juventus (Italy)	H	W 1–0	Hill
			3 Nov 76		A	L 0–3	
1977–78	Cup-Winners' Cup	1	14 Sep 77	St Etienne (France)	A	D 1–1	Hill
			5 Oct 77		H	W 2–0	Pearson, Coppell
		2	19 Oct 77	Porto (Portugal)	A	L 0–4	
			2 Nov 77		H	W 5–2	Coppell 2, own goals 2, Nicholl
1980–81	UEFA Cup	1	17 Sep 80	Widzew Lodz*	H	D 1–1	McIlroy
			1 Oct 80	(Poland)	A	D 0–0	
1982–83	UEFA Cup	1	15 Sep 82	Valencia (Spain)	H	D 0–0	
			29 Sep 82		A	L 1–2	Robson
1983–84	Cup-Winners' Cup	1	14 Sep 83	Dukla Prague	H	D 1–1	Wilkins
			27 Sep 83	(Czechoslovakia)	A	D 2–2*	Robson, Stapleton
		2	19 Oct 83	Spartak Varna	A	W 2–1	Robson, Graham
			2 Nov 83	(Bulgaria)	H	W 2–0	Stapleton 2
		QF	7 Mar 84	Barcelona (Spain)	A	L 0–2	
			21 Mar 84		H	W 3–0	Robson 2, Stapleton

		SF	11 Apr 84	Juventus (Italy)	H	D 1–1	Davies
			24 Apr 84		A	L 1–2	Whiteside
1984–85	UEFA Cup	1	19 Sep 84	Raba Gyor (Hungary)	H	W 3–0	Robson, Muhren, Hughes
			3 Oct 84		A	D 2–2	Brazil, Muhren
		2	24 Oct 84	PSV Eindhoven	A	D 0–0	
			7 Nov 84	(Holland)	H	W 1–0	Strachan
		3	28 Nov 84	Dundee United	H	D 2–2	Strachan, Robson
			12 Dec 84	(Scotland)	A	W 3–2	Hughes, Muhren, own goal
		QF	6 Mar 85	Videoton (Hungary) †	H	W 1–0	Stapleton
			20 Mar 84		A	L 0–1	

NEWCASTLE UNITED

1968–69	Fairs Cup	1	11 Nov 68	Feyenoord (Holland)	H	W 4–0	Scott, Robson (B), Gibb, Davies
			17 Nov 68		A	L 0–2	
		2	30 Oct 68	Sporting Lisbon	A	D 1–1	Scott
			20 Nov 68	(Portugal)	H	W 1–0	Robson (B)
		3	1 Jan 69	Real Zaragoza (Spain)	A	L 2–3	Robson (B), Davies
			15 Jan 69		H	W 2–1*	Robson (B), Gibb
		QF	12 Mar 69	Setubal (Portugal)	H	W 5–1	Robson (B) 2, Gibb, Davies, Foggon
			26 Mar 69		A	L 1–3	Davies
		SF	14 Apr 69	Rangers (Scotland)	A	D 0–0	
			22 May 69		H	W 2–0	Scott, Sinclair
		F	29 May 69	Ujpest Dozsa	H	W 3–0	Moncur 2, Scott
			11 Jun 69	(Hungary)	A	W 3–2	Moncur, Arentoft, Foggon
1969–70	Fairs Cup	1	15 Sep 69	Dundee United	A	W 2–1	Davies 2
			1 Oct 69	(Scotland)	H	W 1–0	Dyson
		2	19 Nov 69	Porto (Portugal)	A	D 0–0	
			26 Nov 69		H	W 1–0	Scott
		3	17 Dec 69	Southampton	H	D 0–0	
			13 Jan 70	(England)	A	D 1–1*	Robson (B)
		QF	11 Mar 70	Anderlecht (Belgium)*	A	L 0–2	
			18 Mar 70		H	W 3–1	Robson (B) 2, Dyson
1970–71	Fairs Cup	1	23 Sep 70	Inter Milan (Italy)	A	D 1–1	Davies
			30 Sep 70		H	W 2–0	Moncur, Davies
		2	21 Oct 70	Pecs Dozsa	H	W 2–0	Davies 2
			4 Nov 70	(Hungary) †	A	L 0–2	
1977–78	UEFA Cup	1	14 Sep 77	Bohemians (Eire)	A	D 0–0	
			28 Sep 77		H	W 4–0	Gowling 2, Craig 2
		2	19 Oct 77	Bastia (France)	A	L 1–2	Cannell
			2 Nov 77		H	L 1–3	Gowling

NEWPORT COUNTY

1980–81	Cup-Winners' Cup	1	16 Sep 80	Crusaders (Northern Ireland)	H	W 4–0	Gwyther, Moore, Aldridge, Bruton
			1 Oct 80		A	D 0–0	
		2	22 Oct 80	Haugar (Norway)	A	D 0–0	
			4 Nov 80		H	W 6–0	Gwyther, Lowndes, Aldridge, Tynan 2, Moore
		QF	4 Mar 81	Carl Zeiss Jena	A	D 2–2	Tynan 2
			18 Mar 81	(East Germany)	H	L 0–1	

NOTTINGHAM FOREST

1961–62	Fairs Cup	1	13 Sep 61	Valencia (Spain)	A	L	0–2	
			4 Oct 61		H	L	1–5	Cobb
1967–68	Fairs Cup	1	20 Sep 67	Eintracht Frankfurt	A	W	1–0	Baker
			17 Oct 67	(West Germany)	H	W	4–0	Baker 2, Chapman, Lyons
		2	31 Oct 67	Zurich (Switzerland)*	H	W	2–1	Newton, Moore (pen)
			14 Nov 67		A	L	0–1	
1978–79	European Cup	1	13 Sep 78	Liverpool (England)	H	W	2–0	Birtles, Barrett
			27 Sep 78		A	D	0–0	
		2	18 Oct 78	AEK Athens (Greece)	A	W	2–1	McGovern, Birtles
			1 Nov 78		H	W	5–1	Needham, Woodcock, Anderson, Birtles 2
		QF	7 Mar 79	Grasshoppers (Switzerland)	H	W	4–1	Birtles, Robertson (pen), Gemmill, Lloyd
			21 Mar 79		A	D	1–1	O'Neill
		SF	11 Apr 79	FC Cologne (West Germany)	H	D	3–3	Birtles, Bowyer, Robertson
			25 Apr 79		A	W	1–0	Bowyer
		F	30 May 79	Malmo FF (Sweden)	N	W	1–0	Francis
1979–80	Super Cup		30 Jan 80	Barcelona (Spain)	H	W	1–0	George
			5 Feb 80		A	D	1–1	Burns
1979–80	European Cup	1	19 Sep 79	Oster (Sweden)	H	W	2–0	Bowyer, own goal
			3 Oct 79		A	D	1–1	Woodcock
		2	24 Oct 79	Arges Pitesti	H	W	2–0	Woodcock, Birtles
			7 Nov 79	(Romania)	A	W	2–1	Bowyer, Birtles
		QF	5 Mar 80	Dynamo Berlin	H	L	0–1	
			19 Mar 80	(East Germany)	A	W	3–1	Francis 2, Robertson (pen)
		SF	9 Apr 80	Ajax (Holland)	H	W	2–0	Francis, Robertson (pen)
			23 Apr 80		A	L	0–1	
		F	28 May 80	SV Hamburg (West Germany)	N	W	1–0	Robertson
1980–81	Super Cup	F	25 Nov 80	Valencia (Spain)*	H	W	2–1	Bowyer 2
			17 Dec 80		A	L	0–1	
1980–81	European Cup	1	17 Sep 80	CSKA Sofia	A	L	0–1	
			1 Oct 80	(Bulgaria)	H	L	0–1	
1983–84	UEFA Cup	1	14 Sep 83	Vorwaerts	H	W	2–0	Wallace, Hodge
			28 Sep 83	(East Germany)	A	W	1–0	Bowyer
		2	19 Oct 83	PSV Eindhoven	A	W	2–1	Davenport, Walsh (pen)
			2 Nov 83	(Holland)	H	W	1–0	Davenport
		3	23 Nov 83	Celtic (Scotland)	H	D	0–0	
			7 Dec 83		A	W	2–1	Hodge, Walsh
		QF	7 Mar 84	Sturm Graz (Austria)	H	W	1–0	Hart
			21 Mar 84		A	D	1–1	Walsh (pen)
		SF	11 Apr 84	Anderlecht (Belgium)	H	W	2–0	Hodge 2
					A	L	0–3	
1984–85	UEFA Cup	1	19 Sep 84	FC Bruges (Belgium)	H	D	0–0	
			3 Oct 84		A	L	0–1	

QUEEN'S PARK RANGERS

1976–77	UEFA Cup	1	15 Sep 76	Brann Bergen	H	W	4–0	Bowles 3, Masson
			29 Sep 76	(Norway)	A	W	7–0	Bowles 3, Givens 2, Thomas, Webb

	2.	20 Oct 76	Slovan Bratislava	A	D	3-3	Bowles 2, Givens
		3 Nov 76	(Czechoslovakia)	H	W	5-2	Givens 3, Bowles, Clement
	3	24 Nov 76	FC Cologne	H	W	3-0	Givens, Webb, Bowles
		7 Dec 76	(West Germany)	A	L	1-4*Masson
	QF	2 Mar 77	AEK Athens (Greece)	H	W	3-0	Francis 2 (2 pens), Bowles
		16 Mar 77		A	L	0-3†
1984–85 UEFA Cup	1	18 Sep 84	KR Reykjavik	A	W	3-0	Stainrod 2, Bannister
		2 Oct 84	(Iceland)	H	W	4-0	Bannister 3, Charles
	2	24 Oct 84	Partizan Belgrade*	H	W	6-2	Gregory, Fereday,
			(Yugoslavia)				Stainrod, Neill, Bannister 2
		7 Nov 84		A	L	0-4

SHEFFIELD WEDNESDAY

1961–62 Fairs Cup	1	12 Sep 61	Lyon (France)	A	L	2-4	Ellis, Young
		4 Oct 61		H	W	5-2	Fantham 2, Griffin,
							McAnearney (pen),
							Dobson
	2	29 Nov 61	AS Roma (Italy)	H	W	4-0	Fantham, Young 3
		13 Dec 61		A	L	0-1
	QF	28 Feb 62	Barcelona (Spain)	H	W	3-2	Fantham 2, Finney
		28 Mar 62		A	L	0-2
1963–64 Fairs Cup	1	25 Sep 63	DOS Utrecht (Holland)	A	W	4-1	Holliday, Layne, Quinn,
							own goal
		15 Oct 63		H	W	4-1	Layne 3 (1 pen), Dobson
	2	6 Nov 63	FC Cologne	A	L	2-3	Pearson 2
		27 Nov 63	(West Germany)	H	L	1-2	Layne

SOUTHAMPTON

1969–70 Fairs Cup	1	17 Sep 69	Rosenborg (Norway)	A	L	0-1
		1 Oct 69		H	W	2-0	Davies, Paine
	2	4 Nov 69	Vitoria Guimaraes	A	D	3-3	Channon, Davies, Paine
		12 Nov 69	(Portugal)	H	W	5-1	Gabriel, Davies 2 (1 pen),
							Channon, own goal
	3	17 Dec 69	Newcastle United	A	D	0-0
		13 Jan 70	(England)*	H	D	1-1	Channon
1971–72 UEFA Cup	1	15 Sep 71	Athletic Bilbao	H	W	2-1	Jenkins, Channon (pen)
		29 Sep 71	(Spain)	A	L	0-2
1976–77 Cup-Winners'	1	15 Sep 76	Marseille (France)	H	W	4-0	Waldron, Channon 2
Cup							(1 pen), Osgood
		29 Sep 76		A	L	1-2	Peach
	2	20 Oct 76	Carrick Rangers	A	W	5-2	Stokes, Channon 2,
			(Northern Ireland)				McCalliog, Osgood
		3 Nov 76		H	W	4-1	Williams, Hayes 2, Stokes
	QF	2 Mar 77	Anderlecht (Belgium)	A	L	0-2
		16 Mar 77		H	W	2-1	Peach (pen), MacDougall
1981–82 UEFA Cup	1	16 Sep 81	Limerick (Eire)	A	W	3-0	Moran 2, Armstrong
		29 Sep 81		H	D	1-1	Keegan
	2	21 Oct 81	Sporting Lisbon	H	L	2-4	Keegan (pen), Channon
		4 Nov 81	(Portugal)	A	D	0-0
1982–83 UEFA Cup	1	15 Sep 82	Norrkoping (Sweden)	H	D	2-2	Williams, Wright
		29 Sep 82		A	D	0-0

1984–85	UEFA Cup	1	19 Sep 84	Hamburg	H	D	0–0	
			3 Oct 84	(West Germany)	A	L	0–2	

STOKE CITY

1972–73	UEFA Cup	1	13 Sep 72	Kaiserslautern	H	W	3–1	Conroy, Hurst, Ritchie
			27 Sep 72	(West Germany)	A	L	0–4	
1974–75	UEFA Cup	1	18 Sep 74	Ajax (Holland)*	H	D	1–1	Smith
			2 Oct 74		A	D	0–0	

SUNDERLAND

1973–74	Cup-Winners'	1	19 Sep 73	Vasas Budapest	A	W	2–0	Hughes, Tueart
	Cup		3 Oct 73	(Hungary)	H	W	1–0	Tueart (pen)
		2	24 Oct 73	Sporting Lisbon	H	W	2–1	Kerr, Horswill
			7 Nov 73	(Portugal)	A	L	0–2	

SWANSEA CITY

1961–62	Cup-Winners'	1	16 Sep 61	Motor Jena	H	D	2–2	Reynolds, Nurse (pen)
	Cup		18 Oct 61	(East Germany)	A	L	1–5	Reynolds
				(in Linz, Austria)				
1966–67	Cup-Winners'	1	21 Sep 66	Slavia Sofia	H	D	1–1	Todd
	Cup		5 Oct 66	(Bulgaria)	A	L	0–4	
1981–82	Cup-Winners'	1	16 Sep 81	Lokomotive Leipzig	H	L	0–1	
	Cup		30 Sep 81	(East Germany)	A	L	1–2	Charles
1982–83	Cup-Winners'	Pr	17 Aug 82	Braga (Portugal)	H	W	3–0	Charles 2, own goal
	Cup		25 Aug 82		A	L	0–1	
		1	15 Sep 82	Sliema Wanderers (Malta)	H	W	12–0	Charles 2, Loveridge 2, Irwin, Latchford, Hadziabdic, Walsh 3, Rajkovic, Stevenson
			29 Sep 82		A	W	5–0	Curtis 2, Gale 2, Toshack
		2	20 Oct 82	Paris St Germain	H	L	0–1	
			3 Nov 82	(France)	A	L	0–2	
1983–84	Cup-Winners'	Pr	24 Aug 83	Magdeburg	H	D	1–1	Walsh
	Cup		31 Aug 83	(East Germany)	A	L	0–1	
1989–90	Cup-Winners'	1	13 Sep 89	Panathinaikos	A	L	2–3	Raynor, Salako
	Cup		27 Sep 89	(Greece)	H	D	3–3	James (pen), Melville 2

TOTTENHAM HOTSPUR

1961–62	European Cup	Pr	13 Sep 61	Gornik Zabrze	A	L	2–4	Jones, Dyson
			20 Sep 61	(Poland)	H	W	8–1	Blanchflower (pen), Jones 3, Smith 2, Dyson, White
		1	1 Nov 61	Feyenoord (Holland)	A	W	3–1	Dyson, Saul 2
			15 Oct 61		H	D	1–1	Dyson
		QF	14 Feb 62	Dukla Prague	A	L	0–1	
			26 Feb 62	(Czechoslovakia)	H	W	4–1	Smith 2, Mackay 2
		SF	21 Mar 62	Benfica (Portugal)	A	L	1–3	Smith
			5 Apr 62		H	W	2–1	Smith, Blanchflower (pen)
1962–63	Cup-Winners'	1		bye				
	Cup	2	31 Oct 62	Rangers (Scotland)	H	W	5–2	White, Greaves, Allen, Norman, own goal
			11 Dec 62		A	W	3–2	Greaves, Smith 2

	QF	5 Mar 63	Slovan Bratislava	A	L	0-2	
		14 Mar 63	(Czechoslovakia)	H	W	6-0	Mackay, Smith, Greaves 2, Jones, White
	SF	24 Apr 63	OFK Belgrade	A	W	2-1	White, Dyson
		1 May 63	(Yugoslavia)	H	W	3-1	Mackay, Jones, Smith
	F	15 May 63	Atletico Madrid (Spain)	N	W	5-1	Greaves 2, White, Dyson 2
1963-64 Cup-Winners' Cup	1		exempt				
	2	3 Dec 63	Manchester United	H	W	2-0	Mackay, Dyson
		10 Dec 63	(England)	A	L	1-4	Greaves
1967-68 Cup-Winners' Cup	1	20 Sep 67	Hajduk Split	A	W	2-0	Robertson, Greaves
		27 Sep 67	(Yugoslavia)	H	W	4-3	Robertson 2, Gilzean, Venables
	2	29 Nov 67	Lyon (France)*	A	L	0-1	
		13 Dec 67		H	W	4-3	Greaves 2 (1 pen), Jones, Gilzean
1971-72 UEFA Cup	1	14 Sep 71	Keflavik (Iceland)	A	W	6-1	Gilzean 3, Coates, Mullery 2
		28 Sep 71		H	W	9-1	Chivers 3, Gilzean 2, Perryman, Coates, Knowles, Holder
	2	20 Oct 71	Nantes (France)	A	D	0-0	
		2 Nov 71		H	W	1-0	Peters
	3	8 Dec 71	Rapid Bucharest	H	W	3-0	Peters, Chivers 2
		15 Dec 71	(Romania)	A	W	2-0	Pearce, Chivers
	QF	7 Mar 72	UT Arad (Romania)	A	W	2-0	Morgan, England
		21 Mar 72		H	D	1-1	Gilzean
	SF	5 Apr 72	AC Milan (Italy)	H	W	2-1	Perryman 2
		19 Apr 72		A	D	1-1	Mullery
	F	3 May 72	Wolverhampton	A	W	2-1	Chivers 2
		17 May 72	Wanderers (England)	H	D	1-1	Mullery
1972-73 UEFA Cup	1	13 Sep 72	Lyn Oslo (Norway)	A	W	6-3	Peters, Pratt, Gilzean 2, Chivers 2
		27 Sep 72		H	W	6-0	Chivers 3, Coates 2, Pearce
	2	25 Oct 72	Olympiakos Piraeus	H	W	4-0	Pearce 2, Chivers, Coates
		8 Nov 72	(Greece)	A	L	0-1	
	3	29 Nov 72	Red Star Belgrade	H	W	2-0	Chivers, Gilzean
		13 Dec 72	(Yugoslavia)	A	L	0-1	
	QF	7 Mar 73	Setubal (Portugal)	H	W	1-0	Evans
		21 Mar 73		A	L	1-2*Chivers	
	SF	10 Apr 73	Liverpool (England)*	A	L	0-1	
		25 Apr 73		H	W	2-1	Peters 2
1973-74 UEFA Cup	1	19 Sep 73	Grasshoppers	A	W	5-1	Chivers 2, Evans, Gilzean 2
		3 Oct 73	(Switzerland)	H	W	4-1	Peters 2, England, own goal
	2	24 Oct 73	Aberdeen (Scotland)	A	D	1-1	Coates
		7 Nov 73		H	W	4-1	Peters, Neighbour, McGrath 2
	3	28 Nov 73	Dynamo Tbilisi (USSR)	A	D	1-1	Coates
		12 Dec 73		H	W	5-1	McGrath, Chivers 2, Peters 2

	QF	6 Mar 74	FC Cologne	A	W	2-1	McGrath, Peters
		20 Mar 74	(West Germany)	H	W	3-0	Chivers, Coates, Peters
	SF	10 Apr 74	Lokomotive Leipzig	A	W	2-1	Peters, McGrath
		24 Apr 74	(East Germany)	H	W	2-0	McGrath, Chivers
	F	21 May 74	Feyenoord (Holland)	H	D	2-2	England, own goal
		29 May 74		A	L	0-2	
1981-82 Cup-Winners'	1	16 Sep 81	Ajax (Holland)	A	W	3-1	Falco 2, Villa
Cup		29 Sep 81		H	W	3-0	Galvin, Falco, Ardiles
	2	21 Oct 81	Dundalk (Eire)	A	D	1-1	Crooks
		4 Nov 81		H	W	1-0	Crooks
	QF	3 Mar 82	Eintracht Frankfurt	H	W	2-0	Miller, Hazard
		17 Mar 82	(West Germany)	A	L	1-2	Hoddle
	SF	7 Apr 82	Barcelona (Spain)	H	D	1-1	Roberts
		21 Apr 82		A	L	0-1	
1982-83 Cup-Winners'	1	15 Sep 82	Coleraine	A	W	3-0	Crooks 2, Archibald
Cup		28 Sep 82	(Northern Ireland)	H	W	4-0	Crooks, Mabbutt, Brooke, Gibson
	2	20 Oct 82	Bayern Munich	H	D	1-1	Archibald
		3 Nov 82	(West Germany)	A	L	1-4	Hughton
1983-84 UEFA Cup	1	14 Sep 83	Drogheda (Eire)	A	W	6-0	Falco 2, Crooks, Galvin, Mabbutt 2
		28 Sep 83		H	W	8-0	Falco 2, Roberts 2, Brazil 2, Hughton, Archibald
	2	19 Oct 83	Feyenoord (Holland)	H	W	4-2	Archibald 2, Galvin 2
		2 Nov 83		A	W	2-0	Hughton, Galvin
	3	23 Nov 83	Bayern Munich	A	L	0-1	
		7 Dec 83	(West Germany)	H	W	2-0	Archibald, Falco
	QF	7 Mar 84	FK Austria (Austria)	H	W	2-0	Archibald, Brazil
		21 Mar 84		A	D	2-2	Brazil, Ardiles
	SF	11 Apr 84	Hajduk Split	A	L	1-2	Falco
		25 Apr 84	(Yugoslavia)	H	W	1-0*Hazard
	F	9 May 84	Anderlecht (Belgium)	A	D	1-1	Miller
		23 May 84		H	D	1-1†	Roberts
1984-85 UEFA Cup	1	19 Sep 84	Sporting Braga	A	W	3-0	Falco 2, Galvin
		3 Oct 84	(Portugal)	H	W	6-0	Stevens, Hughton, Falco, Crooks 3
	2	24 Oct 84	FC Bruges (Belgium)	A	L	1-2	Allen
		7 Nov 84		H	W	3-0	Hazard, Allen, Roberts
	3	28 Nov 84	Bohemians	H	W	2-0	Stevens, own goal
		12 Dec 84	(Czechoslovakia)	A	D	1-1	Falco
	QF	6 Mar 85	Real Madrid (Spain)	H	L	0-1	
		20 Mar 85		A	D	0-0	

WATFORD

1983-84 UEFA Cup	1	14 Sep 83	Kaiserslautern	A	L	1-3	Gilligan
		28 Sep 83	(West Germany)	H	W	3-0	Richardson 2, own goal
	2	19 Oct 83	Levski Spartak	H	D	1-1	Rostron
		2 Nov 83	(Bulgaria)	A	W	3-1	Callaghan, Rostron, Richardson
	3	23 Nov 83	Sparta Prague	H	L	2-3	Rostron, Gilligan
		7 Dec 83	(Czechoslovakia)	A	L	0-4	

WEST BROMWICH ALBION

1966–67	Fairs Cup	1		bye				
		2	2 Nov 66	DOS Utrecht (Holland)	A	D	1-1	Hope
			9 Nov 66		H	W	5-2	Brown (T) 3 (1 pen), Clark, Kaye
		3	2 Feb 67	Bologna (Italy)	A	L	0-3	
			8 Mar 67		H	L	1-3	Fairfax
1968–69	Cup-Winners' Cup	1	18 Sep 68	FC Bruges (Belgium)	A	L	1-3	Hartford
			2 Oct 68		H	W	2-0*	Brown (T), Hartford
		2	13 Nov 68	Dinamo Bucharest	A	D	1-1	Hartford
			27 Nov 68	(Romania)	H	W	4-0	Lovett, Astle, Brown (T) 2 (1 pen)
		QF	15 Jan 69	Dunfermline Athletic	A	D	0-0	
			19 Feb 69	(Scotland)	H	L	0-1	
1978–79	UEFA Cup	1	13 Sep 78	Galatasaray (Turkey)	A	W	3-1	Robson, Regis, Cunningham
			27 Sep 78		H	W	3-1	Robson, Cunningham (pen), Trewick
		2	18 Oct 78	Sporting Braga	A	W	2-0	Regis 2
			1 Nov 78	(Portugal)	H	W	1-0	Brown (A)
		3	22 Nov 78	Valencia (Spain)	A	D	1-1	Cunningham
			6 Dec 78		H	W	2-0	Brown (T) 2 (1 pen)
		QF	7 Mar 79	Red Star Belgrade	A	L	0-1	
			21 Mar 79	(Yugoslavia)	H	D	1-1	Regis
1979–80	UEFA Cup	1	19 Sep 79	Carl Zeiss Jena	A	L	0-2	
			3 Oct 79	(East Germany)	H	L	1-2	Wile
1981–82	UEFA Cup	1	16 Sep 81	Grasshoppers	A	L	0-1	
			30 Sep 81	(Switzerland)	H	L	1-3	Robertson

WEST HAM UNITED

1964–65	Cup-Winners' Cup	1	23 Sep 64	La Gantoise (Belgium)	A	W	1-0	Boyce
			7 Oct 64		H	D	1-1	Byrne
		2	25 Nov 64	Sparta Prague	H	W	2-0	Bond, Sealey
			9 Dec 64	(Czechoslovakia)	A	L	1-2	Sissons
		QF	16 Mar 65	Lausanne	A	W	2-1	Dear, Byrne
			23 Mar 65	(Switzerland)	H	W	4-3	Dear 2, Peters, own goal
		SF	7 Apr 65	Real Zaragoza	H	W	2-1	Dear, Byrne
			28 Apr 65	(Spain)	A	D	1-1	Sissons
		F	19 May 65	Munich 1860 (West Germany)	N	W	2-0	Sealey 2
1965–66	Cup-Winners' Cup	1		bye				
		2	24 Nov 65	Olympiakos Piraeus	H	W	4-0	Hurst 2, Byrne, Brabrook
			1 Dec 65	(Greece)	A	D	2-2	Peters 2
		QF	2 Mar 66	Magdeburg	H	W	1-0	Byrne
			16 Mar 66	(East Germany)	A	D	1-1	Sissons
		SF	5 Apr 66	Borussia Dortmund	H	L	1-2	Peters
			13 Apr 66	(West Germany)	A	L	1-3	Byrne
1975–76	Cup-Winners' Cup	1	17 Sep 75	Lahden Reipas	A	D	2-2	Brooking, Bonds
			1 Oct 75	(Finland)	H	W	3-0	Robson (K), Holland, Jennings
		2	22 Oct 75	Ararat Erevan (USSR)	A	D	1-1	Taylor (A)
			5 Nov 75		H	W	3-1	Paddon, Robson (K), Taylor (A)

	QF	3 Mar 76	Den Haag (Holland)	A	L	2–4	Jennings 2
		17 Mar 76		H	W	3–1*	Taylor (A), Lampard, Bonds (pen)
	SF	31 Mar 76	Eintracht Frankfurt	A	L	1–2	Paddon
		14 Apr 76	(West Germany)	H	W	3–1	Brooking 2, Robson (K)
	F	5 May 76	Anderlecht (Belgium)	N	L	2–4	Holland, Robson (K)
1980–81 Cup Winners' Cup	1	17 Sep 80	Castilla (Spain)	A	L	1–3	Cross
		1 Oct 80		H	W	5–1	Pike, Cross 3, Goddard
	2	22 Oct 80	Poli. Timisoara (Romania)	H	W	4–0	Bonds, Goddard, Stewart (pen), Cross
		5 Nov 80		A	L	0–1	
	QF	4 Mar 81	Dynamo Tbilisi	H	L	1–4	Cross
		18 Mar 81	(USSR)	A	W	1–0	Pearson

WOLVERHAMPTON WANDERERS

1958–59 European Cup	Pr		bye				
	1	12 Nov 58	Schalke 04	H	D	2–2	Broadbent 2
		18 Nov 58	(West Germany)	A	L	1–2	Jackson
1959–60 European Cup	Pr	30 Sep 59	Vorwaerts	A	L	1–2	Broadbent
		7 Oct 59	(East Germany)	H	W	2–0	Broadbent, Mason
	1	11 Nov 59	Red Star Belgrade	A	D	1–1	Deeley
		24 Nov 59	(Yugoslavia)	H	W	3–0	Murray, Mason 2
	QF	10 Feb 60	Barcelona (Spain)	A	L	0–4	
		2 Mar 60		H	L	2–5	Murray, Mason
1960–61 Cup-Winners' Cup	Pr		bye				
	QF	12 Oct 60	FK Austria (Austria)	A	L	0–2	
		30 Nov 60		H	W	5–0	Kirkham 2, Mason, Broadbent 2
	SF	29 Mar 61	Rangers (Scotland)	A	L	0–2	
		19 Apr 61		H	D	1–1	Broadbent
1971–72 UEFA Cup	1	15 Sep 71	Academica Coimbra	H	W	3–0	McAlle, Richards, Dougan
		29 Sep 71	(Portugal)	A	W	3–1	Dougan, McAlle
	2	20 Oct 71	Den Haag (Holland)	A	W	3–1	Dougan, McCalliog, Hibbitt
		3 Nov 71		H	W	4–0	Dougan, own goals 3
	3	24 Nov 71	Carl Zeiss Jena	A	W	1–0	Richards
		8 Dec 71	(East Germany)	H	W	3–0	Hibbitt, Dougan 2
	QF	7 Mar 72	Juventus (Italy)	A	D	1–1	McCalliog
		21 Mar 72		H	W	2–1	Hegan, Dougan
	SF	4 Apr 72	Ferencvaros	A	D	2–2	Richards, Munro
		19 Apr 72	(Hungary)	H	W	2–1	Bailey, Munro
	F	3 May 72	Tottenham Hotspur	H	L	1–2	McCalliog
		17 May 72	(England)	A	D	1–1	Wagstaffe
1973–74 UEFA Cup	1	26 Sep 73	Belenenses (Portugal)	A	W	2–0	Richards, Dougan
		3 Oct 73		H	W	2–1	Eastoe, McCalliog
	2	24 Oct 73	Lokomotive Leipzig	A	L	0–3	
		7 Nov 73	(East Germany)	H	W	4–1	Kindon, Munro, Dougan, Hibbitt
1974–75 UEFA Cup	1	18 Sep 74	Porto (Portugal)	A	L	1–4	Bailey
		2 Oct 74		H	W	3–1	Bailey, Daley, Dougan
1980–81 UEFA Cup	1	17 Sep 80	PSV Eindhoven	A	L	1–3	Gray
		1 Oct 80	(Holland)	H	W	1–0	Eves

WREXHAM

Season	Competition	Round	Date	Opponents (Country)	Venue	Result		Scorers
1972–73	Cup Winners' Cup	1	13 Sep 72	Zurich (Switzerland)	A	D	1–1	Kinsey
			27 Sep 72		H	W	2–2	Ashcroft, Sutton
		2	25 Oct 72	Hajduk Split (Yugoslavia)*	H	W	3–1	Tinnion, Smallman, own goal
			8 Nov 72		A	L	0–2	
1975–76	Cup-Winners' Cup	1	17 Sep 75	Djurgaarden (Sweden)	H	W	2–1	Griffiths, Davis
			1 Oct 75		A	D	1–1	Whittle
		2	22 Oct 75	Stal Rzeszow (Poland)	H	W	2–0	Ashcroft 2
			5 Nov 75		A	D	1–1	Sutton
		QF	3 Mar 76	Anderlecht (Belgium)	A	L	0–1	
			17 Mar 76		H	D	1–1	Lee
1978–79	Cup-Winners' Cup	1	13 Sep 78	Rijeka (Yugoslavia)	A	L	0–3	
			27 Sep 78		H	W	2–0	McNeil, Cartwright
1979–80	Cup-Winners' Cup	1	19 Sep 79	Magdeburg (East Germany)	H	W	3–2	McNeil, Fox, Buxton
			3 Oct 79		A	L	2–5	Vinter, Hill
1984–85	Cup-Winners' Cup	1	19 Sep 84	Porto (Portugal)	H	W	1–0	Steel
			3 Oct 84		A	L	3–4	King 2, Horne
		2	24 Oct 84	Roma (Italy)	A	L	0–2	
			7 Nov 84		H	L	0–1	
1986–87	Cup-Winners' Cup	1	17 Sep 86	Zurrieq (Malta)	A	W	3–0	Massey, Charles, Conroy
			1 Oct 86		H	W	4–0	Massey 2 (1 pen), Steel, Horne
		2	22 Oct 86	Zaragoza (Spain)*	A	D	0–0	
			5 Nov 86		H	D	2–2	Massey, Buxton

Scottish League Clubs

Season	Competition	Round	Date	Opponents (Country)	Venue	Result		Scorers
ABERDEEN								
1967–68	Cup-Winners' Cup	1	6 Sep 67	KR Reykjavik (Iceland)	H	W	10–1	Munro 3, Storrie 2, Smith 2, McMillan, Petersen, Taylor
			13 Sep 67		A	W	4–1	Storrie 2, Buchan, Munro
		2	29 Nov 67	Standard Liege (Belgium)	A	L	0–3	
			6 Dec 67		H	W	2–0	Munro, Melrose
1968–69	Fairs Cup	1	17 Sep 68	Slavia Sofia (Bulgaria)	A	D	0–0	
			2 Oct 68		H	W	2–0	Robb, Taylor
		2	23 Oct 68	Real Zaragoza (Spain)	H	W	2–1	Forrest, Smith
			30 Oct 68		A	L	0–3	
1970–71	Cup-Winners' Cup	1	16 Sep 70	Honved (Hungary) †	H	W	3–1	Graham, Harper, Murray (S)
			30 Sep 70		A	L	1–3	Murray (S)
1971–72	UEFA Cup	1	15 Sep 71	Celta Vigo (Spain)	A	W	2–0	Harper, own goal
			29 Sep 71		H	W	1–0	Harper
		2	27 Oct 71	Juventus (Italy)	A	L	0–2	
			17 Nov 71		H	D	1–1	Harper
1972–73	UEFA Cup	1	13 Sep 72	Borussia Moenchengladbach (West Germany)	H	L	2–3	Harper, Jarvie
			27 Sep 72		A	L	3–6	Harper 2, Jarvie

1973–74	UEFA Cup	1	19 Sep 73	Finn Harps (Eire)	H	W 4–1	Miller (R), Jarvie 2, Graham
			3 Oct 73		A	W 3–1	Robb, Graham, Miller (R)
		2	24 Oct 73	Tottenham Hotspur	H	D 1–1	Hermiston (pen)
			7 Nov 73	(England)	A	L 1–4	Jarvie
1977–78	UEFA Cup	1	14 Sep 77	RWD Molenbeek	A	D 0–0	
			28 Sep 77	(Belgium)	H	L 1–2	Jarvie
1978–79	Cup-Winners' Cup	1	13 Sep 78	Marek Stanke	A	L 2–3	Jarvie, Harper
			27 Sep 78	(Bulgaria)	H	W 3–0	Strachan, Jarvie, Harper
		2	18 Oct 78	Fortuna Dusseldorf	A	L 0–3	
			1 Nov 78	(West Germany)	H	W 2–0	McLelland, Jarvie
1979–80	UEFA Cup	1	19 Sep 79	Eintracht Frankfurt	H	D 1–1	Harper
			3 Oct 79	(West Germany)	A	L 0–1	
1980–81	European Cup	1	17 Sep 80	Austria Vienna	H	W 1–0	McGhee
			1 Oct 80	(Austria)	A	D 0–0	
		2	22 Oct 80	Liverpool (England)	H	L 0–1	
			5 Nov 80		A	L 0–4	
1981–82	UEFA Cup	1	16 Sep 81	Ipswich Town	A	D 1–1	Hewitt
			30 Sep 81	(England)	H	W 3–1	Strachan (pen), Weir 2
		2	21 Oct 81	Arges Pitesti	H	W 3–0	Strachan, Weir, Hewitt
			4 Nov 81	(Rumania)	A	D 2–2	Strachan (pen), Hewitt
		3	25 Nov 81	SV Hamburg	H	W 3–2	Black, Watson, Hewitt
			9 Dec 81	(West Germany)	A	L 1–3	McGhee
1982–83	Cup-Winners' Cup	Pr	18 Aug 82	Sion (Switzerland)	H	W 7–0	Black 2, Strachan, Hewitt, Simpson, McGhee, Kennedy
			1 Sep 82		A	W 4–1	Hewitt, Miller, McGhee 2
		1	15 Sep 82	Dynamo Tirana	H	W 1–0	Hewitt
			29 Sep 82	(Albania)	A	D 0–0	
		2	20 Oct 82	Lech Poznan (Poland)	H	W 2–0	McGhee, Weir
			3 Nov 82		A	W 1–0	Bell
		QF	2 Mar 83	Bayern Munich	A	D 0–0	
			16 Mar 83	(West Germany)	H	W 3–2	Simpson, McLeish, Hewitt
		SF	6 Apr 83	Waterschei (Belgium)	H	W 5–1	Black, Simpson, McGhee 2, Weir
			19 Apr 83		A	L 0–1	
		F	11 May 83	Real Madrid (Spain)	N	W 2–1	Black, Hewitt
1983–84	Super Cup	F	22 Nov 83	SV Hamburg	A	D 0–0	
			20 Dec 83	(West Germany)	H	W 2–0	Simpson, McGhee
1983–84	Cup-Winners' Cup	1	14 Sep 83	IA Akranes (Iceland)	A	W 2–1	McGhee 2
			28 Sep 83		H	D 1–1	Strachan (pen)
		2	19 Oct 83	Beveren (Belgium)	A	D 0–0	
			2 Nov 83		H	W 4–1	Strachan 2 (1 pen), Simpson, Weir
		QF	7 Mar 84	Ujpest Dozsa	A	L 0–2	
			21 Mar 84	(Hungary)	H	W 3–0	McGhee 3
		SF	11 Apr 84	Porto (Portugal)	A	L 0–1	
			25 Apr 84		H	L 0–1	
1984–85	European Cup	1	19 Sep 84	Dynamo Berlin	H	W 2–1	Black 2
			3 Oct 84	(East Germany) †	A	L 1–2	Angus
1985–86	European Cup	1	18 Sep 85	IA Akranes (Iceland)	A	W 3–1	Black, Hewitt, Stark
			2 Oct 85		H	W 4–1	Simpson, Hewitt, Gray, Falconer

		2	23 Oct 85	Servette	A	D	0-0	
			6 Nov 85	(Switzerland)	H	W	1-0	McDougall
		QF	5 Mar 86	IFK Gothenburg*	H	D	2-2	Miller (J), Hewitt
			19 Mar 86	(Sweden)	A	D	0-0	
1986–87	Cup-Winners'	1	17 Sep 86	Sion (Switzerland)	H	W	2-1	Bett (pen), Wright
	Cup		1 Oct 86		A	L	0-3	
1987–88	UEFA Cup	1	15 Sep 87	Bohemians (Eire)	A	D	0-0	
			30 Sep 87		H	W	1-0	Bett (pen)
		2	21 Oct 87	Feyenoord*	H	W	2-1	Falconer, Miller (J)
			4 Nov 87	(Holland)	A	L	0-1	
1988–89	UEFA Cup	1	7 Sep 88	Dynamo Dresden	H	D	0-0	
			5 Oct 88	(East Germany)	A	L	0-2	
1989–90	UEFA Cup	1	13 Sep 89	Rapid Vienna*	H	W	2-1	Robertson (C), Grant
			27 Sep 89	(Austria)	A	L	0-1	

CELTIC

1962–63	Fairs Cup	1	26 Sep 62	Valencia (Spain)	A	L	2-4	Carrol 2
			24 Oct 62		H	D	2-2	Crerand, own goal
1963–64	Cup-Winners'	1	17 Sep 63	Basle (Switzerland)	A	W	5-1	Divers, Hughes 3, Lennox
	Cup		9 Oct 63		H	W	5-0	Johnstone, Divers 2, Murdoch, Chalmers
		2	4 Dec 63	Dynamo Zagreb	H	W	3-0	Chalmers 2, Hughes
			11 Dec 63	(Yugoslavia)	A	L	1-2	Murdoch
		QF	26 Feb 64	Slovan Bratislava	H	W	1-0	Murdoch (pen)
			4 Mar 64	(Czechoslovakia)	A	W	1-0	Hughes
		SF	15 Apr 64	MTK Budapest	H	W	3-0	Johnstone, Chalmers 2
			29 Apr 64	(Hungary)	A	L	0-4	
1964–65	Fairs Cup	1	23 Sep 64	Leixoes (Portugal)	A	D	1-1	Murdoch
			7 Oct 64		H	W	3-0	Murdoch (pen), Chalmers 2
		2	18 Nov 64	Barcelona (Spain)	A	L	1-3	Hughes
			2 Dec 64		H	D	0-0	
1965–66	Cup-Winners'	1	29 Sep 65	Go Ahead Deventer	A	W	6-0	Gallagher 2, Hughes, Johnstone 2, Lennox
	Cup			(Holland)				
			7 Oct 65		H	W	1-0	McBride
		2	3 Nov 65	Aarhus (Denmark)	A	W	1-0	McBride
			17 Nov 65		H	W	2-0	McNeill, Johnstone
		QF	12 Jan 66	Dynamo Kiev (USSR)	H	W	3-0	Gemmell, Murdoch 2
			26 Jan 66		A	D	1-1	Gemmell
		SF	14 Apr 66	Liverpool (England)	H	W	1-0	Lennox
			19 Apr 66		A	L	0-2	
1966–67	European Cup	1	28 Sep 66	Zurich (Switzerland)	H	W	2-0	Gemmell, McBride
			5 Oct 66		A	W	3-0	Gemmell 2 (1 pen), Chalmers
		2	30 Nov 66	Nantes (France)	A	W	3-1	McBride, Lennox, Chalmers
			7 Dec 66		H	W	3-1	Johnstone, Lennox, Chalmers
		QF	1 Mar 66	Vojvodina	A	L	0-1	
			8 Mar 66	(Yugoslavia)	H	W	2-0	Chalmers, McNeill
		SF	12 Apr 67	Dukla Prague	H	W	3-1	Johnstone, Wallace 2
			25 Apr 67	(Czechoslovakia)	A	D	0-0	
		F	25 May 67	Inter Milan (Italy)	N	W	2-1	Gemmell, Chalmers

1967–68	European Cup	1	20 Sep 67	Dynamo Kiev (USSR)	H	L	1–2	Lennox
			4 Oct 67		A	D	1–1	Lennox
1968–69	European Cup	1	18 Aug 68	St Etienne (France)	A	L	0–2	
			2 Oct 68		H	W	4–0	Gemmell (pen), Craig, Chalmers, McBride
		2	13 Nov 68	Red Star Belgrade (Yugoslavia)	H	W	5–1	Murdoch, Johnstone 2, Lennox, Wallace
			27 Nov 68		A	D	1–1	Wallace
		QF	19 Feb 69	AC Milan (Italy)	A	D	0–0	
			12 Mar 69		H	L	0–1	
1969–70	European Cup	1	17 Sep 69	Basle (Switzerland)	A	D	0–0	
			1 Oct 69		H	W	2–0	Hood, Gemmell
		2	12 Nov 69	Benfica (Portugal)	H	W	3–0	Gemmell, Wallace, Hood
			26 Nov 69		A	L	0–3 †	
		QF	4 Mar 70	Fiorentina (Italy)	H	W	3–0	Auld, Wallace, own goal
			18 Mar 70		A	L	0–1	
		SF	1 Apr 70	Leeds United	A	W	1–0	Connolly
			15 Apr 70	(England)	H	W	2–1	Hughes, Murdoch
		F	6 May 70	Feyenoord (Holland)	N	L	1–2	Gemmell
1970–71	European Cup	1	16 Sep 70	KPV Kokkola (Finland)	H	W	9–0	Hood 3, Wilson 2, Hughes, McNeill, Johnstone, Davidson
			30 Sep 70		A	W	5–0	Wallace 2, Callaghan, Davidson, Lennox
		2	21 Oct 70	Waterford (Eire)	A	W	7–0	Wallace 3, Murdoch 2, Macari 2
			4 Nov 70		H	W	3–2	Hughes, Johnstone 2
		QF	10 Mar 70	Ajax (Holland)	A	L	0–3	
			24 Mar 71		H	W	1–0	Johnstone
1971–72	European Cup	1	15 Sep 71	BK 1903 Copenhagen	A	L	1–2	Macari
			29 Sep 71	(Denmark)	H	W	3–0	Wallace 2, Callaghan
		2	20 Oct 71	Sliema Wanderers (Malta)	H	W	5–0	Gemmell, Macari 2, Hood, Brogan
			3 Nov 71		A	W	2–1	Hood, Lennox
		QF	8 Mar 72	Ujpest Dozsa	A	W	2–1	Macari, own goal
			22 Mar 72	(Hungary)	H	D	1–1	Macari
		SF	5 Apr 72	Inter Milan (Italy) †	A	D	0–0	
			19 Apr 72		H	D	0–0	
1972–73	European Cup	1	13 Sep 72	Rosenborg (Norway)	H	W	2–1	Macari, Deans
			27 Sep 72		A	W	3–1	Macari, Hood, Dalglish
		2	25 Oct 72	Ujpest Dozsa	H	W	2–1	Dalglish 2
			8 Nov 72	(Hungary)	A	L	0–3	
1973–74	European Cup	1	19 Sep 73	Turun (Finland)	A	W	6–1	Callaghan 2, Hood, Johnstone, Connelly (pen), Deans
			3 Oct 73		H	W	3–0	Deans, Johnstone 2
		2	24 Oct 73	Vejle (Denmark)	H	D	0–0	
			6 Nov 73		A	W	1–0	Lennox
		QF	27 Feb 74	Basle (Switzerland)	A	L	2–3	Wilson, Dalglish
			20 Mar 74		H	W	4–2	Dalglish, Deans, Callaghan, Murray
		SF	10 Apr 74	Atletico Madrid	H	D	0–0	
			24 Apr 74	(Spain)	A	L	0–2	

Season	Competition	Round	Date	Opponent (Country)	Venue	Result	Score	Scorers
1974–75	European Cup	1	18 Sep 74	Olympiakos Piraeus	H	D	1–1	Wilson
			2 Oct 74	(Greece)	A	L	0–2	
1975–76	Cup-Winners' Cup	1	16 Sep 75	Valur Reykjavik	A	W	2–0	Wilson, McDonald
			1 Oct 75	(Iceland)	H	W	7–0	Edvaldsson, Dalglish, McCluskey (P) (pen), Hood 2, Deans, Callaghan
		2	22 Oct 75	Boavista (Portugal)	A	D	0–0	
			5 Nov 75		H	W	3–1	Dalglish, Edvaldsson, Deans
		QF	3 Mar 76	Sachsenring Zwickau	H	D	1–1	Dalglish
			17 Mar 76	(East Germany)	A	L	0–1	
1976–77	UEFA Cup	1	15 Sep 76	Wisla Krakow	H	D	2–2	McDonald, Dalglish
			29 Sep 76	(Poland)	A	L	0–2	
1977–78	European Cup	1	14 Sep 77	Jeunesse D'Esch (Luxembourg)	H	W	5–0	McDonald, Wilson, Craig 2, McLaughlin
			28 Sep 77		A	W	6–1	Lennox 2, Edvaldsson 2, Glavin, Craig
		2	19 Oct 77	SW Innsbruck (Austria)	H	W	2–1	Craig, Burns
			2 Nov 77		A	L	0–3	
1979–80	European Cup	1	19 Sep 79	Partizan Tirana	A	L	0–1	
			3 Oct 79	(Albania)	H	W	4–1	McDonald, Aitken 2, Davidson
		2	24 Oct 79	Dundalk (Eire)	H	W	3–2	McDonald, McCluskey, Burns
			7 Nov 79		A	D	0–0	
		QF	5 Mar 80	Real Madrid (Spain)	H	W	2–0	McCluskey, Doyle
			19 Mar 80		A	L	0–3	
1980–81	Cup-Winners' Cup	Pr	20 Aug 80	Diosgyor (Hungary)	H	W	6–0	McGarvey 2, McCluskey 2, Sullivan, own goal
			3 Sep 80		A	L	1–2	Nicholas
		1	17 Sep 80	Poli. Timisoara*	H	W	2–1	Nicholas 2
			1 Oct 80	(Romania)	A	L	0–1	
1981–82	European Cup	1	16 Sep 81	Juventus (Italy)	H	W	1–0	MacLeod
			30 Sep 81		A	L	0–2	
1982–83	European Cup	1	15 Sep 82	Ajax (Holland)	H	D	2–2	Nicholas, McGarvey
			29 Sep 82		A	W	2–1	Nicholas, McCluskey
		2	20 Oct 82	Real Sociedad (Spain)	A	L	0–2	
			3 Nov 82		H	W	2–1	MacLeod 2
1983–84	UEFA Cup	1	14 Sep 83	Aarhus (Denmark)	H	W	1–0	Aitken
			28 Sep 83		A	W	4–1	MacLeod, McGarvey, Aitken, Provan
		2	19 Oct 83	Sporting Lisbon	A	L	0–2	
			2 Nov 83	(Portugal)	H	W	5–0	Burns, McAdam, McClair, MacLeod, McGarvey
		3	23 Nov 83	Nottingham Forest	A	D	0–0	
			7 Dec 83	(England)	H	L	1–2	MacLeod
1984–85	Cup-Winners' Cup	1	19 Sep 84	Gent (Belgium)	A	L	0–1	
			3 Oct 84		H	W	3–0	McGarvey 2, McStay
		2	24 Oct 84	Rapid Vienna	A	L	1–3	McClair
			7 Nov 84	(Austria)	H	W	3–0	McClair, MacLeod, Burns
			(match ordered to be replayed by UEFA)					
			12 Dec 84		N	L	0–1	

1985–86	Cup-Winners'	1	18 Sep 85	Atletico Madrid	A	D	1–1	Johnston
	Cup		2 Oct 85	(Spain)	H	L	1–2	Aitken
1986–87	European Cup	1	17 Sep 86	Shamrock Rovers	A	W	1–0	MacLeod
			1 Oct 86		H	W	2–0	Johnston 2
		2	22 Oct 86	Dynamo Kiev (USSR)	H	D	1–1	Johnston
			5 Nov 86		A	L	1–3	McGhee
1987–88	UEFA Cup	1	15 Sep 87	Borussia Dortmund	H	W	2–1	Walker, Whyte
			20 Sep 87	(West Germany)	A	L	0–2	
1988–89	European Cup	1	7 Sep 88	Honved (Hungary)	A	L	0–1	
			5 Oct 88		H	W	4–0	Stark, Walker, McAvennie, McGhee
		2	26 Oct 88	Werder Bremen	H	L	0–1	
			9 Nov 88	(West Germany)	A	D	0–0	
1989–90	Cup-Winners'	1	12 Sep 89	Partizan Belgrade*	A	L	1–2	Galloway
	Cup		27 Sep 89	(Yugoslavia)	H	W	5–4	Dziekanowski 4, Walker

DUNDEE

1962–63	European Cup	Pr	5 Jun 62	FC Cologne (West Germany)	H	W	8–1	Gilzean 3, own goal, Wishart, Robertson, Smith, Penman
			26 Sep 62		A	L	0–4	
		1	24 Oct 62	Sporting Lisbon	A	L	0–1	
			31 Oct 62	(Portugal)	H	W	4–1	Gilzean 3, Cousin
		QF	6 Mar 63	Anderlecht (Belgium)	A	W	4–1	Gilzean 2, Cousin, Smith
			13 Mar 63		H	W	2–1	Cousin, Smith
		SF	24 Apr 63	AC Milan (Italy)	A	L	1–5	Cousin
			1 May 63		H	W	1–0	Gilzean
1964–65	Cup-Winners'	1		bye				
	Cup	2	18 Nov 64	Real Zaragoza (Spain)	H	D	2–2	Murray, Houston
			8 Dec 64		A	L	1–2	Robertson
1967–68	Fairs Cup	1	27 Sep 67	DWS Amsterdam	A	L	1–2	McLean (G)
			4 Oct 67	(Holland)	H	W	3–0	Wilson (S), McLean 2 (1 pen)
		2	1 Nov 67	FC Liege (Belgium)	H	W	3–1	Stuart 2, Wilson (S)
			14 Nov 67		A	W	4–1	McLean (G) 4
		3		bye				
		QF	27 Mar 68	Zurich (Switzerland)	H	W	1–0	Easton
			3 Apr 68		A	W	1–0	Wilson (S)
		SF	1 May 68	Leeds United	H	D	1–1	Wilson (R)
			15 May 68	(England)	A	L	0–2	
1971–72	UEFA Cup	1	15 Sep 71	Akademisk	H	W	4–2	Bryce 2, Wallace, Lambie
			29 Sep 71	Copenhagen (Denmark)	A	W	1–0	Duncan
		2	19 Oct 71	FC Cologne	A	L	1–2	Kinninmonth
			3 Nov 71	(West Germany)	H	W	4–2	Duncan 3, Wilson (R)
		3	24 Nov 71	AC Milan (Italy)	A	L	0–3	
			8 Dec 71		H	W	2–0	Wallace, Duncan
1973–74	UEFA Cup	1	19 Sep 73	Twente Enschede	H	L	1–3	Stewart
			3 Oct 73	(Holland)	A	L	2–4	Johnston, Scott (J)
1974–75	UEFA Cup	1	18 Sep 74	RWD Molenbeek	A	L	0–1	
			2 Oct 74	(Belgium)	H	L	2–4	Duncan, Scott (J)

DUNDEE UNITED

Season	Competition	Round	Date		Opponent	Venue	Result	Scorers
1966–67	Fairs Cup	1			bye			
		2	25 Oct	66	Barcelona (Spain)	A	W 2–1	Hainey, Seeman
			16 Nov	66		H	W 2–0	Mitchell, Hainey
		3	8 Feb	67	Juventus (Italy)	A	L 0–3	
			8 Mar	67		H	W 1–0	Dossing
1969–70	Fairs Cup	1	15 Sep	69	Newcastle United	H	L 1–2	Scott
			1 Oct	69	(England)	A	L 0–1	
1970–71	Fairs Cup	1	15 Sep	70	Grasshoppers	H	W 3–2	Reid (I), Markland, Reid (A)
			30 Sep	70	(Switzerland)	A	D 0–0	
		2	21 Oct	70	Sparta Prague	A	L 1–3	Traynor
			4 Nov	70	(Czechoslovakia)	H	W 1–0	Gordon
1974–75	Cup-Winners' Cup	1	18 Sep	74	Jiul Petrosani	H	W 3–0	Narey, Copland, Gardner
			2 Oct	74	(Romania)	A	L 0–2	
		2	23 Oct	74	Bursaspor (Turkey)	H	D 0–0	
			6 Oct	74		A	L 0–1	
1975–76	UEFA Cup	1	23 Sep	75	Keflavik (Iceland)	A	W 2–0	Narey 2
			30 Sep	75		H	W 4–0	Hall 2, Hegarty (pen), Sturrock
		2	22 Oct	75	Porto (Portugal)	H	L 1–2	Rennie
			5 Nov	75		A	D 1–1	Hegarty
1977–78	UEFA Cup	1	14 Sep	77	KB Copenhagen	H	W 1–0	Sturrock
			27 Sep	77	(Denmark)	A	L 0–3	
1978–79	UEFA Cup	1	12 Sep	78	Standard Liege	A	L 0–1	
			27 Sep	78	(Belgium)	H	D 0–0	
1979–80	UEFA Cup	1	19 Sep	79	Anderlecht (Belgium)	H	D 0–0	
			2 Oct	79		A	D 1–1	*Kopel
		2	24 Oct	79	Diosgyor (Hungary)	H	L 0–1	
			7 Nov	79		A	L 1–3	Kopel
1980–81	UEFA Cup	1	17 Sep	80	Slask Wroclaw	A	D 0–0	
			1 Oct	80	(Poland)	H	W 7–2	Dodds 2, Pettigrew 2, Stark, Hegarty, Payne (pen)
		2	22 Oct	80	Lokeren* (Belgium)	H	D 1–1	Pettigrew
			5 Nov	80		A	D 0–0	
1981–82	UEFA Cup	1	16 Sep	81	Monaco (France)	A	W 5–2	Bannon 2 (1 pen), Dodds 2, Kirkwood
			30 Sep	81		H	L 1–2	Milne
		2	20 Oct	81	Borussia	A	L 0–2	
			3 Nov	81	Moenchengladbach (West Germany)	H	W 5–0	Milne, Kirkwood, Sturrock, Hegarty, Bannon
		3	1 Dec	81	Winterslag	A	D 0–0	
			9 Dec	81	(Belgium)	H	W 5–0	Bannon, Narey, Hegarty, Milne 2
		QF	3 Mar	82	Radnicki Nis	H	W 2–0	Narey, Dodds
			17 Mar	82	(Yugoslavia)	A	L 0–3	
1982–83	UEFA Cup	1	15 Sep	82	PSV Eindhoven	H	D 1–1	Dodds
			29 Sep	82	(Holland)	A	W 2–0	Kirkwood, Hegarty
		2	20 Oct	82	Viking Stavanger	A	W 3–1	Milne 2, Sturrock
			3 Nov	82	(Norway)	H	D 0–0	
		3	24 Nov	82	Werder Bremen	H	W 2–1	Milne, Narey
			8 Dec	82	(West Germany)	A	D 1–1	Hegarty
		QF	2 Mar	83	Bohemians	A	L 0–1	
			16 Mar	83	(Czechoslovakia)	H	D 0–0	

Season	Competition	Round	Date	Opponent	Venue	Result	Score	Scorers
1983–84	European Cup	1	14 Sep 83	Hamrun Spartans	A	W	3–0	Reilly, Bannon, Stark
			28 Sep 83	(Malta)	H	W	3–0	Milne, Kirkwood 2
		2	19 Oct 83	Standard Liege	A	D	0–0	
			2 Nov 83	(Belgium)	H	W	4–0	Milne 2, Hegarty, Dodds
		QF	7 Mar 84	Rapid Vienna (Austria)	A	L	1–2	Stark
			21 Mar 84		H	W	1–0	*Dodds
		SF	11 Apr 84	AS Roma (Italy)	H	W	2–0	Dodds, Stark
			24 Apr 84		A	L	0–3	
1984–85	UEFA Cup	1	19 Sep 84	AIK Stockholm	A	L	0–1	
			3 Oct 84	(Sweden)	H	W	3–0	Sturrock, Milne 2
		2	24 Oct 84	ASK Linz (Austria)	A	W	2–1	Kirkwood, Bannon (pen)
			7 Nov 84		H	W	5–1	Hegarty, Coyne 2, Gough, Beaumont
		3	28 Nov 84	Manchester United	A	D	2–2	Hegarty, Sturrock
			12 Dec 84	(England)	H	L	2–3	Dodds, Hegarty
1985–86	UEFA Cup	1	18 Sep 85	Bohemians (Eire)	A	W	5–2	Sturrock 3, Bannon 2
			2 Oct 85		H	D	2–2	Milne, Redford
		2	23 Oct 85	Vardar Skopje	H	W	2–0	Redford, Gough
			6 Nov 85	(Yugoslavia)	A	D	1–1	Hegarty
		3	27 Nov 85	Neuchatel Xamax	H	W	2–1	Dodds, Redford
			11 Dec 85	(Switzerland)	A	L	1–3	Redford
1986–87	UEFA Cup	1	17 Sep 86	Lens (France)	A	L	0–1	
			1 Oct 86		H	W	2–0	Milne, Coyne
		2	22 Oct 86	Uni. Craiova	H	W	3–0	Redford 2, Clark
			5 Nov 86	(Romania)	A	L	0–1	
		3	26 Nov 86	Hajduk Split	H	W	2–0	McInally, Clark
			10 Dec 86	(Yugoslavia)	A	D	0–0	
		QF	4 Mar 87	Barcelona (Spain)	H	W	1–0	Gallacher
			18 Mar 87		A	W	2–1	Clark, Ferguson
		SF	8 Apr 87	Borussia	H	D	0–0	
			22 Apr 87	Moenchengladbach (West Germany)	A	W	2–0	Ferguson, Redford
		F	6 May 87	IFK Gothenburg	A	L	0–1	
			20 May 87	(Sweden)	H	D	1–1	Clark
1987–88	UEFA Cup	1	15 Sep 87	Coleraine	A	W	1–0	Sturrock
			30 Sep 87	(Northern Ireland)	H	W	3–1	Gallacher, Sturrock, Clark
		2	21 Oct 87	Vitkovice	H	L	1–2	Ferguson
			4 Nov 87	(Czechoslovakia)	A	D	1–1	own goal
1988–89	Cup-Winners' Cup	1	7 Sep 88	Floriana (Malta)	A	D	0–0	
			5 Oct 88		H	W	1–0	Meade
		2	26 Oct 88	Dinamo Bucharest	H	L	0–1	
			9 Nov 88	(Romania)	A	D	1–1	Beaumont
1989–90	UEFA Cup	1	13 Sep 89	Glentoran	A	W	3–1	Cleland, McInally, Hinds
			27 Sep 89	(Northern Ireland)	H	W	2–0	Clark, Gallacher
		2	17 Oct 89	Antwerp (Belgium)	A	L	0–4	
			31 Oct 89		H	W	3–2	Paatelainen, O'Neill, Clark

DUNFERMLINE ATHLETIC

Season	Competition	Round	Date	Opponent	Venue	Result	Score	Scorers
1961–62	Cup-Winners' Cup	1	12 Sep 61	St Patrick's Athletic (Eire)	H	W	4–1	Melrose, Peebles, Dickson, Macdonald
			27 Sep 61		A	W	4–0	Peebles 2, Dickson 2

	2	25 Oct 61	Vardar Skopje (Yugoslavia)	H	W	5-0	Smith, Dickson 2, Melrose, Peebles
		8 Nov 61		A	L	0-2	
	QF	13 Feb 62	Ujpest Dozsa	A	L	3-4	Smith, Macdonald 2
		20 Feb 62	(Hungary)	H	L	0-1	
1962-63 Fairs Cup	1	24 Oct 62	Everton (England)	A	L	0-1	
		31 Oct 62		H	W	2-0	Miller, Melrose
	2	12 Dec 62	Valencia (Spain)	A	L	0-4	
		19 Dec 62		H	W	6-2	Melrose, Sinclair 2, McLean, Peebles, Smith
		6 Feb 63		N	L	0-1	
1964-65 Fairs Cup	1	13 Oct 64	Oergryte (Sweden)	H	W	4-2	McLaughlin 2, Sinclair 2
		20 Oct 64		A	D	0-0	
	2	17 Nov 64	Stuttgart	H	W	1-0	Callaghan (T)
		1 Dec 64	(West Germany)	A	D	0-0	
	3	27 Jan 65	Athletic Bilbao (Spain)	A	L	0-1	
		3 Mar 65		H	W	1-0	Smith
		16 Mar 65		A	L	1-2	Smith
1965-66 Fairs Cup	1		bye				
	2	3 Nov 65	KB Copenhagen (Denmark)	H	W	5-0	Fleming, Paton 2, Robertson, Callaghan (T)
		17 Nov 65		A	W	4-2	Edwards, Paton, Fleming, Ferguson
	3	26 Jan 66	Spartak Brno	H	W	2-0	Paton, Ferguson (pen)
		16 Feb 66	(Czechoslovakia)	A	D	0-0	
	QF	16 Mar 66	Real Zaragoza (Spain)	H	W	1-0	Paton
		20 Mar 66		A	L	2-4	Ferguson 2
1966-67 Fairs Cup	1	24 Aug 66	Frigg Oslo (Norway)	A	W	3-1	Fleming 2, Callaghan (T)
		28 Sep 66		H	W	3-1	Delaney 2, Callaghan (T)
	2	26 Oct 66	Dynamo Zagreb* (Yugoslavia)	H	W	4-2	Delaney, Edwards, Ferguson 2
		11 Nov 66		A	L	0-2	
1967-68 Cup-Winners' Cup	1	18 Sep 68	Apoel (Cyprus)	H	W	10-1	Robertson 2, Renton 2, Barry, Callaghan (W) 2, Gardner, Edwards, Callaghan (T)
		2 Oct 68		A	W	2-0	Gardner, Callaghan (W)
	2	13 Nov 68	Olympiakos Piraeus (Greece)	H	W	4-0	Edwards 2, Fraser, Mitchell
		27 Nov 68		A	L	0-3	
	QF	15 Jan 69	West Bromwich Albion	H	D	0-0	
		18 Feb 69	(England)	A	W	1-0	Gardner
	SF	9 Apr 69	Slovan Bratislava	H	D	1-1	Fraser
		23 Apr 69	(Czechoslovakia)	A	L	0-1	
1969-70 Fairs Cup	1	16 Sep 69	Bordeaux (France)	H	W	4-0	Paton 2, Mitchell, Gardner
		30 Sep 69		A	L	0-2	
	2	5 Nov 69	Gwardia Warsaw	H	W	2-1	McLean, Gardner
		18 Nov 69	(Poland)	A	W	1-0	Renton
	3	17 Dec 69	Anderlecht (Belgium)*	A	L	0-1	
		14 Jan 70		H	W	3-2	McLean 2, Mitchell

HEARTS

1958–59	European Cup	Pr	3 Sep 58	Standard Liege	A	L	1–5	Crawford
			9 Sep 58	(Belgium)	H	W	2–1	Bauld 2
1960–61	European Cup	Pr	29 Sep 60	Benfica (Portugal)	H	L	1–2	Young
			5 Oct 60		A	L	0–3	
1961–62	Fairs Cup	1	27 Sep 61	Union St Gilloise	A	W	3–1	Blackwood, Davidson 2
			4 Oct 61	(Belgium)	H	W	2–0	Wallace, Stenhouse
		2	6 Nov 61	Inter Milan (Italy)	H	L	0–1	
			22 Nov 61		A	L	0–4	
1963–64	Fairs Cup	1	25 Sep 63	Lausanne	A	D	2–2	Traynor, Ferguson
			9 Oct 63	(Switzerland)	H	D	2–2	Cumming, Hamilton (J)
			15 Oct 63		A	L	2–3	Wallace, Ferguson
1965–66	Fairs Cup	1		bye				
		2	18 Oct 65	Valerengen (Norway)	H	W	1–0	Wallace
			27 Oct 65		A	W	3–1	Kerrigan 2, Traynor
		3	12 Jan 66	Real Zaragoza	H	D	3–3	Anderson, Wallace, Kerrigan
				(Spain)				
			26 Jan 66		A	D	2–2	Anderson, Wallace
			2 Mar 66		A	L	0–1	
1976–77	Cup-Winners' Cup	1	15 Sep 76	Lokomotive Leipzig	A	L	0–2	
			29 Sep 76	(East Germany)	H	W	5–1	Kay, Gibson 2, Brown, Busby
		2	20 Oct 76	SV Hamburg	A	L	2–4	Park, Busby
			3 Nov 76	(West Germany)	H	L	1–4	Gibson
1984–85	UEFA Cup	1	19 Sep 84	Paris St Germain	A	L	0–4	
			3 Oct 84	(France)	H	D	2–2	Robertson 2
1986–87	UEFA Cup	1	17 Sep 86	Dukla Prague*	H	W	3–2	Foster, Clark, Robertson
			1 Oct 86	(Czechoslovakia)	A	L	0–1	
1988–89	UEFA Cup	1	7 Sep 88	St Patrick's Athletic	A	W	2–0	Foster (pen), Galloway
			5 Oct 88	(Eire)	H	W	2–0	Black, Galloway
		2	26 Oct 88	FK Austria (Austria)	H	D	0–0	
			9 Nov 88		A	W	1–0	Galloway
		3	23 Nov 88	Velez Mostar	H	W	3–0	Bannon, Galloway, Colquhoun
				(Yugoslavia)				
			7 Dec 88		A	L	1–2	Galloway
		QF	28 Feb 89	Bayern Munich	H	W	1–0	Ferguson
			15 Mar 89	(West Germany)	A	L	0–2	

HIBERNIAN

1955–56	European Cup	1	14 Sep 55	Rot-Weiss Essen	A	W	4–0	Turnbull 2, Reilly, Ormond
			12 Oct 55	(West Germany)	H	D	1–1	Buchanan (J)
		QF	23 Nov 55	Djurgaarden (Sweden)	H	W	3–1	Combe, Mulkerrin, own goal
			28 Nov 55		A	W	1–0	Turnbull (pen)
		SF	4 Apr 56	Reims (France)*	A	L	0–2	
			18 Apr 56		H	L	0–1	
1960–61	Fairs Cup	1		Lausanne (Switzerland) *Lausanne withdrew*				
		QF	27 Dec 60	Barcelona (Spain)	A	D	4–4	McLeod, Preston, Baker 2
			22 Feb 61		H	W	3–2	Kinloch 2 (1 pen), Baker

	SF	19 Apr 61	AS Roma (Italy)	H	D	2-2	Baker, McLeod	
		26 Apr 61		A	D	3-3	Baker 2, Kinloch	
		27 May 61		A	L	0-6		
1961-62 Fairs Cup	1	4 Sep 61	Belenenses (Portugal)	H	D	3-3	Fraser 2, Baird (pen)	
		27 Sep 61		A	W	3-1	Baxter 2, Stevenson	
	2	1 Nov 61	Red Star Belgrade	A	L	0-4		
		15 Nov 61	(Yugoslavia)	H	L	0-1		
1962-63 Fairs Cup	1	3 Oct 62	Stavenet (Denmark)	H	W	4-0	Byrne 2, Baker, own goal	
		23 Oct 62		A	W	3-2	Stevenson 2, Byrne	
	2	27 Nov 62	DOS Utrecht	A	W	1-0	Falconer	
		12 Dec 62	(Holland)	H	W	2-1	Baker, Stevenson	
	QF	13 Mar 63	Valencia (Spain)	A	L	0-5		
		3 Apr 63		H	W	2-1	Preston, Baker	
1965-66 Fairs Cup	1	8 Sep 65	Valencia (Spain)	H	W	2-0	Scott, McNamee	
		12 Oct 65		A	L	0-2		
		3 Nov 65		A	L	0-3		
1967-68 Fairs Cup	1	20 Sep 67	Porto (Portugal)	H	W	3-0	Cormack 2, Stevenson	
		4 Oct 67		A	L	1-3	Stanton (pen)	
	2	22 Nov 67	Napoli (Italy)	A	L	1-4	Stein	
		29 Nov 67		H	W	5-0	Duncan, Quinn, Cormack, Stanton, Stein	
	3	20 Dec 67	Leeds United	A	L	0-1		
		10 Jan 68	(England)	H	D	1-1	Stein	
1968-69 Fairs Cup	1	18 Sep 68	Ljubljana (Yugoslavia)	A	W	3-0	Stevenson, Stein, Marinello	
		2 Oct 68		H	W	2-1	Davis 2 (2 pens)	
	2	13 Nov 68	Lokomotive Leipzig	H	W	3-1	McBride 3	
		20 Nov 68	(East Germany)	A	W	1-0	Grant	
	3	18 Dec 68	SV Hamburg	A	L	0-1		
		15 Jan 69	(West Germany)	H	W	2-1	McBride 2	
1970-71 Fairs Cup	1	16 Sep 70	Malmo FF (Sweden)	H	W	6-0	McBride 3, Duncan 2, Blair	
		30 Sep 70		A	W	3-2	Duncan, McEwan, Stanton	
	2	14 Oct 70	Vitoria Guimaraes	H	W	2-0	Duncan, Stanton	
		28 Oct 70	(Portugal)	A	L	1-2	Graham	
	3	9 Dec 70	Liverpool (England)	H	L	0-1		
		22 Dec 70		A	L	0-2		
1972-73 Cup Winners' Cup	1	13 Sep 72	Sporting Lisbon	A	L	1-2	Duncan	
		27 Sep 72	(Portugal)	H	W	6-1	Gordon 2, O'Rourke 3, own goal	
	2	25 Oct 72	Besa (Albania)	H	W	7-1	Cropley, O'Rourke 3, Duncan 2, Brownlie	
		8 Nov 72		A	D	1-1	Gordon	
	QF	7 Mar 73	Hajduk Split	H	W	4-2	Gordon 3, Duncan	
		21 Mar 73	(Yugoslavia)	A	L	0-3		
1973-74 UEFA Cup	1	19 Sep 73	Keflavik (Iceland)	H	W	2-0	Black, Higgins	
		3 Oct 73		A	D	1-1	Stanton	
	2	24 Oct 73	Leeds United	A	D	0-0		
		2 Oct 73	(England) †	A	D	0-0		
1974-75 UEFA Cup	1	18 Sep 74	Rosenborg (Norway)	A	W	3-2	Stanton, Gordon, Cropley	
		2 Oct 74		H	W	9-1	Harper 2, Munro 2, Stanton 2, Cropley 2 (2 pens), Gordon	

	2	23 Oct 74	Juventus (Italy)	H	L	2-4	Stanton, Cropley
		6 Nov 74		A	L	0-4	
1975-76 UEFA Cup	1	17 Sep 75	Liverpool (England)	H	W	1-0	Harper
		30 Sep 75		A	L	1-3	Edwards
1976-77 UEFA Cup	1	15 Sep 76	Sochaux (France)	H	W	1-0	Brownlie
		29 Sep 76		A	D	0-0	
	2	20 Oct 76	Osters Vaxjo	H	W	2-0	Blackley, Brownlie (pen)
		3 Nov 76	(Sweden)	A	L	1-4	Smith
1978-79 UEFA Cup	1	13 Sep 78	Norrkoping (Sweden)	H	W	3-2	Higgins 2, Temperley
		27 Sep 78		A	D	0-0	
	2	18 Oct 78	Strasbourg (France)	A	L	0-2	
		1 Nov 78		H	W	1-0	McLeod (pen)
1989-90 UEFA Cup	1	12 Sep 89	Videoton (Hungary)	H	W	1-0	Mitchell
		26 Sep 89		A	W	3-0	Houchen, Evans, Collins
	2	18 Oct 89	FC Liege (Belgium)	H	D	0-0	
		31 Oct 89		A	L	0-1	

KILMARNOCK

1964-65 Fairs Cup	1	2 Sep 64	Eintracht Frankfurt	A	L	0-3	
		22 Sep 64	(West Germany)	H	W	5-1	Hamilton, McIlroy, McFadzean, McInally, Sneddon
	2	11 Nov 64	Everton (England)	H	L	0-2	
		23 Nov 64		A	L	1-4	McIlroy
1965-66 European Cup	Pr	8 Sep 65	Nendori Tirana	A	D	0-0	
		29 Sep 65	(Albania)	H	W	1-0	Black
	1	17 Nov 65	Real Madrid (Spain)	H	D	2-2	McLean (pen), McInally
		1 Dec 65		A	L	1-5	McIlroy
1966-67 Fairs Cup	1		bye				
	2	25 Oct 66	Antwerp (Belgium)	A	W	1-0	McInally
		2 Nov 66		H	W	7-2	McInally 2, Queen 2, McLean 2, Watson
	3	14 Dec 66	La Gantoise (Belgium)	H	W	1-0	Murray
		21 Dec 66		A	W	2-1	McInally, McLean
	QF	19 Apr 67	Lokomotive Leipzig	A	L	0-1	
		26 Apr 67	(East Germany)	H	W	2-0	McFadzean, McIlroy
	SF	19 May 67	Leeds United	A	L	2-4	McIlroy 2
		24 May 67	(England)	H	D	0-0	
1969-70 Fairs Cup	1	16 Sep 69	Zurich (Switzerland)	A	L	2-3	McLean (J), Mathie
		30 Sep 69		H	W	3-1	McGrory, Morrison, McLean (T)
	2	19 Nov 69	Slavia Sofia (Bulgaria)	H	W	4-1	Mathie 2, Cook, Gilmour
		26 Nov 69		A	L	0-2	
	3	17 Dec 69	Dynamo Bacau	H	D	1-1	Mathie
		13 Jan 70	(Romania)	A	L	0-2	
1970-71 Fairs Cup	1	15 Sep 70	Coleraine	A	D	1-1	Mathie
		29 Sep 70	(Northern Ireland)	H	L	2-3	McLean (T), Morrison

MORTON

1968-69 Fairs Cup	1	18 Sep 68	Chelsea (England)	A	L	0-5	
		30 Sep 68		H	L	3-4	Thorop, Mason, Taylor

PARTICK THISTLE

1963–64	Fairs Cup	1	16 Sep 63	Glentoran	A	W 4–1	Hainey, Yard 2, Wright
			30 Sep 63	(Northern Ireland)	H	W 3–0	Smith 2, Harvey (pen)
		2	18 Nov 63	Spartak Brno	H	W 3–2	Yard, Harvey (pen),
				(Czechoslovakia)			Ferguson
			27 Nov 63		A	L 0–4	
1972–73	UEFA Cup	1	13 Sep 72	Honved (Hungary)	A	L 0–1	
			27 Sep 72		H	L 0–3	

RANGERS

1956–57	European Cup	Pr		bye			
		1	24 Oct 56	Nice (France)	H	W 2–1	Murray, Simpson
			14 Nov 56		A	L 1–2	Hubbard (pen)
			28 Nov 56		N	L 1–3	own goal
1957–58	European Cup	Pr	4 Sep 57	St Etienne (France)	H	W 3–1	Kichenbrand, Scott,
							Simpson
			25 Sep 57		A	L 1–2	Wilson
		1	27 Nov 57	AC Milan (Italy)	H	L 1–4	Murray
			11 Dec 57		A	L 0–2	
1959–60	European Cup	Pr	16 Sep 59	Anderlecht (Belgium)	H	W 5–2	Millar, Scott, Matthew,
							Baird 2
			24 Sep 59		A	W 2–0	Matthew, McMillan
		1	11 Nov 59	Red Star Belgrade	H	W 4–3	McMillan, Scott, Wilson,
				(Czechoslovakia)			Millar
			18 Nov 59		A	D 1–1	Scott
		QF	9 Mar 60	Sparta Rotterdam	A	W 3–2	Wilson, Baird, Murray
			16 Mar 60	(Holland)	H	L 0–1	
			30 Mar 60		N	W 3–2	Baird 2, own goal
		SF	13 Apr 60	Eintracht Frankfurt	A	L 1–6	Caldow (pen)
			5 May 60	(West Germany)	H	L 3–6	McMillan 2, Wilson
1960–61	Cup-Winners'	Pr	28 Sep 60	Ferencvaros	H	W 4–2	Davis, Millar 2, Brand
	Cup		12 Oct 60	(Hungary)	A	L 1–2	Wilson
		QF	15 Nov 60	Borussia	A	W 3–0	Millar, Scott, McMillan
			30 Nov 60	Moenchengladbach	H	W 8–0	Baxter, Brand 3, Millar 2,
				(West Germany)			Davis, own goal
		SF	29 Mar 61	Wolverhampton	H	W 2–0	Scott, Brand
			19 Apr 61	Wanderers (England)	A	D 1–1	Scott
		F	17 May 61	Fiorentina (Italy)	H	L 0–2	
			27 May 61		A	L 1–2	Scott
1961–62	European Cup	Pr	5 Sep 61	Monaco (France)	A	W 3–2	Baxter, Scott 2
			12 Sep 61		H	W 3–2	Christie 2, Scott
		1	15 Nov 61	Vorwaerts	A	W 2–1	Caldow (pen), Brand
			23 Nov 61	(East Germany)	H	W 4–1	McMillan 2, Henderson,
							own goal
		QF	7 Feb 62	Standard Liege	A	L 1–4	Wilson
			14 Feb 62	(Belgium)	H	W 2–0	Brand, Caldow (pen)
1962–63	Cup-Winners'	1	5 Sep 62	Seville (Spain)	H	W 4–0	Millar 3, Brand
	Cup		26 Sep 62		A	L 0–2	
		2	31 Oct 62	Tottenham Hotspur	A	L 2–5	Brand, Millar
			11 Dec 62	(England)	H	L 2–3	Brand, Wilson
1963–64	European Cup	Pr	25 Sep 63	Real Madrid (Spain)	H	L 0–1	
			9 Oct 63		A	L 0–6	

1964–65	European Cup	Pr	2 Sep 64	Red Star Belgrade	H	W 3–1	Brand 2, Forrest
			9 Sep 64	(Yugoslavia)	A	L 2–4	Greig, McKinnon
			4 Nov 64		N	W 3–1	Forrest 2, Brand
		1	18 Nov 64	Rapid Vienna (Austria)	H	W 1–0	Wilson
			8 Dec 64		A	W 2–0	Forrest, Wilson
		QF	17 Feb 65	Inter Milan (Italy)	A	L 1–3	Forrest
			3 Mar 65		H	W 1–0	Forrest
1966–67	Cup-Winners' Cup	1	27 Sep 66	Glentoran	A	D 1–1	McLean
			5 Oct 66	(Northern Ireland)	H	W 4–0	Johnston, Smith (D), Setterington, McLean
		2	23 Nov 66	Borussia Dortmund	H	W 2–1	Johansen, Smith (A)
			6 Dec 66	(West Germany)	A	D 0–0	
		QF	1 Mar 67	Real Zaragoza (Spain)	H	W 2–0	Smith, Willoughby
			22 Mar 67		A	L 0–2‡	
		SF	19 Apr 67	Slavia Sofia (Bulgaria)	A	W 1–0	Wilson
			3 May 67		H	W 1–0	Henderson
		F	31 May 67	Bayern Munich (West Germany)	N	L 0–1	
1967–68	Fairs Cup	1	21 Sep 67	Dynamo Dresden	A	D 1–1	Ferguson
			4 Oct 67	(East Germany)	H	W 2–1	Penman, Greig
		2	8 Nov 67	FC Cologne	H	W 3–0	Ferguson 2, Henderson
			28 Nov 67	(West Germany)	A	L 1–3	Henderson
		3		bye			
		QF	26 Mar 68	Leeds United	H	D 0–0	
			9 Apr 68	(England)	A	L 0–2	
1968–69	Fairs Cup	1	18 Sep 68	Vojvodina	H	W 2–0	Greig (pen), Jardine
			2 Oct 68	(Yugoslavia)	A	L 0–1	
		2	30 Oct 68	Dundalk (Eire)	H	W 6–1	Henderson 2, Ferguson 2, Greig, own goal
			13 Nov 68		A	W 3–0	Mathieson, Stein 2
		3	11 Jan 69	DWS Amsterdam	A	W 2–0	Johnstone, Henderson
			22 Jan 69	(Holland)	H	W 2–1	Smith, Stein
		QF	19 Mar 69	Athletic Bilbao (Spain)	H	W 4–1	Ferguson, Penman, Persson, Stein
			2 Apr 69		A	L 0–2	
		SF	14 May 69	Newcastle United	H	D 0–0	
			22 May 69	(England)	A	L 0–2	
1969–70	Cup-Winners' Cup	1	17 Sep 69	Steaua Bucharest	H	W 2–0	Johnston 2
			1 Oct 69	(Rumania)	A	D 0–0	
		2	12 Nov 69	Gornik Zabrze	A	L 1–3	Persson
			26 Nov 69	(Poland)	H	L 1–3	Baxter
1970–71	Fairs Cup	1	16 Sep 70	Bayern Munich	A	L 0–1	
			30 Sep 70	(West Germany)	H	D 1–1	Stein
1971–72	Cup-Winners' Cup	1	15 Sep 71	Rennes (France)	A	D 1–1	Johnston
			28 Sep 71		H	W 1–0	MacDonald
		2	20 Oct 71	Sporting Lisbon	H	W 3–2	Stein 2, Henderson
			3 Nov 71	(Portugal)	A	L 3–4*	Stein 2, Henderson
		QF	8 Mar 72	Torino (Italy)	A	D 1–1	Johnston
			22 Mar 72		H	W 1–0	MacDonald
		SF	5 Apr 72	Bayern Munich	A	D 1–1	own goal
			19 Apr 72	(West Germany)	H	W 2–0	Jardine, Parlane

		F	24 May 72	Dynamo Moscow (USSR)	N	W 3-2	Johnstone 2, Stein
1972-73	Super Cup	F	16 Jan 73	Ajax (Holland)	H	L 1-3	MacDonald
			24 Jan 73		A	L 2-3	MacDonald, Young
1973-74	Cup-Winners' Cup	1	19 Sep 73	Ankaragucu (Turkey)	A	W 2-0	Conn, McLean
			3 Oct 73		H	W 4-0	Greig 2, O'Hara, Johnstone
		2	24 Oct 73	Borussia	A	L 0-3	
			7 Nov 73	Moenchengladbach (West Germany)	H	W 3-2	Conn, Jackson, MacDonald
1975-76	European Cup	1	17 Sep 75	Bohemians (Eire)	H	W 4-1	Fyfe, Johnstone, O'Hara, own goal
			1 Oct 75		A	D 1-1	Johnstone
		2	22 Oct 75	St Etienne (France)	A	L 0-2	
			5 Nov 75		H	L 1-2	MacDonald
1976-77	European Cup	1	15 Sep 76	Zurich (Switzerland)	H	D 1-1	Parlane
			29 Sep 76		A	L 0-1	
1977-78	Cup-Winners' Cup	Pr	17 Aug 77	Young Boys	H	W 1-0	Greig
			31 Aug 77	(Switzerland)	A	D 2-2	Johnstone, Smith
		1	14 Sep 77	Twente Enschede	H	D 0-0	
			28 Sep 77	(Holland)	A	L 0-3	
1978-79	European Cup	1	13 Sep 78	Juventus (Italy)	A	L 0-1	
			27 Sep 78		H	W 2-0	MacDonald, Smith
		2	18 Oct 78	PSV Eindhoven	H	D 0-0	
			1 Nov 78	(Holland)	A	W 3-2	MacDonald, Johnstone, Russell
		QF	6 Mar 79	FC Cologne	A	L 0-1	
			22 Mar 79	(West Germany)	H	D 1-1	McLean
1979-80	Cup-Winners' Cup	Pr	21 Aug 79	Lillestrom (Norway)	H	W 1-0	Smith
			5 Sep 79		A	W 2-0	MacDonald (A), Johnstone
		1	19 Sep 79	Fortuna Dusseldorf	H	W 2-1	MacDonald (A), McLean
			3 Oct 79	(West Germany)	A	D 0-0	
		2	24 Oct 79	Valencia (Spain)	A	D 1-1	McLean
			7 Nov 79		H	L 1-3	Johnstone
1981-82	Cup-Winners' Cup	1	16 Sep 81	Dukla Prague	A	L 0-3	
			30 Sep 81	(Czechoslovakia)	H	W 2-1	Bett, MacDonald (J)
1982-83	UEFA Cup	1	15 Sep 82	Borussia Dortmund	A	D 0-0	
			29 Sep 82	(West Germany)	H	W 2-0	Cooper, Johnstone
		2	20 Sep 82	FC Cologne	H	W 2-1	Johnstone, McClelland
			3 Nov 82	(West Germany)	A	L 0-5	
1983-84	Cup-Winners' Cup	1	14 Sep 83	Valletta (Malta)	A	W 8-0	Paterson, McPherson 4, McDonald, Prytz 2
			28 Sep 83		H	W 10-0	Mitchell 2, McDonald 3, Dawson, McKay, Davis 2, Redford
		2	19 Oct 83	Porto (Portugal)*	H	W 2-1	Clark, Mitchell
			2 Nov 83		A	L 0-1	
1984-85	UEFA Cup	1	18 Sep 84	Bohemians (Eire)	A	L 2-3	McCoist, McPherson
			3 Oct 84		H	W 2-0	Paterson, Redford
		2	24 Oct 84	Inter Milan (Italy)	A	L 0-3	
			7 Nov 84		H	W 3-1	Mitchell, Ferguson 2
1985-86	UEFA Cup	1	18 Sep 85	Osasuna (Spain)	H	W 1-0	Paterson
			2 Oct 85		A	L 0-2	

1986–87 UEFA Cup	1	17 Sep 86	Ilves (Finland)	H	W	4–0	Fleck 3, McCoist
		1 Oct 86		A	L	0–2	
	2	23 Oct 86	Boavista (Portugal)	H	W	2–1	McPherson, McCoist
		4 Nov 86		A	W	1–0	Ferguson
	3	26 Nov 86	Borussia	H	D	1–1	Durrant
		10 Dec 86	Moenchengladbach (West Germany)*	A	D	0–0	
1987–88 European Cup	1	16 Sep 87	Dynamo Kiev (USSR)	A	L	0–1	
		30 Sep 87		H	W	2–0	Falco, McCoist
	2	21 Oct 87	Gornik Zabrze	H	W	3–1	McCoist, Durrant, Falco
		4 Nov 87	(Poland)	A	D	1–1	McCoist (pen)
	QF	2 Mar 88	Steaua Bucharest	A	L	0–2	
		16 Mar 88	(Romania)	H	W	2–1	Gough, McCoist (pen)
1988–89 UEFA Cup	1	7 Sep 88	Katowice (Poland)	H	W	1–0	Walters
		5 Oct 88		A	W	4–2	Butcher 2, Durrant, Ferguson
	2	26 Oct 88	FC Cologne	A	L	0–2	
		9 Nov 88	(West Germany)	H	D	1–1	Drinkell
1989–90 European Cup	1	13 Sep 89	Bayern Munich	H	L	1–3	Walters (pen)
		27 Sep 89	(West Germany)	A	D	0–0	

ST JOHNSTONE

1971–72 UEFA Cup	1	15 Sep 71	SV Hamburg	A	L	1–2	Pearson
		29 Sep 71	(West Germany)	H	W	3–0	Hall, Pearson, Whitelaw
	2	20 Oct 71	Vasas Budapest	H	W	2–0	Connolly (pen), Pearson
		2 Nov 71	(Hungary)	A	L	0–1	
	3	24 Nov 71	Zeljeznicar	H	W	1–0	Connolly
		8 Dec 71	(Yugoslavia)	A	L	1–5	Rooney

ST MIRREN

1980–81 UEFA Cup	1	17 Sep 80	Elfsborg (Sweden)	A	W	2–1	Somner, Abercromby
		1 Oct 80		H	D	0–0	
	2	22 Oct 80	St Etienne (France)	H	D	0–0	
		5 Nov 80		A	L	0–2	
1983–84 UEFA Cup	1	14 Sep 83	Feyenoord (Holland)	H	L	0–1	
		28 Sep 83		A	L	0–2	
1985–86 UEFA Cup	1	17 Sep 85	Slavia Prague	A	L	0–1	
		2 Oct 85	(Czechoslovakia)	H	W	3–0	Gallagher, McGarvey 2
	2	23 Oct 85	Hammarby (Sweden)	A	D	3–3	Gallagher 3
		6 Nov 85		H	L	1–2	McGarvey
1987–88 Cup-Winners' Cup	1	16 Sep 87	Tromso (Norway)	H	W	1–0	McDowall
		30 Sep 87		A	D	0–0	
	2	21 Oct 87	Mechelen (Belgium)	A	D	0–0	
		4 Nov 87		H	L	0–2	

Irish League Clubs

ARDS

1958–59 European Cup	Pr	17 Sep 58	Reims (France)	H	L	1–4	Lowry
		8 Oct 58		A	L	2–6	Lawther, Quee

1969–70	Cup-Winners' Cup	1	17 Sep 69	AS Roma (Italy)	H	D	0–0	
			1 Oct 69		A	L	0–10	
1973–74	UEFA Cup	1	12 Sep 73	Standard Liege	H	W	3–2	Cathcart, McAvoy (pen),
				(Belgium)				McAteer (pen)
			19 Sep 73		A	L	1–6	Guy
1974–75	Cup-Winners' Cup	1	18 Sep 74	PSV Eindhoven	A	L	0–10	
			2 Oct 74	(Holland)	H	L	1–4	Guy

BALLYMENA UNITED

1978–79	Cup-Winner's Cup	1	13 Sep 78	Beveren (Belgium)	A	L	0–3	
			27 Sep 78		H	L	0–3	
1980–81	UEFA Cup	1	17 Sep 80	Vorwaerts	H	W	2–1	McQviston, Sloan
			1 Oct 80	(East Germany)	A	L	0–3	
1981–82	Cup-Winners' Cup	1	16 Sep 81	AS Roma (Italy)	H	L	0–2	
			30 Sep 81		A	L	0–4	
1984–85	Cup-Winners' Cup	1	19 Sep 84	Hamrun Spartans	H	L	0–1	
			26 Sep 84	(Malta)	A	L	1–2	Beattie
1989–90	Cup-Winners' Cup	1	13 Sep 89	Anderlecht	A	L	0–6	
			27 Sep 89	(Belgium)	H	L	0–4	

CARRICK RANGERS

1966–77	Cup-Winners' Cup	1	15 Sep 76	Aris Bonnevoie	H	W	3–1	Prenter 2, Connor
			6 Oct 76	(Luxembourg)	A	L	1–2	Irwin
		2	20 Oct 76	Southampton	H	L	2–5	Irwin, Prenter
			3 Nov 76	(England)	A	L	1–4	Reid

CLIFTONVILLE

| 1979–80 | Cup-Winners' Cup | 1 | 20 Sep 79 | Nantes (France) | H | L | 0–1 | |
| | | | 3 Oct 79 | | A | L | 0–7 | |

COLERAINE

1965–66	Cup-Winners' Cup	1	2 Sep 65	Dynamo Kiev (USSR)	H	L	1–6	Curley
			8 Sep 65		A	L	0–4	
1969–70	Fairs Cup	1	17 Sep 69	Jeunesse D'Esch	A	L	2–3	Hunter, Murray
			1 Oct 69	(Luxembourg)	H	W	4–0	Dickson 2, Wilson, Jennings
		2	11 Nov 69	Anderlecht (Belgium)	A	L	1–6	Murray
			20 Nov 69		H	L	3–7	Dickson 2, Irwin
1970–71	Fairs Cup	1	15 Sep 70	Kilmarnock (Scotland)	H	D	1–1	Mullan
			29 Sep 70		A	W	3–2	Dickson 3
		2	20 Oct 70	Sparta Rotterdam	A	L	0–2	
			4 Nov 70	(Holland)	H	L	1–2	Jennings
1974–75	European Cup	1	18 Sep 74	Feyenoord (Holland)	A	L	0–7	
			2 Oct 74		H	L	1–4	Simpson
1975–76	Cup-Winners' Cup	1	16 Sep 75	Eintracht Frankfurt	A	L	1–5	Cochrane
			30 Sep 75	(West Germany)	H	L	2–6	McCurdy, Cochrane
1977–78	Cup-Winners' Cup	1	14 Sep 77	Lokomotive Leipzig	H	L	1–4	Tweed
			28 Sep 77	(East Germany)	A	D	2–2	Guy 2
1982–83	Cup-Winners' Cup	1	15 Sep 82	Tottenham Hotspur	H	L	0–3	
			28 Sep 82	(England)	A	L	0–4	

1983–84	UEFA Cup	1	14 Sep 83	Sparta Rotterdam	A	L	0–4	
			28 Sep 83	(Holland)	H	D	1–1	Healy
1985–86	UEFA Cup	1	18 Sep 85	Lokomotive Leipzig	H	D	1–1	Wade
			2 Oct 85	(East Germany)	A	L	0–5	
1986–87	UEFA Cup	1	17 Sep 86	Stahl Brandenburg	H	D	1–1	Healy (pen)
			1 Oct 86	(East Germany)	A	L	0–1	

CRUSADERS

1967–68	Cup-Winners'	1	20 Sep 67	Valencia (Spain)	A	L	0–4	
	Cup		11 Oct 67		H	L	2–4	Trainor, Magill
1968–69	Cup-Winners'	1	18 Sep 68	Norrkoping (Sweden)	H	D	2–2	Jameson, Parke
	Cup		2 Oct 68		A	L	1–4	McPolin
1973–74	European Cup	1	19 Sep 73	Dinamo Bucharest	H	L	0–1	
			3 Oct 73	(Romania)	A	L	0–11	
1976–77	European Cup	1	14 Sep 76	Liverpool (England)	A	L	0–2	
			28 Sep 76		H	L	0–5	
1980–81	Cup-Winners'	1	16 Sep 80	Newport County	A	L	0–4	
	Cup		1 Oct 80	(Wales)	H	D	0–0	

DERRY CITY

1964–65	Cup-Winners'	1	9 Sep 64	Steaua Bucharest	A	L	0–3	
	Cup		16 Sep 64	(Rumania)	H	L	0–2	
1965–66	European Cup	Pr	31 Aug 65	Lyn Oslo (Norway)	A	L	3–5	Wood (R), Gilbert 2
			9 Sep 65		H	W	5–1	Wilson 2, Crossan, Wood (R), McGeough
		1	23 Nov 65	Anderlecht (Belgium)	A	L	0–9	
				Derry City withdrew				

DISTILLERY

1963–64	European Cup	Pr	25 Sep 63	Benfica (Portugal)	H	D	3–3	John Kennedy, Hamilton, Ellison
			2 Oct 63		A	L	0–5	
1971–72	Cup-Winners'	1	15 Sep 71	Barcelona (Spain)	H	L	1–3	O'Neill
	Cup		29 Sep 71		A	L	0–4	

GLENAVON

1957–58	European Cup	Pr	11 Sep 57	Aarhus (Denmark)	A	D	0–0	
			25 Sep 57		H	L	0–3	
1960–61	European Cup	Pr		*withdrew*				
1961–62	Cup-Winners'	1	13 Sep 61	Leicester City	H	L	1–4	Jones
	Cup		27 Sep 61	(England)	A	L	1–3	Wilson
1977–78	UEFA Cup	1	14 Sep 77	PSV Eindhoven	H	L	2–6	Malone (pen), McDonald
			28 Sep 77	(Holland)	A	L	0–5	
1979–80	UEFA Cup	1	18 Sep 79	Standard Liege	H	L	0–1	
			3 Oct 79	(Belgium)	A	L	0–1	
1988–89	Cup-Winners'	1	7 Sep 88	Aarhus (Denmark)	H	L	1–4	McCann
	Cup		5 Oct 88		A	L	1–3	McConville

GLENTORAN

1962–63	Fairs Cup	1	26 Sep 62	Real Zaragoza (Spain)	H	L	0–2	
			10 Oct 62		A	L	2–6	Doherty 2
1963–64	Fairs Cup	1	16 Sep 63	Partick Thistle	H	L	1–4	Thompson
			30 Sep 63	(Scotland)	A	L	0–3	
1964–65	European Cup	Pr	16 Sep 64	Panathinaikos	H	D	2–2	Turner, Thompson
			30 Sep 64	(Greece)	A	L	2–3	Turner, Pavis
1965–66	Fairs Cup	1	28 Sep 65	Antwerp (Belgium)	A	L	0–1	
			6 Oct 65		H	D	3–3	Hamilton, Thompson 2
1966–67	Cup-Winners' Cup	1	27 Sep 66	Rangers (Scotland)	H	D	1–1	Sinclair
			5 Oct 66		A	l	0–4	
1967–68	European Cup	1	13 Sep 67	Benfica (Portugal)*	H	D	1–1	Colrain (pen)
			4 Oct 67		A	D	0–0	
1968–69	European Cup	1	18 Sep 68	Anderlecht (Belgium)	A	L	0–3	
			2 Oct 68		H	D	2–2	Morrow, Johnston
1969–70	Fairs Cup	1	9 Sep 69	Arsenal (England)	A	L	0–3	
			29 Sep 69		H	W	1–0	Henderson
1970–71	European Cup	1	16 Sep 70	Waterford (Eire)	H	L	1–3	Hall
			30 Sep 70		A	L	0–1	
1971–72	UEFA Cup	1	14 Sep 71	Eintracht Brunswick	H	L	0–1	
			28 Sep 71	(West Germany)	A	L	1–6	McCaffrey
1973–74	Cup-Winners' Cup	1	19 Sep 73	Chimia Ramnicu	A	D	2–2	Jamison, McCreary
			3 Oct 73	(Romania)	H	W	2–0	Jamison, Craig
		2	24 Oct 73	Brann Bergen	A	D	1–1	Feeney
			7 Nov 73	(Norway)	H	W	3–1	Feeney, Jamison 2
		QF	5 May 74	Borussia	H	L	0–2	
			20 May 74	Moenchengladbach (West Germany)	A	L	0–5	
1975–76	UEFA Cup	1	16 Sep 75	Ajax (Holland)	H	L	1–6	Jamison
			1 Oct 75		A	L	0–8	
1976–77	UEFA Cup	1	14 Sep 76	Basle (Switzerland)	H	W	3–2	Feeney 2, Dickenson
			29 Sep 76		A	L	0–3	
1977–78	European Cup	1	15 Sep 77	Valur (Iceland)	A	L	0–1	
			29 Sep 77		H	W	2–0	Robson, Jamison
		2	19 Oct 77	Juventus (Italy)	H	L	0–1	
			2 Nov 77		A	L	0–5	
1978–79	UEFA Cup	1	5 Sep 78	IBV Westmann*	A	D	0–0	
			14 Sep 78	(Iceland)	H	D	1–1	Caskey (W)
1981–82	European Cup	1	16 Sep 81	Progres Niedercorn	A	D	1–1	Cleary
			30 Sep 81	(Luxembourg)	H	W	4–0	Blackledge 2, Jameson, Manley
		2	21 Oct 81	CSKA Sofia (Bulgaria)	A	L	0–2	
			4 Nov 81		H	W	2–1	Cleary, Manley
1982–83	UEFA Cup	1	15 Sep 82	Banik Ostrava	H	L	1–3	Bowers
			29 Sep 82	(Czechoslovakia)	A	L	0–1	
1983–84	Cup-Winners' Cup	1	14 Sep 83	Paris St Germain	H	L	1–2	Jameson
			28 Sep 83	(France)	A	L	1–2	Mullan
1984–85	UEFA Cup	1	18 Sep 84	Standard Liege	H	D	1–1	Bowers
			3 Oct 84	(Belgium)	A	L	0–2	
1985–86	Cup-Winners' Cup	1	21 Sep 85	Fram (Iceland)	A	L	1–3	Bowers
			2 Oct 85		H	W	1–0	Mullan
1986–87	Cup-Winners' Cup	1	17 Sep 86	Lokomotive Leipzig	H	D	1–1	Cleary
			1 Oct 86	(East Germany)	A	L	0–2	

1987–88	Cup-Winners'	1	16 Sep 87	Ropa Rovaniemi*	A	D	0–0	
	Cup		30 Sep 87	(Finland)	H	D	1–1	Caskey
1988–89	European Cup	1	7 Sep 88	Moscow Spartak	A	L	0–2	
			5 Oct 88	(USSR)	H	D	1–1	Moore
1989–90	UEFA Cup	1	13 Sep 89	Dundee United	H	L	1–3	Jameson
			27 Sep 89	(Scotland)	A	L	0–2	

LINFIELD

1959–60	European Cup	Pr	9 Sep 59	Gothenburg (Sweden)	H	W	2–1	Milburn 2
			23 Sep 59		A	L	1–6	Dickson
1961–62	European Cup	Pr	30 Aug 61	Vorwaerts	A	L	0–3	
				(East Germany)	*Linfield withdrew*			
1962–63	European Cup	Pr	5 Sep 62	Esbjerg (Denmark)	H	L	1–2	Dickson
			19 Sep 62		A	D	0–0	
1963–64	Cup-Winners'	1		bye				
	Cup	2	13 Nov 63	Fenerbahce (Turkey)	A	L	1–4	Dickson
			11 Dec 63		H	W	2–0	Craig, Ferguson
1966–67	European Cup	1	7 Sep 66	Aris Bonnevoie	A	D	3–3	Hamilton, Pavis, Scott
			16 Sep 66	(Luxembourg)	A	W	6–1	Thomas 3, Scott 2, Parvis
		2	26 Oct 66	Valerengen (Norway)	A	W	4–1	Scott, Pavis, Thomas, Shields
			8 Nov 66		H	D	1–1	Thomas
		QF	1 Mar 67	CSKA Sofia (Bulgaria)	H	D	2–2	Hamilton, Shields
			15 Mar 67		A	L	0–1	
1967–68	Fairs Cup	1	19 Sep 67	Lokomotive Leipzig	A	L	1–5	Pavis
			4 Oct 67	(East Germany)	H	W	1–0	Hamilton
1968–69	Fairs Cup	1	18 Sep 68	Setubal (Portugal)	A	L	0–3	
			9 Oct 68		H	L	1–3	Scott
1969–70	European Cup	1	17 Sep 69	Red Star Belgrade	A	L	0–8	
			1 Oct 69	(Yugoslavia)	H	L	2–4	McGraw 2
1970–71	Cup-Winners'	1	16 Sep 70	Manchester City*	A	L	0–1	
	Cup		30 Sep 70	(England)	H	W	2–1	Millen 2
1971–72	European Cup	1	15 Sep 71	Standard Liege	A	L	0–2	
			29 Sep 71	(Belgium)	H	L	2–3	Magee, Larmour
1975–76	European Cup	1	17 Sep 75	PSV Eindhoven	H	L	1–2	Malone (P)
			1 Oct 75	(Holland)	A	L	0–8	
1978–79	European Cup	1	13 Sep 78	Lillestrom (Norway)	H	D	0–0	
			27 Sep 78		A	L	0–1	
1979–80	European Cup	Pr	29 Aug 79	Dundalk (Eire)	A	D	1–1	Feeney
			5 Sep 79	*(in Haarlem, Holland)*	H	L	0–2	
1980–81	European Cup	1	16 Sep 80	Nantes (France)	H	L	0–1	
			30 Sep 80		A	L	0–2	
1981–82	UEFA Cup	1	16 Sep 81	Beveren (Belgium)	A	L	0–3	
			29 Sep 81		H	L	0–5	
1982–83	European Cup	1	15 Sep 82	17 Nendori (Albania)*	A	L	0–1	
			29 Sep 82		H	W	2–1	Gibson, Anderson
1983–84	European Cup	1	14 Sep 83	Benfica (Portugal)	A	L	0–3	
			28 Sep 83		H	L	2–3	Walsh, own goal
1984–85	European Cup	1	19 Sep 84	Shamrock Rovers	H	D	0–0	
			3 Oct 84	(Eire)	A	D	1–1	*Jeffrey
		2	24 Oct 84	Panathinaikos	A	L	1–2	Totten
			7 Oct 84	(Greece)	H	D	3–3	McGaughey 2 (1 pen), Maxwell

1985–86	European Cup	1	18 Sep 85	Servette	H	D	2–2	Anderson, McKeown
			2 Oct 85	(Switzerland)	A	L	1–2	Anderson
1986–87	European cup	1	17 Sep 86	Rosenborg (Norway)	A	L	0–1	
			1 Oct 86		H	D	1–1	McKeown (pen)
1987–88	European Cup	1	16 Sep 87	Lillestrom (Norway)	A	D	1–1	Baxter
			30 Sep 87		H	L	2–4	McGaughey 2
1988–89	UEFA Cup	1	7 Sep 88	TPS Turun (Finland)	A	D	0–0	
			5 Oct 88		H	D	1–1	*O'Boyle
1989–90	European Cup	1	13 Sep 89	Dnepr (USSR)	H	L	1–2	Mooney (pen)
			27 Sep 89		A	L	0–1	

PORTADOWN

1962–63	Cup-Winners'	1		bye				
	Cup	2	7 Nov 62	OFK Belgrade	A	L	1–5	Clements
			22 Nov 62	(Yugoslavia)	H	W	3–2	Burke, Jones, Cush
1974–75	UEFA Cup	1	18 Sep 74	Valur (Iceland)	A	D	0–0	
			1 Oct 74		H	W	2–1	MacFaul, Morrison (pen)
		2	23 Oct 74	Partizan Belgrade	A	L	0–5	
			6 Nov 74	(Yugoslavia)	H	D	1–1	Malcolmson

League of Ireland Clubs

ATHLONE TOWN

1975–76	UEFA Cup	1	18 Sep 75	Valerengen (Norway)	H	W	3–0	Martin, Davis 2
			1 Oct 75		A	D	1–1	Martin
		2	22 Oct 75	AC Milan (Italy)	H	D	0–0	
			5 Nov 75		A	L	0–3	
1981–82	European Cup	1	16 Sep 81	KB Copenhagen	A	D	1–1	O'Connor (M)
			30 Sep 81	(Denmark)	H	D	2–2	Davis 2
1983–84	European Cup	1	14 Sep 83	Standard Liege	H	L	2–3	Collins, Salmon
			28 Sep 83	(Belgium)	A	L	2–8	Salmon, Hitchcock

BOHEMIANS

1970–71	Cup-Winners'	Pr	26 Aug 70	Gottwaldov	H	L	1–2	Swan (pen)
	Cup		2 Sep 70	(Czechoslovakia)	A	D	2–2	O'Connell, Dunne
1972–73	UEFA Cup	1	13 Sep 72	FC Cologne	A	L	1–2	Daly
			27 Sep 72	(West Germany)	H	L	0–3	
1974–75	UEFA Cup	1	18 Sep 74	SV Hamburg	A	L	0–3	
			2 Oct 74	(West Germany)	H	L	0–1	
1975–76	European Cup	1	17 Sep 75	Rangers (Scotland)	A	L	1–4	Flanagan
			1 Oct 75		H	D	1–1	O'Connor (T)
1976–77	Cup-Winners'	1	15 Sep 76	Esbjerg (Denmark)	H	W	2–1	Ryan (B), own goal
	Cup		29 Sep 76		A	W	1–0	Mitten
		2	20 Oct 76	Slask Wroclaw	A	L	0–3	
			3 Nov 76	(Poland)	H	L	0–1	
1978–79	European Cup	1	13 Sep 78	Omonia Nicosia	A	L	1–2	O'Connor (P)
			27 Sep 78	(Cyprus)	H	W	1–0	Joyce
		2	18 Oct 78	Dynamo Dresden	H	D	0–0	
			1 Nov 78	(East Germany)	A	L	0–6	
1979–80	UEFA Cup	1	19 Sep 79	Sporting Lisbon	A	L	0–2	
			3 Oct 79	(Portugal)	H	D	0–0	

1984–85	UEFA Cup	1	18 Sep 84	Rangers (Scotland)	H	W	3–2	O'Brien 2, Lawless
			3 Oct 84		A	L	0–2	
1987–88	UEFA Cup	1	15 Sep 87	Aberdeen (Scotland)	H	D	0–0	
			30 Sep 87		A	L	0–1	

CORK CELTIC

1964–65	Cup-Winners' Cup	1	30 Sep 64	Slavia Sofia (Bulgaria)	A	D	1–1	Leahy
			7 Oct 64		H	L	0–2	
1974–75	European Cup	1		walkover				
		2	23 Oct 74	Ararat Erevan (USSR)	H	L	1–2	Tambling
			6 Nov 74		A	L	0–5	
1989–90	Cup-Winners' Cup	1	13 Sep 89	Moscow Torpedo	A	L	0–5	
			27 Sep 89	(USSR)	H	L	0–1	

CORK HIBS

1970–71	Fairs Cup	1	16 Sep 70	Valencia (Spain)	H	L	0–3	
			26 Sep 70		A	L	1–3	Wigginton
1971–72	European Cup	1	15 Sep 71	Borussia	H	L	0–5	
			29 Sep 71	Moenchengladbach (West Germany)	A	L	1–2	Dennehy
1972–73	Cup-Winners' Cup	1	10 Sep 72	Pezoporikos (Cyprus)	A	W	2–1	Lawson (pen), Sheehan
			13 Sep 72		H	W	4–1	Wallace, Lawson 2, Dennehy
		2	25 Oct 72	Schalke 04	H	D	0–0	
			8 Nov 72	(West Germany)	A	L	0–3	
1973–74	Cup-Winners' Cup	1	19 Sep 73	Banik Ostrava	A	L	0–1	
			3 Oct 73	(Czechoslovakia)	H	L	1–2	Humphries

DERRY CITY

1988–89	Cup-Winners' Cup	1	7 Sep 88	Cardiff City (Wales)	H	D	0–0	
			5 Oct 88		A	L	0–4	
1989–90	European Cup	1	13 Sep 89	Benfica (Portugal)	H	L	1–2	Carlyle
			27 Sep 89		A	L	0–4	

DROGHEDA

1983–84	UEFA Cup	1	14 Sep 83	Tottenham Hotspur	H	L	0–6	
			28 Sep 83	(England)	A	L	0–8	

DRUMCONDRA

1958–59	European Cup	Pr	17 Sep 58	Atletico Madrid	A	L	0–8	
			1 Oct 58	(Spain)	H	L	1–5	Fullam (pen)
1961–62	European Cup	Pr	23 Aug 61	FC Nuremberg	A	L	0–5	
			13 Sep 61	(West Germany)	H	L	1–4	Fullam
1962–63	Fairs Cup	1	3 Oct 62	Odense BK 09 (Denmark)	H	W	4–1	Dixon 2, Morrissey, McCann
			17 Oct 62		A	L	2–4	Rice, Morrissey
		2	4 Dec 62	Bayern Munich	A	L	0–6	
			12 Dec 62	(West Germany)	H	W	1–0	Dixon
1965–66	European Cup	Pr	15 Sep 65	Vorwaerts	H	W	1–0	Morrissey
			22 Sep 65	(East Germany)	A	L	0–3	

1966–67	Fairs Cup	1	21 Sep 66	Eintracht Frankfurt	H	L	0–2	
			5 Oct 66	(West Germany)	A	L	1–6	Whelan

DUNDALK

1963–64	European Cup	Pr	11 Sep 63	Zurich (Switzerland)	H	L	0–3	
			25 Sep 63		A	W	2–1	Cross, Hasty
1967–68	European Cup	1	20 Sep 67	Vasas Budapest	H	L	0–1	
			11 Oct 67	(Hungary)	A	L	1–8	Hale
1968–69	Fairs Cup	1	11 Sep 68	DOS Utrecht (Holland)	A	D	1–1	Stokes
			1 Oct 68		H	W	2–1	Stokes, Morrissey
		2	30 Oct 68	Rangers (Scotland)	A	L	1–6	Murray (pen)
			13 Nov 68		H	L	0–3	
1969–70	Fairs Cup	1	16 Sep 69	Liverpool (England)	A	L	0–10	
			30 Sep 69		H	L	0–4	
1976–77	European Cup	1	15 Sep 76	PSV Eindhoven	H	D	1–1	McDowell
			29 Sep 76	(Holland)	A	L	0–6	
1977–78	Cup-Winners' Cup	1	14 Sep 77	Hajduk Split	H	W	1–0	Flanagan
			28 Sep 77	(Yugoslavia)	A	L	0–4	
1979–80	European Cup	Pr	29 Aug 79	Linfield (Northern Ireland)	H	D	1–1	Devine
			5 Sep 79	(in Haarlem, Holland)	A	W	2–0	Muckian 2
		1	19 Sep 79	Hibernians (Malta)	H	W	2–0	Carlyle, Devine
			26 Sep 79		A	L	0–1	
		2	24 Oct 79	Celtic (Scotland)	A	L	2–3	Muckian, Lawlor
			7 Nov 79		H	D	0–0	
1980–81	UEFA Cup	1	16 Sep 80	Porto (Portugal)	A	L	0–1	
			1 Oct 80		H	D	0–0	
1981–82	Cup-Winners' Cup	1	16 Sep 81	Fram (Iceland)	A	L	1–2	Fairclough
			30 Sep 81		H	W	4–0	Flanagan (pen), Fairclough, Lawlor, Duff
		2	21 Oct 81	Tottenham Hotspur	H	D	1–1	Fairclough
			4 Nov 81	(England)	A	L	0–1	
1982–83	European Cup	1	14 Sep 82	Liverpool (England)	H	L	1–4	Flanagan
			28 Sep 82		A	L	0–1	
1987–88	Cup-Winners' Cup	1	16 Sep 87	Ajax (Holland)	A	L	0–4	
			30 Sep 87		H	L	0–2	
1988–89	European Cup	1	7 Sep 88	Red Star Belgrade	H	L	0–5	
			5 Oct 88	(Yugoslavia)	A	L	0–3	
1989–90	UEFA Cup	1	13 Sep 89	Wettingen	A	L	0–3	
			27 Sep 89	(Switzerland)	H	L	0–2	

FINN HARPS

1973–74	UEFA Cup	1	19 Sep 73	Aberdeen (Scotland)	A	L	1–4	Harkin
			3 Oct 73		H	L	1–3	Harkin
1974–75	Cup-Winners' Cup	1	18 Nov 74	Bursaspor (Turkey)	A	L	2–4	Ferry, Bradley
					H	D	0–0	
1976–77	UEFA Cup	1	15 Sep 76	Derby County	A	L	0–12	
			29 Sep 76	(England)	H	L	1–4	own goal
1978–79	UEFA Cup	1	12 Sep 78	Everton (England)	H	L	0–5	
			26 Sep 78		A	L	0–5	

GALWAY UNITED

1985–86	Cup-Winners' Cup	1	18 Sep 85	Lyngby (Denmark)	A	L	0–1	
			2 Oct 85		H	L	2–3	Murphy, Bonner
1986–87	UEFA Cup	1	16 Sep 86	Groningen (Holland)	A	L	1–5	McGee (pen)
			1 Oct 86		H	L	1–3	Murphy

HOME FARM

1975–76	Cup-Winners' Cup	1	17 Aug 75	Lens (France)	H	D	1–1	Brophy
			1 Oct 75		A	L	0–6	

LIMERICK

1960–61	European Cup	Pr	31 Aug 60	Young Boys	H	L	0–5	
			5 Oct 60	(Switzerland)	A	L	2–4	Lynam, O'Reilly
1965–66	Cup-Winners' Cup	1	7 Oct 65	CSKA Sofia (Bulgaria)	H	L	1–2	O'Connor
			13 Oct 65		A	L	0–2	
1971–72	Cup-Winners' Cup	1	15 Sep 71	Torino (Italy)	H	L	0–1	
			29 Sep 71		A	L	0–4	
1980–81	European Cup	1	17 Sep 80	Real Madrid (Spain)	H	L	1–2	Kennedy
			1 Oct 80		A	L	1–5	Kennedy
1981–82	UEFA Cup	1	16 Sep 81	Southampton	H	L	0–3	
			29 Sep 81	(England)	A	D	1–1	Morris
1982–83	Cup-Winners' Cup	1	15 Sep 82	AZ 67 (Holland)	H	D	1–1	Nolan
			30 Sep 82		A	L	0–1	

SHAMROCK ROVERS

1957–58	European Cup	Pr	25 Sep 57	Manchester United	H	L	0–6	
			2 Oct 57	(England)	A	L	2–3	McCann, Hamilton
1959–60	European Cup	Pr	26 Aug 59	Nice (France)	A	L	2–3	Hamilton, Tuohy
			23 Sep 59		H	D	1–1	Hennessy
1962–63	Cup-Winners' Cup	1		bye				
		2	24 Oct 62	Botev Plovdiv	H	L	0–4	
			14 Nov 62	(Bulgaria)	A	L	0–1	
1963–64	Fairs Cup	1	18 Sep 63	Valencia (Spain)	H	L	0–1	
			10 Oct 63		A	D	2–2	O'Neill, Mooney
1964–65	European Cup	Pr	16 Sep 64	Rapid Vienna (Austria)	A	L	0–3	
			30 Sep 64		H	L	0–2	
1965–66	Fairs Cup	1		bye				
		2	17 Nov 65	Real Zaragoza (Spain)	H	D	1–1	Tuohy
			24 Nov 65		A	L	1–2	Fullam
1966–67	Cup-Winners' Cup	1	28 Sep 66	Spora (Luxembourg)	H	W	4–1	Fullam, Dixon, Kearin, O'Neill (pen)
			5 Oct 66		A	W	4–1	Kearin, Dixon 2, O'Neill
		2	9 Nov 66	Bayern Munich	H	D	1–1	Dixon
			23 Nov 66	(West Germany)	A	L	2–3	Gilbert, O'Neill
1967–68	Cup-Winners' Cup	1	20 Sep 67	Cardiff City (Wales)	H	D	1–1	Gilbert
			4 Oct 67		A	L	0–2	
1968–69	Cup-Winners' Cup	1	18 Sep 68	Randers Freja	A	L	0–1	
			2 Oct 68	(Denmark)	H	L	1–2	Fullam
1969–70	Cup-Winners' Cup	1	17 Sep 69	Schalke 04	H	W	2–1	Barber 2
			1 Oct 69	(West Germany)	A	L	0–3	
1978–79	Cup-Winners' Cup	1	13 Sep 78	Apoel Nicosia	H	W	2–0	Giles, Lynex
			27 Sep 78	(Cyprus)	A	W	1–0	Lynex

		2	18 Oct 78	Banik Ostrava	A	L	0-3	
			1 Nov 78	(Czechoslovakia)	H	L	1-3	Giles
1982-83	UEFA Cup	1	15 Sep 82	Fram (Iceland)	A	W	3-0	Murphy, Campbell, Gaynor
			30 Sep 82		H	W	4-0	O'Carroll, Buckley, Beglin, Gaynor
		2	21 Oct 82	Uni. Craiova	H	L	0-2	
			3 Nov 82	(Romania)	A	L	0-3	
1984-85	European Cup	1	19 Sep 84	Linfield*	A	D	0-0	
			3 Oct 84	(Northern Ireland)	H	D	1-1	Eccles
1985-86	European Cup	1	18 Sep 85	Honved (Hungary)	A	L	0-2	
			2 Oct 85		H	L	1-3	Coady
1986-87	European Cup	1	17 Sep 86	Celtic (Scotland)	H	L	0-1	
			1 Oct 86		A	L	0-2	
1987-88	European Cup	1	16 Sep 87	Omonia Nicosia	H	L	0-1	
			30 Sep 87	(Cyprus)	A	D	0-0	

SHELBOURNE

1962-63	European Cup	Pr	19 Sep 62	Sporting Lisbon	H	L	0-2	
			27 Sep 62	(Portugal)	A	L	1-5	Hennessy
1963-64	Cup-Winners' Cup	1	24 Sep 63	Barcelona (Spain)	H	L	0-2	
			15 Oct 63		A	L	1-3	Bonham (pen)
1964-65	Fairs Cup	1	16 Sep 64	Belenenses (Portugal)	A	D	1-1	Barber
			14 Oct 64		H	D	0-0	
			28 Oct 64		N	W	2-1	Hannigan, Conroy (M)
		2	25 Nov 64	Atletico Madrid	H	L	0-1	
			2 Dec 64	(Spain)	A	L	0-1	
1971-72	UEFA Cup	1	15 Sep 71	Vasas Budapest	A	L	0-1	
			29 Sep 71	(Hungary)	H	D	1-1	Murray

SLIGO ROVERS

1983-84	European Cup	1	14 Sep 83	Haka Valkeakosken	H	L	0-1	
			28 Sep 83	(Finland)	A	L	0-3	

ST PATRICK'S ATHLETIC

1961-62	Cup-Winners' Cup	Pr	12 Sep 61	Dunfermline Athletic	A	L	1-4	O'Rourke
			27 Sep 61	(Scotland)	H	L	0-4	
1967-68	Fairs Cup	1	13 Sep 67	Bordeaux (France)	H	L	1-3	Hennessy
			11 Oct 67		A	L	3-6	Campbell 2, Ryan
1988-89	UEFA Cup	1	7 Sep 88	Hearts (Scotland)	H	L	0-2	
			5 Oct 88		A	L	0-2	

UCD

1984-85	Cup-Winners' Cup	1	19 Sep 84	Everton (England)	H	D	0-0	
			2 Oct 84		A	L	0-1	

WATERFORD

1966-67	European Cup	Pr	31 Aug 66	Vorwaerts Berlin	H	L	1-5	Lynch
			9 Sep 66	(East Germany)	A	L	0-6	
1968-69	European Cup	1	18 Sep 68	Manchester United	H	L	1-3	Matthews
			2 Oct 68	(England)	A	L	1-7	Casey

1969–70	European cup	1	17 Sep 69	Galatasaray (Turkey)	A	L	0–2	
			1 Oct 69		H	L	2–3	Buck, Morley
1970–71	European Cup	1	16 Sep 70	Glentoran	A	W	3–1	O'Neill, McGeough, Casey
			30 Sep 70	(Northern Ireland)	H	W	1–0	Casey
		2	21 Oct 70	Celtic (Scotland)	H	L	0–7	
			4 Nov 70		A	L	2–3	Matthews, own goal
1972–73	European Cup	1	13 Sep 72	Omonia Nicosia	H	W	2–1	Hale 2
			27 Sep 72	(Cyprus)	A	L	0–2	
1973–74	European Cup	1	19 Sep 73	Ujpest Dozsa	H	L	2–3	Kirby, O'Neill
			3 Oct 73	(Hungary)	A	L	0–3	
1979–80	Cup-Winners' Cup	1	19 Sep 79	Gothenburg (Sweden)	A	L	0–1	
			3 Oct 79		H	D	1–1	Keane
1980–81	Cup-Winners' Cup	1	17 Sep 80	Hibernians (Malta)	A	L	0–1	
			1 Oct 80		H	W	4–0	Kirk 2, Finucane, Fitzpatrick
		2	22 Oct 80	Dynamo Tbilisi	H	L	0–1	
			5 Nov 80	(USSR)	A	L	0–4	
1986–67	Cup-Winners' Cup	1	17 Sep 86	Bordeaux (France)	H	L	1–2	Synnott
			30 Sep 86		A	L	0–4	

Welsh Non-League Clubs

BANGOR CITY

1962–63	Cup-Winners' Cup	1	5 Sep 62	Napoli (Italy)	H	W	2–0	Matthews, Birch (pen)
			26 Sep 62		A	L	1–3	McAlister
			10 Oct 62		N	L	1–2	McAlister
1985–86	Cup-Winners' Cup	1	18 Sep 85	Fredrikstad	A	D	1–1	Williams (E)
			2 Oct 85	(Norway)	H	D	0–0*	
		2	24 Oct 85	Atletico Madrid	H	L	0–2	
			6 Nov 85	(Spain)	A	L	0–1	

BOROUGH UNITED

1963–64	Cup-Winners' Cup	1	15 Sep 63	Sliema Wanderers	A	D	0–0	
			3 Oct 63	(Malta)	H	W	2–0	Duffy, Pritchard (M)
		2	11 Dec 63	Slovan Bratislava	H	L	0–1	
			15 Dec 63	(Czechoslovakia)	A	L	0–3	

MERTHYR

| 1987–88 | Cup-Winners' Cup | 1 | 16 Sep 87 | Atalanta (Italy) | H | W | 2–1 | Rogers, Ceri Williams |
| | | | 30 Sep 87 | | A | L | 0–2 | |

Representative Team

LONDON

1955–58	Fairs Cup	Gp. C	4 Jun 55	Basle (Switzerland)	A	W	5–0	Firmani 2, Holton 3
			4 Jun 56		H	W	1–0	Robb
			26 Oct 56	Frankfurt	H	W	3–2	Jezzard 2, Robson
			27 Mar 57	(West Germany)	A	L	0–1	
		SF	16 Sep 57	Lausanne	A	L	1–2	Haverty
			23 Oct 57	(Switzerland)	H	W	2–0	Greaves, Holton
		F	5 Mar 58	Barcelona (Spain)	H	D	2–2	Greaves, Langley (pen)
			1 May 58		A	L	0–6	

European Club Competition Records

Highest scores

14-0 Ajax v Red Boys, UEFA Cup 1st Round, 3 Oct 1984

12-2 Feyenoord v KR Reykjavik, European Cup 1st Round, 17 Sep 1969

11-0 Dinamo Bucharest v Crusaders, European Cup 1st Round, 3 Oct 1973

16-1 Sporting Lisbon v Apoel Nicosia, Cup Winners' Cup 1st Round, 13 Nov 1963

13-0 Cologne v Union Luxembourg, Fairs Cup 1st Round, 15 Oct 1965

Highest scores involving British clubs

13-0 Chelsea v Jeunesse Hautcharage, Cup Winners' Cup, 29 Sep 1971

12-0 Derby County v Finn Harps, UEFA Cup, 15 Sep 1976

12-0 Swansea City v Sliema Wanderers, Cup Winners' Cup, 15 Sep 1982

11-0 Liverpool v Stromsgodset, Cup Winners' Cup, 17 Sep 1974

Goalscoring in European competitions

European Cup individual aggregate

49, Alfredo di Stefano (Real Madrid) 1955-56 to 1963-64

46, Eusebio (Benfica) 1961-62 to 1973-74

36, Gerd Muller (Bayern Munich) 1969-70 to 1976-77

European Cup in one season

14, José Altafini (AC Milan) 1962-63

Cup Winners' Cup

14, Lothar Emmerich (Borussia Dortmund), 1965-66

Top British marksmen in European competitions

Leading scorers

30 goals Peter Lorimer (Leeds United) 1965-66 to 1976-77

28 goals Denis Law (Manchester United) 1963-64 to 1968-69

20 goals Kenny Dalglish (Celtic and Liverpool) 1972-73 to 1983-84

5 goals in one match

Ray Crawford (Ipswich Town) v Floriana, European Cup 1st Round 2nd leg, 25 Sep 1962

Peter Osgood (Chelsea) v Jeunesse Hautcharage, Cup Winners' Cup, 29 Sep 1971

Aggregate scores by individuals

11 goals, Stan Bowles (Queen's Park Rangers) UEFA Cup, 1976-77

7 goals in one tie (five in first leg) Kevin Hector (Derby County) UEFA Cup, 1976-77

4 goals on two occasions, Trevor Whymark (Ipswich Town) v Lazio, UEFA Cup, 24 Oct 1973; v Landskrona Bois, UEFA Cup 28 Sep 1977

The Golden Boot

Awarded to Europe's leading goalscorer

Season	Gold		Silver		Bronze	
1967-68	Eusebio (Benfica)	43	Antal Dunai (Ujpest Dozsa)	36	Bobby Lennox (Celtic)	32
1968-69	Petar Jekov (CSKA Sofia)	36	George Sideris (Olympiakos)	35	Helmut Kogelberger (FC Austria)	31
					Antal Dunai (Ujpest Dozsa)	31
1969-70	Gerd Muller (Bayern Munich)	38	Jan Devillet (Spora Lux)	31		
			Petar Jekov (CSKA Sofia)	31		
1970-71	Josip Skoblar (Marseilles)	44	Salif Keita (St Etienne)	42	George Dedes (Panionios)	28
1971-72	Gerd Muller (Bayern Munich)	40	Antonis Antoniadis (Panathinaikos)	39	Joe Harper (Aberdeen)	33
					Slobodan Santrac (OFK Belgrade)	33
					Francis Lee (Man City)	33
1972-73	Eusebio (Benfica)	40	Gerd Muller (Bayern Munich)	36	Petar Jekov (CSKA Sofia)	29

1973–74	Hector Yazalde (Sporting Lisbon)	46	Hans Krankl (Rapid Vienna)	36	Gerd Muller (Bayern Munich)	30
					Jupp Heynckes (Borussia Moenchengladbach)	30
					Carlos Bianchi (Reims)	30
1974–75	Dudu Georgescu (Dinamo Bucharest)	33	Hector Yazalde (Sporting)	30		
			Ruud Geels (Ajax)	30		
			Delio Onnis (Monaco)	30		
1975–76	Sotiris Kaiafas (Omonia Nicosia)	39	Carlos Bianchi (Reims)	34	Peter Risi (Zurich)	33
1976–77	Dudu Georgescu (Dinamo Bucharest)	47	Bela Varadi (Vasas Budapest)	36	Ruud Geels (Ajax)	34
					Dieter Muller (FC Cologne)	34
1977–78	Hans Krankl (Rapid Vienna)	41	Carlos Bianchi (Paris SG)	37	Ruud Geels (Ajax)	34
1978–79	Kees Kist (AZ 67 Alkmaar)	34	Thomas Mavros (AEK)	31		
			Laszlo Fekete (Ujpest Dozsa)	31		
1979–80	Erwin Van Den Bergh (Lierse)	39	Laszlo Fazekas (Ujpest Dozsa)	36	Walter Schachner (FK Austria)	34
1980–81	Georgi Slavkov (Trakia Plovdiv)	31	Tibor Nyilasi (Ferencvaros)	30	Karl-Heinz Rummenigge (Bayern Munich)	29
1981–82	Wim Kieft (Ajax)	32	Kees Kist (AZ 67 Alkmaar)	29	Allan Hansen (Odense BK)	28
			Delio Onnis (Tours)	29		
1982–83	Fernando Gomes (Porto)	36	Peter Houtman (Feyenoord)	30	Nikos Anastopoulos (Olympiakos)	29
					Charlie Nicholas (Celtic)	29
1983–84	Ian Rush (Liverpool)	32	Marco Van Basten (Ajax)	28	Nico Claesen (Seraing)	27
1984–85	Fernando Gomes (Porto)	39	Martin McGaughey (Linfield)	34	Vahid Halilhodzic (Nantes)	28
1985–86	Marco Van Basten (Ajax)	37	Oleg Protasov (Dnepr)	36	Toni Polster (FK Austria)	33
					Tanju Colak (Samsunspor)	33
1986–87	Rodion Camataru (Dinamo Bucharest)	44	Toni Polster (FK Austria)	39	Nasko Sirakov (Vitosha)	36
1987–88	Tanju Colak (Galatasaray)	39	John Eriksen (Servette)	36	Tommy Coyne (Dundee)	33
1988–89	Dorin Mateut (Dinamo Bucharest)	43	Baltazar (Atletico Madrid)	35	Aykut (Fenerbahce)	29
1989–90	Hugo Sanchez (Real Madrid)	38			Gerhard Rodax (Admira Wacker)	35
	Christo Stoichkov (CSKA Sofia)	38				

International Goalscoring Records

For club

16 goals, Stephan Stanis (Stanikowski and sometimes known as Dembicki), Racing Club Lens v Aubry-Asturies, French Cup, 13 Dec 1942.

International matches

10 goals, Sofus Nielsen, Denmark v France, 1908 Olympics
Gottfried Fuchs, Germany v Russia (as Russia), 1912 Olympics

World career records

1329 goals, Artur Friedenreich, in Brazilian football, 1910–30
1216 goals, Edson Arantes do Nascimento (Pelé) 1956–74, in Brazilian football, later in USA for New York Cosmos taking total to 1281 and then to 1283 after two farewell performances
1006 goals, Franz 'Bimbo' Binder, in Austrian football, 1921–50

European Championship Finals

European Nations Cup 1960–68

Year	Winners		Runners-up	Venue	Attendance	Referee	Entries	Top scorer (3 or more goals in final tournament)	
1960	USSR	2–1	Yugoslavia	Paris, France	17 966	Ellis, England	17	—	
1964	Spain	2–1	USSR	Madrid, Spain	120 00	Holland, England	29	—	
1968	Italy	1–1	Yugoslavia	Rome, Italy	60 000	Dienst, Switzerland	31	—	
		2–0			75 000				
1972	West Germany	3–0	USSR	Brussels, Belgium	43 437	Marschall, Austria	32	Gerd Muller (West Germany)	4
1976	Czechoslovakia	2–2*	West Germany	Belgrade, Yugoslavia	45 000	Gonella, Italy	32	Dieter Muller (West Germany)	4
	(Czechs won 5–3 on penalties)								
1980	West Germany	2–1	Belgium	Rome, Italy	47 864	Rainea, Rumania	32	Klaus Allofs (West Germany)	3
1984	France	2–0	Spain	Paris, France	48 000	Christov, Czechoslovakia	33	Michel Platini (France)	8
1988	Holland	2–0	USSR	Munich, West Germany	72 308	Vautrot, France	33	Van Basten (Holland)	5

* after extra time

Marco Van Basten achieved an impressive treble for club and country by scoring in a major European final in three consecutive seasons. He scored in the 1987 Cup-Winners' Cup Final for Ajax, in the 1988 European Championship Final for Holland and in the 1989 European Cup Final for AC Milan (Colorsport)

WORLD FOOTBALL

The World Cup 1930–1990

Year	Final	Venue	Attendance	Referee
1930	Uruguay 4 Argentina 2	Montevideo, Italy	90 000	Langenus, Belgium
1934	Italy 2 Czechoslovakia 1 (aet)	Rome, Italy	50 000	Eklind, Sweden
1938	Italy 4 Hungary 2	Paris, France	45 000	Capdeville, France
1950	Uruguay 2 Brazil 1	Rio de Janeiro, Brazil	199 854	Reader, England
1954	West Germany 3 Hungary 2	Berne, Switzerland	60 000	Ling, England
1958	Brazil 5 Sweden 2	Stockholm, Sweden	49 737	Guigue, France
1962	Brazil 3 Czechoslovakia 1	Santiago, Chile	68 679	Latychev, USSR
1966	England 4 West Germany 2 (aet)	Wembley, England	93 802	Dienst, Switzerland
1970	Brazil 4 Italy 1	Mexico City, Mexico	107 412	Glockner, East Germany
1974	West Germany 2 Holland 1	Munich, West Germany	77 833	Taylor, England
1978	Argentina 3 Holland 1 (aet)	Buenos Aires, Argentina	77 000	Gonella, Italy
1982	Italy 3 West Germany 1	Madrid, Spain	90 080	Coelho, Brazil
1986	Argentina 3 West Germany 2	Mexico City, Mexico	114 580	Filho, Brazil
1990	West Germany 1 Argentina 0	Rome, Italy	73 603	Codesal, Mexico

World Cup: Winners Records

Year	Winners	P	W	D	L	F	A	Players used
1930	Uruguay	4	4	0	0	16	3	15
1934	Italy	5	4	1	0	12	3	17
1938	Italy	4	4	0	0	11	5	14
1950	Uruguay	4	3	1	0	15	5	14
1954	West Germany	6	5	0	1	25	14	18
1958	Brazil	6	5	1	0	16	4	16
1962	Brazil	6	5	1	0	14	5	12
1966	England	6	5	1	0	11	3	15
1970	Brazil	6	6	0	0	19	7	15
1974	West Germany	7	6	0	1	13	4	18
1978	Argentina	7	5	1	1	15	4	17
1982	Italy	7	4	3	0	12	6	15
1986	Argentina	7	6	1	0	14	5	18
1990	West Germany	7	5	2	0	15	5	17

Bobby Moore with the Jules Rimet Trophy accompanied by George Cohen after the 1966 World Cup triumph (JR)

Dino Zoff the Italian goalkeeper who captained his team to the 1982
World Cup success (Associated Sports Photography)

World Cup: Gates and goals

Year	Aggregate attendances	Average attendance	Matches	Goals	Average	Top Scorer	Goals
1930	434 500	24 139	18	70	3.88	Guillermo Stabile (Argentina)	8
1934	395 000	23 235	17	70	4.11	Angelo Schiavio (Italy)	4
						Oldrich Nejedly (Czechoslovakia)	
						Edmund Cohen (Germany)	
1938	483 000	26 833	18	84	4.66	Leonidas Da Silva (Brazil)	8
1950	1 337 00	60 772	22	88	4.00	Ademir (Brazil)	9
1954	943 000	36 270	26	140	5.38	Sandor Kocsis (Hungary)	11
1958	868 000	24 800	35	126	3.60	Just Fontaine (France)	13
1962	776 000	24 250	32	89	2.78	Drazen Jerkovic (Yugoslavia)	5
1966	614 677	50 458	32	89	2.78	Eusebio (Portugal)	9
1970	1 673 975	52 312	32	95	2.96	Gerd Muller (West Germany)	10
1974	1 774 002	46 685	38	97	2.55	Grzegorz Lato (Poland)	7
1978	1 610 215	42 374	38	102	2.68	Mario Kempes (Argentina)	6
1982	1 766 277	33 967	52	146	2.81	Paolo Rossi (Italy)	6
1986	2 401 480	46 184	52	132	2.53	Gary Lineker (England)	6
1990	2 510 686	48 282	52	115	2.21	Salvatore Schillaci (Italy)	6

South American Championship

Year	Venue	Teams	Matches	Goals	Champions	Pts
1916	Buenos Aires, Argentina	4	6	18	Uruguay	5
1917	Montevideo, Uruguay	4	6	21	Uruguay	6
1919	Rio de Janeiro, Brazil[1]	4	7	26	Brazil	7
1920	Valparaiso, Chile	4	6	16	Uruguay	5
1921	Buenos Aires, Argentina	4	6	14	Argentina	6
1922	Rio de Janeiro, Brazil[2]	5	11	23	Brazil	7
1923	Montevideo, Uruguay	4	6	18	Uruguay	6
1924	Montevideo, Uruguay	4	6	15	Uruguay	5
1925	Buenos Aires, Argentina[3]	3	6	26	Argentina	7
1926	Santiago de Chile, Chile	5	10	55	Uruguay	8
1927	Lima, Peru	4	6	37	Argentina	6
1929	Buenos Aires, Argentina	4	6	23	Argentina	6
1935	Lima, Peru*	4	6	18	Uruguay	6
1937	Buenos Aires, Argentina[4]	6	16	68	Argentina	10
1939	Lima, Peru	5	10	47	Peru	8
1941	Santiago de Chile, Chile*	5	10	32	Argentina	8
1942	Montevideo, Uruguay[5]	7	21	81	Uruguay	12
1945	Santiago de Chile, Chile*	7	21	89	Argentina	11
1946	Buenos Aires, Argentina*	6	15	61	Argentina	10
1947	Guayaquil, Ecuador	8	28	102	Argentina	13
1949	Rio de Janeiro, Brazil[6]	8	29	130	Brazil	14
1953	Lima, Peru[7]	7	21	67	Paraguay	10
1955	Santiago de Chile, Chile	6	15	73	Argentina	9
1956	Montevideo, Uruguay*	6	15	38	Uruguay	9
1957	Lima, Peru	7	21	101	Argentina	10
1959	Buenos Aires, Argentina	7	21	86	Argentina	11
1959	Guayaquil, Ecuador*	5	20	39	Uruguay	7
1963	La Paz & Cochabamba, Bolivia	7	21	91	Bolivia	11
1967	Montevideo, Uruguay	6	15	49	Uruguay	9
1975	(Reorganized	10	25	79	Peru	N/A
1979	on home and	10	25	63	Paraguay	N/A
1983	away basis)	10	24	55	Uruguay	N/A
1987	Argentina	10	13	33	Uruguay	N/A
1989	Brazil	10	26	56	Brazil	N/A

* extraordinary tournaments
[1] play-off; Brazil 1 Uruguay 0
[2] play-off; Brazil 3 Paraguay 1; Uruguay withdrew
[3] two legs were played (home and away)
[4] play-off; Argentina 2 Brazil 0
[5] Chile withdrew
[6] play-off; Brazil 7 Paraguay 0
[7] play-off; Paraguay 3 Brazil 2 (organized by the Paraguayan Football League)

South American Cup (Copa Libertadores)

Year	Winner	Entries	Matches	Goals	Year	Winner	Entries	Matches	Goal
1960	Penarol (Uruguay)	8	13	39	1975	Independiente	21	76	208
1961	Penarol	9	16	52	1976	Cruziero (Brazil)	21	77	211
1962	Santos (Brazil)	10	25	101	1977	Boca Juniors (Argentina)	21	75	152
1963	Santos	9	19	63	1978	Boca Juniors	21	75	181
1964	Independiente (Argentina)	10	25	89	1979	Olimpia (Paraguay)	21	74	211
1965	Independiente	10	27	72	1980	Nacional	21	75	160
1966	Penarol	17	94	218	1981	Flamengo (Brazil)	21	77	220
1967	Racing (Argentina)	19	114	355	1982	Penarol	21	73	163
1968	Estudiantes (Argentina)	21	93	232	1983	Gremio (Brazil)	21	74	179
1969	Estudiantes	17	74	211	1984	Independiente	21	75	206
1970	Estudiantes	19	88	253	1985	Argentios Juniors (Argentina)	21	71	181
1971	Nacional (Uruguay)	21	73	196	1986	River Plate (Argentina)	19	64	166
1972	Independiente	20	69	176	1987	Penarol	21	76	207
1973	Independiente	19	66	190	1988	Nacional	21	82	169
1974	Independiente	21	76	178	1989	Nacional (Colombia)	21	91	233

Roberto Rivelino, who has made more appearances for Brazil than any of his fellow countrymen (Syndication International)

World Club Championship 1960–89

Year	Winners		Runners-up	Venue	Attendance	Referee
1960	Real Madrid	0–0	Penarol	Montevideo	75 000	Praddaude (Argentina)
		5–1		Madrid	125 000	Aston (England)
1961	Penarol	0–1	Benfica	Lisbon	55 000	Ebert (Switzerland)
		5–0		Montevideo	57 358	Nay Foino (Argentina)
		2–1		Montevideo	62 300	Praddaude (Argentina)
1962	Santos	3–2	Benfica	Rio de Janeiro	90 000	Ramirez (Paraguay)
		5–2		Lisbon	75 000	Schwinte (France)
1963	Santos	2–4	AC Milan	Milan	80 000	Harbseliner (Austria)
		4–2		Rio de Janeiro	150 000	Brozzi (Argentina)
		1–0		Rio de Janeiro	121 000	Brozzi (Argentina)
1964	Internazionale	0–1	Independiente	Buenos Aires	70 000	Armando Marques (Brazil)
		2–0		Milan	70 000	Geroe (Hungary)
		1–0		Madrid	45 000	De Mendibil (Spain)
1965	Internazionale	3–0	Independiente	Milan	70 000	Kreitlein (West Germany)
		0–0		Buenos Aires	70 000	Yamasaki (Peru)
1966	Penarol	2–0	Real Madrid	Montevideo	70 000	Vicuna (Chile)
		2–0		Madrid	70 000	Lo Bello (Italy)
1967	Racing Club	0–1	Celtic	Hampden Park	103 000	Gardeazabal (Spain)
		2–1		Buenos Aires	80 000	Esteban Marino (Spain)
		1–0		Montevideo	65 172	Osorio (Paraguay)
1968	Estudientes	1–0	Manchester United	Buenos Aires	65 000	Miranda (Paraguay)
		1–1		Old Trafford		
1969	AC Milan	3–0	Estudiantes	Milan	80 000	Machin (France)
		1–2		Buenos Aires	65 000	Massaro (Chile)
1970	Feyenoord	2–2	Estudiantes	Buenos Aires	65 000	Glockner (East Germany)
		1–0		Rotterdam	70 000	Tejada (Peru)
1971	Nacional	1–1	Panathanaikos	Athens	60 000	
		2–1		Montevideo	70 000	
1972	Ajax	1–1	Independiente	Buenos Aires	65 000	Bakhramov (USSR)
		3–0		Amsterdam	65 000	Romey (Paraguay)
1973	Independiente	1–0	Juventus	Rome	35 000	Belcourt (Belgium)
1974	Atletico Madrid	0–1	Independiente	Buenos Aires	60 000	Corver (Holland)
		2–0		Madrid	45 000	Robles (Chile)
1975	Independiente and Bayern Munich could not agree on dates to play					
1976	Bayern Munich	2–0	Cruzeiro	Munich	22 000	Pestarino (Argentina)
		0–0		Belo Horizonte	114 000	Partridge (England)
1977	Boca Juniors	2–2	Moenchengladbach	Buenos Aires	50 000	Doudine (Bulgaria)
		3–0		Karlsruhe	21 500	Cerullo (Uruguay)
1978	Not contested; Liverpool declined to play					
1979	Olimpia	1–0	Malmo	Malmo	4 811	Partridge (England)
		2–1		Asuncion	35 000	Cardellino (Uruguay)
1980	Nacional	1–0	Nottingham Forest	Tokyo	62 000	Klein (Israel)
1981	Flamengo	3–0	Liverpool	Tokyo	62 000	Vasquez (Mexico)
1982	Penarol	2–0	Aston Villa	Tokyo	62 000	Siles (Costa Rica)
1983	Gremio	2–1	Hamburg	Tokyo	62 000	Vautrot (France)
1984	Independiente	1–0	Liverpool	Tokyo	62 000	Filho (Brazil)
1985	Juventus	2–2*	Argentinos Juniors	Tokyo	62 000	Roth (West Germany)
	(Juventus won 4–2 on penalties)					

1986	River Plate	1-0	Steaua Bucharest	Tokyo	62 000	Bazan (Uruguay)
1987	Porto	2-1*	Penarol	Tokyo	45 000	Wohrer (Austria)
1988	Nacional	2-2*	PSV Eindhoven	Tokyo	62 000	Palacio (Colombia)
	(Nacional won 7-6 on penalties)					
1989	AC Milan	1-0*	Nacional (Colombia)	Tokyo	62 000	Fredriksson (Sweden)

* after extra time

International Records

Most capped players in the world

Player	Caps	Career
Hector Chumpitaz (Peru)	*150	1963–82
Peter Shilton (England)	125	1970–90
Robert Rivelino (Brazil)	*120	1968–79
Pat Jennings (Northern Ireland)	119	1964–86
Bjorn Nordqvist (Sweden)	115	1963–78
Dino Zoff (Italy)	112	1968–83
Pele (Brazil)	*111	1957–71
Tarak (Tunisia) †	110	1976–90
Oleg Blokhin (USSR)	109	1972–88
Attouga (Tunisia)	109	1963–79
Bobby Moore (England)	108	1962–73
Ladislau Boloni (Rumania)	108	1975–88
Djalma Santos (Brazil)	*107	1952–68
Bobby Charlton (England)	106	1958–70
Billy Wright (England)	105	1936–59
Thorbjorn Svenssen (Norway)	104	1947–62
Leonel Sanchez (Chile)	*104	1955–67
Franz Beckenbauer (West Germany)	103	1965–67
Grzegorz Lato (Poland)	103	1971–82
Kenny Dalglish (Scotland)	102	1971–87
Kazimierz Deyna (Poland)	102	1968–78
Joachin Streich (East Germany)	102	1971–84
Morten Olsen (Denmark)	102	1970–89
Heinz Hermann (East Germany) †	101	1978–90
Jozsef Bozsik (Hungary)	100	1947–62
Hans-Jurgen Dorner (East Germany)	100	1971–85
Gylmar (Brazil)	*100	1953–69

Most international goals

Player		
Pele (Brazil)	97	1957–71
Ferenc Puskas (Hungary)	83	1945–56
Sandor Kocsis (Hungary)	75	1948–56
Gerd Muller (West Germany)	68	1966–74

* includes matches against representative teams and others
† still adding to total

Joachim Streich made his 100th appearance for East Germany against England at Wembley in 1984 (Associated Sports Photography)

Kazimierz Deyna was the first Pole to reach 100 caps for his country (Associated Sports Photography)

The World Football Scene

Withdrawal symptoms

In February 1990 Dynamo Tbilisi were instructed to withdraw from the Soviet championship by their Georgian federation. The following month Lithuania withdrew Zhalgiris Vilnius from the championship. Another Georgian club, Guria Lanchkuti, also failed to signify their intention of participating in the season.

Back home

In February 1990 East Germany announced that three foreigners would be permitted per club. The first 'foreigner' turned out to be a former East German, Jens Koenig of Wismut Aue, who had taken the offer of automatic citizenship in West Germany.

Not again!

On 13 February 1990 Montpellier sacked their manager Aime Jacquet exactly a year after he had been dismissed by Bordeaux.

Coffee break

On 24 February 1990 Cannes suspended their former international midfield player Luis Fernandez after a row with coach Jean Fernandez (unrelated) because he ordered a cup of coffee in a restaurant while still at the dinner table, instead of waiting until the players had entered the lounge.

East of Eden

In 1989 the Venezuelan championship was increased to 16 clubs. The winners proved to be Mineros de Guayana, the first team from the eastern part of the country to win the title; and the runners-up were Pepeganga from Margarita, the tourist paradise island whose home ground was a park pitch!

Manni's many games

On 25 February 1989 Manni Kaltz equalled Klaus Fichtel's record of 552 Bundesliga games in a 2–2 draw with Fichtel's former club Borussia Dortmund.

Devilish Turkey

On 29 March 1989 Greece met Turkey in Athens for the first time since 1952. Turkey won 1–0 with a goal from Ridvan Dilmen, known as 'The Devil'. It was the seventh meeting between the two neighbours; Turkey have won five times and Greece twice.

Soviet niet

The Dutch club Vitesse Arnhem signed two Soviet players in January 1990. They were Valeri Masalitin, top scorer in the USSR with 32 goals, and Sergei Krutov, a midfield player, both from TSKA Moscow, the Army club. The two clubs had a twinning arrangement. Krutov was later denied a work permit.

Swiss migration

In 1989 there were 64 foreigners playing in the Swiss Division One. Of these, 13 were Italians, eight Swedes, eight West Germans, six Yugoslavs, four Danes, four Chileans, three Dutch, three Argentines, two Poles, two Spaniards and one each from 11 other countries.

Unlimited success

In 1988 Rosenborg Trondheim celebrated becoming the first limited company among Norwegian clubs by winning the League and Cup double. Their average attendance was 12 000.

Pontoons only

On 14 December 1988 Partizan Belgrade and Celik established a Yugoslav record after their League game had ended 2–2. In the subsequent penalty shoot-out Partizan won 11–10.

Chinese chequers

In 1988 Qixin Pharmaceutica, a factory in China's city of Guangzhou, agreed to a one-year sponsorship of the national team and also the national women's team.

Dividends divided

In 1989 the Placido Galindo national championship in Peru was divided into metropolitan, northern, central and southern sections. Penalties were used for the first time to decide drawn games.

Kiwis close call

The finish of the Air New Zealand National Soccer League in 1989 was a close affair. Before the last day of the season, Mount Maunganui had a two point lead over Napier City Rovers. Maunganui had a home game with mid-table Manurewa, Napier were away to bottom place Papatoetoe. Napier were fortunate to win 2–1 thanks to a defensive error, but Maunganui had more of a struggle in their match. With the score

0–0 they were awarded a penalty only for Frank Van Hattum, the 1982 World Cup goalkeeper and ex-Maunganui himself, to save it. This left both teams on the same points with the same record of wins, draws and losses. But Napier edged it by a one goal difference.

Goalkeepers turned poachers

Jose Rene Higuita the Nacional Medellin and Colombian international goalkeeper had scored 26 penalties and missed three for his club, and converted four successfully for his country before the World Cup qualifying game with Paraguay on 27 August 1989. Colombia equalised at 1–1 with three minutes remaining. But in the last minute Higuita conceded a penalty. Jose Luis Chilavert, the Paraguayan goalkeeper, ran the length of the field to score from the spot kick to give Paraguay a 2–1 win.

Fillol the matches

Ubaldo Fillol, the Argentina goalkeeper in their successful 1978 World Cup team, celebrated his 39th birthday on 21 July 1989. He had completed 542 matches in the Argentine Division One since his debut for Quilmes in 1969. Subsequently he had played for Racing Club, River Plate, Argentinos Juniors, Flamengo (Brazil), Atletico Madrid (Spain) and Racing again. He had won 53 caps for Argentina. His total number of Division One goals conceded had been 554, an average of 1.02 per game.

Out of pocket

Harald Schumacher, the former West German international goalkeeper and captain of Fenerbahce when they won the 1988–89 Turkish championship, paid more than £100,000 out of his own pocket in bonuses to players because the club president was hard-up.

Luxembourg Lille

The Luxembourg Football Federation was ordered by FIFA to find a different venue for their World Cup qualifying match with Belgium on 1 June 1989, as the national stadium was being redeveloped. Luxembourg wanted to play at Lille, but Switzerland, Belgium's rivals in the qualifying group, objected, saying that it would be like a home game for the Belgians. However the game went ahead at Lille and Belgium won 5–0.

In the right place

On 30 December 1989 Lionello Manfredonia collapsed with a heart attack after taking a corner kick for Roma at Bologna. He was revived thanks to a defibrillator installed at the ground, the only one in an Italian stadium. He came out of a coma on 1 January and left hospital eight days later.

Blowing the whistle

On 3 January 1990 the Bulgarian national referees association severed all links with their FA and threatened a token strike if Bulgarian TV refused to broadcast a weekly programme aimed at educating players and public on refereeing.

Now you see them . . .

On 18 January 1990 Dublin City, a team in name only, had their application to join the Scottish League rejected.

The numbers game

In 1989 the 20 Division One clubs in Mexico came from 13 different cities and utilised 16 different grounds. The Division Two clubs numbered 40 from 37 places and the Division Three teams amounting to 60 came from 54 sources. Full professional football had started in Mexico in 1943–44.

Rule of Thom

In January 1990 Andreas Thom became the first East German to be transferred to West Germany officially, when he moved from Dynamo Berlin to Bayer Leverkusen. The fee was said to be £1.6 million although the method of payment was not disclosed. However, Dynamo refused to allow Rainer Ernst to join Borussia Dortmund even though he had been training there for a week. The reason they gave was that Ernst had not been playing well enough to deserve a move. Dynamo Berlin, the club of the Ministry of State Security and the hated 'Stasi' secret police, subsequently changed their name to FC Berlin. Meanwhile Thom scored the first Bundesliga goal after the winter break.

It pays to advertise

Sweden's Malmo celebrated their first year as a professional club in January 1990. They made a profit of £850 000, chiefly through income derived from advertising and television.

No place for a teenager

When Blendi Nallbani kept goal for Albania against England at Wembley on 26 April 1989 he was only 17 years and 19 days old. He was the youngest senior international to play at the stadium. England won 5–0.

Right off the Bolivia

When the Bolivian national team was preparing for the qualifying tournament in the 1990 World Cup, no club in La Paz would allow them to train on their ground. The players first trained in a local park before deciding to move to Oruro some 240 km away. Bolivia failed to qualify.

The wanderer

In 1989 FK Austria signed Yevgeni Milevsky, a striker, from Spartak Moscow. He had previously been with Dougava Riga, the Latvian club, and left the Soviet Union as an emigrant but had to surrender his passport, thus becoming stateless. He was also of Jewish origin.

Crazy custodians?

Goalkeepers are supposed to be mad. Certainly the French variety includes some odd names – Bats, Dropsy and Rust have all featured in international games in the 1980s. The list of goalkeepers in Divisions One and Two for 1989–90 also included Hours, Mary and Simonella.

Capping it all

Jan Ceulemans won his 82nd cap for Belgium in a World Cup qualifying match against Denmark on 23 August 1989 to establish a new record. He was presented with a special cap with 82 embroidered stars on it by Paul Van Himst, holder of 81 Belgian caps. Belgium won the game 3–0.

Freedom to stay away

On the 40th anniversary in 1989 of the founding of Honved, the crack Hungarian Army club which produced so many internationals for the national team which dominated the 1950s, the club gave free admission to the game with Vasas. The gates of the Joszef Bozsik stadium, named after the club's midfield player from the same era, were flung open and Zoltan Czibor, the legendary left-winger, ceremoniously kicked off. Unfortunately only 5000 spectators turned up.

Wizards of Aus

In 1989 Marconi won the Australian National Soccer League championship for the second successive year, beating Sydney Olympic 1–0 in the Grand Final. Zlatko Nastevski headed the injury-time winner before a crowd of 23 387 in the Parramatta Stadium. It was a record crowd for the competition and the third highest for a club game in the country.

Uruguayan players have increasingly had to venture abroad in search of a living. Even this 1966 World Cup squad contained several who sought foreign shores. Front row left to right: Cortes, Veira, Rocha, Silva, Perez. Back: Caetano, Troche, Mazurkiewicz, Goncalvez, Ubinas and Manicera. Troche played in West Germany and Mazurkiewicz in nearby Brazil (Syndication International)

The export game

In the year up to 1989, nine South American countries had transferred 245 Division One players to foreign leagues. Uruguay, with 575 Division One players registered, had lost 800 players to other countries in the previous ten years. Argentina had 232 players in action in 23 different countries abroad including eight in Japan and one in Greece.

No score or roar

In 1988–89 attendances in the West German Bundesliga barely reached 5.6 million. The average of 18 292 per game was the fourth worst since the competition was established in 1963–64. But the total of 852 goals was the poorest on record at 2.78 per game.

Lifetime association

Gerald Vanenburg, who was transferred to PSV Eindhoven from Ajax in 1986 for £500 000, signed a new eight-year contract with his new club in 1989. It guaranteed him £300 000 a year and subsequently a £20 000-a-year pension until he reaches 60.

No Yorke bar

On 22 November 1989 Trinidad's World Cup striker Dwight Yorke joined Aston Villa awaiting a work permit to be allowed to play. He subsequently made his debut as a substitute against Crystal Palace in the 82nd minute of a Division One match at Selhurst Park.

No substitute
In the aftermath of the Romanian revolution in the winter of 1989, Dinamo Bucharest attempted to change their name. As the team of the Ministry of the Interior associated with the hated Securitate secret police, they were understandably anxious to distance themselves from such a connection. The first name which sprang to mind was Unirea Tricolor, from a long-since defunct club. UEFA even accepted the alteration as Dinamo were still competing in the Cup-Winners' Cup. Unirea Tricolor had gained promotion from the old Division Two to Division One in 1938–39 and won the title in their second season. The war finally caused the championship to be abandoned and when it resumed Unirea Tricolor were back in Division Two. They did regain Division One status but then came the reorganisation of the sport on Soviet lines and the club disappeared. But when the 1989–90 championship was resumed, Dinamo Bucharest continued to play under that name.

Poles together
In 1989–90 two Polish internationals were transferred to Celtic from Legia Warsaw. Striker Dariusz Dziekanowski cost £540 000 and defender Dariusz Wdowczyk £400 000.

Draw not war
On 5 November 1989 in the aftermath of the Gulf War between Iraq and Iran, the two countries met each other in Kuwait in the Islamic Friendship and Peace Festival. Appropriately enough the game ended in a 0–0 draw. The two teams each received two copies of the Koran.

Never on a weekday
In the first leg of the Concacaf Champions Cup match between Herediano and Universidad Guadalajara in San Jose, Costa Rica on 13 October 1989, rain caused the game to be stopped at half-time with the score 0–0. The pitch became unplayable and it was decided to finish the match the following day. Unfortunately the law prevented any spectators to be present as it was during working hours on a weekday. Herediano, the local team, won 2–1.

A Grecian earn
On 4 February 1990 Olympiakos beat Ionikos 3–0 and Panayiotis Tsaluhidis set up a new record for the Greek League by having scored in five consecutive games.

The famous five
Colo Colo, the most popular club in Chile, regained the championship in 1989. The club name is a Chilean expression meaning wildcat and the nickname of 'The Chiefs'. They were founded in 1925 by five disgruntled members of Magallanes.

Not too late to Lucerne
When Lucerne won the Swiss championship in 1989 it was their first such title in 88 years of existence. Promoted to Division One for the first time in 1936, their only other honour had been winning the Swiss Cup in 1960.

Game of two halves?
The longest match staged in Spain might well have been the Division One fixture between Osasuna and Real Madrid in the 1988–89 season. On 27 January 1989 Osasuna were leading Real 1–0 after 43 minutes in Pamplona when the Madrid players walked off the field following the pelting of their goalkeeper by a variety of missiles from the crowd. The match was re-scheduled for a neutral ground in Zaragoza on 3 May, but beginning with the moment that the previous game had been abandoned. In the remaining 47 minutes, Real managed to score and drew this marathon match 1–1.

Remote control
On 4 June 1989 the USA played Peru in the final of the Marlborough Cup at East Rutherford, New Jersey. The national coach Bob Gansler was not at the match, but at Milwaukee attending his two sons' graduation ceremony. He watched the game on TV, telephoning half-time instructions to his No. 2, Joe Machnik. The USA, leading 1–0 at half-time, won 3–0 before a crowd of 33 133.

Close Finnish
On 31 May 1989 a record crowd for a football match in Finland watched the World Cup qualifying game with Holland in Helsinki. Holland won 1–0 with a goal from Wim Kieft in the 87th minute. The attendance was 46 217.

All-Ireland
Derry City were members of the Irish League in Northern Ireland from 1929 to 1972. They disbanded and did not re-appear again until 1985 when they gained admission to the League of Ireland in the Republic. In 1988–89 they won three trophies: League, Cup and League Cup.

Napoli surrendered their championship in 1988–89 but the players had plenty to celebrate, winning the UEFA Cup, and the groundsman still had to keep the pitch in perfect order (Allsport)

Italian gates
In 1988–89 average attendances in the Italian Serie A (Division One) fell from 30 493 to 29 813 per game. AC Milan were the best supported with an average of 72 340, while Napoli had 61 792.

Inter-record
When Internazionale won the 1988–89 Italian League championship with a 4–2 win over Atalanta they reached 56 points from their 32 games, to beat the record for a 16-team programme in the country set up 29 years earlier by Juventus with 55 points.

Double century
Morten Olsen made his 100th international appearance for Denmark on 26 April 1989 against Bulgaria. He appeared in his 101st on the occasion of the centenary of the Danish Football Association on 10 May.

Title contenders
When Luis Angel Firpo won the El Salvador championship in 1989 it was their first honour in 66 years in the Division One. They beat Cojutepeque 6–5 on penalties after a 2–2 draw which went into extra time. The club is named after a famous Argentine boxer.

About the size of it
Brazil is 65 times the size of England. Of the 25 states and two territories all but three of the states and both territories have their own championships. The leading states are: Sao Paulo, Rio de Janeiro, Bahia, Rio Grande do Sul and Minas Gerais. Of the 17 others only Parana and Pernambuco have competitions considered Division One status.

Farewell to arms
Dukla Prague are probably the poorest supported of any club to have achieved as many League and Cup honours in one of the leading European countries. They are rarely blessed with crowds of 2000 and then only when playing in a local derby with either Bohemians, Slavia or Sparta in Prague when the visiting supporters swell the gate. As the Czechoslovakian Army club they are not popular.

Hugo a-go-go
On 31 March 1990 Hugo Sanchez, the Real Madrid and Mexican international centre-forward, was shown the yellow card after he criticised the official in a half-time interview on the radio during a match in Zaragoza. Real won 1–0.

Brazilian flavour
In 1988–89 there were 177 foreign players in the Portuguese Division One including 110 from Brazil. Eight teams could field a complete eleven of imported players.

Extra Time

Hunt for goals
In 1938–39, Walter Hunt scored four, four and three goals respectively in Division Three (North) matches against Lincoln City, Accrington Stanley and Rochdale for Carlisle United, the three clubs in question having been his former teams.

Family fare
On 17 February 1973 in a Division One match, Newcastle United drew 1–1 with Wolverhampton Wanderers, at Molineux. Kenny Hibbitt put Wolves ahead in the first half and his brother Terry equalised after the interval.

Lighting up the Light Blues
The first Scottish League game played under floodlights was on 7 March 1956 when Rangers beat Queen of the South 8–0 in Division One. Don Kichenbrand scored five goals.

Harris survives
Martin Harris scored two goals for Workington when they were beaten 6–3 at Doncaster Rovers in a Division Four match on 19 April 1977. Doncaster-born Harris was the only survivor from Workington's team which met Doncaster Rovers in the FA Cup first round at Workington on 20 November 1982 as substitute. Doncaster won 2–1.

Varying results
In 23 Division Three (North) home matches in the 1950–51 season, Scunthorpe United conceded only nine goals. In the same season and division, Hartlepools United scored just nine goals away and failed to score in any of their last 11 away fixtures. Only four places separated the two teams at the end of the season, Scunthorpe finishing 12th with 44 points and Hartlepools 16th with 39.

Anfield astounds
When Liverpool were beaten 1–0 by Bradford City in a League Cup second round first leg match at Valley Parade on 27 August 1980, it was their first away defeat in a competitive match against a club from below Division Two since 1959, when they had lost 2–1 to Worcester City in an FA Cup tie. No team below Division Two has won a cup-tie at Anfield since Norwich City, then members of the Southern League, did so 3–2 in 1909.

Asa Hartford, intense as ever, in Albion colours early in his long career (Tony Matthews, West Bromwich Albion)

All heart
For a player rejected by Leeds United early in his career because of a heart condition, Asa Hartford has shown remarkable durability. After service with West Bromwich Albion, Manchester City, Nottingham Forest, Everton, Manchester City (again), Norwich City, Bolton Wanderers, Stockport County and Oldham Athletic he joined Shrewsbury Town at the start of 1989–90. His first-class career had spanned two decades and seen 735 League appearances.

Steve's unique duo
Bangor-born centre-forward Steve Balcombe scored on his League debut for Leeds United against Aston Villa on 3 October 1981 in a 1–1 draw in Division One. He also made one substitute appearance for the Welsh Under-21 side against France in Troyes on 24 February 1982 in a goalless draw. These were his only senior appearances.

Smee: it's mine

Reading-born striker Roger Smee was re-signed by his local club in 1973, three years after they had given him a free transfer. He had been on the books of Chelsea at one time. In 1983 he was the leader of a movement which made a takeover bid for Reading FC and he subsequently became chairman.

Miner importance

George Richardson was working in the pit at Manton Colliery on the morning of Saturday 8 April 1933. In the afternoon he played in the Colliery team and immediately afterwards was transferred to Huddersfield Town, playing in their Central League side on the Monday and the first team on the Wednesday.

Harold's one-off

Harold McNaughton had the unusual distinction of appearing in a Merseyside derby for Liverpool against Everton, keeping a clean sheet as the unbeaten goalkeeper, yet never again playing for them in the League. It happened on 23 October 1920 when Liverpool won 1–0.

Villa at the double

For three months in 1947, Aston Villa held two unusual records of quick scoring. On 3 December 1938 Bob Iverson, playing at left-half against Charlton Athletic at Villa Park, achieved the feat of scoring a goal 9.6 seconds after the kick-off, then a British record. On 17 September 1947 the Australian Rugby Union team scored a try against Midland Counties after seven seconds on the same ground. Villa's football record remained until Willie Sharp scored for Partick Thistle after seven seconds against Queen of the South in a Scottish League Division One match on 20 December 1947.

Bristol fashion

The relegation of Bristol City and Bristol Rovers from Division Two at the end of the 1980–81 season was the first time two teams from the same provincial town or city had gone down in the same season since Bradford City were relegated from Division One and Bradford Park Avenue from Division Two at the end of 1921–22.

Money matters

The 1979–80 season produced the first instance of a club making a million-pound profit and another losing a similar amount. Nottingham Forest's profit was £1 258 000 while Manchester City lost £1 663 000.

A youthful-looking Emlyn Hughes (centre) defends the Blackpool goal from a Spurs attack in October 1966 (Associated Sports Photography)

Crazy Horse's marathon

Emlyn Hughes holds the record for the highest number of first-class matches in which any player has appeared in one season. In 1972–73 he made 74 appearances. They comprised 41 for Liverpool in Division One, four in the FA Cup, eight in the League Cup and 12 in the UEFA Cup. He also played in eight full internationals for England and in the Common Market Entry match at Wembley for The Three against The Six.

Black days for the 'B's

In 1970–71 Lancashire suffered badly from relegation. Burnley and Blackpool went down from Division One to Division Two, Blackburn Rovers and Bolton Wanderers from Two to Three and Bury from Three to Four. Barrow had to seek re-election after finishing bottom of Division Four.

Lure of the cup

After beating Derby County 2–1 in November 1971, Huddersfield Town failed to win another Division One game. Yet during the same period they won three FA Cup ties at Burnley and at home to Fulham and West Ham United.

North–South divide
Of the original 22 clubs in Division Three (South) on its formation in 1920 only Merthyr Town and Newport County have since lost Football League status. Gillingham were voted out in 1938 but returned on the expansion of the Third Division in 1950. But of the original 20 in Division Three (North) in 1921, there have been the following permanent casualties: Wigan Borough, Nelson, Barrow, Durham City, Ashington, Accrington Stanley, Southport and Stalybridge Celtic.

Away goals rule, OK?
York City had the misfortune to be knocked out of the League Cup in successive seasons on the away goals rule. In 1979–80 Mansfield Town beat them in a first round tie while in 1980–81 it was Bristol Rovers who eliminated them in the second round.

Amateur Gunners
When Arsenal beat Stoke City 1–0 on 19 October 1946 they included three amateurs in their side: Bernard Joy, Kevin O'Flanagan and Albert Gudmundsson.

Deepdale deep down
Preston North End have occupied their Deepdale ground longer than any other contemporary Football League club. They have been in residence since their formation in 1881.

Easy for Easson
Dave Easson was given a free transfer by Dundee and joined Arbroath, for whom he scored a club record of 45 League goals in 1958–59 without any other player in the club reaching double figures. Their overall total was 86.

The not so Real times
Real Madrid had a justifiable reputation as the leading club on the continent in the 1950s. But they suffered on several occasions at the hands of Scottish teams in former years. Motherwell beat them 3–1 in Madrid in 1927 while Dundee had beaten them 2–0 in a tour four years earlier.

Topsy turvy Mariners
Grimsby Town have become the Football League's champion shuttlecock through having changed their divisional status more than 20 times. Promotion to Division Three in 1990 represented their 24th move which included losing League status for one season in 1910–11.

Numbering the players
In 1933 Tottenham Hotspur proposed that players should be numbered in Football League matches but it was defeated at the Annual General Meeting. In the Cup Final that year, both teams were numbered for the first time but from 1–22. Numbering of players in the Football League became official from the start of the 1939–40 season.

Legal niceties
Illegally approaching players is not a new facet of the game. In the 1890–91 season Wolverhampton Wanderers induced Sam Thomson, a Preston North End player, to join them without that club's permission and they were fined £50 for their misconduct.

Player power
In March 1902 the Stockport County team, unpaid for some weeks in Division Two, revolted against the club's management, selected their own team and shared out the gate money to compensate for the lack of wages. They did manage to avoid bottom place that season.

Priorities!
When Workington increased their board of directors to 13 in October 1966, it was reported that they then had more directors than professionals on their books.

Ubiquitous (1)
Brentford became the first club to play against all other 91 teams in the Football League during their first season in Division Four in 1962–63. Grimsby Town are the only League team to have met more than 100 different sides in the competition. At the start of the 1989–90 season their total of opponents had risen to 120. But with the introduction of Maidstone United, the figure was 121.

Jimmy's unique double
Jimmy McAlinden, an Irish international inside-forward, became the only player in history to appear in successful Irish Cup and FA Cup teams in consecutive seasons. He picked up winners medals for Belfast Celtic in 1937–38 and Portsmouth in 1938–39.

Women's lib
In February 1979 Mrs Millie Allen became the first woman to join a Football League club's board of directors. Her husband Bill Allen, who had died a month earlier, had been Bury's chairman for seven years.

Geographical error
Between 1937 and 1947 Mansfield Town operated in Division Three (South) while Crewe Alexandra were members of Division Three (North), even though Mansfield is some 20 miles north of Crewe.

Juventus twice
Only once have two Football League clubs in the same town or city been knocked out of the same European cup competition in the same season by the same team. In the 1976–77 UEFA Cup, Manchester City were beaten in the first round and Manchester United in the second by Juventus each time.

Cup overflows
On 24 January 1934 in a Third Division (South) Cup match at Exeter, there were 17 goals scored. Exeter City won 11–6 against Crystal Palace.

Straw in pole position
Ray Straw appeared in all six divisions of the Football League between 1952 and 1960, for Derby County and Coventry City in Divisions One, Two, Three (South), Three (North), Three and Four. In 1956–57 he was top scorer in Division Three (North) with 37 goals for Derby.

Six of one . . . half a dozen . . .
Shrewsbury Town met Swindon Town six times in 1960–61 in League, League Cup and FA Cup matches and did not lose. Huddersfield Town and Plymouth Argyle met six times in 1963–64 in League, League Cup and FA Cup games.

Ubiquitous (2)
James Gordon of Rangers was selected to play for the club in all eleven positions, including goalkeeper, during his career at Ibrox Park from 1910 to 1930.

Lincolnshire handicap
Between 1908 and 1922 the three Lincolnshire clubs, Lincoln City, Grimsby Town and Gainsborough Trinity were engaged in moving in and out of the Football League at regular intervals. In 1908 Lincoln failed to gain re-election, but returned a year later. In 1910 Grimsby went out but returned in place of Lincoln in 1911. A year afterwards Gainsborough were replaced by Lincoln. In 1919–20 both Grimsby and Lincoln were not re-elected. Grimsby found a place in the new Third Division in 1920 and Lincoln returned when the Northern Section was added in 1921. But Gainsborough did not re-appear.

Magnificent six
Since the creation of the Third Division in 1920 there have been six FA Cup victories achieved by non-league teams over Division One clubs:
1923–24 Corinthians 1 Blackburn Rovers 0;
1947–48 Colchester United 1 Huddersfield Town 0;
1948–49 Yeovil Town 2 Sunderland 1;
1971–72 Hereford United 2 Newcastle United 1;
1974–75 Burnley 0 Wimbledon 1;
1988–89 Sutton United 2 Coventry City 1.
But in 1919–20, Darlington, as members of the Northern League, beat Sheffield Wednesday 2–0 at Hillsborough after a 0–0 draw.

Hands off
Until 1912 goalkeepers were allowed to handle the ball anywhere in their own half. In 1910 this allowed Jimmy Brownlie of Third Lanark and Clem Hampton of Motherwell to score in the same game, the only known instance in first-class football of both goalkeepers scoring in one match.

Travel hazard
Derby County travelled to Roker Park, Sunderland for the opening Division One match of the 1894–95 season on 1 September. The referee failed to arrive but the match started with a linesman officiating. At half-time Derby were losing 3–0 but as the referee had appeared by now, the teams elected to start again. Sunderland proceeded to win 8–0 officially (11–0 unofficially).

Cap in hand
Before the 1986–87 season when the bottom club in Division Four was automatically relegated to the GM Vauxhall Conference, the most applications for re-election to the Football League from the division had come from Hartlepool United on 11 occasions. Under the regional divisions of the Third Division, Walsall had made seven applications.

Away day gloom
Exeter City went ten months without scoring an away goal in any first-class fixture between 12 April 1923 and 16 February 1924. Rochdale managed to exist from 7 November 1931 to 3 September 1932 without a win of any kind.

Loyal villans
In 1971–72 Aston Villa attracted an average of 31 952 spectators to their Division Three matches. It was the thirteenth highest average that season in the entire Football League. Villa were champions of the division.

Bob Gregg was an inside-forward who first entered the League with Darlington after playing for several non-league teams. He later turned out for Sheffield Wednesday, Birmingham, Chelsea, Boston United and Sligo Rovers. His greatest disappointment was with Birmingham in the 1931 Cup Final (Colorsport)

Early galling for Gregg

Bob Gregg had the galling experience of scoring after only six minutes in the 1931 FA Cup Final for Birmingham against West Bromwich Albion only to have his header disallowed for offside. It was a well-timed goal attempt from a free-kick by Jimmy Cringan and is often referred to as the greatest Cup Final goal that never was. Albion went on to win 2–1.

The first test

Test Matches were used to determine the promotion and relegation places between Divisions One and Two from 1892–93 to 1897–98. The highest score during the various games was in 1895–96 when Small Heath beat Manchester City 8–0 but still failed to retain Division One status.

Magnificent seven

Sunderland goalkeeper Chris Turner was unbeaten for 573 minutes during the 1982–83 season, the sequence including seven matches without conceding a goal, a club record.

No defence perk

In 1973–74 Manchester United conceded only 48 goals in Division One for the best record of goals let in by a relegated club from 42 games. In 1901–02 Small Heath were relegated after conceding just 45 in 34 matches.

Floods of fans

In 1967–68 Manchester United had a League attendance average of 57 758, a record in the history of the competition. The following season they sold 1 554 540 copies of their official programme, *United Review*, a record for a club programme.

Unusual

At the start of the 1950–51 season, all the promoted teams lost on the first day, all the relegated sides won and the newly-elected clubs to the regional sections of the Third Division drew.

Quick return

Alan Mullery was a Fulham player 24 hours before helping Tottenham Hotspur into the 1971–72 UEFA Cup Final. On loan to the Craven Cottage club, he was recalled in time to play against AC Milan in the semi-final.

Alan Mullery with one foot off the ground; but he almost had no time to touch it when whisked back to Tottenham from Fulham for a European game (Associated Sports Photography)

At home and abroad

Edwin Dutton was born in England in 1890 of English parents but was raised in Berlin where his father had a sports business. He developed as a footballer playing outside right for Prussen Berlin and was even given an international appearance for Germany against Hungary in Budapest on 4 April 1909, the match ending in a 3–3 draw.

Old trophy

When Arsenal won the Littlewoods Cup in 1987 it was not the first time the trophy had been presented. Made in the last century, it was originally called the Viscountess Furness Football Cup, contested by the workers at Furness, Withy and Co, the north-east shipbuilders. The cup bears the mark of Turner Bradbury, a plate worker registered in 1889. Among previous winners were The Platers Helpers in 1923 and The Welders in 1966.

Goalscoring Keetleys

Mr and Mrs William Keetley of Graham Street, Derby, had 11 sons and one daughter. Nine of the boys played for Victoria Ironworks, though not Charlie, the youngest at five. Frank, Harold, Joe and Tom were the sons who played in the Football League. Four others, Bill, Albert, Arthur and John also played professionally while Lawrence and Sid were amateur footballers. Most of them were goalscoring forwards.

Tom, a centre-forward with Bradford Park Avenue, Doncaster Rovers, Notts County and Lincoln City scored 282 goals in 366 League games. He once scored six goals for Doncaster against Ashington on 16 February 1929. Frank also managed six in 21 minutes for Lincoln against Halifax Town on 16 January 1932. In February 1926 Joe, Tom and Harold played in the same Doncaster team and the following season Frank, Tom and Harold were with Rovers. Charlie scored 108 League goals for Leeds United.

The north-east dynasty

The Milburn family of the north-east provided the rearguard for Leeds United at one time before the Second World War. Brothers Jim and Jack were at full-back while brother-in-law Jim Potts was in goal. Another Milburn brother, George, played with Leeds until his transfer to Chesterfield in 1937 while a fourth brother, Stan, made his debut for Chesterfield in 1946–47. Their cousin Jackie was a Newcastle United and England centre-forward in the wartime and post-war period while his nephews were the Charlton brothers, Jack and Bobby.

Traditional knots

Tottenham Hotspur are the only non-league club to have won the FA Cup since the formation of the Football League and at the celebration dinner in 1901 members tied blue and white ribbons on the handles of the trophy, a custom which has since become a tradition.

U-turn sinks the U's

In 1950–51 Colin McDonald, an RAF National Serviceman stationed at Moreton-in-Marsh, was a professional goalkeeper with Burnley but signed for Headington United (later Oxford United) as an amateur under FA rules applying to footballers on National Service. The following season Headington had a run in the FA Cup from the first qualifying round onwards beating neighbours Oxford City, after a replay, and Chesham United.

They were then drawn against Wycombe Wanderers at The Manor in the third qualifying round. McDonald was in goal throughout the cup run and helped Headington to a 3–2 win over Wycombe. However Wycombe subsequently claimed that goalkeeper McDonald was eligible only for Burnley in the FA Cup and protested to the FA. Having apparently given the impression they were happy for McDonald to play for Headington in the competition, Burnley changed their attitude.

Despite pleas by Headington to Burnley, Wycombe's protest was upheld on the grounds that the registration of a professional footballer on National Service differed from that of a player in the regular forces, although it was unlikely that any professional soldier, sailor or airman would be signed as a professional footballer. Wycombe were awarded the game, McDonald returned to Burnley and was capped eight times by England including four games in the 1958 World Cup finals.

Talisman Rush

Ian Rush joined Liverpool from Chester in May 1980 for £300 000 and for the next seven years proved to be an amazing scoring talisman for the Anfield club. Whenever Rush scored a goal, Liverpool remained unbeaten. The spell was finally broken at Wembley on 5 April 1987 when Rush scored against Arsenal in the Littlewoods Cup final, only for two goals from Charlie Nicholas to give the Gunners a 2–1 victory. Overall Rush scored in 146 games for Liverpool before his transfer to Juventus in May 1987 and in 144 of them the Reds were unbeaten.

The great League v Pools dispute

The Football League clubs need the Pools firms, without whose massive annual rake-off many, no doubt, would have gone out of existence before now. And it is equally true to say that the Pools firms cannot manage without the League clubs, whose fixtures are what make their coupons possible. So the two have to work 'hand in glove' in a two-way mutually beneficial process, and there is constant and essential cooperation between them.

But it was not always that way. At one time, in fact, they were at odds with each other in their non-stop attempts to frustrate 'the opposition'. The League's top brass would have nothing to do with gambling or betting in any shape or form, and the Pools people 'pinched' the fixtures without making any payment, though they made an offer that was turned down.

It led to the League hierarchy astounding the football world by actually resorting to the sensational move of scrapping sets of their original scheduled fixtures and substituting others, which were kept so secret that they were not even notified to the clubs until it was too late for the Pools to print the new matches on their coupons. Clubs were not told until late on the Thursday afternoon, by telephone, where and against what opponents they would be playing two days later! Imagine the wholesale upheavals it all caused and how club officials and players had to make frantic last-minute plans.

The ploy was put into effect during the spring of 1936, and the only thing that was not changed, in what many felt to be a hare-brained League move, was that the clubs, under the new arrangement, were still at home or away just as had been planned in the original fixtures. This for example, was how the Division One fixtures were altered for Saturday 7 March:

Home teams	Original opponents	New opponents
Arsenal	Brentford	Huddersfield Town
Birmingham	Preston North End	Bolton Wanderers
Blackburn Rovers	Bolton Wanderers	Wolverhampton Wanderers
Chelsea	Huddersfield Town	Sheffield Wednesday
Grimsby Town	Aston Villa	Preston North End
Leeds United	Wolverhampton Wanderers	Brentford
Liverpool	Middlesbrough	Portsmouth
Manchester City	Derby County	Middlesbrough
Stoke City	Everton	Aston Villa
Sunderland	Portsmouth	Everton
West Bromwich Albion	Sheffield Wednesday	Derby County

A similar scheme applied in the other divisions and the re-shuffle operated on three consecutive Saturdays – 29 February, 7 March and 14 March – but it did not have the desired effect, for the Pools people were able to issue makeshift coupons, and the League realised that they could not win. They were compelled to abandon their endeavours to frustrate the 'enemy', and it became a case of . . . Panel Result: Pools 3, League 0!

To adjust the rearranged fixtures after the upsets caused by those three Saturdays involved a major operation, with clubs and players thrust into all manner of inconveniences. Swansea Town, for instance, actually had to play a Division Two match at Plymouth on Good Friday 10 April and another a day later at Newcastle! That remains to this day as the longest distance ever travelled in League history by any team in fulfilling two fixtures within 24 hours.

'Wiser counsels' just had to prevail, and in the long run the 'war' ended with the two sides getting together, with the Pools firms paying the League an agreed annual fee, increased from time to time since then, for the use of the fixtures.

In reserve

The Central League is now restricted to the reserve teams of Football League clubs, but it was not always so. Crewe Alexandra, Port Vale, Rochdale, Southport and Tranmere Rovers all played in the Central League immediately before they entered the Football League just after World War One.

You're the boss

In 1938 outside-right George Raynor and inside-right Bill Chalmers became wing partners with Aldershot. Both were experienced players, Raynor having played for Sheffield United, Mansfield Town, Rotherham United and Bury; Chalmers for Queen's Park, Glasgow Rangers, Newcastle United, Bury, Notts County. They had previously played together at Bury.

Both players assisted their club when wartime service duties permitted, and in 1945 Raynor was appointed assistant trainer and Chalmers trainer to Aldershot. In 1947 Chalmers became manager of Ebbw Vale and became a qualified FA coach. Meanwhile Raynor had been recommended to the Swedish national team as coach by Stanley Rous, the FA secretary, who had seen him organise an international team in Iraq.

Raynor guided Sweden to the Olympic Games gold medal in 1948, third place in the 1950 World Cup and 1952 Olympics, then to the runners-up spot in the 1958 World Cup. The same year as he was taking charge of the Swedes his former colleague Chalmers was being appointed coach and technical director of Juventus in Italy.

Soviets meet match

On 10 March 1990 two Soviet Union internationals opposed each other for the first time in England during a Division Two match between Ipswich Town and Brighton and Hove Albion. It happened in the 81st minute when Sergei Baltacha came on as a substitute for Ipswich to face Sergei Gotsmanov of Brighton.

Back on familiar soil

Leslie Smith made his last pre-war appearance for Brentford against Huddersfield Town on 2 September 1939 and his next for them against Lincoln City on 28 August 1952. But in between he had played in wartime regional matches for the club and was later transferred to Aston Villa. Brentford goalkeeper Ted Gaskell spent 12 years with the club before making his first appearance in the senior side in 1949, when he had already received two benefits.

Much-travelled Dave Mangnall – in Huddersfield colours (Hulton-Deutsch)

Mangnall on the move

For someone who did not play football until he was 16 years old, Dave Mangnall had an exceptionally long and varied career as a player and then as a manager. He played for Maltby New Church FC in the Rotherham Sunday School League, scoring over 50 goals in one season for them. He moved to Maltby Colliery and after 35 goals in their colours was offered trials by Huddersfield Town, Rotherham United and finally Doncaster Rovers in 1922–23 with whom he remained for half a season as an amateur.

In November 1927 he gave up his job as a miner to sign as a professional for Leeds United and after scoring six goals in nine games was transferred to Huddersfield Town for £3000 in December 1929. There he scored 61 goals in 79 games as an inside forward, including 31 in 1931–32. In February 1934 he was transferred to Birmingham, but remained only 13 months during which time he scored 14 goals in 37 matches.

In March 1935 he moved again, this time to West Ham United for £2950. Twenty-nine goals in 37 League games and he was off to Millwall briefly and then Queen's Park Rangers in 1939. During the war he also guested for Fulham, Southend and Millwall. In 1944 he was appointed QPR manager, successfully guiding them to the Division Three (South) championship in 1947–48. Overall he registered 120 peacetime goals in around 180 games.

Soccer Specials

The London and North-Eastern Railway introduced a batch of 23 locomotives for express passenger work in East Anglia during 1936–37 with Football League club names on them. The engines were scrapped between 1958–60.

Original Engine No.	Name	Panel Colours	Br No.
2848	Arsenal	Red	61648
2849	Sheffield United	Red and white	61649
2850	Grimsby Town	Black and white	61650
2851	Derby County	White	61651
2852	Darlington	Black and white	61652
2853	Huddersfield Town	Blue and white	61653
2854	Sunderland	Red and white	61654
2855	Middlesbrough	Red	61655
2856	Leeds United	Blue and old gold; white latterly	61656
2857	Doncaster Rovers	Red and white	61657
2858	Newcastle United*	Black and white	61658
2859	Norwich City†	Dark green and yellow	
2839			61659
2860	Hull City	Blue; chrome yellow and black post-War	61660
2861	Sheffield Wednesday	Blue and white	61661
2862	Manchester United	Red	61662
2863	Everton	Blue	61663
2864	Liverpool	Red	61664
2865	Leicester City	Blue	61665
2866	Nottingham Forest	Red	61666
2867	Bradford	Black, yellow and red	61667
2868	Bradford City	Claret and amber	61668
2869	Barnsley	Red	61669
2870	Tottenham Hotspur‡	White, with cockerel badges	
2830			61670
2871	Manchester City	Blue	—
2872	West Ham United	Claret and blue; red post-War	61672

Single-colour panels were usually edged with a ³⁄₁₆ in wide white surrounding lining, though *Nottingham Forest*, *Tottenham Hotspur*, *Manchester City* and *West Ham United* (post-War) had blue linings instead. Where two or three colours appeared on the panel they were arranged in stripes with a black edging (red in the case of *Grimsby Town*). The width and number of stripes varied considerably, whilst the stripes themselves could be vertical or horizontal. There were even variations over the years in the interpretation of any one arrangement – for example, *Doncaster Rovers* had horizontal stripes pre-War, vertical stripes post-War, all-red panels by 1958 and finally vertical stripes again when restored after withdrawal for presentation.

When No. 2854 *Sunderland* was needed for working a Cup Final special in 1937 (the year Sunderland won the Cup), it was under general repair at Gorton from 10 April to 15 May. So on 17 April No. 2851 went to Gorton to acquire 2854's number and nameplates. Its own number and nameplates were replaced during another short visit to Gorton from 9 to 13 May. It should perhaps be mentioned that there is in existence an official photograph taken at Darlington showing No. 2849 when named *Darlington*. This was taken for Works photographic purposes only, and is doubly confusing in that this engine was originally allotted the name *Derby County*.

*Name changed to *The Essex Regiment*.
†Originally named *Rendelsham Hall* but the nameplates were incorrectly spelled and in 1938 the Norwich City nameplates were put on it as 2859 had had a name change of its own to *East Anglian* in 1937.
‡Originally named *Manchester City* and later *City of London*.

Forrest fire

In the 1987–88 season, Robert Forrest scored in eight successive Second Division matches for Arbroath. During this period he was responsible for ten of the team's 14 goals. Overall he scored 12 goals in 22 matches.

History repeats

From 1973–74 to 1979–80 inclusive, the teams finishing seventh in Division Four achieved promotion the following season. It happened in succession to Chester, Reading, Exeter City, Watford, Barnsley, Portsmouth and Lincoln City.

Like father

When George Camsell was a youngster before his days with Middlesbrough he turned out in a Sunday game with some miners. The local vicar ticked him off for it and asked Camsell what his father would say if he knew. Camsell informed the cleric that dad was playing in goal!

The troubled times

On 3 November 1983 Watford placed an advertisement in *The Times* asking for players, either male or female between the ages of 18–80, preferably with two arms and two legs!

Players with the same name and attached to the same club have often caused problems through the years. The Billy Richardsons at West Bromwich were a case in point. One of them had to be given a fictitious initial 'G' to separate them. It stood for 'Ginger' (GSL)

The name's the same

In 1932–33 Grimsby Town had two Charlie Wilsons on their staff. In 1949–50 Bradford City had two players by the name of Johnny Millar, both Scots. They frequently drew each other's pay by mistake. In the immediate pre-war period, Newport County signed two players called Bill Owen. Neither had another initial, so a local newspaper decided to add a fictitious one to each, giving the former Exeter City player an 'E' and the ex-Manchester City one an 'M'. And as WE and WM they remained during their careers.

West Bromwich Albion had two forwards in the 1930s, Billy 'Ginger' Richardson and Bill Richardson. Billy was given the added initial 'G' to distinguish them. In 1989–90 Hereford United had a Mark Jones and a Mark A Jones in their Division Four team. They also had a Richard Jones and a Shane Jones in the side. Crewe Alexandra had a Paul Edwards and a Paul R Edwards. They also had a Rob Edwards. Burnley's Steve Davis was temporarily joined by Steve Davis on loan from Southampton. In the 1930s Fulham had a Sam Gibbon and a Sid Gibbons on their staff at the same time. Both were defenders, but Gibbon was tragically killed in a motor accident.

Tales of the unexpected

On 22 February 1939 Wolverhampton Wanderers, who were second in the Division One table at the time, beat the League leaders Everton 7–0. For Harry Morton in the Everton goal it was a harrowing afternoon in what was his only game of the season in the first team. At the end of the season he was transferred to Burnley. But unusual events were not rare for him.

Born in Oldham he attended school at Chadderton and represented Oldham Boys before having trials for Bury and Bolton Wanderers. In 1930 he joined the Royal Welsh Fusiliers and in November of that year played in goal for the Army in a friendly against Aston Villa. Already a Corporal, he had impressed Villa who invited him for further trials. They bought him out and signed him as a professional in March 1931.

His League debut came in odd circumstances. Attending Villa's game at Maine Road against Manchester City as a spectator in the stand he watched the Villa goalkeeper Fred Biddlestone injure himself in the pre-match kick-in. He was summoned and played in a 3–3 draw. Morton went on to make 192 League appearances for Villa and 29 for Everton, whom he joined in March 1937. He retired during the war.

However, that was not the end of the Wolves–Everton saga. Following their 7–0 win, Wolves had to play Liverpool at Anfield three days later. Clearly feeling on Merseyside was running high, because spectators threw various missiles, notably oranges, at the visiting team! Wolves won 2–0. Liverpool were fined 20 guineas (£21) and warned.

Even so, Wolves had to be content at the end of the season by being runners-up in the championship and beaten finalists in the FA Cup. Everton, on the other hand, won the First Division title.

Long wait

Tommy Harris made his debut for Watford against Brighton & Hove Albion on 2 May 1936 in a Division Three (South) game and had to wait until 5 October 1946 for his next senior appearance at Reading. Although he made a number of wartime appearances for the club, it was more than ten years between official games.

Young Sam's record

Sam McMillan was 15 years 212 days old when he made his debut for Ayr United away to Queen's Park on 14 March 1953 in Division Two. A Ballochmyle Thistle player from the Ayr juvenile club, he did not sign as a professional until 1955.

Dynamic Dynamoes

Colne Dynamoes were formed in 1963 playing in the Colne & Nelson League. Player-organiser Graham White did practically everything for the club including washing the strip and marking the pitch. Their list of honours is almost unique and in July 1989 the club decided to become full-time professional, employing 22 full-time players, five trainees, coaching staff, secretary, commercial manager, public relations officer, chief scout, physiotherapist, schools liaison officer and groundsman. All this has been achieved as the ambition of White, a successful businessman, to build a club capable of competing with the best in the country.

In March 1990 a punter placed a bet that Colne would win the Division One championship in 2000. He stands to win £500 000 if his wager succeeds.

Honours:

1963–64	Colne & Nelson League **Champions**
1964–65	Colne & Nelson League **Champions** and Cup **Winners**
1965–66	Amos Nelson Cup **Winners**
1966–67	Colne & Nelson League **Champions**
1967–68	Burnley Combination League **Champions** and Cup **Winners**
1969–70	Burnley Combination League **Champions** and Cup **Winners**
1970–71	West Lancs Division Two **Champions** and Cup **Winners**
1971–72	West Lancs Division One **Champions**
1972–73	West Lancs Division One **Champions** and Challenge Cup **Winners**
1973–74	West Lancs Division One **Champions**, Lancashire Amateur Shield **Winners** and Challenge Cup **Winners**
1974–75	West Lancs Division One **Champions** and Cup **Winners**
1975–76	Lancs Combination Cup Runners-up
1977–78	Lancs Combination George Watson Trophy **Winners**
1978–79	Lancs Combination George Watson Trophy Runners-up
1979–80	Lancs Combination Runners-up and Bridge Shield **Winners**
1980–81	Lancashire Combination Runners-up and Bridge Shield Runners-up
1981–82	Lancashire Combination Runners-up
1982–83	North West Counties Division Three **Champions**
1986–87	North West Counties League Challenge Cup **Winners** & League **Champions** v Cup **Winners** Trophy
1987–88	FA Vase **Winners**, Bass North West Counties Division One **Champions** & League **Champions** v Cup **Winners** Trophy
1988–89	HFS Loans League Division One **Champions** & ATS Challenge Trophy **Winners**
1989–90	HFS Loans League Premier Division **Champions** & ATS Challenge Trophy **Winners**

Willis Edwards had a diverting experience before becoming a
professional (Colorsport)

Timely award

In 1982–83 Cambridge United completed 1159
minutes in home games in Division Two without
conceding a goal. The sequence began in the 11th
minute of the game with Queen Park Rangers on 20
November and ended in the 68th minute against
Oldham Athletic on 14 May. Oldham actually scored
four times in eight minutes to win 4–1. Ironically,
goalkeeper Malcolm Webster had received a special
award to commemorate his performance at half-time.

Unlucky for who?

Scott Crabbe, the Heart of Midlothian striker,
discovered that the week ending 13 May 1989 was
anything but unlucky for him. He scored a hat-trick of
penalties plus another goal to help Hearts retain the
East of Scotland Shield, then holed his tee-shot at
Carrickknowe during a round of golf for his first hole-
in-one.

Naff Daf

Hereford United lost their Leyland Daf Cup quarter-
final at Edgar Street to Notts County on 21 February
1990. The game finished 1–1 after extra time but only
after Mark Jones had missed a 47th minute penalty
for Hereford. In the subsequent penalty shoot-out,
Mark A Jones and Richard Jones both failed from the
spot and Notts won 4–3.

Third time unlucky

When Halifax Town missed a penalty against
Maidstone United on 25 November 1989 in a Division
Four match, it was the third successive home fixture
in which they had failed with a spot kick.

There's no substitute

On 16 December 1989 in a Division Two game at
Bournemouth, the Barnsley substitute Ian Banks was
sent off after 65 minutes without taking part in the
game. As he was warming-up he was alleged to have
made a remark to a linesman just after Bournemouth
had scored a controversial goal from an apparent
offside position. Bournemouth won 2–1.

A miner diversion

Willis Edwards was setting out to play a trial with
Blackburn Rovers when he was signed by
Chesterfield. A pit lad, he moved to Leeds United in
1925 and went on to play 16 times for England as a
wing-half.

Treble centurions

In 1959–60, Wolverhampton Wanderers became the
first club to score a century or more goals in three
successive seasons. In 1957–58 they won the
Division One championship with 103 goals, the
following season they retained the title by scoring
110 and in 1959–60 they were runners-up having
scored 106. Then in 1960–61 they made in four
hundreds in a row by scoring 103 in third place.

Seaside pools dividend

The Football League disposed of some of the money
taken from the pools promoters to purchase the
Sandown Hotel at St Annes-on-Sea as the new
official headquarters in 1959–60.

Take your pick

John Toshack, who made 40 appearances for Wales
between the 1968–69 season and 1979–80, scoring
13 goals, was born in Cardiff, son of a Welsh mother
and a Scottish miner father from Fife. He was
qualified for both countries.

In 1988–89 Southampton created a record with the Wallace brothers making appearances in the Football League. Twins Rodney and Ray joined brother Danny (above) for the first time in October (Allsport)

Brothers abound

In 1919–20 Clapton Orient had three brothers in their Division Two team: the Tonner brothers, Samuel, James and Jack. In 1988–89 Southampton fielded three Wallace brothers, twins Ray and Rodney plus Danny, in Division One.

Blood money

The first time that West Bromwich Albion paid as much as £4000 for a player was to Port Vale in February 1921 for the signature of Bobby Blood. He averaged almost a goal every two games with 26 in 53 appearances in the League side before moving to Stockport County in 1924.

Buoyant boyo – but . . .

Neil Kinnock, leader of the Labour Party and a Cardiff City supporter for 43 years, has never seen Cardiff lose and witnessed a 1–0 win at Brentford on 21 February 1990. But at the end of the season, Cardiff were relegated to Division Four and there was equally bad news for Kinnock's No. 2 Roy Hattersley, who watched his beloved Sheffield Wednesday suffer a simiar fate in descending to Division Two.

Historic spot kicks

On 6 January 1990 history was created at Rugby Park, Kilmarnock when a Scottish Cup tie was decided on penalty kicks for the first time. The match had finished 0–0 after extra time but Stranraer won 4–3 on penalties. Tommy Burns and Paul Flexney both failed to score for Killie.

Keeping up with the Jones'

Chris Jones made League appearances for nine different League clubs: Manchester City, Swindon Town, Oldham Athletic, Walsall, York City, Huddersfield Town, Doncaster Rovers, Darlington and Rochdale. His League career spanned the middle 1960s to the late 1970s. Later he played for Le Havre, Frickley as player-manager, Bridlington Trinity and Rowntree-Mackintosh, for whom he was still playing at the age of 40. A centre-forward, he was involved in a piece of cup history during his time with Trinity in the 1980–81 season. Their tie with Netherfield in the FA Trophy lasted 13 hours, a record for an FA competition. It was in the Second Qualifying round and the original game ended in a goalless draw at Netherfield. The replay at Bridlington was 1–1, the second replay at Goole was 2–2, the third at Chorley was 1–1 as was the fourth replay at the same venue. The fifth replay at Netherfield finished 2–2 but at Goole in attempt number seven Netherfield won 2–0. It was as disappointing for Jones as it had been when he was dropped from Swindon's League Cup final team against Arsenal in 1969 after playing in earlier rounds.

Chris Jones, a goalscorer at many levels and for many different teams up and down the country (Coloursport)

Never strikes twice

In May 1963 Arthur Lightening, Middlesbrough's South African-born goalkeeper, was given permission to return home to attend his brother's wedding. He did not come back.

Alan Shearer (Southampton) became the youngest player to score a Division One hat-trick in April 1988 at the age of 17 years, 240 days (Sporting Pictures)

Young at start

On 9 April 1988, Alan Shearer scored a hat-trick in Southampton's 4–2 win over Arsenal at The Dell, to become the youngest player in the First Division to achieve such a feat. He was 17 years 240 days old at the time. It was also his first full appearance after two outings as substitute in the League side. Jimmy Greaves had been 17 years 10 months when he scored a hat-trick for Chelsea against Portsmouth in Division One on 25 December 1957.

A Gordon for me

On 17 October 1987 the Berwick Rangers physiotherapist Bobby Gordon was forced to take over in goal for the first six minutes of the Second Division game with Albion Rovers at Shielfield Park, because goalkeeper John Thomson's car had broken down en route. Gordon was replaced by substitute goalkeeper David Sanderson. Thomson did not play again in the League side. Berwick lost the game 3–0.

Tangerine travellers

Dundee United competed in 67 different matches during the 1986–87 season. They comprised 44 in an enlarged Scottish Premier Division, four in the Skol Cup, seven in the Scottish Cup and 12 UEFA Cup games. Unfortunately they did not succeed in winning any honours. They finished third in the League, reached the semi-final of the Skol Cup and were beaten finalists in the other two competitions.

Thank you and goodbye

Stranraer goalkeeper Ronnie Tracey was an ever-present in the 1986–87 season during which the club finished 10th out of 14 teams in Division Two. He was voted Player of the Year, but at the end of the season he was given a free transfer.

No seventh haven

Kilmarnock played the entire match away to Port Glasgow Athletic in Division One on 4 January 1908 with seven players. The other four failed to arrive, but Port Glasgow only managed to win 4–1.

All the threes

Berwick Rangers had more goalkeeping problems when they were forced to use three in their Division Two match against Hamilton Academical on 24 August 1955. Alex Paterson was carried off after only ten minutes and his replacement Runciman lasted only another six minutes before he departed injured. A third defender, Mitchell, took over and remained on duty. Despite playing for most of the game with ten men, Berwick drew 3–3.

Shots at random

Although Aldershot remained unbeaten in their first eight matches of the 1933–34 season in Division Three (South), they could finish no higher than 14th. By Boxing Day they had won only five matches and scored 17 goals. However this was the second game in a further sequence of eight games without defeat, followed by a 9–2 reverse on 10 February at Clapton Orient. Yet they managed three wins in succession to end the season.

Bringing home the goals

Arthur Bacon had an eventful first season with Coventry City in 1933–34. Born in Chesterfield, he had previously played for his home town club, Reading and Derby County. In a remarkable spell of five matches in two weeks during December–January his scoring record was 2–1–2–5–4.

Left to right: Dave Watson, Mick Channon, Kevin Keegan and Alan Ball – a quartet of England captains in one Southampton line-up (Associated Sports Photography)

Captains quartet
On 7 March 1981 Southampton fielded four players who had captained England: Mick Channon, Dave Watson, Alan Ball and Kevin Keegan. Keegan scored the only goal of the Division One game against Manchester United.

Blades repeat
Sheffield United had the distinction of being the team with the longest unbeaten run in the Football League in matches from the start of the season on four consecutive occasions. In 1896–97 their Division One programme opened with eight unbeaten games. The following season it was extended to 14, in 1898–99 it was 11 and in 1899–1900 it was impressively extended to 22. Their end-of-season positions were respectively 2nd, 1st, 16th and 2nd.

Handling code
Kilmarnock were actually formed to play under Rugby rules and their Rugby Park ground bears testimony to this fact. They were formed in 1869 and by 1873 had entered the first Scottish Cup competition.

Sad ending
The last day of 1938 was an unhappy one in the Football League. There were three serious injuries: Edward Dawson, the Bristol City goalkeeper, fractured his wrist; John Roberts, centre-forward for Port Vale, dislocated a shoulder and Eddie Perry, the Doncaster Rovers centre-forward, broke an arm. In addition, David Ford, an Arsenal reserve goalkeeper, died of peritonitis.

The goal difference
In 1954–55 Brentford won 16 and lost 16 of their Division Three (South) matches, scored 82 goals and conceded 82 and obtained 46 points from 46 games. They finished joint 11th with Norwich City who scored 60 and conceded 60 goals. Under goal difference, Brentford would have been higher than Norwich by virtue of scoring more goals.

Vengeful Toffees
In the 1930–31 season Everton not only made a quick return to Division One after their first experience in the lower division, but were able to take revenge on Crystal Palace for the humiliation of a 6–0 FA Cup defeat they had suffered at Goodison Park in 1921–22. Everton themselves won by six goals at Selhurst Park with Dixie Dean scoring four times.

O'Grady says move
Harry O'Grady was an inside-forward who joined Leeds United from Southampton in August 1932. He played eight League games, scoring two goals before moving to Burnley in May 1933. In succeeding summers he joined Bury, Millwall, Carlisle United, Accrington Stanley and then Tunbridge Wells Rangers. Oddly enough he had spent just one season with Southampton after signing from Port Vale.

Rams in Lions' clothing
On 12 April 1969 Derby County won 1–0 at Milwall to clinch the Division Two championship. The Rams had intended to play in an all-white strip only to discover that Millwall were planning to do the same. The Lions loaned the Rams their second strip of red shirts and black shorts.

One game Millar
Scottish-born Johnny Millar was 34 years and 220 days old when he made his debut for West Bromwich Albion against Burton United in a Division Two game on 8 October 1904. Signed from Sunderland, he captained Albion in a 4–0 win playing at centre-forward. He did not play again and joined Chelsea the following season.

Non-stop blank
Leeds United full-back Grenville Hair played 411 League games before scoring a goal against Middlesbrough on 7 April 1962. The time taken to achieve this milestone was three weeks, four days and 16 hours of non-stop football.

York centurions
York City became the first Football League club to score a century of points. They achieved the feat in 1983–84 in Division Four when winning the championship with 101 points, 15 more than the runners-up. Their 96 goals was also a club record and more than half the total was contributed by two players: John Byrne with 27 and Keith Walwyn with 25.

Rare Stranraer
The first occasion that Stranraer finished as high as fourth in Division Two was in 1960–61. At the end of December they had taken 26 points, but then managed only three from the next possible ten. However a recovery brought 15 from a maximum of 20. Their best wins were at home: 6–0 v Montrose, 5–0 v Hamilton Academical, 5–1 v Arbroath and 6–2 v East Fife.

Smith's problem is rare
Stockport County signed centre-forward Joe Smith from Bolton Wanderers in 1927. He made his first appearance on 19 March against Stoke City and a record crowd of 22 500 packed into Edgeley Park to see him. But a few minutes before kick-off a telegram arrived at the ground from the Football League which read: 'Don't play Smith. Registration not in order.' The County chairman Ernest Barlow received the telegram and was faced with a dilemma: to withdraw Smith and break faith with the capacity crowd or risk the wrath of the League and suffer the consequences.

He put the telegram in his pocket and said nothing until after the match. County drew 2–2 with Stoke. In the subsequent inquiry County were fined £100 and had to forfeit two points. Worse still, Smith was only allowed to play that season in matches where the League management committee granted permission. Stockport's case had been that they signed Smith on the last day of the transfer deadline. The letter was posted and it was thought that the date on the postmark would be sufficient proof of the signing and registration.

Crowd onus
In 1960–61 the Morton club introduced a scheme for bonus payments based on the extent of the home attendances. At the end of the season they were bottom of the Division Two table with 21 points from 36 games and 16 players were released.

Bill's bullet
Bill Rawlings scored ten hat-tricks, including two which led to four goals, for Southampton during a career between 1919 and 1928. Having joined the Army at 18 he served in the First World War with the Wessex Field Ambulance and came to Southampton as an amateur in 1918, turning professional the following year. His most memorable goal did not figure among them. That was a fiercely struck free-kick from an acute angle which divided the Saints and Liverpool in an FA Cup tie in the fourth round on 7 March 1925.

Borrowed time
On 27 January 1951 Southampton played at Sunderland in a fourth round FA Cup tie wearing a kit of amber jerseys and black shorts borrowed from the Hampshire Regiment. Sunderland used a set of black and white striped shirts loaned from Newcastle United, who played in Sunderland's jerseys of red and white stripes against Bolton Wanderers. The colour changes benefited both north-east teams.

Hamish McAlpine proved to be a goalscorer as well as a shot-stopper in his career (Allsport)

Raith from the back

On 12 September 1987 in the First Division match between Kilmarnock and Raith Rovers at Rugby Park the scores were level at 3–3 when Hamish McAlpine, the Raith goalkeeper, scored with a long clearance to give Raith victory at 4–3. His goal came in the 79th minute. At the time, Rovers had lost all three of their home matches.

Lost in space

On 30 January 1988 Stranraer travelled to Celtic for a Scottish Cup third round tie. At the time Stranraer were second from bottom in Division Two, Celtic top of the Premier Division. Celtic took the lead through Frank McAvennie after five minutes but failed to make any further impression on the game. Stranraer centre-forward Bruce Cleland, who had postponed taking a job in the US aerospace industry to play in the game, missed a penalty and an open goal near the end as Celtic hung on to win 1–0.

Indelible Marker

On 24 March 1990 Nick Marker, the Plymouth Argyle captain, conceded a penalty from which Leicester City scored, equalised and was later sent off in this Division Two match.

Fair shares

When Gillingham defeated Chesterfield 10–0 at Priestfield Stadium in a Division Four match on 5 September 1987, it was the first time in 61 Football League matches with a double figure score that no player had managed to score a hat-trick. Six different players shared the scoring.

Top that

Alisdair D'Arcy scored ten goals for Dundee Harp in the 35–0 win over Aberdeen Rovers in the Scottish Cup on 12 September 1885. But neither he nor Dundee were top scorers that day. John Petrie scored 13 in Arbroath's 36–0 victory over Bon Accord.

The Mac-trick

Liverpool's first League goal was scored by Malcolm McVean. Previously Hugh McQueen had hit the woodwork with a shot. Joe McQue scored the second goal and John McBride the first home goal.

Super Celts

Celtic's performance in 1966–67 outshone any other club in the history of the game in the British Isles. They won the Scottish League, League Cup and Scottish Cup as well as the Glasgow Cup and added the European Cup.

Penalty cause (1)

On 14 December 1935 three penalties were awarded in seven minutes, all for handball, in the match between Charlton Athletic and West Ham United. Charlton converted both of their spot kicks, West Ham their one. The Division Two game ended 2–2.

Penalty cause (2)

On 19 November 1988 Gerry McCoy of Partick Thistle scored from a penalty after ten seconds of the Division One game at Ayr United. Partick won 3–1. On 29 August 1956 Sammy Collins had converted a penalty for Torquay United in a Division Three (South) match against Walsall only ten seconds from the kick-off. Torquay won 2–0.

Penalty cause (3)

The highest number of penalties awarded in a Football League match is five. On 27 March 1989 in the Division Two game between Crystal Palace and Brighton & Hove Albion at Selhurst Park, Palace were awarded four (missing three) and Brighton one (scored). Palace won 2–1. Three of the penalties were awarded in a five minute spell during a game which also saw five bookings and a Brighton player sent off.

Index

Page numbers in *italics* refer to captions and illustrations.